Destination Dissertation

Destination Dissertation

A Traveler's Guide to a Done Dissertation

Sonja K. Foss and William Waters

Rowman & Littlefield Publishers, Inc.
Lanham • Boulder • New York • Toronto • Plymouth, UK

ROWMAN & LITTLEFIELD PUBLISHERS, INC.

Published in the United States of America
by Rowman & Littlefield Publishers, Inc.
A wholly owned subsidary of The Rowman & Littlefield Publishing Group, Inc.
4501 Forbes Boulevard, Suite 200, Lanham, Maryland 20706
www.rowmanlittlefield.com

Estover Road, Plymouth PL6 7PY, United Kingdom

British Library Cataloguing in Publication Information Available

Library of Congress Cataloging-in-Publication Data
Foss, Sonja K.
　Destination dissertation : a traveler's guide to a done dissertation / Sonja K. Foss and William Waters.
　　p. cm.
　Includes bibliographical references and index.
　ISBN-13: 978-0-7425-5439-9 (cloth : alk. paper)
　ISBN-10: 0-7425-5439-2 (cloth : alk. paper)
　ISBN-13: 978-0-7425-5440-5 (pbk. : alk. paper)
　ISBN-10: 0-7425-5440-6 (pbk. : alk. paper)
　1. Dissertations, Academic--Authorship--Handbooks, manuals, etc. 2. Academic writing--Handbooks, manuals, etc. I. Waters, William. II. Title.

LB2369.F59 2007
808'.02--dc22
　　　　　　　　　　　　　　　　　　　　　　　　　2007000391

Printed in the United States of America

∞™ The paper used in this publication meets the minimum requirements of American National Standard for Information Sciences—Permanence of Paper for Printed Library Materials, ANSI/NISO Z39.48-1992.

CONTENTS

CONTENTS

CONTENTS

ACKNOWLEDGMENTS

We have had the companionship of many fine people on the journey that has resulted in this book. We are especially grateful to those who helped us develop our ideas about writing dissertations throughout the years—Sonja's graduate students, those who have attended our Scholars' Retreats and workshops, and the students with whom we have worked as coaches. Marianne DiPierro of Western Michigan University deserves a special note of thanks for helping us think in new ways about how our ideas could be applied and for providing us with many opportunities to develop and test our ideas.

Karen A. Foss and Melissa McCalla Manassee read our chapters and gave us comments that significantly improved the book. Karen A. Foss, Stephen W. Littlejohn, and Teri Tapp offered ideas that were particularly helpful in conceptualizing chapter 11, and Anthony J. Radich provided a key idea for chapter 10. Raquel Vasquez's delightful drawings in chapters 5 and 7 helped us communicate our processes more clearly.

We appreciate the willingness of the scholars whose samples we have included in the book to share their work. Their excellent models will make the journeys of others easier. Thanks to: Bernard J. Armada, Francis S. Bartolomeo, Dawn O. Braithwaite, Abby L. Braun, Gail J. Chryslee, Karen A. Foss, Kimberly D. Barnett Gibson, Nicki M. Gonzales, Debra Greene, Daniel D. Gross, Laura K. Hahn, D. Lynn O'Brien Hallstein, Wendy Hilton-Morrow, Marla R. Kanengieter, Patrick M. Krueger, Theodore Matula, Madeline Perez, Gabrielle (Bree) Picower, Raina K. Plowright, Anthony J. Radich, Arthur L. Ranney, Diana Brown Sheridan,

ACKNOWLEDGMENTS

Michelle Fabian Simmons, Sharon M. Varallo, Catherine Egley Waggoner, Jean Guske Ward, Daniel L. Wildeson, Mary Rose Williams, and Naima T. Wong.

Our editor at Rowman & Littlefield, Brenda Hadenfeldt, was wonderful from the start. We very much appreciate her enthusiasm for the book and her trust in our vision for it. We're delighted to have met someone like her to go with us on our way.

Sonja wishes to acknowledge Anthony J. Radich, the most fun traveling companion one could have. Thanks to him for serving as the base camp for Scholars' Retreats, for his superb problem-solving and wordsmithing abilities, for putting up with yet another book, and for his love and support.

William would like to thank Kathleen Longwaters, Bob Long, Barbara Waters, Rebecca Aronson, Tim Ackerman, Robin Gallaher, Wayne Chandler, and Michael Hobbs for their support, advice, and good cheer.

These many wonderful companions have made our own trip a fun and exciting adventure.

PREPARING TO GO: THE DISSERTATION JOURNEY

C hances are, if you have found your way to this book, you're a graduate student just beginning to work on your dissertation or thesis or one who is stuck. We're delighted that you've chosen to take a look at what we can offer you, and we're confident that we can help you—whichever situation you're in. Over the years, we've had the opportunity to work with hundreds of graduate students like you, and we've seen the processes we offer help them move on to life after dissertation. If you're an advisor who advises graduate students and who wants to do a better job of it, you're welcome here, too. We won't be directing our comments explicitly toward you and your interests, but you'll be able to pick up lots of advising tips in the book.

Let's begin with some examples of the kinds of students we've helped in the past. Sylvie had been ABD in history for two years. She took a year off work to try to finish her dissertation, but she made virtually no progress. She was frustrated and despairing. Sylvie is not unique. She is smart and writes well, but she was struggling to complete her dissertation because she didn't know some basic processes that would allow her to move ahead.

Adem, on the other hand, had been ABD in sociology for three years. He had all the data collected for his project—he had conducted and transcribed his interviews. But he didn't know what to do with all the data he had. He knew he was supposed to code it and come up with a theory or explanation from it all, but the process of dealing with so much of it seemed unmanageable to him.

For Frederick, the literature review was the problem. He had so many books and articles to review for his dissertation in public administration that he didn't know where to begin. How was he supposed to get what he needed from all that literature? How was he supposed to keep track of all of those ideas? How should he organize the review once he did figure all of that out? He felt utterly exhausted just looking at what lay in front of him.

Using the techniques in this book, Sylvie, Adem, and Frederick were able to overcome the particular blocks that were holding them back, and they each drafted their dissertations in less than nine months. "Why didn't someone teach me these processes before?" they asked repeatedly. Sylvie, Adem, and Frederick had one thing in common: They had a strong desire to complete their dissertations, but they were stuck. This book is about getting unstuck so you can move forward on your dissertation. If you're not stuck but want to learn how to move forward more efficiently, this book is for you as well. It's designed to help you end up at your desired destination: a done dissertation.

Can a Dissertation Really Be a Trip?

As our title, *Destination Dissertation*, suggests, we're conceptualizing writing a dissertation using a travel metaphor. As you undoubtedly know, this is a very different way to talk about the dissertation process from the metaphors that are usually used, which present the dissertation as a difficult obstacle to surmount. Writing a dissertation, according to the folks who thought up those other metaphors, is like making your way through a Byzantine maze, running a marathon, climbing a mountain, or learning a Martian language. We think that how we talk about something affects our experience of it in significant ways, so we believe metaphors of struggle are part of the reason many students fail to finish. These kinds of metaphors simply make the process seem too difficult or painful to accomplish.

That's why we want you to look at the dissertation as a fun and exciting trip. We want you to call up all of those positive things you associate with trips as you think about your dissertation: discovering new things; the excitement of greeting each new day, not knowing what you'll encounter; developing new skills; acknowledging that you'll sometimes be frustrated, but those periods will be overshadowed by the fun you're having; a confidence that you'll be able to deal with whatever comes your way; and an expectation that you'll be on the trip for a limited amount of time. Writing a dissertation, in other words, will be a vacation from normal routine for a fixed amount of time and will be exciting and stimulating.

Packing Your Bags

If your dissertation journey is going to be a smooth and easy one, you need to start by packing your bags with the gear that will be most useful for your trip. The gear you want to bring along includes beliefs or assumptions about the dissertation process that we believe help make the trip an easy and pleasant one. You might find you have to pull some old assumptions out of your bag to fit these in. Or maybe you'll cling to a couple of old ones for a while but then will feel comfortable ditching them a bit later in your journey. Pull out that suitcase, and let's get started. We're asking you to pack enjoyment, doability, competence, agency, and support.

Enjoyment

What? We don't really mean that writing a dissertation should be enjoyable, do we? We certainly do. Writing a dissertation, like taking a trip, should be fun and interesting—not something to be suffered through. Joy and pleasure aren't usually emotions that are associated with writing a dissertation, but think about it: Aren't the processes of creating something new, discovering new ideas, figuring things out, and sharing what you've learned enjoyable? These are the basic processes involved in a dissertation. And aren't these processes why earning a PhD appealed to you in the first place? We'll be sharing with you some ways to make the actual writing almost magical, so you'll find that even that can be enjoyable, too. When the process is pleasurable, of course, you'll be more interested in doing the work of the dissertation, which means you'll be more efficient at completing it.

Doability

The chief characteristic of a good dissertation is doability. You must be able to get it done, which means that the way you design the project and the way you approach it should facilitate—not hinder—your completion of the project. We want to be clear that we're not saying that, because it's doable, your dissertation is not going to be of high quality. We believe your dissertation should and can follow criteria for good research design, make an original contribution, and showcase your ideas instead of simply applying and extending the ideas of others. We think these are the marks of a good dissertation and research in general, and they're the criteria our processes help you achieve. There's nothing about them, though, that precludes finishing efficiently.

One way to design a dissertation that is doable is by perceiving the function of a dissertation properly. The function of a dissertation is not to change the world or to make an earth-shattering contribution to your discipline. And the dissertation is definitely not supposed to be the culmination of your scholarly career. (If it is, you are going to have a very short career.) In the years to come, you'll have many opportunities to rethink the ideas of your dissertation and to do research that goes beyond what you're doing in your dissertation. Your dissertation marks the beginning of your academic career and research program, not the end, and it is not the best work you'll ever produce. Remember: You are a student trying to finish your doctorate.

One way to help put the function of a dissertation in perspective is to remember that only a few people will read it—you, your committee members, perhaps a family member or two, and maybe a scholar with a particular interest in your topic or another doctoral student looking for a good model for her own dissertation. That's all. More will read it, of course, when you transform it into a journal article (or perhaps a book), but then you'll have a chance to revise and develop your ideas. So slip a little doability into the outside pocket of your suitcase.

Competence

You are beginning the trip that is your dissertation because you are well prepared for it. This trip is not unprecedented or unexpected. You are an experienced and competent scholar, and the dissertation is your opportunity to apply those skills, so we're asking you to pack the confidence of your competence. You might believe that you know nothing about writing a dissertation, but, in fact, you are well under way in the process. You know a great deal on which your dissertation can build. After all, you've been learning how to do research and how to write it up from the beginning of your graduate study.

What's the evidence for your competence? For starters, the fact that you've passed your comprehensive exams. Passing your exams means that faculty members in your department believe you are ready to undertake original scholarship and are qualified to do the work that is the dissertation. They have agreed that you now have the capacity to begin to make original contributions to your discipline. (This is why the exams are sometimes called *qualifying* exams.) You'll see that, over and over again along the route, we trust that you know things and encourage you to listen to the wealth of knowledge within you. This doesn't mean you know everything you need to know about writing a dissertation, but because you are competent, you can confidently and eagerly tackle this project.

As we started talking about how competent you are just now, did you begin to contemplate the possibility that you are one of the few graduate students to whom our words don't apply? Although you probably haven't articulated it to anyone before, do you believe you somehow got admitted to a graduate program because of a mistake? Then you slid by in your coursework, completing assignments and earning good grades only because of the generosity of your professors? As you attempt to write your dissertation, do you believe that you'll be found out for what you are: a fraud? Someone who doesn't belong? Someone who isn't as smart as the other graduate students and professors? Someone who can't think or write in the ways you're supposed to in the academy?

Well, guess what? Your skill levels and intelligence are probably exactly where they should be. And almost everyone feels like a fraud in some ways, even accomplished and seasoned professors. Academia is a conversation about ideas, and you are able to contribute ideas to a conversation as well as anyone else. You can't do it as well right now as you will later, but that's simply a matter of practice. And the dissertation is an excellent place to get some of that practice. So put on your traveling shoes, put those self-doubts on hold (after all, you haven't even given yourself a chance to see what you can do yet), and take the first steps on the path to the dissertation.

Agency

Agency is much talked about these days. It means that you have influence on or control over the affairs of your world—that you are able to do what needs to be done to accomplish your goals. We're asking you to pack agency because we are firm believers in the idea that you are the one who has agency in your dissertation—not your advisor, not other graduate students, not your family, not your discipline. This means that you are going to have to be the one who does the work of the dissertation. Sure, there are all sorts of things that can make finishing a dissertation difficult: You have all that freedom to work as you please with no deadlines, you have a very busy dissertation advisor, you didn't learn all of the skills you need to write a dissertation, your family obligations are heavy, you have to work at many jobs to support yourself.

But there are always going to be conditions of various kinds around you, and if you give them the agency to determine what happens with your dissertation, you won't get done. You have a choice about how to interpret these conditions and how to respond to them. They aren't controlling. You are the one who wants to complete the dissertation, so the responsibility for doing it falls to you. This doesn't mean that you can't ask for help or that others can't help you. But it does mean that, ultimately, this is your dissertation. You are the one who took it on. You are the one to whom it belongs. You are the one who will finish it. Into your bag, then, goes your own agency and a commitment to claim and enact it.

Support

You've got room in your suitcase for one more piece of gear, and it's something that comes from your advisor. It's the idea that advisors want to be helpful to their advisees. They want you to finish and to be successful. There are a number of reasons why helping you finish is good for your advisor. At most universities, faculty members are asked to report how many graduate students they advised and how many they finished each year, and that number may affect the pay increase they get. More important, if you're a good student and go on to a successful academic career, your advisor will get the accolades for having mentored you. Your advisor wants you to finish, then, so you can begin reflecting well on him. Finishing is also good for your department and university. Universities must graduate certain numbers of students with doctoral degrees each year to maintain rankings and accreditation. So must departments to keep their graduate programs.

With few exceptions, advisors are not malevolent, wanting to block you, stymie you, or squash you. After all, they wouldn't have taken you on as an advisee if they had these intentions toward you. If, in fact, it's true that advisors want to be helpful, why do they sometimes seem to be so unhelpful? There are a couple of reasons. One is that they often have limited experience with dissertations and advise you on the basis of that limited experience. For many advisors, the only experience they've had with writing a dissertation was writing their own, so they extrapolate from that process to dissertation writing in general. If it took your advisor six years to write her dissertation, for example, she might assume that everyone should take six years to write a dissertation, including you.

There's a second reason why advisors sometimes don't seem as helpful as they could be: They are very busy people. They are teaching classes, doing their own research, doing service of all kinds for the university and the discipline, advising many graduate students, and trying to have personal lives, too. Sometimes, their advising is not as high quality as it should be simply because they are short on time. That's why we give you ideas for helping your advisor be the best advisor for you in chapter 11. In the meantime, assume that you have the support of your advisor along with you on the trip—because you probably do.

Our Guarantees

Despite careful planning and research, making use of the best resources available, and even the purchase of travel insurance, no trip is perfect. No travel agency or cruise line or hotel will guarantee that it will be. There's a good reason for that: A trip is largely what you make it. Despite obstacles or conditions that aren't exactly what you thought they would be, you have choices at virtually every minute about how to respond to what you are experiencing. The pillow at the hotel may be lumpy, or the train you are on may arrive late, or it may be raining on the one day you have to see a major site. But your choices in terms of these responses—much more than the external conditions you are experiencing—make the trip a good one or not. Whatever is going on, you can still have an enjoyable trip. There are some things we can't guarantee about your trip, then, because they depend on you:

- **We do not guarantee that you will not encounter difficulties.** Research is about solving problems, not avoiding them, and you will be asked to solve problems as you go through the dissertation process. You'll find, though, that the problems are manageable and that you have strategies, resources, and resilience that you can apply to the task.

- **We do not guarantee that your advisor or your committee members will approve or accept your dissertation.** Even if they don't, however, if you write a complete draft of your dissertation, you have a product to which they can specifically and constructively respond and that you can defend and revise. You are still ahead of where you would have been had you not produced a draft.

- **We do not guarantee that every process of the dissertation will be enjoyable.** Yes, we know: We promised you enjoyment when you packed your bag. Now we have to admit that some steps of doing research aren't creative or fun—they're tedious and boring. But none of these processes lasts very long, especially if you do them quickly, and they give you a break from thinking and writing. Even more, the fact that they are concrete and limited helps you enjoy them a bit more because you have control over them and see the efficient progress you're making as you complete them.

- **We do not guarantee that our dissertation model replaces basic skills.** If you are a poor writer or haven't learned to think in the complex and sophisticated ways required of a graduate student, our processes will take you only so far.

- **We do not guarantee that you will finish your dissertation.** In fact, as a result of reading this book and applying the processes that lead to a dissertation, you may decide that it's not something you want to do. Even if you do want to finish, to get it done, you have to do the things that produce a dissertation. If you don't, you won't.

There are some things, though, that we happily guarantee if you follow the processes outlined in this book:

- **We guarantee that our suggested route for writing a dissertation is tested and sound.** We've seen it work with hundreds of graduate students.

- **We guarantee that you will move forward on your dissertation if you apply the processes we outline.** If you follow the steps, there is no way you will not make progress, and your dissertation will be a short trip.

- **We guarantee that you will be intellectually engaged.** The processes we outline invite and, in fact, require this kind of engagement.

- **We guarantee that the findings you generate will go beyond the obvious.** You will be able to develop new ideas—your own ideas—instead of simply applying and extending the ideas of others, which means that what you produce will be insightful and original.

- **We guarantee that your dissertation will be yours.** You will be making the major decisions about it, and you will write it out of your voice.

- **We guarantee more productive conversations with your advisor.** You will be clearer and more confident in these conversations and will be able to defend your dissertation better. This, in turn, will help your advisor advise you better.

- **We guarantee that you will be able to use most of the processes involved in writing your dissertation in your future research.** You can use the techniques to succeed with your research projects after the dissertation is done.

Your Travel Agents

Who are we—these people who think you can write a good dissertation efficiently and even enjoy doing it? This is probably a good time to introduce ourselves to you—your travel agents, in effect, who will take you on a trip to a done dissertation. Sonja began to develop her expertise in this area when she wrote her own dissertation. She was finishing up her coursework in her second year of her doctoral program at Northwestern University when she discovered she had a bit of extra time. She began her dissertation in the late fall and completed it in the spring of that second year of coursework. It wasn't half bad, either—it was 400 pages long and won a dissertation award. As a result of this experience, she knew she was probably doing something right, and she certainly knew that quality dissertations could be written efficiently. When she began teaching in universities where she advised doctoral students, she saw firsthand where students were getting stuck, and she began experimenting with ways to facilitate their processes.

For the most part, Sonja's advising of doctoral students went smoothly, and her students all finished on time. (She has served as the advisor for 35 doctoral students, and all of them finished.) But then one advisee accepted a teaching job before he had finished his dissertation, and he never could quite seem to get around to completing it, no matter how many reminders he got from Sonja. One day, in exasperation, she told him to come stay at her house for a week, and she would make sure he got done. She didn't know what she would do in that week to make sure that happened, but she trusted she would figure something out.

He finally took her up on her invitation, and what happened in that week was that Sonja began to develop some of the processes in this book. Whenever he got stuck, they would talk things through and figure out how to proceed. At the time, Sonja's strategies were largely intuitive and accidental and directed at what she perceived to be the particular needs and working style of that one student. But the strategies seemed to work. By the end of the week, he had completed the entire draft of his dissertation. A year later, another student found himself unable to finish because of the demands of the teaching position he had taken, and Sonja invited him to stay for a week and got similar results.

With these successes behind her, Sonja wondered whether other students might be helped by the approaches she had used with her two advisees. She began to offer Scholars' Retreats to graduate students in all disciplines, providing a place where they could come to work on their dissertations. The first retreat was held in 1997 in Denver and was attended by five bright, eager women from the fields of communication and education who wanted to complete their dissertations.

William entered the picture when he attended one of Sonja's Scholars' Retreats to finish his dissertation in English from the University of New Mexico. He had been ABD for several years and had been trying to write his dissertation in various coffee shops in Albuquerque. Sonja's sister, Karen, who is also a professor, frequently saw him in these coffee shops and said to him one day, "You should attend my sister's Scholars' Retreat." He did and, in fact, he came for two sessions of the retreat. He left with a draft of his dissertation done.

William was so excited about his progress and by the strategies Sonja was developing that he began to organize Scholars' Retreats in New Mexico. His role gradually changed from coordinator of the New Mexico workshops to codirector of our Scholars' Retreats. He has now successfully mentored many PhD students to completion and routinely works as an advisor for faculty members working on publications. As we have worked together, articulating and developing our strategies, our Scholars' Retreat projects have grown. We now conduct Scholars' Retreats each summer in Denver and at other universities, workshops for advisees and advisors, and workshops on publishing for faculty members; we also do individual dissertation coaching. In all of these activities, we continue to try out our processes to see what works and what doesn't, to modify and refine what doesn't, and to develop new processes to make writing dissertations easier.

What we offer you in this book, then, is not based on theoretical knowledge about how to do research and write a dissertation. It is also not built on our experiences with only our individual dissertations. Because we've worked with hundreds of doctoral and master's students at our Scholars' Retreats and in other kinds of workshops, our prescribed route to the dissertation is a collection of answers to practical problems that we've seen trip students up. That they work is evident in the feedback students have given us. Here's just a sampling:

- "For the first time since I started the dissertation process, I know I can finish! Thank you!"

- "I am totally excited about writing again. I actually look forward to my writing sessions now that I know how much I can get done."

- "I have renewed energy about my work and better focus on how I can go about getting my work done. Now, when I'm not writing, I find myself eager to get back to it."

- "You helped me so very much. Not only did you help me with the actual writing process, but you helped me put things in perspective so that I can have the necessary (although often uncomfortable) discussions with my advisor and begin claiming my project for myself."

- "I can't really begin to tell you what your guidance has meant to me. Completion became possible with your instruction and your belief in my abilities. I learned more about research and who I am as a researcher, through my time working with you, than I did through all of my traditional schooling. Thank you for sharing your amazing gift."

- "I followed the pattern you gave me. Although I resisted at first, I finally did it—your tools work if they are used."

- "I'll spare you all the details, but there were some pretty good sobs when I contemplated calling my mother and telling her that I had a draft of the entire dissertation done."

- "Well, it is over! My orals went well. After about an hour of discussion, the chair turned to the other members and said, 'Do we really have to send him out into the hall since it's obvious?' Then they congratulated me. The next day, I presented the dissertation to the library, and it was accepted without change."

Pretty heady praise for a route to a dissertation, huh? We must admit we get a little embarrassed reading these comments, but we want you to know that many students have found that the route we present in this book works and, in the end, offers something more than a dissertation.

How to Use This Guide

There are many ways to travel—you can take a cruise, or make a cross-country road trip, or go backpacking and camping, or stay in a five-star hotel. At the end of all of these trips, you will have reached your destination and undoubtedly will have had many enjoyable experiences. We're presenting one route for doing a dissertation here, but it isn't the only way to write a dissertation. We invite you to take a look at the routes others have suggested and compare them with ours. If ours looks like it might provide you with the guidance you need to make your dissertation process an exciting adventure and that's what you're looking for, we invite you to try it. If not, we hope you find one that works for you. We can perhaps help you make the decision about which road to take by being clear about what our route and this guidebook offer.

Our route emphasizes processes that are concrete and manageable. If you continue reading beyond this chapter, you'll see that, whenever possible, we divide big processes into small ones and make small, chunkable, discrete steps out of something that has to be done. With each step, you know exactly what you have to do and when you're done with that step. Instead of thinking "I have to write my dissertation," these steps change your thinking to, "I have to code eight books today." That's manageable and concrete, and you know exactly what to do and when you're done. "I have to write my chapter on research design" can be replaced with something like, "Right now, I just have to justify why I chose the data I did. I know what goes into the section and the function it performs, so this is something I can do easily."

Remember what that most famous of travelers, Neil Armstrong, said when he set foot on the moon: "That's one small step for a man, one giant leap for mankind." That's a pretty good description of our philosophy—a belief that, by taking small steps, something much bigger—your dissertation—is the result. There's another bonus, too: Because the process can be divided into clear and concrete steps, they can be done when you have small amounts of time. Once you engage the processes, they carry you forward. If you follow them, it will be impossible not to get your dissertation done.

You might find people encouraging you to start writing on your dissertation as soon as you can. We don't. We think you should be working on your dissertation right from the start but not doing the actual writing. You're less likely to get stuck and will be able to move more quickly when you have a sense of the whole picture before you begin to write. Spending more time in the beginning figuring out exactly what you are doing—whether conceptualizing your topic or creating a schema for your literature review or explaining your findings after coding your data—makes any process go much more quickly. When you have the whole picture, you always know where you are, how it fits into the whole, and what you have to do next.

But when you don't have a big picture, every step is a scary unknown. It's like being given a map that shows only a quarter of an inch of a route that is going to cover a long distance. Plus, you waste a lot of time going in different directions that don't pan out and lead you right back to where you started—not exactly the kind of progress you want to make on a trip. The result is captured in the statement that some travelers—especially the ones who don't want to stop for directions—make as they are zooming along the freeway: "I'm lost, but I'm making good time." You're writing lots of pages, but until you know where you're going, it's not where you want to be, and you don't know how to get back to the main highway. That's why we'll give you guidance in this book so that you'll always have a big picture of where you are going or at least the ability to ask for directions.

You will also notice that we have incorporated into this book many actual examples of the processes and sections of a dissertation. Many students have no idea what these should look like, so we want to reveal the mysteries. We don't just tell you how to do something; we show you. This means that those concrete processes we'll be explaining will be very clear, so you won't have any difficulty doing them.

You might be surprised at what is not included in this book. We don't cover topics that are not the reasons students have difficulty finishing their dissertations. Other books on writing dissertations cover things like setting up a workspace, finding sources, finding a dissertation support group, writing an abstract, and using your computer. We left these out because, in our experience, these aren't the reasons students have difficulty finishing their dissertations. Students with whom we work never come to us because they can't use their computers, can't find a dissertation support group, or can't set up a workspace. Our focus in this book is on those places where students like you actually get stuck.

We've also left out some things that are covered in other sources in more detailed, comprehensive, and useful ways. We don't cover research methods, for example, because there are many excellent books on qualitative and quantitative research methods. If you don't know what you need to know about research methods to complete your dissertation, you'll find those sources far more useful than any quick summary of qualitative methods or overview of statistical tests that we could provide here.

Your bags are packed, but you're traveling light with a suitcase of gear that will make your journey easy—enjoyment, doability, competence, agency, and support. Are you ready to make your dissertation into a trip? If so, climb aboard!

CHAPTER TWO
THE JOURNEY BEFORE YOU: 29 STEPS

You're all packed with a set of beliefs and assumptions that will make your travels easier. You're familiar with your travel agents and the guarantees we offer. Now let's get specific about the route you'll be covering in the dissertation process. We'll be talking a lot about making the dissertation into a series of small, concrete steps. The first place to do that is in conceptualizing the basic processes of the dissertation. There are 29 of them. Already, the dissertation seems more manageable, doesn't it? There are just 29 steps.

Many people believe that the 29 steps required to complete a dissertation have to take a long time—that there's no way to cover the route quickly. Typical estimates range from one to five years following your exams, with two to three years the most common. We strongly disagree. We believe most students can complete dissertations within nine months or less, even while they are working part-time. Yes, you heard correctly. Nine months from start to finish, including everything, starting with figuring out your topic all the way through defending.

We don't pretend that everyone can complete a dissertation in nine months. Your particular project may require that you take more time to do some of the 29 steps. If you have steps other than the ones we've conceptualized that you have to do along the way, those will add time, too. But remember that you get to make choices about the kind of project you do for your dissertation. If you make choices that add steps or that add to the length of any of these steps, you are extending the time it takes to cover the route. And, of course, if certain processes take you less than the allotted time, you can complete your dissertation in less than nine months.

A word to the wise: To complete your dissertation in nine months, you have to spend the hours doing the actual work of the dissertation—focused work that actually moves you forward. You have to spend time sitting down and writing. You can't be doing work that doesn't contribute to the dissertation—things like cleaning out your kitchen cupboards or reading e-mail or transcribing tapes in needless detail. (If you're prone to such things, you'll want to pay particular attention to chapter 12, which deals with avoiding delays and annoyances.) Our timetable will work only if you are making good use of the hours you put in.

Our Timetable

So here's our suggested timetable for covering the route. We've put it in hours because that makes the processes ones you can do when you have even an hour here and there and not something you need large blocks of time to do. Put in the hours, and you'll get a dissertation.

- **Step 1. Engaging in a conceptual conversation**: This step is the heart of the planning process for your dissertation. This is a conversation where you (and, ideally, your advisor) map out the preproposal for your dissertation. We explain this process in chapter 3. Time: 10 hours

- **Step 2. Creating the dissertation preproposal**: In this step, you make the key decisions about your dissertation—the research question, categories of your literature review, data, methods of collecting and analyzing your data, significance of your study, and what your chapters will be. The preproposal is the subject of chapter 4. Time: 5 hours

- **Step 3. Approval of the preproposal by your advisor**: Here's where you talk through your preproposal with your advisor, modifying it as necessary. You want to end this conversation with agreement on the elements of your preproposal. Time: 2 hours

- **Step 4. Collecting the literature**: You collect the literature relevant to your project, which you mapped out in your preproposal. Time: 40 hours

- **Step 5. Coding the literature**: Review and code your literature. Time: 60 hours

- **Step 6. Writing the literature review**: Create a conceptual schema for the literature review and write the review. The literature review is the subject of chapter 5. Time: 40 hours

- **Step 7. Writing the proposal**: Write the proposal using your preproposal as your guide. Writing the proposal is discussed in chapter 6. Time: 30 hours

- **Step 8. Review of the proposal by your advisor**: Your advisor reads and suggests revisions to your proposal. This might be a good time to review chapter 11, which deals with working with your advisor, to be sure your interactions are productive. Time: 40 hours (of course, you are doing other work to move your dissertation along during this time)

- **Step 9. Revising the proposal**: Revise your proposal in line with your advisor's suggestions. The revisions should not be major because the proposal follows the preproposal your advisor approved earlier. Time: 10 hours

- **Step 10. Defending the proposal**: If your department requires a defense of your proposal, defend it before your advisor and members of your committee. Because many of the same strategies apply, check out chapter 10, which is about the final defense. Time: 120 hours or three weeks (this isn't all time on task but allows time for committee members to read the proposal)

- **Step 11. Obtaining human subjects' approval**: Obtaining the approval to collect your data from your university's human subjects review committee. Time: Add hours if this step is required for your study

- **Step 12. Collecting the data**: Collect your data. Time: 150 hours

- **Step 13. Transforming the data to codable form**: Transcribe your interviews, or run your statistics, or do whatever is required to get your data in a form you can work with and analyze. Time: Add between 40 and 120 hours if this step is required for your study

- **Step 14. Coding the data**: Code your data based on your research question. Time: 40 hours

- **Step 15. Developing a schema to explain the data**: Develop an explanatory schema that explains and captures in an insightful and coherent way the major pieces of your data. Chapter 7 is about collecting and coding data and developing a schema from the data. Time: 10 hours

- **Step 16. Writing a sample analysis**: Write a sample section of your analysis—something along the lines of five pages—so that your advisor can take a look at it and tell you if there are any problems with your approach. You want to know before you've written up a whole chapter or chapters in that same way. Time: 5 hours

- **Step 17. Review of the sample analysis by your advisor**: Your advisor reviews and provides feedback on your sample analysis. Time: 2 hours

- **Step 18. Writing the findings chapter or chapters**: Write your findings or analysis chapter(s) featuring your explanatory schema. If you feel yourself getting stuck, go to chapter 12. Time: 40 hours per chapter (if three chapters, for example, 120 hours)

- **Step 19. Writing the final chapter**: Write the final chapter of your dissertation—the discussion or conclusion chapter. We talk about this chapter in chapter 8. Time: 20 hours

- **Step 20. Transforming the proposal into a chapter or chapters and preparing the front matter**: Revise your proposal to turn it into your first chapter or your first three chapters, depending on the format you are using for your dissertation. Also prepare your abstract, table of contents, acknowledgments, and lists of figures and tables. This process is discussed in chapter 8. Time: 5 hours

- **Step 21. Editing the chapters**: Editing all of your chapters for substance and form. See chapter 9 for suggestions on editing. Time: 80 hours

- **Step 22. Review of the dissertation by your advisor**: Your advisor reads the dissertation and makes suggestions for revision. Time: 80 hours (of course, you are doing other work during this time, such as formatting the manuscript)

- **Step 23. Revising the dissertation**: Following your advisor's suggestions, revise the dissertation. Time: 40 hours

- **Step 24. Approval of the dissertation by the graduate school**: At many universities, the format of your final draft is reviewed by someone in the graduate school. Time: 40 hours (this process varies greatly from university to university, so check what is involved at yours—you may not need this much time)

- **Step 25. Making final formatting revisions**: Make any formatting changes required by the graduate school. Time: 5 hours

- **Step 26. Review of the dissertation by your committee members**: After your advisor has approved your dissertation, distribute the dissertation to the other members of your committee and give them two weeks to read it. Time: 80 hours

- **Step 27. Defending the dissertation**: If an oral defense is required at your university, defend the dissertation. Chapter 10 gives you strategies for doing this successfully. Time: 2 hours

- **Step 28. Revising the dissertation**: Complete any revisions your committee wants you to make. Time: 40 hours

- **Step 29. Submitting the dissertation**: Submit the dissertation either electronically or in hard copy, whichever your graduate school requires. Time: 2 hours

Total hours required is 1,078. If you are working 40 hours a week on your dissertation, that translates into 27 weeks or 6½ months. Let's frame this another way: The average person watches about 20 hours of television a week. At a minimum, you could finish your dissertation in one year if you write when everyone else you know is watching TV.

Our timetable doesn't include the time for human subjects approval or putting your data into codable form, so add time if you'll need to do either of those. These are the cases when your dissertation is likely to take closer to nine rather than six months. Yes, despite what we said at the beginning of this chapter, we actually think most people can finish in a little over six months, but we thought telling you that earlier might have been hard for you to believe. But now we're ready to acknowledge what we really think: A high-quality dissertation can be done in six to seven months. In fact, we know it can because we've seen many students do exactly that.

Yeah, But . . .

After reviewing the 29 steps, you might be thinking to yourself that the dissertation process we have outlined is too simple and that we have trivialized what should be a complex, sophisticated, intellectual endeavor. As an academic, you've been rewarded for being intellectually savvy, critiquing ideas, and thinking deeply. You might be inclined to dismiss our 29 steps just because they aren't complex or sophisticated. But we've seen the steps succeed time and again precisely because they aren't complex. We encourage you to save your complex thinking for your data analysis and to give the steps a try.

You also might be thinking that if we only knew the unique circumstances that you are experiencing, we'd have to adjust our time frame of 1,078 hours. Because you are unique, you think, what has worked for hundreds of other students simply won't work for you. That might be, but we doubt it. We're asking you to suspend your assumptions about your unique difficulties temporarily and to give our processes a chance. We're pretty confident about how well they work, but you won't have the opportunity to experience success with them if you don't give them a try. If you find yourself struggling to accept our 29 steps or our short timetable, you might want to turn to chapter 12, which deals with delays and annoyances, and read it before you go any farther. If you find yourself saying, "This sounds great, but my advisor will never go for it," you might want to read chapter 11 first—it deals with making your advisor into a good advisor for you.

We certainly acknowledge that there are hundreds of reasons why students don't finish. We are choosing, however, not to focus on them. Instead, our processes are designed to move you forward and get you finished. Stay with us—we'd love to show you how.

Dissertation Checklist

_____ Step 1. Engaging in a conceptual conversation
_____ Step 2. Creating the dissertation preproposal
_____ Step 3. Approval of the preproposal by your advisor
_____ Step 4. Collecting the literature
_____ Step 5. Coding the literature
_____ Step 6. Writing the literature review
_____ Step 7. Writing the proposal
_____ Step 8. Review of the proposal by your advisor
_____ Step 9. Revising the proposal
_____ Step 10. Defending the proposal
_____ Step 11. Obtaining human subjects approval
_____ Step 12. Collecting the data
_____ Step 13. Transforming the data to codable form
_____ Step 14. Coding the data
_____ Step 15. Developing a schema to explain the data
_____ Step 16. Writing a sample analysis
_____ Step 17. Review of the sample analysis by your advisor
_____ Step 18. Writing the findings chapter or chapters
_____ Step 19. Writing the final chapter
_____ Step 20. Transforming the proposal into a chapter or chapters and preparing the front matter
_____ Step 21. Editing the chapters
_____ Step 22. Review of the dissertation by your advisor
_____ Step 23. Revising the dissertation
_____ Step 24. Approval of the dissertation by the graduate school
_____ Step 25. Making final formatting revisions
_____ Step 26. Review of the dissertation by your committee members
_____ Step 27. Defending the dissertation
_____ Step 28. Revising the dissertation
_____ Step 29. Submitting the dissertation

CHAPTER THREE
PLANNING THE TRIP:
THE CONCEPTUAL CONVERSATION

Step 1 (10 hours)

You have decided that you want to take a trip. But where to? So many possibilities lie before you. Do you want to go bicycling along the coast of Denmark? Cruise to the Caribbean islands? Visit the ancient archaeological sites of Greece? Spend a week on the beaches of Thailand? Or explore someplace closer to home like New York City?

You begin to narrow the options almost immediately because of your own preferences and the constraints of time and money. Perhaps you've been intrigued by China ever since you saw the film *Raise the Red Lantern*. Maybe you've always wanted to go to Africa because you trace your ancestors to that region of the world. Perhaps you're interested in going to Russia because a friend traveled there and really enjoyed it. Maybe because you studied Spanish in school, you want to go to someplace like Mexico or Spain so you can try out your language skills. Maybe you only have a week for a trip, so you want to go someplace close. Or perhaps you have friends living in Australia, and staying with them would make your trip affordable.

You have the same kinds of preferences and resources when you begin contemplating your dissertation topic. You have taken many courses for your graduate degree, and some of them were more interesting to you than others. Some theories appeal to you because they explain things in ways that make sense to you, and you like working with some kinds of methods more than others. You enjoy writing papers on some topics more than others. You also chose to develop expertise in particular areas in your comprehensive exams. All of these experiences helped prepare you to choose your dissertation topic, and they are resources on which to draw as you make that decision.

But how do you bring all of your resources to bear to actually choose a topic and then create a plan for your dissertation? This is where a conceptual conversation comes in. This is a conversation you have with someone to work out a preproposal for your dissertation. It's a discussion designed to help you conceptualize your project by funneling your knowledge and preferences efficiently and effectively into a dissertation topic and preproposal. The conceptual conversation happens before you write your proposal because the decisions you make in this conversation become the key components of your dissertation preproposal and then your proposal. A conceptual conversation gives you a specific time period—usually no more than a week—to make all of the key decisions about your dissertation. Writing your proposal on the basis of these decisions then becomes a very efficient process.

A conceptual conversation is based on the premise that you intuitively know some or all of the key pieces you want in the research you will do for your dissertation. Because no one has asked you to articulate these pieces, however, you often don't consciously know what they are and haven't pulled them together in a way that enables you to come up with a dissertation topic. Articulating the pieces you want in your dissertation out loud through conversation makes them evident to you and allows you to probe and explore them in a focused way. Nelle Morton came up with a label we like a lot for the process that characterizes a conceptual conversation—*hearing to speech*. She describes this as a process of articulating thoughts and ideas we don't know we know until someone fully listens to us and allows us to articulate them.[1]

The conceptual conversation replaces the serendipity by which most students pick their dissertation topics. The serendipitous method assumes many forms. Usually, it involves going off on your own, searching through literature to see if something strikes you as interesting. Another variation is to get a vague idea of a topic and to write and write on your proposal, hoping to figure out what you want to research. A third version is when you periodically run into your advisor and chat for a few minutes about your latest idea, hoping for a response that affirms and solidifies your idea. All of these variations on serendipity will significantly delay the completion of your dissertation because they delay its real start. A conceptual conversation gives you the start you need.

Selecting and Orienting a Partner

Conversations involve more than one person, so who is your partner in this conversation? The preferred conversational partner is your advisor. Your advisor will assume the role of your tour guide during the dissertation process, and, ideally, she would be involved in creating the preproposal for your study. Sometimes, though, your advisor is not your best conversational partner for any number of reasons. Maybe your advisor is unwilling to take the time required for this kind of conversation, not realizing that spending the time with you now will cut down on the amount of advising she has to do later. Maybe you don't know your advisor well and don't feel you can ask her to have this kind of conversation with you. You might be intimidated by your advisor, or she might believe the dissertation is something you should figure out by yourself. Or you simply might not feel comfortable with your advisor as your conversational partner. (If you want help making your advisor into the kind of person who could have a conceptual conversation with you, check out chapter 11.)

If you are unable to have your advisor as your conversational partner, you'll have to find someone else to assume this role for you. Maybe another faculty member with whom you have a good relationship is willing to have this kind of conversation with you—perhaps someone in another department if not your own. Maybe a fellow graduate student will be your partner for a conceptual conversation. If someone in your academic circle is not available, a spouse or partner or other friend will work. Sometimes, in fact, someone who doesn't know a lot about research or your field of study can be a particularly good choice as a partner in a conceptual conversation. These people are often good at asking the naive or "silly" questions during the conversation that can help you design a good study.

After you've identified someone you believe would be a good person with whom to have a conceptual conversation, you probably will have to explain what this kind of conversation is and give him an idea of what happens during it. Here are the key points to include in your invitation to your partner: You need a block of uninterrupted time for the conversation—something in the neighborhood of two to three hours. If you don't get your preproposal figured out in this amount of time, you and your conversational partner will want to schedule another session. If possible, this second session should take place within a few days of the first one so you can maintain the momentum you've developed and you remember where you are in the process. Also key is to hold this meeting someplace where you won't be interrupted—in your home or at a coffee shop, for example, rather than in your office if other people are likely to be stopping by to chat. You want uninterrupted time to focus just on creating your dissertation preproposal.

What should each of you bring to the conceptual conversation? For you, your luggage is light but brimming with resources. Bring your interests (those resources you have been developing throughout your coursework), your enthusiasm, a tablet to write on, something to write with, and perhaps a tape recorder. Recording the conversation is sometimes useful in helping you identify key ideas later. And your partner? Ask her to bring a commitment to spend a significant amount of time with you, excitement about what she will figure out with you, a tablet to write on, and something to write with. A pot of tea or coffee wouldn't hurt, either.

Asking and Answering Questions

Now is the time for the conversation to begin. So what exactly goes on in it? What do the two of you do to produce the preproposal for your dissertation? Your partner begins by asking you questions designed to help you identify some key pieces or elements you want to include in your dissertation. Here are some of the questions your partner might want to ask:

- What are your major interests in your discipline?

- What personal experiences have you had that were particularly significant or meaningful for you that are relevant to your discipline?

- What coursework did you take that you found most exciting?

- What theories and concepts are most interesting to you?

- Are there some ideas you have studied that you are curious about and want to explore more?

- What bodies of literature have you encountered that intrigue you?

- Are there some theories you want to avoid?

- With what kinds of data do you enjoy working?

- Do you have ideas for specific data, texts, or artifacts you would like to study?

- Are there resources to which you have access that could provide participants or data for your study? Does your job offer any of these resources? How about your volunteer activities? Is there someone you know who could give you access to these kinds of resources? Is there an archive, organization, or upcoming event in your community that is ripe for analysis?

- What kinds of methods do you like to use when you do research?

- What are your career goals when you finish your degree?

As you answer the questions, your partner should encourage you to continue talking by asking exploratory, open-ended, follow-up questions. For example, he might ask you defining questions such as: "What do you mean by. . . ?" He might ask you doubting questions that encourage you to think and explain more: "Why do you think that's the case? What are you seeing here?" He might ask you questions that ask you to make connections between some of your ideas: "What connection do you see between theory X and theory Y? How do they relate for you?" Some of his questions will be probing questions: "Can you elaborate on what interests you about that theory?" These questions are not intended to intimidate or bully you in particular directions or show you what you don't know. Their purpose is to get you to articulate the key pieces you want in your dissertation. If you don't know the answer to a question your partner asks, try to make a good guess. The point is less to provide a precise and correct answer to a question and more to use the questions to stimulate your thinking.

Your partner should keep asking you questions, all designed to encourage you to produce more talk about your interests. As you answer the questions, she'll sometimes provide new input by introducing ideas, especially if she is also a scholar in your discipline. She might ask you, for example, if a particular concept is relevant to what you are thinking about: "Is Foucault's notion of the discursive formation something like what you're talking about?" or "This sounds a lot to me like how things were in the frontier days of the West. Is that an accurate way to think about this idea?" This new input might help you form dissertation pieces out of your interests that you didn't see how to do before.

Your partner should be doing other things in this conversation besides asking questions. You want him to listen closely and carefully. Encourage your partner to take notes as completely as possible so that you have a record of your ideas in the order in which they came to you. He is taking the notes so that you are free to think and talk. You can also record this conversation so that neither one of you has to take detailed notes. We often find, however, that note taking is one more technique for making connections among ideas that you are articulating. Regardless of how you are documenting the session, your partner should note in some way the ideas that seem most important to you to include in your study. He should not be telling you what he is noting as he does it because his goal is to keep you talking. But you want him, in effect, to do a meta-analysis of your talk, transcending the details of it to try to see the larger picture that is emerging for you and that will form the basis for your dissertation. If he has ideas about possibilities for your dissertation that incorporate some of the ideas you are talking about, he'll want to note those, too, so he can share them with you later in the conversation.

The two of you don't want to be doing any evaluating or sorting of ideas at this stage of the conversation. None of the ideas that you or your partner articulates should be dismissed. Even the ideas that seem the silliest and the most irrelevant should be written down. Silly ideas can lead you to new places and to significant new ideas.

You might discover, as you answer your partner's questions, that you are repeating yourself, saying some ideas over and over again. Don't worry about that, and don't stop yourself. These cycles help you understand what is most important to you. You will tend to go through one cycle of ideas and then repeat the cycle, perhaps with a few additions. When you begin to repeat yourself frequently, with no new additions—when you can't think of anything else you want to add—that's an indication that you are done. All of the pieces that you know at this moment that you want to have in your dissertation have come out. Repetition without any new pieces means you are ready to formalize those key pieces.

Identifying Key Pieces

Now is the time for you and your partner to use the information produced in your conceptual conversation to identify the key pieces that you want to be part of your dissertation study. What are key pieces? They are elements that will be used to form the preproposal for your dissertation. They will be more formally articulated later, but they have to do with the key components of a study:

- A research question to guide your study

- Some data you will analyze

- A method of data collection

- A method of data analysis

- The areas of your literature review

One piece you might identify for your dissertation is that you are interested in discovering something about a particular concept or phenomenon. For example, you might know that you want to figure out something about how gender affects social movements. Another piece might be that you want to work with a certain set of data—perhaps an archive of land ownership records that exists in your community or popular artifacts such as the *Harry Potter* books. Maybe you have access to a particular group of individuals such as clergy wives and want to make use of that group as participants. Perhaps you really like a particular theory such as chaos theory and want to be sure you get to work with it in your dissertation. These are all the kinds of pieces that turn into key components of your dissertation.

Identifying your key components can happen in many different ways. Your partner might tentatively suggest what those pieces are from the notes she has been taking and the ideas she has marked in her notes as ones that seem most important to you. Maybe you both know what the pieces are as a result of your conversation and can name them together. You might know the data you want to analyze but not your research question or the categories of your literature review. Or maybe you know what you want to ask and a relevant body of literature with which you want to work but nothing else. That's OK. The point here is to identify the key pieces of which you are certain—those things you know you really want in your dissertation. You'll fill in the missing pieces later as you create your dissertation preproposal.

What you want to be able to do at this moment is to answer "yes" to this question when your conversational partner asks it: "Are these key pieces you want in your dissertation?" All of the key components of your study probably won't have been identified yet, but your partner's statement of the key elements you know so far will look something like this: "From what I understand, you want to use grounded theory as the method of analysis in your dissertation, you want to analyze the conversation among participants in your online classes for your data, and you are interested in dealing somehow with Paolo Freire's ideas. Are these key pieces you want in your dissertation?" Another example is: "You want to do something with organizations that only exist online, you are interested in Anthony Giddens' idea of structuration and want to use it somehow, and you don't want to use statistical methods to analyze your data. Are these key pieces you want in your dissertation?" And another: "You want to ask a research question that gets at the role of gender in resistance strategies used in social movements, you want to use biographies of Native American activists, and you know a lot about narrative analysis and would like to use it as a method. Are these key pieces you want in your dissertation?"

Maybe your partner suggests what he thinks are the key pieces of your dissertation and, when you hear him articulate them, you disagree. You might not be interested in what your partner names as the key components, or maybe he is close, but his articulation of the ideas isn't quite right. Or maybe your partner is articulating what *he* wants you to do in your dissertation and not what *you* want. He might think he has articulated a perfect dissertation topic for you that encapsulates a lot of your interests, but it's not what you want to do. (This occurs most often when your conversational partner is your advisor.) If your partner is pushing you in a direction in which you're not interested, you both want to remind yourselves whose dissertation you are planning—yours! Your partner should not try to convince you that his proposed topic is a good one and that you should use it if the topic simply doesn't interest you. His role is to help you design a project that you really want to do and in which you really believe.

The problem with doing someone else's idea for a project is that if you get stuck in the doing of the study, you have less motivation and knowledge and fewer resources available to work through the difficulties. If your dissertation is part of your advisor's funded research, of course, you're going to have less say about your dissertation topic and cannot easily dismiss your advisor's articulation of a possible study for you. Even in this case, though, you need to work out the particulars of *your* study in the context of your advisor's larger research project, and it still must be a study in which you have some interest.

But back to our question. If you can't answer "yes" to your partner's articulation of the key pieces of your dissertation, what you need to do is to articulate what is missing from the key pieces that your conversational partner proposed. What was not included in the key pieces your partner articulated? What was included that you don't want to be there? Together, sculpt and whittle at the key pieces to get them closer to your interests. Yes, you both want the process to be over at this point. You are eager for the dissertation topic to be decided. But rushing at this stage will only make the dissertation take longer in the end.

With the help of your conversational partner, you've identified some of the key pieces you want your dissertation to include, articulated them, and written them down. You have made the first decision about where you want to go on the trip that is your dissertation. The next step is to build on these key pieces to develop your itinerary or create your preproposal by filling in missing pieces.

Notes

1. Nelle Morton, *The Journey Is Home* (Boston: Beacon, 1985), 202.

CHAPTER FOUR

DEVELOPING YOUR ITINERARY:
THE PREPROPOSAL

Steps 2–3 (7 hours)

You're off to a good start in planning for your trip. You have a topic that interests you and have worked out a few key pieces of your dissertation. You still want to do more planning before you go, though, because your trip is not inexpensive, and you want to get as much as you can from the experience. Although you might be tempted to begin writing your proposal now, don't go to the computer yet. Beginning to write now will significantly delay the completion of your dissertation because you will be delaying its real start. When you begin writing before you've made the key decisions about your dissertation and without a real understanding of where you're going, you usually get stuck fairly quickly. When you clarify your intentions at the beginning, you have a more successful trip.

What you want to do now is to create a dissertation preproposal. The preproposal you develop for your dissertation is not unlike the itinerary travelers develop for their trips. They know a couple of key pieces—their destination, the amount of time they have to spend, or the kind of transportation they will take, for example—and make their other travel plans around those pieces. If your conversational partner is willing to stay with you for a little while longer, ask him to join you in developing this preproposal. Talking through the elements of your preproposal with the person who facilitated your topic selection often makes the creation of the preproposal go more quickly. The quality of the decisions you make tends to be higher, too.

To create your preproposal, take a look at the key pieces that you know you want in your dissertation that you identified in the conceptual conversation. These key pieces might be a variety of things—theories you want to use or ideas about how you might like to collect or analyze data, for example. Have you identified your research question and data as part of the key pieces? If you haven't identified one or both of these—the research question and the data—now is the time to turn your attention to these two decisions. If you have formulated your research question, you still want to turn your attention to it—not to develop it but to assess it. We'll start at the beginning of the process of developing a research question, and you can join in at whatever point is appropriate for where you are in the process.

Formulating Your Research Question

The research question is what you are trying to find out by doing your study. It guides your research process, tells you what to look at and what to ignore, and is captured in the title of your dissertation. As a result of your conceptual conversation, you might already have a question that you want to ask in your study that is quite close to what your actual research question will be. What is more likely, though, is that you have several key pieces of your dissertation figured out but not the research question. That's because the research question is the most important part of the dissertation and takes the most effort and care to develop.

If you don't have a question that could turn into your research question, how do you get one? One of the easiest ways is to review the key pieces you identified that you would like in your dissertation and to ask how they might be connected to various theoretical conversations in your field. If you know you are interested in dealing with Paolo Freire's ideas, for example, you might identify as relevant theoretical conversations liberatory pedagogy and online pedagogy. Brainstorm possible questions that allow you to use the key pieces you have identified for your dissertation and connect them to constructs or phenomena that are part of these theoretical conversations. Write down all of the questions that you (and your partner, if she is still involved) suggest, even if you know they are not questions you would want for your study. By writing them down, you can see how to build on them, how to combine them, and how to mold a question from them that captures your interests.

Criteria for a Good Research Question

What are you aiming for as you create a question for your dissertation? A good research question meets six criteria. The first criterion for a good research question is that it *clearly identifies the theoretical construct* you are studying. For example, if you are interested in figuring out the processes by which parents transmit their political perspectives to their children, the theoretical construct you are studying is "transmission of political perspectives." If you are interested in whether grades motivate students' learning, your theoretical construct is "students' motivation." If you are interested in how television networks attract and retain viewers through branding, your theoretical concept is "branding." Notice that the theoretical construct is the phenomenon, event, or experience you want to learn more about.

A second criterion that a research question should meet is that it should contain some suggestion of *recognizability* of the theoretical construct. This means that the research question articulates the theoretical construct in a specific enough way so that you'll know it when you see it when you are coding for it in your data. In other words, it supplies a clear unit of analysis that allows you to tell the difference between that construct and other constructs relatively easily. To accomplish recognizability, word the construct in a way that is concrete and specific.

An example will help clarify this idea of recognizability. Celeste started her dissertation planning with a theoretical construct of "the experience of nontraditional women in college." While certainly a construct that would be important to explore, it is too large because Celeste would have a difficult time recognizing the construct when she sees it in her data. It involves a potentially large number of different constructs, including women's experiences of raising children while going to school, degree of support from family members, responses of other students, educational accomplishments, use of technology, emotions the women experience, and on and on and on. There is virtually nothing having to do with nontraditional women college students that would not count as part of the construct of "the experience of nontraditional women in college." A more specific theoretical construct would be "nontraditional women's experiences of discrimination in the classroom" or "nontraditional women's use of support services on campus." The recognizability here is that the theoretical construct is focused on one aspect of nontraditional women's experiences and allows Celeste to discriminate between it and other constructs that are a part of nontraditional women's experiences in college. Identifying recognizability in this way allows Celeste to find more examples—and more nuanced examples—of these experiences in her data because she can ask herself, as she sees an experience discussed, "Is this an example of ____?"

Here's another example: You begin with a theoretical construct of "group purpose in therapeutic settings." Again, you have many options for theoretical constructs as part of this construct, including the importance of achieving the group's purpose, therapists' strategies for achieving group purpose, obstacles to achieving it, and so on. You might choose to settle on "participants' methods of sabotaging group purpose" as your recognizable theoretical construct for your research question. As you formulate your research question, then, think about how you will code data with that question, looking for examples of the theoretical construct you are considering featuring in your research question. Will you be able to locate it and distinguish it easily from other constructs that appear in your data?

There's another criterion you want your research question to meet, and that is *transcendence of data*. Except in a few instances (and we'll talk about what these are shortly), your research question should not include mention of the specific data you are using to investigate your question. Many different kinds of data can be used to answer your research question, so don't confine your question to the one type of data you plan to study. You want your question to be more abstract than those specific data.

For example, if you want to study resistance strategies used by marginalized groups to challenge institutions, you can use as your data a social movement, works of art by politically motivated artists, the songs sung by union organizers, or the strategies used by Mexican immigrants to improve their status in the United States, to name a few. You want your study to contribute to a significant theoretical conversation in your field, and it can do that more easily if your question is not tied to one particular kind of data. A research question on the topic of resistance that transcends the data, then, might be, "What is the nature of the resistance strategies used by subordinate groups in their efforts to challenge hegemonic institutions?"

Let's look at an example where the criterion of transcendence of data was violated in a research question. Larry initially proposed as part of his research question a theoretical construct of "accounting practices used in children's theaters in Detroit." Here, his theoretical construct is the same as his data—he is conflating the construct in the research question with the data he will use to answer the question. As a result, Larry's story has limited interest to other readers. Larry certainly could collect data for his study concerning accounting practices in children's theater groups in Detroit, but the construct he wants to understand in his study is larger than that—perhaps something like "accounting practices in nonprofit arts organizations."

There are a few kinds of dissertations where the criterion of transcendence of data in the research question does not apply. These are dissertations in which researchers want to find out about a particular phenomenon, so the research is specifically about that phenomenon. For example, someone who is interested in the strategies used by Alcoholics Anonymous to attract members would want to include *Alcoholics Anonymous* in the research question. In this case, the researcher sees something unique and significant about that particular organization, in contrast to other treatment approaches, and sets out to understand it specifically.

There are some fields, too, where the data are typically included in the research question in dissertations. History is one. Dissertations in this field are about a particular place and time, and their purpose is to explore that place and time. Thus, those particulars are included in the theoretical construct of the research question. For example, a research question for a history dissertation might be, "How was a counterculture identity sustained in Humboldt County, California, in the 1980s and 1990s?" The discipline of English is another one where research questions may include mention of data. Scholars in English are often interested in a writer or group of writers or a particular type of literature, and those would be included in the research question. An example is: "How do troll images function in the narratives of Scandinavian writers between 1960 and 1990?"

Your research question also should meet the criterion of identifying your study's *contribution to an understanding of the theoretical construct*. Your research question should name what happens to the theoretical construct in your study—what you are doing with it in your study or what interests you about it. This contribution should be developed from the theoretical conversations in your discipline and should reflect a specialized knowledge of your discipline. For example, the new contribution you might be making is to begin to suggest the communication processes by which political beliefs are transmitted within families. You know that such beliefs (the theoretical construct) get transmitted. Your new contribution will be to explain some of the processes by which the transmission happens. Or let's say your theoretical construct is stay-at-home mothers. The new contribution you might make is to explain how stay-at-home mothers legitimize the role in an era when most women work. Meeting this criterion in your research question forecasts the contributions to the discipline you'll discuss in your conclusion.

A fifth criterion your research question should meet is *capacity to surprise*. You should not already know the answer to the research question you're asking. You want to be surprised by what you find out. If you already know the answer to your question, you don't need to do the study. Moreover, if you know the answer, you aren't really doing research. Instead, you are selecting and coding data to report on and advocate for a position you already hold. Zaila, for example, had selected as her data immigrant narratives, and her research question was, "How do traumatic events produce long-term negative effects on individuals?" She was already assuming that immigration inevitably traumatizes individuals and that there are no possibilities other than to experience immigration negatively. She was not likely to be surprised by her findings because her question articulated what she was expecting to discover. If she continued in this direction, she certainly could have found examples of negative effects, but her contribution to her discipline (and her future ability to publish) would have been greatly diminished. And, by the way, don't worry about not coming up with any significant findings when you ask a question and don't already know the answer to it. Whatever findings you get are your findings, and they tell you something useful about your theoretical construct.

The final criterion for judging a research question is *robustness*, the capacity to generate complex results. Your question should have the capacity to produce multiple insights about various aspects of the theoretical construct you are exploring. It should not be a question to which the answer is "yes" or "no" because such an answer is not a complex result. The following list provides examples of how to begin research questions that typically produce robust findings.

Research Questions that Produce Robust Findings Often Begin With . . .

- What is the nature of
- What are the functions of
- What are the mechanisms by which
- How do . . . perceive
- What factors affect
- What strategies are used
- How do . . . respond

- How do . . . affect
- What are the effects of
- What is the relationship between
- How are . . . defined
- How do . . . differ
- Under what conditions do

When you are formulating your research question, work carefully on wording it so that the question meets the six criteria for a good research question: It clearly identifies the theoretical construct you are studying, it contains some suggestion of recognizability of the theoretical construct, it (usually) transcends your data, it identifies your study's contribution to an understanding of the theoretical construct, it has a capacity to surprise, and it can produce robust results. A question formulated according to these criteria ensures that your study has a solid center that can hold all of the pieces of the study together.

Once you have the core of a question that you think is a good one, work with your conversational partner (if he is still hanging in there with you) to formulate the exact wording for the question. This is important to do now because it helps test the viability of the research question before you get too far along. Here are samples of some poorly worded research questions that don't meet one or more of the criteria for a good research question. Notice how easily they can be revised into good questions:

- **Research Question 1**: "Are minority mentoring programs effective in mentoring minority undergraduate students?" This question does not meet the criterion of robustness because it is a yes-no question that will not produce complex and insightful findings. **A better question is**: "What factors characterize successful mentoring relationships for minority undergraduate students?"

- **Research Question 2**: "What is the history of public education in Washington, D.C.?" This question for a study in the discipline of history is inappropriate because it contains no identification of the contribution the study will make to an understanding of the theoretical construct—education in Washington, D.C. Because no contribution the history will make is specified in the question, anything can count as data to include in the study (history of minority relations within the schools, history of school finances, history of assessment of students, history of pedagogical practices used in the schools), thus violating the criterion of recognizability. **A better question is**: "How did the relationship between teachers and unions in Washington, D.C., affect pedagogical practices within the schools in the decade of the 1960s?"

- **Research Question 3**: "How do climate-driven changes in the biophysical environment of the Great Lakes region affect the sustainability of wetlands?" This question violates the criterion of transcendence of data. It names the particular data that will be collected to answer the question—the biophysical environment of the Great Lakes region. **A better question is**: "How do climate-driven changes in the biophysical environment affect the sustainability of wetlands?"

- **Research Question 4**: "How do Amish parents ensure that their children actively contribute to the survival of the Amish community?" This question does not have a recognizable theoretical construct. Virtually any practice in which Amish parents engage could be seen as a possible mechanism for ensuring active contributions by their children, and collecting and coding data to answer this question would be very difficult. **A better question is**: "What disciplinary practices do Amish parents use to facilitate their children's active participation in contributing to the survival of the Amish community?" "Disciplinary practices" focuses the theoretical construct and enables the researcher to be clear about what will answer the question. Notice that the data are named in this question. That's because the researcher is interested in the Amish community in particular, so lack of transcendence of data is not a problem here.

- **Research Question 5**: "How does the Starbucks chain engage in oppressive practices toward consumers?" Let's assume the researcher really wants to study only Starbucks for some reason, so this question doesn't violate the criterion of transcendence of data. But it does violate the capacity to surprise. The researcher is already assuming that Starbucks performs a particular function. **A better question is**: "What are the impacts of Starbucks on the consuming patterns of its patrons?"

- **Research Question 6**: "Are the learning strategies used by law students at St. Louis University's School of Law effective?" There are three problems with this question. It includes the data in the question, violating the criterion of transcendence of data. It asks a yes-no question, violating the criterion of robustness. And it has a vague theoretical construct—strategies to learn what? **A better question is**: "What learning strategies do first-year law students use to develop their case-analysis skills?"

- **Research Question 7**: "What happens when motivational techniques from the business world are applied to nonprofit arts organizations?" This question lacks specificity in identification of the contribution to an understanding of the theoretical construct. "What happens" does not provide a clear and specific understanding about what interests the researcher about nonprofit arts organizations. **A better question is**: "What motivational techniques are reported as effective by the staff of nonprofit arts organizations?"

- **Research Question 8**: "How do union organizations use the strategy of enactment to retain their radicalism over time?" The trouble with this question is that the answer will not be a surprise because the researcher has already assumed that retention of radicalism is due to one strategy. **A better question is**: "What strategies do union organizations use to retain their radicalism over time?"

Multiple Research Questions

You undoubtedly have seen dissertations or journal articles in which there is more than one research question. Should you have more than one question in your study? Maybe, but we discourage it, and here's why: In some cases, studies contain more than one question because researchers have not thought carefully enough about what they want to find out. As a result, they take a scattershot approach and try to get close to the question they want to answer by asking about many things. A better approach is to aim for one research question and to think carefully about what it is. Refine it sufficiently so that it really gets at the key thing you want to find out. All research designs have one central question that is guiding them, and taking the time to figure out precisely what it is will make it easier to create and execute your dissertation preproposal and help you analyze your data.

Another reason studies sometimes include many research questions is because students confuse research questions with the questions they will use as prompts for coding their data. The many research questions are really just guides for coding data. In her study about online chat rooms and whether they have the capacity for deep culture, Frankie had such a list of research questions:

- What artifacts do chat rooms use as the basis for developing culture?

- What norms characterize chat rooms?

- What processes are used to socialize new members into chat rooms?

- What mechanisms are used in chat rooms to repair breaches of organizational norms?

These questions are not separate research questions as much as they are questions that Frankie will use to guide her analysis of her data. They are methodological guidelines that will help her know what to look for as she codes her data. Remember that a research question is what the dissertation is about—it produces the title of the dissertation. None of these questions is major enough to assume that role in Frankie's study, so they aren't really her research questions.

There are some cases when more than one research question is warranted. When a study has more than one research question, it tends to be when basic information about a theoretical construct does not exist, and you need to know basic information before you can investigate a process that characterizes the construct. Frankie, for example, knew from the literature she had read that online interaction is not supposed to have the capacity to develop a deep culture the way that organizations typically do, but she had been observing and participating in a chat room that she thought had such a culture. One question she wanted to ask, then, was, "Can chat rooms develop deep culture?" She did not know whether chat rooms can have this kind of culture, and she wanted to find out. The answer to this question alone, though, does not meet the criterion of robustness for a research question because it would produce an answer of "Yes, chat rooms can have deep culture" or "No, they can't." That finding is not complex enough for a dissertation.

Frankie needed another question in addition to the question about whether chat rooms can develop deep culture—something that would produce more complex findings. Frankie also wanted to find out how participants in chat rooms create deep culture if, in fact, they do. So she had a second research question for her study: "What mechanisms do participants in chat rooms use to create deep culture?" Because she needed to validate that these kinds of interactions have a viable culture before she could ask how this culture is created, her study has two research questions.

Another example of a situation in which more than one research question is warranted is Sam's study. He was interested in differences for students between online and face-to-face courses. He could find nothing that answered the question he wanted to ask: "Are there differences in students' retention of subject matter between online and face-to-face courses?" That was his first question. But he would not have had much of a study by just reporting yes or no concerning whether differences exist. He also wanted to know more about those differences, so he added two other questions: "If so, what are the differences?" and "Do the differences correlate with students' learning styles?"

Some studies contain, in addition to a research question or questions, a set of hypotheses. When research questions are developed for quantitative research designs, they lead to hypotheses. Because quantitative designs produce as their primary data measures of significance or measures of relationship among some number of factors, the research question is extended to include one or more hypotheses about whether the relationship exists. The hypotheses make predictions in a testable form, and they are either rejected or accepted as a result of the study. If you are doing an experimental study, you know that hypotheses are of different types—such as null, alternative, directional, and nondirectional—and that there are specific rules for these different forms. Because you know how to construct hypotheses if you are doing this kind of study, we won't be providing any more information about that process here.

So here's where we are now: You have created one key piece of your study for your dissertation preproposal—your research question. You have worked on the wording of the question so that it meets the criteria of identifiability of theoretical construct, recognizability, contribution to understanding the theoretical construct, transcendence of data, capacity to surprise, and robustness. Now is the time to turn your attention to your data.

Selecting Your Data

The second key piece of your dissertation that you have to work out as you move toward creating the preproposal is the data you want to analyze in your study. Perhaps you decided on this in your conceptual conversation. If not, this is the next decision to make. What, exactly, are you going to collect and analyze? A particular set of art works by one artist? The narratives of a group of people around a specific event? Newspaper coverage of an event for a particular period of time? Historical accounts of an event? Census data? The data you choose to study also must meet criteria, just as research questions do. While the criteria for your research question help you create a significant study, the two criteria for data help make your study doable and efficient.

The first criterion to consider as you think about your data is *accessibility*. Try to conceptualize your project so that you can collect the data easily and in a reasonable amount of time. Don't formulate something as your data that will be procedurally difficult or time consuming to collect. You are conceptualizing a doable dissertation here, so make sure your data don't inhibit doability.

One way to ensure accessibility is to choose as your data something you can control because you don't have to rely on others to gain access to those data. You don't want your data to be subject to the decisions of others or complicated bureaucratic procedures about whether they can be released, for example. Accessibility also takes into account time, money, and location. If you must travel great distances and at great expense to collect data, you have chosen data that are not very accessible. Do you have options closer to home that would be less expensive?

Remember your own resources, too, as you settle on your data. Nagesh was looking for data to use to study the processes involved in starting environmental activist groups, and we discovered that he had been an environmental activist for most of his adult life, had been involved in starting several environmental organizations, and had all the files and materials related to the founding of the organizations. He had a major data source in his own file cabinet! Sally wanted to study the impact of technology on students' openness to multiculturalism. She was scheduled to teach an online class on multiculturalism the next semester and had an excellent source of data for her project already available to her. Tatjana stumbled accidentally onto a ready source of data for her dissertation: She found years of correspondence between two people in the attic of the house she was renting and used the letters as her data in a dissertation on interpersonal communication.

Contrast Nagesh's, Sally's, and Tatjana's decisions about their data with Martha's. She wanted to use as her data interviews she would conduct with child soldiers fighting in Sudan. These data required that she postpone data collection until she became fluent in a language she had not studied before, involved hazardous travel, and required that she try to gain the confidence of young children from another culture and under great political pressure simply to collect her data. Cheng also selected some inaccessible data for his dissertation. A Chinese student studying in the United States, he wanted to return to China to interview CEOs of companies there, but if he did, he would not have been allowed back into the United States to finish his degree because of visa problems. Both Martha and Cheng had many more options open to them for data to make a doable dissertation.

There is another common problem with conceptualizing data that you want to avoid, too, and it suggests the second criterion for your data to meet: *limitability*. Students have a tendency to collect much more data than they need for a study. The analysis of the data, not the amount of data collected, determines the originality and significance of your study. What answers your research question is your analysis of your data, not your data. When you collect too much data, your analysis tends to be superficial because it must take so much into account. You are only able to attend to the high points of the data and are prevented from doing in-depth analysis because you are trying to fit in and explain so many findings from all of your data. As you try to fit more and more pieces into the findings, you have to homogenize the data, often resulting in abstract overgeneralization that is not very insightful and that is difficult to write up.

Ian's study provides an example of over-collection of data. He was studying the kinds of questions asked by teachers who adhere to a particular educational philosophy. He videotaped and transcribed 30 two-hour class sessions taught by the same instructor, kept a journal of his observations of those 30 class sessions, and collected the teacher's lesson plan for each day. The result was a massive amount of data that almost overwhelmed him and ultimately produced a superficial, broad-brush analysis that made less of a contribution to his discipline than he had hoped. So keep a close watch on accessibility and limitability. Both are key in designing a doable, high-quality dissertation.

Aligning Your Research Question and Your Data

Up until now, you have focused on your research question and your data because these two elements determine everything else in your study. Your research question and data must be settled on and assessed to make sure they work together well before you finalize the other elements of your study. The next step in the development of your preproposal, then, is checking the alignment between the research question and the data. If the data you want to analyze can't answer the research question you have proposed, you have to change either the research question or the data. You are doing the study to answer your question, and the study can't be completed if your data don't allow you to answer that question.

One thing to be clear about here is that alignment between research question and data does not mean that your data should be the only data that are appropriate for answering your question. If other sets of data besides yours could answer the question, that's not a problem. Your concern is not whether yours are the best data to use but whether they have the capacity to answer your question.

Let's take a look at a few examples of alignment between a research question and data:

- **Research Question**: "How do successful female university professors account for their success?"

  Data: Stories by female university professors about success in their careers

- **Research Question**: "What strategies are used by founder-centered arts organizations to ensure viability following the departure of the founder?"

  Data: Minutes of board meetings, publicity materials, and interviews with the board members and staff of a ballet company whose founder had died

- **Research Question**: "What is the ideology concerning leadership implicit in canonical literature for young adults?"

  Data: Children's books that won the Newbery Medal

- **Research Question**: "What is the nature of the process used in small governmental agencies to decide whether to privatize public service?"

  Data: Case studies of two cities in Nebraska of comparable size, one that has privatized a particular service and one that has not, using minutes of meetings; newspaper articles; press releases about the decisions; and interviews with mayors, city managers, and others involved in the privatization decision

These examples of alignment make it seem easy. You would be surprised, though, at how often misalignment exists between a research question and the data selected to answer it. For example, Ty formulated as his research question, "How is identity constructed through social interaction in conflict situations?" The data he wanted to use to answer the question were individual interviews with participants in a conflict. Those data can't answer the question, though, because interviews will not provide information about how the participants construct identity through interaction with others. Ty needs to see the people in action with others in the conflict to see that.

Maggie's study provides another example of misalignment between a research question and data. She wanted to use as her data interviews with directors of war movies and the actors who starred in them and formulated as her research question, "How do war movies function to promote particular attitudes toward war?" Her data, however, are incompatible with her research question. To answer this research question, she must analyze the movies themselves from audience members' perspectives—not what the directors and actors say about what they were trying to do in the films.

One more example: Miguel wanted to use as his data participant observations of the creation and daily practices a dance troupe uses to choreograph its dances, and he proposed as his research question, "How do independent dance companies balance economic viability with commitment to an artistic vision?" That question cannot be answered with the data he wanted to use because he would not be collecting any data about the dance company's financial status or budgetary decision-making processes. Methods of creating and developing dances provide little or no information about dance companies' finances.

If you discover an incompatibility between the question you are proposing and the data you want to study, you have two choices: You can change the focus of your question or change your data. At this point, most students have a greater commitment to the data they want to analyze than they do to the research question, so tweaking the question so it can be answered using the data is probably the easiest way to fix a misalignment. Miguel, for example, can change his research question to something like, "How is leadership enacted among members of a dance company to create an artistic product?" If you do not have much commitment to a particular set of data, though, making some changes in the data you study can be an easy way out of misalignment. Miguel could choose different data for his study: He could collect the budgets and financial records of the dance company and interview the director and other staff members about how they reconcile financial viability with their artistic visions.

Identifying Your Method of Data Collection

Once you have alignment between the research question and the data, the next decision you want to make is how to collect the data. Of course, if the method of data collection were one of the key pieces you identified in the conceptual conversation, you might already have made this decision. This is a particularly important decision because it has a lot to do with how efficiently you can complete your dissertation.

Picking a relatively quick method of collection—either because you have easy access to the data or because you fully understand the method of collection—will greatly increase the speed with which you can work. For example, let's say you want to analyze the ideology of a particular group for some reason. You can choose to do an analysis of the group's public documents or to conduct interviews with members of the group. The public documents are easily accessible and obtainable, whereas you don't know any of the individuals you would want to interview. Choosing a textual analysis of the documents would be the more efficient choice for your method of data collection. If you choose the route of the interviews, you might need to use a snowball sample just to identify possible group members, you would have to locate individuals from the group who would be willing to be interviewed, and you would have to expend considerable time and resources scheduling and conducting interviews and transcribing at least parts of them. Plus, you would have to apply and wait for the approval of your university's human subjects review committee. You have added months to your dissertation simply because of the method you have chosen for collecting your data.

Identifying Your Method of Data Analysis

Once you decide how to collect your data, you must decide how you are going to analyze the data. Again, the method of analysis might be something you decided in the conceptual conversation. If you haven't made this decision yet, remember that the kinds of explanations that methods can supply vary widely, so select a method that has units of analysis that can provide an answer to the question you are asking.

If you have as your data a particular category of protest songs and want to understand why protest music is effective for mobilizing people to join social movements, the method should have the potential to provide this kind of explanation. The cluster method of communication analysis, for example, might be able to do so. It asks the researcher to look for key terms in the data and then to identify the terms that cluster around them to discover the meanings the terms have for their creators and audience.

Perhaps you are intrigued by the many instances of religious discourse that are appearing in the political realm and want to analyze Congressional speeches to discover how religious discourse functions in political contexts. You probably would not find feminist methods of analysis, which focus in part on the construction of gender, to be very useful in helping you answer this question.

There are also instances when your question and your data will almost require that you use a particular method to analyze your data. If you are asking a question about which factors correlate with one another to produce a particular effect, you would want to calculate the correlation coefficient to discover the type and strength of that relationship as your method of analysis. If you are doing a feminist study—asking a question about gender roles and using data such as the gender constructions of characters on television shows—not to use a feminist method of analysis as your method would seem highly unusual. If you are asking a question where little is known about a phenomenon and where you don't want to impose a theoretical framework on your data, the grounded-theory method of analysis is the most appropriate choice because it allows concepts and themes to emerge from the data without an a priori framework.

Sometimes, students believe that they will complete their analyses more quickly if they choose a quantitative method that uses statistics and computer-processed data. Your study is likely to stall indefinitely, however, if you don't understand your research design, the specific measurements you are using, or how to interpret the findings the statistical analysis produces. In other cases, students choose a particular method of analyzing data because they have never used it before and want to learn it. We applaud this commitment to learning new things, but such a decision doesn't contribute to an efficient dissertation. A good rule to follow in choosing your method of analysis is to choose one with which you feel comfortable and that you already fully understand.

Identifying the Literature to Review

At this step in the process of making decisions on the way to a dissertation prepoposal, you have a well-constructed research question, data to answer the question, a method for collecting your data, and a method for analyzing your data. Now is the time to conceptualize the categories of your literature review. What you want to work out for your preproposal are the major areas of literature to include in the review.

You might be surprised that we are suggesting you do a literature review after you have conceptualized your topic. Aren't you supposed to figure out your topic from a gap in the literature? We don't think so, and here's why: If you read literature relevant to a topic you might want to use for your dissertation, hoping to find a gap or other idea, you will find yourself seeing interesting possibilities with every new book and article you read. "That sounds interesting. I think I want that in my dissertation," you'll think in response to virtually everything you read.

Because all of the studies you read seem fascinating, you keep going down one path after another, and you get lost. You don't know where you are, what you think, or what your interests are. You are being driven by something external to you as you pursue various ideas, and you probably begin to feel overstimulated and overwhelmed because you have no reason to pick one path over another. The literature suggests so many possible topics for you that seem interesting and useful that you become paralyzed. Not to mention the fact that, if you are looking for a gap in the literature to produce a topic, you have to read a great deal of literature just to find one gap you might want to fill.

The purpose of the literature review suggests why it comes at this point in the process. The purpose is not to show everything you know about the topic, and it's not the place to show that you have uncovered every single book and article ever published in an area. It's also not the place to summarize everything you read that led you to develop your topic (this is a particularly common misconception about what literature reviews are supposed to do).

Here's a better way to think about your literature review: It is a convention for familiarizing the readers of your dissertation with critical terms and findings that contextualize your research question. Your literature review is designed to provide contextual knowledge the reader will need to know to fully understand the significance of your study. The literature review provides what readers need to know, in other words, for your study to make sense to them. The literature allows you to enter the conversation about a topic in your field by acquainting yourself with what others are saying so you don't have to repeat what they already know and can extend the conversation they have begun.

Working out the categories of literature to cover in your literature review is not hard to do because the categories come directly from the terms of your research question. The key terms of your research question become the major areas of your literature review. For example, if your research questions are, "Are the arguments that female and male legislators make in relation to children's issues different? If so, how?", the categories to cover for the literature review are: (1) Gender differences in decision making, (2) Gender differences in legislative actions, (3) Gender differences in argumentation, and (4) Kinds of arguments used in relation to children's issues. The terms *female* and *male* suggest literature reviewed regarding gender, *legislator* suggests decision and legislative actions, *arguments* suggest argumentation, and *children's issues* suggests argumentation strategies in terms of policies related to children. These, then, would be the literature you want to cover.

If your research question is, "What factors characterize a successful mentoring relationship for minority students?", the bodies of literature to cover are: (1) Characteristics of successful mentoring, (2) Characteristics of successful academic mentoring of minority students, (3) Characteristics of successful academic mentoring of university students, and (4) Factors that affect the completion of graduate degrees (you would include this body of literature because you are defining *successful* in the question as completion of degree).

There's one other source for developing bodies of literature to include in a literature review—your data. In addition to looking to your research question for clues about what your literature review should contain, also look to your data, particularly if they are texts or artifacts that are well-known, produced by prominent individuals, or significant for other reasons. You want to see if studies of your data have been done, how they might inform your own analyses of the data, and whether they shed any light on the question you are asking about the data. If, for example, you are going to use as your data works of art by Judy Chicago, see if studies have been done on her art in the past and include them in your literature review. If your data are Walt Disney cartoons, see what studies have been done of these data and what kinds of findings about what kinds of questions those studies produced.

As you work to formulate the categories of literature to review, be careful to avoid one of the most common problems of literature reviews:

covering a body of literature at an inappropriate level of abstraction. You always have choices about the level of abstraction at which to conceptualize and talk about things, ranging from the very concrete, which deals with specific instances or material objects, to the very abstract, where many different things are grouped in a way that homogenizes them and focuses on a few characteristics they have in common. Finding the right level of abstraction focuses the literature review so that your readers can clearly and easily see the salient points involved and how they relate to your research question.

As you select the categories of literature for your literature review, keep the level of each category as concrete as possible. Let's say you are studying how parents transmit political perspectives to their children. You are thinking that one of the categories of your literature review should be political participation in the United States in general. This is much too broad to be a category in your literature review. If the level of abstraction is too high, you mislead the reader by focusing on ideas that are too general because you miss key specific characteristics that distinguish your construct from other constructs. Because the theoretical construct in your research question is "political perspective," include only studies that deal specifically with political perspective—how political perspectives are defined, how individuals develop their political perspectives, and how they change over time, for example.

On the other hand, if the categories of your literature review are too concrete, you will under-collect the literature. Students sometimes are tempted to do this because they let their data instead of their research question guide them to the categories of the literature review. Say you have chosen as your data stories of the transmission of political perspectives by parents. If you were to look only at literature that deals with the transmission of political perspectives by families with these particular traits, you will not be using the full resources of other scholars to inform your thinking about your study—and, in fact, you may find no studies that deal with these exact constructs. If there are no studies that deal specifically with this topic, move up one level of abstraction to search for literature on the ways in which political perspectives are developed or methods used by families to indoctrinate children generally.

Let's try another example with the research question, "How do independent dance companies balance economic viability with commitment to an artistic vision?" One category of your literature review would be strategies used by nonprofit arts groups (a more abstract form of independent dance companies) to balance economic viability and artistic vision. Other categories to use for searching for relevant literature would be strategies to ensure maintenance of artistic vision by nonprofit arts organizations and strategies arts organizations use to maintain economic viability.

Sometimes, there are bodies of literature relevant to your research question that readers are likely to know exist and that they want to know you considered and assessed for their relevance to your study. These categories of literature, however, don't contribute to the argument you are making in your study and are at too high a level of abstraction to include in a literature review. Typically, including them in your literature review would make your literature review huge. You can handle these kinds of bodies of literature by acknowledging that a body of literature exists on that topic, and, in one or two paragraphs, identifying the category and giving a sample or two of the types of studies in this category.

An example of this strategy will clarify what we mean. Your research question is, "What coping strategies do caregivers use in caring for stroke victims?" You might include in your literature a paragraph that references the studies that have been done on the factors that affect the severity of strokes and the degrees of recovery possible. These studies have some relevance to your study because the severity of the stroke affects the kind of caregiving required, but the factors themselves are too far away from your interests to be directly relevant. A paragraph in which you characterize the kinds of findings these studies produce and provide a couple of samples of studies in this category shows you checked into this large body of literature and did not find it directly relevant to your study.

There's another mistake that students often make about literature reviews. They include in them literature about the method they are using either to collect or analyze the data. Any literature you believe you need to cover related to your method belongs in the discussion of your method in your section or chapter on research design and not in your literature review. Ana, for example, thought she needed a discussion of narrative theory and the narrative method in her literature review because she was using a narrative method to analyze her data. She came to see, however, that this material does not belong there because *narrative* is not one of the terms in her research question. Because your method is one way to investigate the question but not the only way, it is not part of your research question. As a result, it is not a major term and thus not one of the categories of your literature review.

Identifying the Significance of Your Study

Only a couple of decisions remain to be made to complete your pre-proposal. One is to work out something that should be easy at this point: The significance of your study. You will develop this in more detail when you actually write your proposal and do your study, but you want to be able to explain in a sentence or two why your study is important. What will knowing what you are going to find out do for you and your discipline? This is often called the "so what?" question. Try to formulate at least three reasons why your study is significant.

Your research question and the categories of the literature you are going to review should provide clues as to why your study will be significant because they suggest the theoretical debates to which you are contributing. In your earlier conversation about your interests, you also might have articulated a desire to make a contribution in some area. Use all of these resources to develop the reasons for the significance of your study. Common ways of talking about significance include:

- The study constitutes a starting place from which to understand a phenomenon.

- Understanding this phenomenon may help restore something.

- How a phenomenon is understood comes from one perspective, and the study provides a different perspective that will expand understanding.

- A complex relationship exists between two phenomena, and this study helps explain it.

- The phenomenon being studied does not fit existing theories, and the study will explore the nature of the phenomenon to see if the theories need to be expanded or revised to account for it.

- The phenomenon being studied produces or affects something important, so understanding what that is requires an understanding of the phenomenon that generates it.

- The study legitimizes a phenomenon by articulating and theorizing it.

- The study provides a missing piece in the understanding of a phenomenon.

- The study theorizes a phenomenon that has been under-theorized but that is key to understanding a larger picture.

- Current theories provide a limited array of options for individuals. The study seeks to expand the options available.

- The study helps solve a problem.

- The study provides a model for doing something.

- Individuals are engaged in a particular practice that seems not to be working. The study provides ideas for practices that work.

- The major way in which individuals try to solve a problem is by engaging in a particular practice, but there has been no evaluation of whether that practice is effective. The study investigates and assesses that practice.

- Those who work in this area or with this population will find the study useful because it provides information that enables them to be more effective in some way.

We want to caution you against using a very common justification for a study: The study is important because no one has done it before. This is rarely a good reason for doing a study. Many things have not been done before that should not be because they are foolish, silly, stupid, dangerous, or pointless. As far as we know, no one has ever run a marathon facing backwards or taught a university class standing on her head, but that doesn't mean these activities need to be done. The same is true of the rationale for doing studies. Just because something hasn't been investigated doesn't mean that it should be. Instead of using this as your reason, then, articulate your reasons for the significance of the study by explaining specifically what readers will learn and why such understanding is important.

Identifying Your Chapters

The last thing to do in the decision-making process for your preproposal is to develop an outline of the chapters for your dissertation. This simply means that you work out what your chapters are going to be. You might choose to do a five-chapter dissertation, which is the kind of dissertation that students who are using quantitative research methods typically choose (it also may be selected by students using qualitative methods). In this kind of dissertation, your first chapter is an introduction to the topic, the second chapter is the literature review, the third chapter is a description of the research design, the fourth chapter reports the results or the findings, and the fifth chapter is a discussion of the findings.

For qualitative dissertations, select a format for your chapters that fits your unique study. Qualitative dissertations usually include an introduction chapter that contains the introduction, research question, research design, literature review, significance of the study, and outline of the study. These dissertations might contain a second chapter that provides history or context for the study or the data. Next come the chapters analyzing the data. There might be two, three, four, or more of these chapters, depending on the kind of data you are studying. If you are analyzing three novels, you might have a chapter devoted to each novel. For a historical dissertation, you might have four chapters that chronicle key historical events supporting your argument, each from a different time period. If you are studying the literary development of an author, you might have separate chapters for the major periods of her life. If you discover four major outcomes from your analysis across all of your data, you might want a chapter devoted to each outcome. Perhaps you discover different contributory factors to a phenomenon; each factor could be the subject of a chapter.

If your chapters will be organized around your findings (and, obviously, you don't know what those findings will be yet), simply say, at this stage of your planning, that chapter 1 will be an introduction, and you will have however many chapters are appropriate once you have done your analysis. The final chapter will be the conclusion chapter.

There's another kind of structure for a dissertation that is becoming increasingly common. This is where students write three or four discrete essays that they plan to submit to journals for possible publication. Dissertations organized in this way usually have an introductory chapter, the three or four publishable essays as the three or four middle chapters, and a conclusion chapter that discusses what unites the essays and the collective implications that can be drawn from the studies.

Writing Your Preproposal

You've now made decisions about your research question, your data, your methods of data collection and analysis, the categories of literature to review, the significance of your study, and the outline of your study. With these decisions made, you are ready to write up the decisions into a preproposal—to book your itinerary. A preproposal is a one-page summary of your dissertation that contains these elements:

- Research question

- Research design
  - Data
  - Method(s) for collecting data
  - Method(s) for analyzing data

- Categories of literature to cover in the literature review

- Reasons why the study is significant

- Outline of the chapters of the dissertation

Preproposal Sample #1
(for a five-chapter dissertation)
Research question: "What factors facilitate or constrain the institutionalization of reproductive health-care policy in Nigeria?"
Areas of literature to review: Literature concerning: (1) The process of institutionalization in developing countries; (2) Reproductive health-care policies in Africa, particularly the factors that affect such policies; and (3) Reproductive health-care policies in Nigeria, focusing on those factors that facilitate or constrain institutionalization
Data: Documents related to health-care policy produced by the government of Nigeria and interviews with health-care policymakers and educators employed by the government

Data collection: (1) Unstructured interviews, and (2) Request of documents from the government of Nigeria

Data analysis: Grounded-theory analysis of documents and interviews to discover factors

Significance: The study will inform those who are contributing monetary assistance to Nigeria to improve health care. Currently, those funds do not seem to be having any positive effect on health care.

Outline of the study:

Chapter 1: Introduction, including background of the problem, research question, significance, and outline of the study

Chapter 2: Literature review

Chapter 3: Research design

Chapter 4: Results

Chapter 5: Conclusion or discussion

Preproposal Sample #2

(for a dissertation with multiple findings chapters)

Research question: "What factors affect the effectiveness of appeals in the high school admission process?"

Areas of literature to review: Literature concerning: (1) Educational opportunity and school choice, (2) Critical perspectives on the family-school relationship, and (3) Strategies used by the marginalized to effect social change

Data: Documents and narratives related to families' applications to high schools in the New York City public school system

Data collection: (1) Semistructured interviews (using a snowball sample) of individuals who successfully and unsuccessfully appealed admission decisions, and (2) Request of documents from families, the New York City Department of Education, and organizations that assist families with the admission and appeal processes

Significance: This study will provide a counternarrative to studies of deficit thinking about parents by highlighting successful practices used by families to appeal admission decisions. It will show actions by parents as opposed to reactions, in which their agency is typically viewed only as something shaped by public school officials. The research will also expand our understanding of parental involvement in the education of their children by focusing on a nontraditional form of such involvement.

Outline of the study:
    Chapter 1: Introduction, including background of the problem,
        research question, significance, and outline of the study
    Chapter 2: Literature review
    Chapter 3: Research design
    Chapters 4–?: Findings (unsure at this time how many chapters
        will be dedicated to findings)
    Final chapter: Conclusion[1]

Preproposal Sample #3

(for a dissertation with three distinct artifacts or texts as data)

Research questions: (1) "What are the characteristics of quilts that
    protest?" (2) "Does the study of protest quilts change communi-
    cation theorists' notions about protest rhetoric?"

Areas of literature to review: Literature concerning: (1) Functions of
    quilts, (2) Rhetoric of protest, and (3) Feminist analyses of
    movement and protest rhetoric

Data: Four quilts: the *Secession Quilt*, the Women's Christian Tem-
    perance Union's *Crusade Quilt*, the *AIDS Memorial Quilt*, and the
    Eugene Peace Quilt

Data collection: (1) Analysis of a photograph of the *Secession Quilt*;
    (2) Viewing of the *Crusade Quilt* in the WCTU's museum in
    Evanston, Illinois; (3) Analysis of photographs of some of the
    panels of the *AIDS Memorial Quilt* and viewing of panels stored
    at the NAMES Project's headquarters in San Francisco; and (4)
    Viewing of the *Eugene Peace Quilt* in the 5th Street Public Mar-
    ket in Eugene, Oregon

Data analysis: Generative method of rhetorical criticism or the
    grounded-theory method of analyzing qualitative data

Significance: Theories of protest have been developed largely from
    analyses of the rhetoric of men, focusing on rhetorical patterns
    practiced by men. In this study, I want to analyze protest by
    women, using a type of rhetoric in which their voices can be heard,
    to discover if our theories of protest need to be expanded and/or re-
    vised to incorporate women's voices. I hope to formulate a more
    comprehensive and inclusive theory of protest rhetoric as a result.

Outline of the study:
    Chapter 1: Introduction, including research question; literature
        review; research design (data, data collection, data analysis);
        significance; and outline of the study

Chapter 2: Analysis of the *Secession Quilt*
Chapter 3: Analysis of the *Crusade Quilt*
Chapter 4: Analysis of the *AIDS Memorial Quilt*
Chapter 5: Analysis of the *Eugene Peace Quilt*
Chapter 6: Conclusion[2]

Preproposal Sample #4

(for a dissertation with two research questions and a data chapter to answer each question)

Research questions: (1) "What meaning do individuals attribute to a feeling of loneliness if they feel it within the context of what they perceive to be an intimate relationship that is healthy and strong?" (2) "How does communicating with one's partner (or choosing not to communicate) about this feeling affect the intimate relationship?"

Areas of literature to review: Literature concerning: (1) Typologies of loneliness, (2) Characteristics of good intimate relationships, and (3) Loneliness within relationships

Data: Information from people in healthy, committed, romantic relationships about their perceptions of loneliness

Data collection: Face-to-face interviews with individuals, both heterosexual and homosexual, who do not have children living with them, using a snowball sample to locate participants

Data analysis: Grounded-theory analysis of interviews

Significance: The study might assure people who have good relationships that their relationships are not necessarily lacking if they experience a sense of loneliness within them. It might help reassure them that feeling something like loneliness and articulating it may be perfectly natural in the process of human relating.

Outline of the study:

Chapter 1: Introduction, including research question, literature review; research design, significance, and outline of the study

Chapter 2: Thematic representations of loneliness (findings related to the first research question)

Chapter 3: Loneliness and communication (findings related to the second research question)

Chapter 4: A theory of relational loneliness[3]

Preproposal Sample #5

(for a dissertation with a history or context chapter)

Research questions: (1) "In situations where contractual agreement is achieved, is narrative agreement achieved?" (2) "If so, what characteristics do the narratives have in common?"

Areas of literature to review: Literature concerning: (1) Narrative as argument, (2) Nature and processes involved in narrative agreement, and (3) Characteristics of contractual agreement

Data: Narratives told by participants in a teachers' strike in Eugene, Oregon

Data collection: Face-to-face interviews with participants in the teachers' strike. My plan is to interview six participants who represent the teachers' perspective and six who represent the perspective of the district administration. I will tape and transcribe the interviews.

Data analysis: Narrative criticism

Significance: On many occasions, humans must find agreement on some empirical product—for example, in a divorce settlement, negotiations between a professor and a student over a grade, the creation of a political party's platform, and negotiation of a labor-management contract. Obviously, there is contractual agreement in these cases, but what is the impact of that agreement on narrative? The possible effects on narrative could range from no change in either one of the narratives to a change in both to total acceptance by both parties of one of the narratives. What happens to the initial narratives when agreement is reached may provide clues to an understanding of how such negotiations and conflicts might be more readily solved.

Outline of the study:

Chapter 1: Introduction, including research question; literature review; research design (data, data collection, data analysis); significance; and outline of the study

Chapter 2: Context for the teachers' strike

Chapter 3: Characteristics of the teachers' narrative

Chapter 4: Characteristics of the district's narrative

Chapter 5: Hypotheses of narrative agreement following contractual agreement[4]

Preproposal Sample #6
(for a dissertation composed of three distinct studies)

Overview: Research on adolescent health is dominated by an adult-centric, pathologically focused perspective that views youth as a risk for problems instead of as agents for health promotion. Feminist, critical pedagogical scholars and some practitioners advocate instead an approach of positive youth development that encourages meaningful youth participation in the development of health programs and policies. This dissertation uses a framework of positive youth development to explore young people's ideas about ways to develop more effective health-promotion programs and the kinds of processes and practices that enhance youth voice and participation.

Paper 1: Strategies for Preventing Youth Violence Contributed by Youth

Research question: "What are the strategies that youth suggest for preventing youth violence?"

Research design: Qualitative study in which the grounded-theory method is used to analyze 391 student essays about the prevention of youth violence collected in Flint, Michigan, in a competition, "Do the Write Thing," sponsored by the National Campaign to Stop Violence

Significance: The study will provide information about a health issue and what can be done to prevent it from the perspective of young people, enabling more effective prevention programs to be designed.

Paper 2: Violence-Prevention Programs: Incorporation of Youth-Derived Strategies

Research question: "How do the strategies that youth suggest for preventing youth violence compare to the strategies used in violence-prevention programs?"

Research design: Qualitative comparison and contrast of the strategies identified in Paper 1 with the programs of a major violence-prevention center in the United States

Significance: One way to assess the effectiveness of violence-prevention programs is to compare them with what the audience for those programs suggests are ways to prevent violence. By incorporating the voice of youth into program design, violence-prevention programs can be more effective.

Paper 3: Self-Empowerment in Interventions Designed to Prevent Youth Violence

Research question: "In what ways do youth enact power and power-lessness in interventions designed to prevent youth violence?"

Research design: Qualitative analysis using grounded theory of the essays used in Paper 1 to discover whether the writers give power to violence or see themselves in control of violence; identification of the strategies used to disempower and empower

Significance: Because young people writing about violence prevention are not only suggesting substantive ways to prevent violence but also enacting their own agentic stances concerning violence in various ways, an analysis of the strategies they use to empower or disempower themselves vis-à-vis the issue of violence also may contribute to the design of more effective violence-prevention programs. Understanding these strategies may provide an additional area of attention to consider in the design of the programs—one that may be more important than many of the other elements these programs consider.

Outline of the study:

Chapter 1: Introduction (statement of the overall problem, significance, and preview of the papers to follow)

Chapter 2: Paper 1

Chapter 3: Paper 2

Chapter 4: Paper 3

Chapter 5: Conclusion[5]

Preproposal Sample #7

(for a dissertation composed of four distinct studies)

Overview: Hendra virus (HeV) is one of a cluster of new viruses that have recently emerged from bats of the genus *Pteropus* (flying foxes or fruit bats). All outbreaks have involved transmission of the virus from flying foxes to pasture-fed horses and subsequent transmission to humans with a 50% fatality rate. My goal is to address the lack of information about the biology of Hendra virus in flying foxes. This research will combine fieldwork, mathematical and simulation modeling, and conceptual approaches to generate four dissertation chapters that address the ecology and emergence of Hendra virus in Australian flying foxes.

Paper 1: The epidemiology of Hendra virus in little red flying foxes

Research questions: (1) "How is Hendra virus transmitted within flying fox populations?" (2) "How do age, sex, and reproductive status of flying foxes affect disease risk?" (3) "How do seasonality and population size of flying foxes affect disease risk?"

Research design: Sample little red flying foxes over multiple seasons over two years. Anesthetize each animal and take a blood sample for Hendra virus serology. Analyze teeth to construct age-specific seroprevalence curves. Use logistic regression and stratified data analysis to examine individual and population-level risk factors for disease.

Significance: Understanding why Hendra virus emerged is hindered by our lack of understanding of the basic ecology of the virus within its natural hosts. In particular, we do not yet understand the nature of transmission and the spatiotemporal dynamics of the virus within flying fox populations. This first longitudinal field study of Hendra virus in flying foxes is designed to develop insight into potential mechanisms of transmission as well as population-level factors such as seasonality and metapopulation dynamics.

Paper 2: Spatiotemporal dynamics of Hendra virus in flying foxes

Research questions: (1) "How does Hendra virus persist in flying fox populations?" (2) "What are the characteristics of the spatiotemporal dynamics of the virus?"

Research design: Create and parameterize spatially structured mathematic and simulation models of the dynamics of Hendra virus in flying foxes.

Significance: Outbreaks of Hendra virus are temporally and geographically sporadic, making surveillance and prevention challenging. This is further confounded by lack of information on viral dynamics within the reservoir hosts, which have a nomadic lifestyle and exist in complex, socially structured populations. The model will be used as a framework for examining the population-level consequences of information collected in laboratory and field studies.

Paper 3: Anthropogenic environmental change and the emergence of
Hendra virus from flying foxes

Research question: "Can changes in flying fox ecology cause the
emergence of Hendra virus?"

Hypothesis: The combination of habitat fragmentation, urbanization,
and increased aggregation of flying foxes caused the emergence
of Hendra virus.

Research design: Use mathematical models of the dynamics of Hendra virus in flying fox populations to simulate observed changes
in flying fox population biology. Use the results to assess the impact of land-use change on Hendra virus epidemiology and
emergence.

Significance: Since 1994, four novel pathogens have emerged from
bats of the genus *Pteropus*—Hendra virus, Nipah virus,
Menangle virus, and Australian bat lyssavirus. The unprecedented emergence of four pathogens from a single host genus
in such a short period of time suggests that changes in host
ecology may play a role in disease emergence. Investigation of
these changes may help us understand environmental factors
that impact disease emergence and how interventions can impact them.

Paper 4: Investigating ecological drivers of disease emergence

Research question: "How can theories and strategies from the literature on scientific thinking be applied to disease ecology to understand the cause of disease emergence?"

Research design: Outline a conceptual approach to examining the
causation of disease emergence

Significance: The use of a strong inference approach and triangulation methods should advance our understanding of the causes
and mechanisms of disease emergence, leading to more strategic
interventions for their control and prevention.

Outline of the study:

Preproposal Sample #8

(for a thesis, a shorter and more limited study)

Research question: "What practices by arts advocates discourage individuals from arts participation?"

Areas of literature to review: Studies about reasons for individuals' lack of participation in the arts

Data: Information from individuals who do not participate in the arts about what arts advocates do to discourage them from participating

Data collection: Five focus groups composed of individuals who do not attend arts events

Data analysis: Grounded-theory analysis of focus groups

Significance: Attendance at many arts events is declining, and the reasons may have to do with practices in which arts advocates unintentionally engage that exclude potential participants. Discovery and identification of some of these practices will help arts advocates avoid them and build better cases for arts participation.

Outline of the study:

Chapter 1: Introduction, including research question; literature review; research design (data, data collection, and data analysis); significance; and outline of the study.

Chapter 2: Findings

Chapter 3: Conclusion

Assessing Your Decisions

All of your decisions about your dissertation are now summarized on one sheet of paper. These decisions are your research question, your research design (including your data and the procedures for collecting and analyzing the data), the categories of your literature review, reasons why your study is important, and an outline of your chapters.

Now is the time to assess your preproposal for internal consistency among all of the elements. You have a good preproposal if you can answer yes to these questions:

- Does everything align with the research question?

- Are the data a good example of the phenomenon you want to study?

- Can your question be answered with the method you have proposed?

- Are the categories of the literature review derived from the key terms of the research question?

- Do the reasons for doing the study relate to the research question and the categories of literature covered in the literature review?

- Do the chapters you are planning make sense given your data and your method?

- Can the dissertation be done with the resources and time that you have?

- Is this project of interest and even exciting to you? (It will be very surprising if it's not because the idea for it came directly from you and your interests.)

Making sure that all of the components of the preproposal line up with the research question and are internally consistent is one of the keys to doing an efficient dissertation. If there is misalignment among some elements in your preproposal, you will discover that you frequently get stuck and can't get unstuck simply because your project hasn't been conceptualized clearly and coherently.

There is something else to check after you've written your preproposal, but it is something you need a bit more time to do. When you actually begin to collect and code the literature in the categories you identified for your literature review, check to see if the study you've mapped out has been done before. If the preproposal for your dissertation comes from your interests and knowledge, you are likely to have a pretty good idea of whether the study you designed has been done before, but this is the time to make sure. If you discover that a study very similar to what you have planned has already been done, don't start completely over and design a whole new dissertation project. Tweak your research question, your method, or your data in some way to create a preproposal for a study that extends or elaborates in some way on that previous study. For example, if you discover that someone else has already done a study of how political perspectives are transmitted to children by parents (the study you wanted to do), you could ask instead the degree to which children learn and adopt the political perspectives their parents attempt to transmit to them.

Committing to the Preproposal with Your Advisor

You have made your key decisions about your dissertation, have written them up in a preproposal, and have assessed it. You are happy with your preproposal and are looking forward to doing your study. If your advisor was not your conversational partner in the conceptual conversation that led you to your preproposal, now is the time to bring the preproposal to your advisor.

There are several advantages to going to your advisor with a completed preproposal instead of vague and incomplete ideas about what you want to do for your dissertation. You are providing your advisor with a document that she can give you advice about. Your advisor wants to be helpful to you and may think that giving you all sorts of ideas in all sorts of directions is the best way to help. A preproposal keeps her ideas focused because she has a specific document to which to respond. Another advantage of going to your advisor with a complete, clearly conceptualized, and coherent preproposal is that you are positioning yourself as an expert. You signal to your advisor that you are a scholar who can generate ideas for research projects and that you are going to be enacting the scholarly role with competence throughout the dissertation process.

What if your advisor is surprised by your preproposal, has a different idea about what you should do for your dissertation, or raises serious objections to some part of your preproposal? Here is where your dissertation defense begins. Your response to your advisor in such cases should be something like this: "I'm excited about the study I've designed. Can you help me do this project?" or "How can my preproposal be tweaked so that I can do the study I would like to do?" The manner in which you conduct the conversation around your preproposal is important. Your goal is not to argue with your advisor but to seek advice about how to make your preproposal both doable and one your advisor can support without dramatically changing it.

After you and your advisor agree on the dissertation preproposal, make two copies of it (and, of course, you'll have it on your computer).

Keep one handy for your own reference, and give one to your advisor. Advisors are busy people, and they can't be expected to remember all of the decisions you've made together about your dissertation. When your advisor has your preproposal in his file cabinet or on his computer, he can easily pull it out and remind himself of those decisions when you ask him a question or give him chapters to read. A preproposal also makes it easy for him to be respectful of you and the progress you're making on your dissertation.

You always have the option, too, of printing out another copy of the preproposal and attaching it when you submit your proposal or chapters to your advisor as a gentle jog to her memory. Shakir's advisor refused to let him use grounded theory as his method of analysis because she was tired of so many of her students using it, and she suggested the narrative method instead. Shakir acceded to her wishes. After he had analyzed his data and brought his analysis chapters in for her to review, his advisor asked why he was using the narrative method instead of grounded theory. Had Shakir clipped a copy of the preproposal to his analysis chapters, his advisor would not have been able to forget the decision they had made about his method of analysis. His advisor had agreed to a particular method, and it would been there in writing in the preproposal as a prompt for her.

Once you and your advisor have agreed on your dissertation preproposal, you both should be devoted nontyrannically to it. This means that your primary commitment is to following the preproposal but acknowledging that it can be changed, if necessary, in minor ways. Questions and challenges are certain to come up as you actually do the research and writing for your dissertation, and you will have to work out such kinks as they come up. If you encounter a problem in your study, however, your basic commitment should be to avoid changing the preproposal in major ways. Instead, what you and your advisor want to do is to innovate to solve the problem so that the basic elements of the preproposal remain intact.

Creating the dissertation preproposal is the core of a high-quality and efficient dissertation. Even if you don't make use of any of the other ideas in this book, if you apply this one alone, it will cut down significantly on the amount of time you spend on your dissertation. If the dissertation preproposal is fully developed and scrutinized at the start of the dissertation process, we promise that you'll save yourself a lot of time later.

Your preproposal makes it easy for you to stay on track. Just like an itinerary when you travel, anything that takes you away from the dissertation, as represented by the preproposal, is not relevant to what you should be doing. Diverging means missed planes and trains and not visiting places you really want to visit. You will get many good ideas that you would like to pursue while you are working on your dissertation. If they don't fit into your preproposal, don't pursue them. Start a promise file—a file of promising research ideas to pursue later—and jot those ideas down and slip them into it. When you are done with your dissertation, you will have great fun going through the file and deciding what you want to do for your next research project. But research unrelated to the dissertation is not what you should be doing now. Sticking to the preproposal is the promise of doability and completeability of your dissertation.

Notes

1. Constructed from conversations with Madeline Perez about her dissertation, "Race, Class, and Social Capital in the High School Admissions Process" (PhD diss., City University of New York, forthcoming).

2. Constructed from the dissertation of Mary Rose Williams, "A Re-Conceptualization of Protest Rhetoric: Characteristics of Quilts as Protest" (PhD diss., University of Oregon, 1990).

3. Constructed from the dissertation of Sharon M. Varallo, "Communication, Loneliness and Intimacy" (PhD diss., Ohio State University, 1997).

4. Constructed from the dissertation of Daniel Dwight Gross, "Narrative Agreement Surrounding Contractual Agreement" (PhD diss., University of Oregon, 1989).

5. Constructed from conversations with Naima T. Wong about her dissertation, as yet untitled (PhD diss., University of Michigan, forthcoming).

6. Constructed from the dissertation of Raina K. Plowright, "The Ecology and Epidemiology of Hendra Virus in Flying Foxes" (PhD diss., University of California, Davis, 2006).

CHAPTER FIVE

ADVICE FROM OTHER TRAVELERS: THE LITERATURE REVIEW

	Steps 4–6 (140 hours)

You are not the first one to go traveling among the sites of your topic. Others who have gone before you are eager to share their discoveries with you, and the literature review is your opportunity to hear the tales and advice of previous travelers. Your study will contribute to a theoretical debate in your field, and that debate takes place through literature. You want to know what others are saying in that debate.

As part of your dissertation preproposal, you figured out the major categories of your literature review from the key terms of your research question. Now is the time to head to the library and the Internet to collect sources of information in these areas. Keep your preproposal clearly in front of you as you do this. You'll discover all sorts of interesting books and articles out there, but resist the temptation to be terrorized by the literature. Don't check them out from the library or download them from the Internet if they do not clearly pertain to the categories you identified earlier for your literature review. This means that you can skip huge bodies of literature because they aren't relevant to your study.

Coding the Literature

You have gathered your literature. You have all the books that are relevant to the categories you developed earlier for your literature review in

75

front of you. You have another stack of the articles from journals you copied or printed off the Internet that are about those categories. You are probably facing several huge piles of books and several piles of articles. Now what do you do? How are you supposed to begin to tackle and process all of this material? It seems utterly overwhelming. Even if you felt like you could get through it, how are you supposed to keep track of everything you read? How will you synthesize it all and put it together in some way that is interesting and useful? You remember writing research papers where you had underlined almost every paragraph of all of the articles you were using and had many different colors of sticky notes marking particular passages in your books. That was a nightmare to figure out, and you were using much less literature than what you see before you now.

There's a method you can use that will make processing and writing your literature efficient and manageable. It makes the process concrete so you have proof right in front of you that you are making good progress. There's an added bonus, too. After you've completed the process, the literature review almost writes itself.

Ready to begin? Take a book from the top of the pile of books in front of you that you have determined is relevant to one of the categories of your literature review. Open it to the table of contents. Look through the table of contents to see what chapters appear to be relevant to that category of your literature review. When you see a chapter that seems like it relates, turn to that chapter and look at the section headings. If you find a section that seems relevant to your study, skim it, looking for these things:

- Claims, conclusions, and findings about the constructs you are investigating

- Definitions of terms

- Calls for follow-up studies relevant to your project

- Gaps you notice in the literature

- Disagreements about the constructs you are investigating

Let's say, for example, that you have the following page in front of you and that the concept with which you are dealing in your literature review is agency:

Foucault suggests a number of rules that govern the discursive formation. One category of rules controls the fact that something is able to be talked about and governs the appearance of objects of discourse. Rules in this category include, for example, prohibitions against talking about certain things—rules that silence certain dimensions of experience simply by not recognizing them as objects of discourse.[25] In the Victorian Age, for example, children's sexuality simply was not an object of discourse, so children's sexuality was not discussed and that aspect of children's experience was repressed.

Some rules that govern objects of discourse concern the function of insituational bodies in creating such objects. Particular institutions may be rec-ognized as the ones with the authority to name and thus distinguish one object from another. One such authority was nineteenth-century medicine, which distinguished madness from other concepts and became the major authority that established madness as an object. Educational experts currently recognize and diagnose children with attention deficit disorder, for example, thus making it a condition that can be perceived and about which individuals are able to speak.

A second category of rules concerns not what is talked about but who is allowed to speak and write. Such rules dictate that individuals listen to certain people and reject the discourse of others. The discourse of those who are not heard is considered null "and void without truth or significance, worthless as evidence, inadmissible in the authentification of acts or contracts." Their words are "neither heard nor remembered."[26] Only those deemed qualified by satisfying certain conditions are heard when they engage in discourse. Among the conditions are legal requirements that give the right to speak in certain ways. Lawyers, for example, must pass the bar examination in order to practice law. Other such rules involve criteria of competence and knowledge. Individuals listen to medical doctors speak about issues involving health because discursive rules attribute competence to them in this area, while the discourse of alternative medicine generally is not heard because its practitioners have not fulfilled the conditions for competence established for speakers of medical discourse.

Another condition imposed on those whose speech is heard is the production of certain kinds of discourse, formulated in certain ways. Those who wish to speak in the academic world, for example, must produce certain types of statements and use certain forms to be allowed to participate in scholarly discourse. An academic paper or article must evidence particular forms of argument and particular kinds of language, put together in complex ways. It also must contain citations to other scholarly articles, and these citations must follow the form of an established style manual such as that published by the Modern Language Association.

Other rules that govern the nature of the speaker defines the gestures, behaviors, and circumstances, that must accompany speakers as they talk. The wearing of particular clothing and the enactment of behaviors such as genuflection, for example, often must accompany religious discourse of the

Read the page, looking for any sentences, paragraphs, or excerpts that include one or more of the items on the previous bulleted list. Read quickly. You are not reading for deep meaning. You are not reading to remember. Do not try to figure out at this point what you are going to do with any information you find in your literature review. The process is going to do that automatically for you. Right now, you are skimming, looking for ideas relevant to the categories of your literature review.

Sit down at your computer and open a new document. When you find a relevant idea or passage, type it into your computer single-spaced. Typing the actual words you see instead of trying to paraphrase them is usually faster because typing exactly what you see doesn't require that you do any major thinking. Type as fast you can, ignoring typos. You're not going to use these notes as any part of your finished document, so perfection is not your goal here. You also will check any quotes you use in your dissertation against the originals later.

After you've typed an excerpt that is relevant, follow it with the page number on which it appears and a shorthand reference to the book. For example, if the excerpt comes from a book called *Contemporary Perspectives on Rhetoric* by Sonja K. Foss, Karen A. Foss, and Robert Trapp and is on page 349, you might type after the excerpt *CPR 349*, or you might reference it by the authors' names and put *Foss, Foss, Trapp 349*. After you've typed the excerpt and the source, double or triple space before you type the next excerpt (you'll see the reason for the space in a minute). The finished note might look like this:

> A second category of rules concerns not what is talked about but who is allowed to speak and write. Such rules dictate that individuals listen to certain people and reject the discourse of others. The discourse of those who are not heard is considered null "and void, without truth or significance, worthless as evidence, inadmissible in the authentification of acts or contracts." Their words are "neither heard nor remembered." Only those deemed qualified by satisfying certain conditions are heard when they engage in discourse. CPR 349

Keep reading. Let's say you see another idea that is useful for your thinking about your project on the same page. Type it into your computer. Once again, put the source and page number after it. Then double or triple space, and look for the next relevant excerpt. When you find it, type it in.

Read quickly through the chapter, looking for headings and sections that are relevant for you and skipping those that aren't. You can read quickly because you know what you are looking for.

You'll end up with pages upon pages that look something like this:

> A second category of rules concerns not what is talked about but who is allowed to speak and write, Such rules dictate that individuals listen to certain people and reject the discourse of others. The discourse of those who are not heard is considered null "and void, without truth or significance. worthless as evidence, inadmissible in the authentification of acts or contracts." Their words are "neither heard nor remembered." Only those deemed qualified by satisfying certain conditions are heard when they engage in discourse. Foss, Foss, Trapp 349
>
> Another condition imposed on those whose speech is heard is the production of certain kinds of discourse, formulated in certain ways. Those who wish to speak in the academic world, for example, must produce certain types of statements and use certain forms to be allowed to participate in scholarly discourse. Foss, Foss, Trapp 349
>
> It is commonplace to describe rhetorical agency as political action. From such a starting point, rhetorical agency describves a communicative process of inquiry and advocacy on issues of public importance. As political action, rhetorical agency often takes on the characteristics of a normative theory of citizenship: a good citizen persuades and is persuaded by the gentle force of the better argument. Greene 188
>
> Greene's purpose is to offer an escape route from theorizing rhetorical agency as a model of political communication. He imagines rhetorical agency as a form of living labor. He argues that rhetorical agency belongs to the domain of communicative labor, a form of labor increasingly necessary to the workings of contemporary capitalist production. I want to replace a political-communicative model of rhetorical agency with. a materialiswt-communica-tive model. 189 Greene
>
> Greene wants to abandon communication as a political model for imagining rhetorical agency. 198 Rhetorical agency as political communica-tion suspends dialectically between structures of power and the possibility of social change. 198 Greene
>
> Rhetoricians need to bo beyond studies of those whose agency is taken for granted, and attend as well to the "ever present complications of who has access to rhetorical agency and how rhetorical agency is obtained." Geisler 10
>
> Definition: the capacity of the rhetor to act. Geisler 12
>
> What I am most interested in probing is "agentic invention" or perhaps "subversive invention." By agenic or subversice invention I mean that process by which rhetors/subjects/agents formulate rhetorical strateties to break free from dominant subjectivities. The potential for agenic/, subversive invention loiters at sites of discursive tension. Zaeske 1

Now that you're beginning to see how efficient this process is going to make you, you might think to yourself that you can save even more time by putting the source on a page only once—perhaps at the top of the page—so you don't have to repeat it with every excerpt. Or what about when you have two excerpts from the same page of the same source? Why not use one page number to cover them both? You'll see why you don't want to use these kinds of shortcuts in a minute. You want to be sure you have a source and a page number next to every excerpt you type.

If you find something that is interesting that you would like to know more about, but it's not related to your project, avoid the temptation to read it now. Jot the page number, source, and a brief reminder of the topic on a piece of paper and file it in your promise file so you can find it later when you are not working on your dissertation. (Remember that this is that file you have begun to keep of promising research ideas to pursue later.) Don't let any of these kinds of distractions keep you from the task at hand: reading and coding the relevant literature. Anything that is not relevant should fall by the wayside or be inserted into your promise file.

When you're done reading and coding the relevant sections of a chapter, go back to the table of contents. Are there other chapters that might be relevant? If so, review and code the relevant sections of those chapters. When you have coded all of the chapters that seem relevant, go to the index of the book. Look up key terms related to your project, and go to the pages to which they direct you. If you find ideas you didn't pick up in your earlier coding of the chapters, type those excerpts into the computer, making sure to type the source and page number after each one.

Use the same process to code your articles that you are using to code your books. Look through the article to see which sections seem relevant to the categories of your literature review. When you see a section that might be useful, skim it, seeing if there are excerpts you want to pick up.

Be careful when you are coding articles that you don't get lost in the details of a study. Highlight only the findings of the study. Because you are only looking for claims and conclusions that are relevant to your research question, you usually don't need to know anything about how the knowledge that you are including in a literature review came to be generated—the participants, data, or methods used in a study. You are interested in the findings of the study because the findings are contributing to a theoretical discussion about your topic. There are some exceptions, of course. If one study produced very different findings from the others and you believe the explanation lies in the method used to conduct the study, note the method for that study. But generally, focus on findings. This means that you can review most journal articles very quickly because you are likely to be interested only in the sections where the findings are explained and discussed.

Using our system of coding literature, a book might take you 45 minutes to read and code and an article 10 or 15 minutes. How is this possible? Because you are reading with a very clear focus. You're not reading every word. You are constantly asking, "Is this chapter relevant for my study?" "Is this section relevant for my study?" "Is this paragraph relevant for my study?" If not, skip it. This is a very different kind of reading from the reading you did for your comprehensive exams, which required that you have a deep understanding of the books and articles you read. In contrast, when you are coding literature for your literature review, you aren't reading or typing in the complete oeuvre of someone, the entire history of a theory, or all of the critiques of a theory. You are getting a snapshot view of the literature directly relevant to the project you've conceptualized.

What if you miss an idea that is relevant to your project because you are moving so quickly through the literature? The cost of finding that idea is much greater than the cost of missing it. To do the kind of reading that would be required to ensure that you never miss a relevant idea would be incredibly time consuming, and you are trying to write a dissertation efficiently. If an idea is critical to your study, it is likely to show up someplace else. Some other source will quote, summarize, or allude to it, and you will pick it up through that source. In addition, your committee members will have the opportunity to advise you about sources that can strengthen your argument, and they won't let you miss major ideas.

Coding the literature happens at the very beginning of the reading process. You are doing the coding of the literature and typing excerpts from it the very first time you read a book or an article in your stack. In other words, you are doing your reading while sitting at your computer, typing excerpts into it. Don't read your books and articles first and then sit down to code them. Reading and coding and typing are all the same process in this method. This means that you are not sitting in a coffee shop, reading and reflecting on one of the books in your stack, underlining, highlighting, or marking the interesting passages with sticky notes.

You are at your computer, whizzing through your literature. If you have trouble reading quickly like this, you might try putting your laptop on the kitchen counter and standing up while you read and type in your excerpts. This will keep you from settling into your old reading patterns.

We have assumed, in our description of this method for coding literature, that you are a relatively fast keyboarder or typist. But typing may not be one of the skills you bring to your dissertation project. If typing into your computer all of the relevant excerpts from your sources would be a slow, tedious, and painful process for you, there are other ways. You'll sometimes find these other methods useful for coding literature even if you are a fast typist.

One alternative way of processing what you are picking up in your coding of the literature is to mark the passages that are relevant for you. Instead of typing them into the computer, put a line in the margin by the excerpt you want with a pencil or pen. At the end of reading a book or an article, you will probably have many pages where you have sentences or paragraphs marked with a line in the margin that tells you where the relevant passage starts and stops. A page from a book or an article you have coded in this way might look like this:

Michel Foucault 349

Foucault suggests a number of rules that govern the discursive formation. One category of rules controls the fact that something is able to be talked about and governs the appearance of objects of discourse. Rules in this category include, for example, prohibitions against talking about certain things—rules that silence certain dimensions of experience simply by not recognizing them as objects of discourse.[25] In the Victorian Age, for example, children's sexuality simply was not an object of discourse, so children's sexuality was not discussed and that aspect of children's experience was repressed.

Some rules that govern objects of discourse concern the function of institutional bodies in creating such objects. Particular institutions may be rec-ognized as the ones with the authority to name and thus distinguish one object from another. One such authority was nineteenth-century medicine, which distinguished madness from other concepts and became the major authority that established madness as an object. Educational experts currently recognize and diagnose children with attention deficit disorder, for example, thus making it a condition that can be perceived and about which individuals are able to speak.

A second category of rules concerns not what is talked about but who is allowed to speak and write. Such rules dictate that individuals listen to certain people and reject the discourse of others. The discourse of those who are not heard is considered null "and void without truth or significance, worthless as evidence, inadmissible in the authentification of acts or contracts." Their words are "neither heard nor remembered."[26] Only those deemed qualified by satisfying certain conditions are heard when they engage in discourse. Among the conditions are legal requirements that give

CPR 349

the right to speak in certain ways. Lawyers, for example, must pass the bar examination in order to practice law. Other such rules involve criteria of competence and knowledge. Individuals listen to medical doctors speak about issues involving health because discursive rules attribute competence to them in this area, while the discourse of alternative medicine generally is not heard because its practitioners have not fulfilled the conditions for competence established for speakers of medical discourse.

Another condition imposed on those whose speech is heard is the production of certain kinds of discourse, formulated in certain ways. Those who wish to speak in the academic world, for example, must produce certain types of statements and use certain forms to be allowed to participate in scholarly discourse. An academic paper or article must evidence particular forms of argument and particular kinds of language, put together in complex ways. It also must contain citations to other scholarly articles, and these citations must follow the form of an established style manual such as that published by the Modern Language Association.

Other rules that govern the nature of the speaker defines the gestures, behaviors, and circumstances, that must accompany speakers as they talk. The wearing of particular clothing and the enactment of behaviors such as genuflection, for example, often must accompany religious discourse of the

After you've read all of your books and articles (or even a portion of them) and have marked them in this way, go to a copy machine. (Footnote: We think one of the best investments you can make if you plan to spend your life as an academic is to buy a small copy machine for your home. It can greatly increase your efficiency in many ways.) Page through your book or article, and whenever you find a page that has one of your margin marks, copy that page. After you have made a copy of that one page, write an abbreviation for the source and the page number in the margin of the passage on the copy. Again, do this with every passage, even if some are on the same page. Every marked passage that you copy should have a source and a page number next to it.

There's a third method besides typing excerpts or marking and photocopying them that you can use to code your literature. It involves voice-activated software, where you read the excerpts relevant to your project into your computer. This is really the same method as the typing process mentioned above, except that you are reading the selected passages into a microphone that translates them into text on your computer. Several accurate voice-to-text programs (such as Dragon NaturallySpeaking) are available that cost less than $100. One minor drawback to using such software is that these programs need to be trained to the speech patterns of your voice, but after a few hours of training the software, they usually are fairly accurate.

Now comes the point in the process when you'll see why you left those spaces between excerpts and why you noted the reference citation next to each excerpt. If you typed excerpts into the computer or used voice-activated software, print out your notes. Keep the pages separate for each category of your literature review. In other words, put all the pages about one major topic or category together and keep them separate from the pages on your other categories. And, yes, you will have pages and pages and pages of excerpts for each category of your literature review when you print them out.

Get out your scissors, and cut each note apart. You'll end up with many slips of paper, each one containing one excerpt and a reference and page number. If you copied pages from books and articles, cut out the passages you marked from the pages you copied. Sometimes, a relevant passage will continue from one page to another. When that happens, tape the two parts of the passage together. At the end of this process, you will have reduced a book or a journal article to a stack of little slips of paper, each containing a passage that has a reference to the source from which it came and the page number on which you can find that passage.

Sorting Your Codes

You now have a huge pile of slips of paper containing excerpts from your literature that are either typed or photocopied. Whatever form your "codings" are in, you are going to do the same thing with them: Sort the pieces of paper according to like topic. Put everything that is about the same thing in the same pile.

For example, let's say your dissertation and literature review have something to do with agency. You might discover that several of the excerpts from your coding of your literature talk about the origins or sources of agency, so make a pile out of the slips that contain those excerpts. As you come across other slips on that same subject, put them into that same pile. You might have another pile that contains excerpts that all have to do with definitions of agency and maybe another pile that contains excerpts on the topic of mechanisms for enacting agency. Use sticky notes to label your piles as you are building them. Your labels should be abstract terms that express succinctly what all the excerpts in that one pile are all about. You might label the first pile above, for example, *SOURCES OF AGENCY*.

Often, you'll figure out after you have been sorting for a while that one of your piles is conceptually too large. You initially thought some topics belonged together, but now you see that there are important distinctions among them. Maybe the pile is too general as a category or contains too many different subareas. That's OK. Take a few minutes and sort the excerpts in that one pile, making two or more smaller piles from it. Label those new piles with sticky notes, too.

You'll also find, as you sort, that for some excerpts, you just can't figure out where they go. Maybe the excerpt doesn't make sense to you now, doesn't seem important enough to be a part of your literature review, or doesn't seem as relevant to your project as you originally thought. Put those excerpts in a pile labeled something like *DON'T KNOW*. You will deal with them later.

Notice that you are not making any judgments at this point about what is going to happen to your piles and the topics in them. You are simply putting similar topics together. We like this part of the process because it is very mechanical and concrete and doesn't require any difficult thinking. You don't have to come up with a sophisticated way of conceptualizing your literature at this stage of the process. You are just putting things together that go together for some reason. You can see that you are making progress as your piles with labels on them grow, and the huge pile with which you began shrinks.

Checking Your Codes

You now have many different piles of excerpts, and you've labeled each one. Now check your piles to be sure that all of the excerpts in each pile are relevant to the label you've given it. Take each pile in turn and look at the excerpts it contains, checking to be sure that all the excerpts deal with the topic summarized by the label you gave to that pile. You might find that some excerpts don't belong in a particular pile and belong in another. And remember that *DON'T KNOW* pile? Now is also the time to look through it. Can any of the excerpts in this pile go into other piles? There will still be some excerpts in this pile that you can't convince yourself belong in another pile or are important enough to do anything with. Set them aside, but don't throw them away because they might be relevant later as your project develops, or they might be relevant for a future research project.

Once you are convinced that your piles all contain excerpts dealing with the same topics, put the piles into envelopes and label the envelopes. An envelope labeled *DON'T KNOW* will probably be among them. Storing excerpts in envelopes prevents you from losing track of the piles or having the piles messed up by unwitting animal or human companions.

Creating Your Conceptual Schema

You have before you many different envelopes with labels on them containing many excerpts from your literature. What you really have, of course, is a filing system for the major ideas relevant to your project and thus the major subareas of a category of your literature review. You might discover that some envelopes have many excerpts in them but that others have only a few. Those small envelopes are minor topics and probably will not be important enough to include in your literature review, so set them aside. Focus on the envelopes where you have many slips of paper because you know those are topic areas that are receiving substantial attention in the category of literature you are reviewing.

Your next task is to turn the ideas represented by the remaining envelopes into a conceptual schema or creative synthesis for your literature review. A conceptual schema is a way of organizing your literature review that connects the literature relevant to your study in a way that shows how the pieces of the literature relate and talk to one another. Another way to think of a schema is as an explanation for what you are seeing across your piles of excerpts. A conceptual schema allows you to tell a story about the content of your literature review and features the themes you want to highlight.

A conceptual schema is not a chronological description of literature in which you take each study and talk about it in the order in which it was done. You've seen these kinds of literature reviews, where studies on a common theme are merely strung together. They're tedious because they don't make an argument or connect the studies to one another. These are the kinds of literature reviews that readers tend to skip when reading a study. Your literature review, in contrast, is going to be organized by major topics and not by individual studies. In fact, you may find that the same study appears in more than one of the subareas of your literature review. If you want to do research that is insightful, you want to position your study within the theoretical conversation of your field, and that means engaging your literature in a coherent and sophisticated way.

You have the mechanism for creating your conceptual schema for your literature right in front of you. Go back to your computer and make a list of the labels that are on your envelopes. Once again, leave a couple of spaces between each of the labels as you type the list. Make the font for the list large—perhaps in 26 point—and then print it out. Just as you did with the excerpts from your sources, cut the labels apart.

Take the labels to your desk, a table, a bed, or the floor. Lay them out in any order and begin to play around with the relationships you see among the topics represented in the labels. Do you have some topics that disagree with a position? Some that agree? If so, group them together. Do you have several major topics that are subsets of one of the other topics?

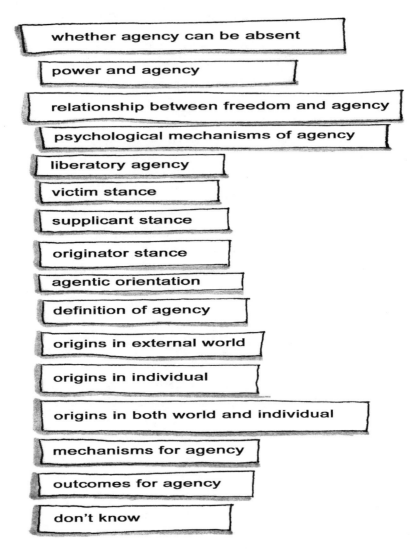

whether agency can be absent

power and agency

relationship between freedom and agency

psychological mechanisms of agency

liberatory agency

victim stance

supplicant stance

originator stance

agentic orientation

definition of agency

origins in external world

origins in individual

origins in both world and individual

mechanisms for agency

outcomes for agency

don't know

If so, lay them out under that label. Maybe you have three different topics that are the major variables that have been studied. Group those three labels together. Are there other labels or topics that belong under them? Perhaps you have some labels or topics that are less important, and some are more important. Physically lay them out in that order. Perhaps you discover that the literature can be organized by different influences on a phenomenon, by different components of a phenomenon, by functions, by outcomes, by models, by components of a model, by different ways of doing something, by different parts of a process, by different perspectives on a phenomenon, by a comparison and contrast among different perspectives. You can try out different ways of organizing the literature just by moving the labels into different patterns. Keep trying alternatives until you come up with a schema that encompasses all or most of the labels.

Here's an example of a conceptual schema developed from labels that discusses literature on agency according to what agency is and how it functions.

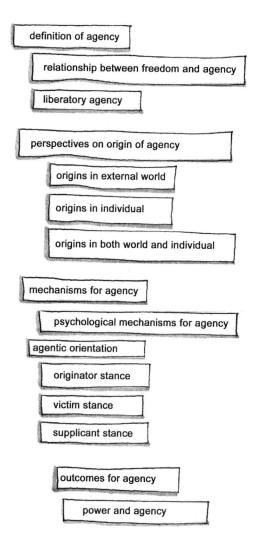

definition of agency

relationship between freedom and agency

liberatory agency

perspectives on origin of agency

origins in external world

origins in individual

origins in both world and individual

mechanisms for agency

psychological mechanisms for agency

agentic orientation

originator stance

victim stance

supplicant stance

outcomes for agency

power and agency

There is no right or wrong conceptual schema for a body of literature. Someone else could review, code, and sort the same literature you did and come up with a different conceptual schema. That's not a problem. You want to organize the literature in a way that makes sense to you, helps you enter the theoretical conversation of your discipline about that topic in a meaningful way, and connects the major parts of the literature. Developing your schema from the labels enables you to accomplish all of these objectives in a way that is grounded in your unique interpretation of the literature.

Schema for Literature Review Sample #1

Research question: "How is a rhetorical response to visual art constructed by lay viewers?"

Categories of the literature review:

- Object-centered theories of response
  - Semiotic theories
  - Prescriptive models
  - Message-formation theories
  - Media-aesthetics theories
  - Theories of form
- Audience-centered theories of response
  - Theories concerned with qualities inherent in the viewer
  - Theories concerned with culturally shared visual codes
  - Theories concerned with the locus of difference
- Performance-centered theories of response[1]

Schema for Literature Review Sample #2

Research question: "What contribution does divergence in national languages make to a divergence in national literature?"

Categories of the literature review:

- Linguistic relativity
  - Strong form
  - Weak form
- Effect on worldview
  - Language and individual worldviews
  - Language and national worldviews

- Great writers as model national thinkers
- Literature as hegemonic education
- Language change
  - Immigration
    - Contact languages
      - Pidgins
      - Creoles
    - New ideas
  - Migration
  - Technology
  - Nature

- Language change in America between 1776 and 1850
- Language change in Great Britain between 1776 and 1850[2]

Schema for Literature Review Sample #3

Research question: "What effects do alternative intervention methods have on the frequency and intensity of disruptive behavior in troubled students?"

Categories of the literature review:

- Disruptive behavior among troubled students
- Extent of problem
- Types of disruptive behaviors exhibited
  - Emotional
  - Physical
  - Social

- Causes of disruptive behaviors in schools
  - Physical
  - Psychological
  - Social

- Interventions commonly used to handle behavior
  - Punishment
  - Definition of punishment
    - Examples of punishment
    - Effects of punishment
  - Positive reinforcement
    - Definition of positive reinforcement
    - Examples of positive reinforcement

- Previous applications of interventions
  - Staff development
  - Transition room
  - Token economy/earning rewards

Writing It Up

You have your conceptual schema for your literature review, which means that you have physically laid out the labels that represent your envelopes on the desk or floor in front of you. This layout is a visual representation of your conceptual schema. Write the schema down so you won't forget it.

Choose a section of the literature review that you want to write. You can begin with any section because you know exactly what your sections are, how they relate to each other, and the order in which you want to discuss them. Find the envelope with the excerpts related to that topic, take all the excerpts from that envelope, and lay them out in front of you. By moving them around and playing with different ways of arranging them, create a miniconceptual schema that presents the literature about that subarea. In other words, do the same thing you did with the whole literature review on a smaller scale, and arrange the excerpts about that topic so that they make the argument you want to make about what the literature says in that subarea.

As you develop the miniconceptual schema for this topic, you'll discover that some excerpts say the same thing. Group them together and then choose the one that says the idea best or the one from the best source. If several important sources make the same point, you can cite them in one parenthetical citation or a footnote following your discussion of that idea, alleviating the need to repeat the same idea multiple times. You'll also discover that some excerpts are not as relevant as you thought they would be to the topic. Take those out, too.

What is left is a layout in front of you of the literature on a particular subarea you want to talk about and in what order. The excerpt you want to talk about first is at the top of your workspace, the second one next, and on down through the entire pile of excerpts in the envelope. You have in front of you something that looks like the figure on the next page.

Greene wants to abandon communication as a political model for imagining rhetorical agency. 198 Rhetorical agency as political communication suspends dialectically between structures of power and the possibility of social change. 198 Greene

It is commonplace to describe rhetorical agency as political action. From such a starting point, rhetorical agency describbves a communicative process of inquiry and advocacy on issues of public importance. As political action, rhetorical agency often takes on the characteristics of a normative theory of citizenship: a good citizen persuades and is persuaded by the gentle force of the better argument. Greene 188

Agency may be defined as the capacity (in persons and things) through which something is created or done. If so, a rhetorical approach to agency would afford opportunities to inquire after the palce of rhetoric in the capacity to act. Clark 1

For most participants, the question of how to amend the concept of rhetorical agency in order to address the ideology of agency was central. Some of the most interesting advances appear to be coming when rhetoricians bgo beyond traditional political contexts. Indeed, developmens on two fronts suggest that the concept of rhetorical agency may be on the cusp of a major rethinking. The first has concerned itself with describing how rhetorical agency functions in subaltern social groups that have not had access to mainstream public forums. . . . . Instead of characterizing rhetors in terms of what they lack, these scholars seem to be moving us toward a richer understanding of rhetorical agency by examining how rhetors without taken-for-granted access do, nevertheless, manage to exercise agency. 10-11 Geisler

Rhetoricians need to go beyond studies of those whose agency is taken for granted, and attend as well to the ever present complications of who has access to rhetorical agency and how rhetorical agency is obtained. Geisler 10

The central problem with the traditional notion of rhetorical agency is its assumption of a public capable of hearing the speaker and of a speaker capable of gaining access to relevant public forums. Many potential agents including women, foreigners, and racial or etnic minorities have been excluded from the only forums that could make a difference to their pleas. One should not, however, assume that the only form of rhetorical agency is that observable in the public sphere. In every culture agerncy has many faces, voices, forums and genres. Campbell 1

I have grappled with the question from the particular position of one interested in learning how certain peole who at particular historical moments are denied access to political power use symbols to attempt to gain political power. Zaeske 1

Any politics of transformation or change is a good bit more complicated than the direct application of political power to particular identities. Instead, transformation or change is predicated on the reconfiguration of context or, put differently, the articulation, disarticulation, and rearticulation of surfaces of emergence. Biesecker 1

And, yes, there are all sorts of typos in the excerpts, but that's OK. The student who typed these was typing fast as she coded her literature, and the typos don't keep her from understanding the content of the excerpt.

Now comes the magical part because the literature review almost writes itself. Start with the first excerpt and type it into your computer. You are literally writing your way through the pile as you type the second excerpt, the third excerpt, the fourth excerpt, and all the way through your layout. Of course, you have to add introductions, overviews, your argument about the excerpts, and transitions between the excerpts, but those are easy now because you see your argument and know exactly where you're going. You can even type all of the relevant points from the excerpts into your computer in the order in which you want them and then add the argument around them in a later draft.

Because you are using the ideas of others, the substance of the literature review is not yours, of course. But how you present the literature review and the connections you make among the pieces of the literature are your own unique inventions. By coding your literature to create an innovative conceptual schema, you have begun to do original scholarship and have an excellent start on your dissertation proposal. And that's your next step.

Literature Review Sample #1

The research questions posed for this study touch upon three primary areas of scholarship: literature on quilts, protest literature, and feminist analyses of movement and protest rhetoric. The vast quantity of available literature in each of these areas prohibits a comprehensive review of the literature in each category, nor would such profiles of sources be useful for the purposes of this study. Therefore, I will provide synopses of the literature in each of these areas that is the most relevant to my study.

Functions of Quilts

There are a vast number of texts, articles, and how-to books on quilts on library and bookstore shelves. In addition, the quilt encyclopedia, *The Quilt Digest*, and magazines such as *Uncoverings* and *The Quilter's News Magazine* contain volumes of quilt stories and information about patterns and a variety of other quilt subjects. I will focus my review of literature on quilts on sources that deal primarily with the functions quilts serve. Because the emphasis of my study is on the function of quilts as a vehicle of discourse, sources that highlight the various functions that are fulfilled by the quilt and the quilt-making process are the most relevant.

Through a review of the literature, I have discovered that the *functions* of quilts are the keys to understanding the significance of quilts in American society. For what are quilts used? How has the activity of quilt making functioned as a form of socialization? How have quilts facilitated community building? What are the aesthetic functions of quilts? How do quilts serve as a mouthpiece through which their creators can speak? These questions—addressed consistently in the literature—will serve as the organizing principle for my review of the literature on quilts.

Utility

Quilts traditionally have been made with some sort of filler material—straw; feathers; cotton; or old, worn quilts—sandwiched between two pieces of material and held in place by knotting or stitching. A primary use of quilts is for warmth. Although the first quilts were used as protective clothing in battle and for mattresses, quilts later came to be used as bed and/or window coverings to keep the warmth in and the cold and drafts out.

The quilt as a source of comfort, warmth, and protection often is discussed as a preface to a text or article that deals with one or more of the other functions of a quilt. For example, in the introduction of their book, *Kentucky Quilts 1800–1900*, Holstein and Finley tell the reader: "Quilts were at once the most efficient answer to a pressing need—warm bed coverings."[4] Holstein's introduction in *American Pieced Quilts* includes his claim that quilting was "a very efficient method of protecting against both heat and cold."[5]

Efficiency seems to be one of the more common words used to describe the quality of quilts that made them such an integral part of the early American household. For example, Holstein states in *How to Know American Folk Art* that the "harsh winters demanded warm bed clothing for survival, and quilts were quicker to make and more efficient as insulators than blankets that were woven from home-grown wool."[6] Bresenhan, Patterson, and Puentes point out that the efficient nature of the quilt was in its thermal qualities and the materials from which a quilt could be made, rather than in the process of its creation. For instance, to make a quilt in early Texas,

> cotton had to be grown, cultivated, chopped, picked, ginned, and carded. Thread had to be spun on spinning wheels, cloth woven on looms and dyed by hand, then the quilt top pieced. The cotton for the batting had to be grown, picked, ginned and carded. Then the quilt could be quilted. None of this was easy, nor was it fast. . . . [I]t was a slow, tedious process.[7]

Whether the basic fiber was cotton, wool, or flax, quilt making consumed a great deal of the early American woman's time; thus, the quilt was energy efficient for its user but not necessarily for its creator.

Literature on quilts contains documentation of one other form of protection for which quilts were used. Early Americans often wrapped their dead in a quilt; in fact, often the best quilts were used for a burial. For example, in *The Quilters*, quilter Lois Hand recalls that, when a neighbor's baby died, women in the community quilted a precious piece of blue silk into a lining for the casket and made a blue silk cover for the baby.[8] A pictorial documentation of the quilt as a cover for the dead is included in *Hearts and Hands: The Influence of Women & Quilts on American Society*.[9] Quilts used for burial also are referenced in the novel, *Captain Gray's Company; or, Crossing the Plains and Living in Oregon* by Abigail Scott Duniway. Pioneers who died during the journey to Oregon often were wrapped in quilt coffins and buried in shallow, hurriedly dug graves: "No coffins could be procured, but heavy bed-clothes were used in their stead. The clods descended with a muffled sound upon the quilted linings of the last resting places of the sleepers."[10]

The primary purpose of the quilt was to ward off the elements for both the living and the dead. As such, quilts became symbolic of the comfort and shelter of home. How, then, did such a functional object become a platform for public speech? While sources that document the utility of the quilt do not address this question directly, they do provide the basis for an understanding of the subconscious and conscious associations people make with quilts. These associations may be an important factor in discovering the characteristics of quilts that protest.

Socialization of Woman

In a larger sense, the process of quilt making was an integral part of the maintenance of a complex social system. Learning the fundamentals of needlework required for quilt making was a form of gender socialization; thus, women's role as builders and keepers of the domestic/private sphere was dictated and reinforced through their sewing. Several sources represent the attention given to the socialization process in the literature on quilts. Parker, for example, lays the historical foundation for the development of the notion that women should receive limited education. She provides detailed accounts of the processes through which men reasoned and the claims they made that women should not receive too much education: "All writers and educators were in agreement that no matter what other skills or knowledge a woman strove to attain, skill in needlework was of first priority."[11]

Another example of literature that highlights the socialization function of quilt making is Swan's "Quilt-Making Within Women's Needlework Repertoire." She admits that, after the American Revolution, women's opportunities expanded; however, even during this time of the Enlightenment, "women still practiced needlework for two days of the school week."[12] How the process of quilt making functioned to socialize women for their domestic role also is discussed by Holstein, who explains that "in the eighteenth and early nineteenth centuries young girls' education in stitchery was started when they were as young as three, and it continued, through much practical application, until they left home."[13] Fox notes that the quilt given to a young girl for her doll was more than a token of love from a mother to her daughter; with doll quilts, a little girl could play the "little mother." Thus, doll quilts facilitated a girl's indoctrination for her role as mother.[14]

Much of the literature on quilts includes discussion of how women's role as mother and protector of the family has been woven into the fabric of the quilts they have made and in those that have been made for them. Trained for and consigned to the private sphere, women were discouraged or prohibited from participating in the public arena. Yet, women were able to transcend their domestic confinement via an object that symbolized this confinement—the quilt. The allusion to quilts as suasive artifacts—in domestic role training—makes this literature relevant to my study of the quilt as a channel for public persuasion.

Community Building

Many quilt sources attend to the community activity of quilt making—an activity out of which more than a finished quilt was produced. For example, as Hedges and Wendt note, "Quilting bees were usually festive occasions, opportunities to renew and cement friendships, to reestablish social bonds among women otherwise isolated, especially on the western frontier, to exchange news and ideas and to express feelings."[15] While they constructed a quilt, women also created a communication network through which they were able to satisfy some of their emotional and intellectual needs.

Another example of a text that highlights the function of quilt making as a community-building activity is *The Quilters*. In this book, several women recall the times in their lives when the nearest neighbor was ten to twenty miles away. Also, they remember when their mothers or they would be left alone for weeks while their fathers and husbands were off in search of work, seed, or livestock. During these times, the quilting bee helped to alleviate some of the isolation.[16] Clarke includes a description of the event at which "there used to be fifteen or even more women invited to come in and make a quilt.[17] Similarly, Dewhurst, MacDowell, and MacDowell claim that the bee was a "uniquely American Institution," in which the "greater value lay in the opportunity it afforded women for getting together to exchange news, recipes, home remedies, fabric scraps and patterns, to discuss political issues and personal problems.[18]

The community-building function of the quilt-making process also is discussed by Lasansky and Holstein. Lasansky credits the quilting bee with building women's sense of community with one another and with children—she points out that young girls were included in the quilting bee despite their inexperience.[19] Holstein includes men in one of his discussions of the quilting bee. When the last stitch of a quilt was completed, many bees culminated in a social gathering—attended by males—in which everyone indulged "in all of those festivities which were part of that era of American social life."[20]

How the quilt-making process involved and affected entire communities is emphasized in many references that deal with quilts. Because these sources focus more on process than on the actual quilt produced, they do not address directly the characteristics that make quilts protest symbols. However, the social and community function of the quilt-making process may be one of the features of quilts that makes them a persuasive change agent.

The quilt as a utilitarian item, girls' and women's forced training in needlework, and the isolation that periodically was alleviated through the communal process of quilt making are three areas that commonly receive treatment in literature on quilts. Some recent publications have begun to emphasize the aesthetic qualities of quilts and the artistic abilities of quilts and quilt makers.

Aesthetic Qualities

Another function that quilts perform is an aesthetic one. Harris claims that the "[f]irst official recognition of the painterly qualities in quilts came . . . at New York's Whitney Museum of American Art" in a sixty-piece quilt exhibit in 1971.[21] This exhibit, entitled "Abstract Design in American Quilts," was the first in which quilts were hung as art rather than needlework.[22] Since then, quilt making has been accepted as an art form.

Women long ago "unofficially" recognized the artistic qualities of quilts. The discrepancy between official and unofficial recognition of the quilt as art is apparent in the quilt literature. For instance, Mondale claims that women "had the cleverness and the insight to . . . make art in the home as part of one's regular routine."[23] Holstein suggests, in contrast, that art was distinguished from utility by women in the nineteenth century. Appliqué quilts were considered "the best" quilts; pieced ones were the utility quilts.[24] Thus, among quilters, standards were set that distinguished the non-art quilt from the art quilt.

An example of a text that specifies the standards women set for the best quilts is *Kentucky Quilts 1800–1900: The Kentucky Quilt Project*, in which the authors state: "Traditional criteria for judging excellence in quilts in addition to overall beauty, were the craft aspects, the quality of stitching in the piecing or appliquéing, fineness and elaborateness of the quilting, the intricacy of design, number of pieces used in the patterns, how well complicated maneuvers (sewing curves, making points meet etc.) had been done."[25] According to Holstein and Finley, the quality of the various aspects of quilt construction was the primary criterion used by women in judging quilts.

Distinguishing between the artist and the folk artist is the topic of many books and articles about quilts. Samples of these sources include Irwin's book, *A People and Their Quilts*, in which the author claims: "When our great-grandmothers made a beautiful quilt . . . they were not trained in color schemes, pattern creation or needlework, and never even thought of the work as art, but they were true folk artists."[26] Texts such as *Quilts, Coverlets, Rugs and Samplers*,[27] *How to Know American Folk*

Art,[28] and *Artists in Aprons: Folk Art by American Women*[29] include discussions of the unschooled and unsophisticated nature of women artists whose quilts warmed the body and brightened people's lives. These sources exemplify the notion espoused in much of the literature on quilts that the lack of formal training is the factor that distinguishes an art quilt from a folk-art quilt.

While many women may not have called themselves *artists* or thought of themselves as such, their artistry has been credited by Hedges and Wendt. They assert that women "responded to the technical challenge implicit in quilt-making, just as a painter might set and solve a technical problem of shading or perspective or design."[30] The traditional quilter's artistry is apparent when one considers the "pieced quilt that contains 30,000 pieces, each one-half inch by three-quarters inch in size."[31] Hedges and Wendt focus less on formal training and more on the nature of the task and product as criteria for designating the quilt maker as artist.

In Roe's compilation of essays, formally trained quilt artists talk about quilts as art. For example, James laments, "Now in the 1980's *all* quilts seem to be art, and all quilters are artists."[32] Nixon distinguishes the artist from the non-artist on the basis of purpose: "for some, [quilting may] evoke warmth, comfort, security, tradition and on-going continuity. For others, the quilt provides a marvelous vehicle to express their creativity."[33]

Holstein also discusses the quilt as art and the criteria for distinguishing between an art quilt and a utility quilt. He explains how the art quilt was distinguished from the non-art quilt when determining those to be included in a 1972 quilt exhibit at the Renwick Gallery in Washington, D.C. The primary criterion used was whether the quilt worked as a painting—whether it formed a cohesive, strong, and important visual statement.[34] This criterion was very different from the standards of elaborate needlework, fineness of the quilting, and complicated maneuvers by which traditional quilters judge their quilts.

The aesthetic function of quilts afforded traditional quilters the opportunity to document the events of their lives in a colorful and artistic way. This form of self-expression continues through contemporary quilt artists' efforts to explore new approaches to quilts and quilt making. Whether creating new images or reproducing old ones, quilts are a medium through which people have and continue to express themselves. Although literature on quilts often emphasizes the aesthetic function of quilts, these sources have not addressed directly the message that traditional or contemporary artists intend or hope to communicate to the viewer through their art. Therefore, while authors of quilt literature credit the quilt with serving as a vehicle of self-expression, they stop short of in-depth analyses of how and what people communicate through their quilts.

<u>Voice</u>

Much of the literature about quilts includes some mention of the function of quilts as a means of women's expression. There are several sources that primarily deal with the communicative qualities of quilts. *Hearts and Hands: The Influence of Women & Quilts on American Society,*[35] for example, is an outstanding text in its coverage of quilts as historical records, purveyors of traditional values and morals, women's ballots, and symbols of protest. The authors do not limit their discussion to White American women's quilts. How slave and Indian women influenced and were influenced by quilts also are discussed in this book.

Another excellent example of a source that emphasizes the communicative qualities of quilts is Hedges and Wendt's *In Her Own Image: Women Working in the Arts.* This text includes an extensive discussion of how quilt patterns and the names given to quilt patterns often represent historical/political events. The authors explain that, although quilts usually were named on the basis of their patterns, over time, there were small variations introduced in response to sectional and national events. For instance, "during the Civil War a traditional rose pattern was modified by the addition of a black patch at its center and renamed the *Radical Rose* in recognition of the slavery controversy."[36] The names given to traditional patterns were (and are) excellent historical records. The authors claim that there are about three-hundred quilt patterns; however, these patterns have been given thousands of different names.

Lasansky also discusses the history of quilts and their makers, providing a chronological narrative of the quilt's place in America and a general overview of quilts as they mirror the various roles of women. In addition, Lasansky discusses how quilts function as a chronicle of regional and national events, past and present:

> Frontier quilts, no matter where they were made, should share common factors. But, because the frontier period of one location is chronologically different from that of another, the quilts also reflect national trends of that particular era, both in the fabrics available and the designs popular at the time. Within this broad framework one then considers the individuals at work: an older,

middle-aged, or younger woman whose attitudes are formed by her past and current lives. . . . Thus each quilt is a complex response to a unique combination of circumstances.[37]

Through their quilts, women's role as communicator is evidenced—women speak about economic trends, fabric and design, their environments, and local life styles.

A collection of papers presented in a symposium at Bucknell University in 1985 is a good example of a source that focuses on quilt history, social and economic influences on quilts, quilt patterns, and the dating of quilts. The symposium papers, edited by Lasansky, include two that are particularly important to the study of quilts as women's mouthpieces. In "The Typical Versus the Unusual/Distortions of Time," Lasansky compares and analyzes the unusual quilts—those that people consider their best—and the typical quilts—ones that people think are more mundane. Lasansky believes that much of what women lived and felt is said in the "mundane" quilts.

In her efforts to find and study mundane quilts, Lasansky encouraged people in the middle and eastern regions of Pennsylvania to bring as many quilts as their families owned to an exhibit. Rather than limiting their contributions to the fanciest quilts or the ones that were in the best condition, people also brought plain, old, worn, and discolored quilts. From these, Lasansky was able to surmise which patterns and fabrics were the most popular and available in a given time period. Lasansky claims that many of the quilts, well worn and dating back several decades, contained messages that the quilters wished to send to succeeding generations. One such message was attached by a daughter to her mother's quilt in 1903 and read:

Not to be sold out of the family This quilt was peiced [sic] by Christena Pontius 75 years or more the black star was her mother's dress probabaly [sic] the only calico dress she had because they wore homemade linen and wool in the winter. She thought in this way she would remember it P.S. in Mifflinburg her fingers lying in the dust homemade thread.[38]

This note expresses how much Catherine Gemberling appreciated the importance of a special dress to her mother. It also suggests that Gemberling wanted to keep both Christena's memory and part of her mother's private self alive within the family—a self disclosed in the material Christena stitched into her quilt.

Focusing more on the rhetorical qualities of quilts, Clark's paper in the collection includes information on historic events and traditions that can give us "insight into the language of quilts and the world-views of their makers."[39] Clark claims that "quilts themselves are rich resources that strongly document the continuity and changes in women's attitudes and roles over time."[40] Women have found voice in quilts to talk about social and political events and to talk about themselves.

Clark's essay is replete with examples of quilts that have symbolized the makers' moral values, fears, and political beliefs. For example, *The Peace Ribbon*, conceived by Justine Merritt as a protest to nuclear war, and the *Secession Quilt*, made by Jemima Cook, ostensibly supporting the South's cause in the Civil War, were vehicles of expression of the political stances of two politically powerless women.

Traditionally denied full participation in society, their ideas largely ignored, their work discounted, and their needs subsumed by those of men, women have found voice in their quilts. Whether women made quilts as part of a fund-raising effort—as did the "Nineteenth Century evangelical Protestant women who joined forces to spread the Gospel, help the needy, and protect their homes from threats posed by an increasingly complex society"[41]—or to celebrate the release of the Iranian hostages in the late twentieth century, the quilts were public statements of the women's private beliefs and feelings.

Clark acknowledges that quilts carried messages of a large number of people who were the "backbone of a growing America."[42] For example, referring to quilts made by members of the Boston Female Anti-Slavery Society, Clark quotes an inscription from one quilt: "When the pin cushions are periodicals and needlebooks are tracts, discussion can hardly be stifled or slavery perpetuated."[43] Such quilts "reflect the world-views of their makers," claims Clark, as do the "many quilts which record private and public events, rites of passage, and interpersonal relationships."[44] Clark documents quilt messages and discusses how quilts can convey much about the social, economic, and political fabric of the nation.

A primary source for first-hand testimony of how quilts have functioned to express women's voices is *The Quilters: Women and Domestic Art*. In this book, women who have been quilting for more than sixty years talk about what quilting means to them: "their quilts were journals in cloth on which they could focus their remembrances."[45] The memories they recorded included childhood experiences; family blessings and tragedies; and social, economic, and political events. Quirl Thompson Havenhill, for example, made her first quilt in the winter of her eighth year. She quilted a garden of flowers reminiscent of the flower garden she had planted the previous spring. Hattie Wooddell made a Dutch Doll quilt during her first pregnancy, and Mrs. Herron made a Tracks to Oklahoma quilt—a reference to the days when people had to clear rocks in order to make their road and way westward.

Contemporary artists and quilters have designed and created quilts that are intended to express views on a variety of issues. Some of these quilts have received extensive media coverage; perhaps the most well-known contemporary quilt is the *AIDS Memorial Quilt*. In her book on this quilt, Ruskin emphasizes the rhetorical significance of this quilt.[46] The quilt "speaks" of those who have died as a result of AIDS and is a forum through which its creators can express their grief for the dead and concern for the living. One example of a panel in this quilt that pays tribute to the dead and carries a message to the living is the creation of JoAnne Melody. The panel contains eighteen squares; on each square is sewn the name of either *John Doe* or *Jane Doe*, his or her occupation, and age. The occupations range from teacher and priest to journalist and musician. This variety of professions demonstrates the wide range of individuals who are infected with the AIDS virus. The anonymous names—representing individuals who have died from AIDS but whose death certificates have been falsified to hide the fact—demonstrate the denial of the straight community to acknowledge gay behavior as legitimate behavior. The anonymity of the victims also represents the lack of commitment and involvement of the straight community in caring about and finding a cure for victims and their illness.[47]

Another example of a panel from the *AIDS Memorial Quilt* demonstrates the simplicity of the design of some panels. On a rectangular piece of teal-colored material, the name of *Steve Abrahms* is sewn in black letters. Next to his name, three appliqués of record albums appear vertically. Musical notes of various colors line each side of the albums.[48] While the design is simple, the message indicates a depth and complexity of feeling expressed by the panel maker, evidenced by at least two factors. First, Abrahms was loved *publicly* by the maker; thus, the creator rejects the taboos society places on gays. Second, by featuring record albums and colorful musical notes, the panel's maker seems to be saying that Abrahms appreciated the many melodies life had to offer both in music and in everyday living. Whether the albums refer to personal taste, a career, or a general attitude toward life, the panel maker felt that music and vibrant colors best represented the person whom she or he wished to honor. Such a representation begins to give life to a person who, to many, is no more than another statistical casualty of the AIDS virus.

While the *AIDS Memorial Quilt* honors the dead and dying, quilt art that celebrates birth and female sexuality is Judy Chicago's *The Birth Project*. *The Birth Project* is a series of needlework pieces, with some quilt works among them, that represent women's life force—a connection to the "ecstasy of existence and the complexity of life."[49] Chicago's book, *The Birth Project*, identifies how ideas for the various pieces were conceived, shows them in various stages of their development, and presents many of the final products.[50] This book is an excellent example of a source on quilts that treats quilts both as art and as a vehicle for social commentary and persuasive communication.

The stories women have been telling with their quilts have been recognized and acknowledged in an exhibition at the Williams College Museum of Art in Massachusetts. The show, entitled "Stitching Memories," contains narrative quilts created by slaves and African Americans. Quilts in the exhibit are a mix of traditional and new forms. For example, on Elizabeth Scott's *Plantation Quilt*, brightly embroidered stars depict the sky as it appears over the farmhouse porch where her ancestors sat at night, talking and singing as they pieced their quilts together. A non-traditional quilt included in the exhibit is one made by Winnie McClean of Macon, Georgia. This quilt is made with Xeroxed photographs of McClean's family stitched over cloth sacks to make what the artist calls her "Family Tree."[51]

Functions of quilts—how they are used, women's socialization, community building, aesthetic, and vocal qualities of quilts—are topics that are addressed regularly in quilt literature. The literature that includes discussions of these functions has relevance to my study in five ways. First, the fact that quilts have been used by children and adults of both sexes for several centuries influences how messages carried by protest quilts are received. Second, women—trained for domestic duties and confined to the private sphere—adapted their talents to fulfill the need to express themselves. The effectiveness of this adaptation is reflected in how quilts are used as protest symbols. Literature on the function of community building is a third category relevant to my study because the inclusion of all members of a community in the quilting process makes the quilt a "mainstream" rhetorical artifact—one used to challenge the system that helps to create it. Fourth, the elements of quilts that are considered to be art must be studied as part of the effort to identify the features of quilts that make them protest symbols. Finally, sources that deal with how quilts have functioned to facilitate speech form the foundation of my study of the characteristics of quilts that function as protest symbols.

Protest Rhetoric

The literature on protest rhetoric generally falls into two broad categories: (1) Studies that purport to define protest rhetoric and social movements; and (2) Studies that deal with specific elements within a movement or time period—strategies, speakers, particular speeches, effects, audience, or specific events. My study is geared toward defining what constitutes an artifact of protest through an analysis of a specific element—a quilt. Therefore, I will include a discussion of relevant protest literature in both of the categories.

Studies on the rhetoric of protest that begin with an explicit definition of protest rhetoric are rare. In fact, those that include an explicit definition refer to "agitation" or "confrontation" rhetoric rather than the rhetoric of protest. McEdwards, for example, offers a definition of agitation rhetoric, claiming that "[a]gitative language belongs to a particular type of rhetoric whose end is movement away from the *status quo* . . . usually a complete reversal of existing conditions or situation."[52] Further, "agitative language is jolting, combative and passionate—in the fullest sense of the term."[53] Key to McEdwards' definition is the notion of extreme rhetoric used to promote extreme action or change.

For Cathcart, agitation is "a necessary concomitant to change in any established system . . . (by those who are) seeking reform within the system (as distinguished) from those who produce a dialectical enjoinment. . . ."[54] Whereas Cathcart views agitation as conventional behavior that is part of the normal process of change and growth in a system, Bowers and Ochs view the rhetoric of agitation as a phenomenon that occurs outside of the normal discursive boundaries of a system: "Agitation exists when (1) people outside the normal decision-making establishment (2) advocate significant social change and (3) encounter a degree of resistance within the establishment such as to require more than the normal discursive means of persuasion."[55] The definitions by Cathcart and Bowers and Ochs of agitation rhetoric share one common characteristic—both definitions involve communication directed toward changing a system.

More closely aligned with Bowers and Ochs' definition of agitation rhetoric is Cathcart's notion of confrontation rhetoric. Cathcart claims that confrontation rhetoric is distinguished from agitation rhetoric in that the former rejects the system, its hierarchy and its values, while the latter upholds and reinforces the established order or system.[56] Similarly, Scott and Smith,[57] Bailey,[58] Andrews,[59] and Burgess[60] view confrontation rhetoric as an extension of communication adopted by confronters who have exhausted all acceptable channels of communication with those in power. Scott and Smith claim, for example, that confrontation is used "as a tactic for achieving attention and an importance not readily attainable through decorum."[61]

Studies that do not include specific definitions of protest/agitation/confrontation rhetoric leave the reader to assume or infer a definition. For example, Ash's definition of protest rhetoric can be discerned from the definition she provides of a social movement. A social movement, she claims, is "the set of attitudes and self-conscious actions of people directed toward change . . . that is carried on outside of the ideologically legitimated channels or channels used in innovative ways."[62] Protest rhetoric, then, is communication that challenges the system in a way that is not condoned or acceptable to the system.

Another way some scholars have defined protest rhetoric is through example. Haiman cites Aristotle's definition of rhetoric and provides examples of "available means of persuasion" that have been employed: "With respect to the Vietnam war we have witnessed everything from vigils, sit-ins at draft boards, and picket signs accusing the President of murder, to the burning of draft cards and self-immolation."[63] Throughout his essay, Haiman interchangeably uses such phrases as "a new array of rhetorical expression" or "expressing deviant views" as he speaks about the "new rhetoric [that is] persuasion by a strategy of power and coercion rather than by reason and democratic decision making."[64] Although he does not identify it as such, these statements seem to constitute Haiman's definition of protest rhetoric.

As some authors discuss the features of protest rhetoric, they include a definition of the people who engage in protest activities. McEdwards asserts that agitators are people who "deliberately [try] to select the diction, the imagery, the syntax that will move [their] audience emotionally and intellectually to call for change."[65] Writing about the 1968 Presidential campaign, White was less kind to protesters. He defined those who protest as "naïve and exploited people, exploited by the police; television; and those calculating organizers who can manipulate them as a skirmish line into the forefront of confrontation. . . ."[66] Simons distinguishes between the moderate and the radical protester. He claims that moderate protesters tend to be easily controlled and are more orderly. Unlike radical protesters who are not so easy to control, moderate protesters' inclinations toward orderly behavior make them an asset for the leader during bargaining sessions; however, moderate tactics may effect change slowly, or possibly not at all.[67]

Based on the examples of protest literature provided, there does not appear to be one definite, distinctive definition of protest rhetoric. Yet, there do seem to be some common elements or assumptions to all of the definitions explicated thus far. All of the above essays on protest rhetoric recognize such rhetoric as designed to effect a change in the status quo. Protest rhetoric and the people who use it, to some extent, challenge a system in which the protesters are not members of the dominant social order. Finally, traditional definitions of the rhetoric of protest indicate that this type of communication is combative in nature.

Studies that include definitions or explanations of the features of protest rhetoric are marginally useful for my study of the characteristics of quilts that protest. Because the creators of protest quilts have been members of non-dominant groups who have sought to challenge a system, there is some basis for comparison between current literature and my study. Existing studies on protest rhetoric, however, are limited to one perspective. According to these studies, rhetoric that is not combative in nature—where the rhetors do not receive a confrontative response from the control or establishment group—is not considered a protest form. Because quilts do not evoke an aggressive response from the establishment, they do not qualify as legitimate protest forms by traditional standards. However, I propose to question the traditional definitions of protest rhetoric.

Because women largely have been excluded from utilizing the usual channels of communication, such as public address, publishing, and standing for public office, they have been forced to find other means to express themselves. While other non-dominant groups—such as minorities, students, and laborers—have had similar problems that led them to protest, they have had to overcome only one major obstacle as they confronted the system—their low-power position. Women, on the other hand, have had to overcome several major obstacles.

By their very socialization, women have been conditioned to be cooperative with and self-sacrificing for God, man, and country. They also have been relegated to the private sphere of the home and family. Thus, they have been forced to design methods of protest that enable them to overcome their low-power position in a participatory way and in a way that would not threaten the stability of the family structure.

Given their training, women's development of non-aggressive protest strategies would seem to be reasonable and expected. Unfortunately, scholars of protest rhetoric have ignored women's perspectives on rhetorical strategies of protest. In fact, by their very definitions of protest rhetoric, rhetorical scholars have discounted any non-confrontational strategies women have devised. Through my analysis of quilts that have been used as a channel to communicate dissatisfaction with the status quo, I will begin to explore new definitions of protest. Such exploration will lay the groundwork for a different conceptualization of the nature of protest rhetoric—one based on a feminist perspective.

A second category of literature on protest rhetoric covers specific elements of protest events and movements. Such elements as rhetorical strategies and their effects, significant rhetorical events, and particular speakers and their rhetoric form the basis for analysis and theory verification in these studies. Klumpp, for example, discusses the process and implications of the radical strategy of protest employed by students during the Columbia University student revolt of 1968.[68] Windt focuses his study on several aspects of the rhetoric primarily used by the Yippies: obscenities, strident moralism, and the "counter-culture" lifestyle.[69] The focus of Andrews' essay on the confrontation at Columbia University is on the coercive versus persuasive nature of the protesters' rhetoric.[70] Kaye analyzes the rhetorical qualities of protest music of the 1960s,[71] while Jurma studies moderate leadership tactics in his essay.[72] As with my study, these articles are focused on one component of a protest movement. The elements featured in these studies, however, are confrontative strategies that received a direct response from control or establishment groups. Therefore, these articles will be marginally useful for my purposes.

Studies of a particular speaker and/or a specific speech are the subject of studies by many rhetorical scholars. Sampson's dissertation on the antislavery speaking of Joshua Reed Giddings[73] and Andrews' essay on Richard Cobden's rhetoric[74] are two examples of such analyses. Similarly, Bezayiff analyzes John Adams' use of the courtroom in pre-Revolutionary America to express colonial dissatisfaction and opposition to England's authority.[75] Such studies have little bearing on the research I will conduct. The discourse and persuasive strategies used by men such as Giddings, Cobden, and Adams generally conform to the traditional notions of confrontation rhetoric; thus, this type of scholarship—in which a particular speaker or speech is featured—will be of little relevance to a study in which the traditional notions of protest rhetoric are questioned.

Protest movements in which women have been visibly involved and the public oratory they have produced have received some attention from rhetorical scholars. For example, in his anthology of American public address, Reid includes critical commentaries of and speeches on the topics of equal rights and women's suffrage presented by historically noteworthy women—Sojourner Truth, Lucretia Mott, Elizabeth Stanton, and Susan B. Anthony.[76] Similarly, Anderson's anthology of women's speeches includes a brief biographical and historical sketch of each speaker.[77] More extensive treatment of women rhetors is provided in Campbell's *Man Cannot Speak for Her*, a two-volume text that focuses on early feminist rhetoric and key texts of early feminist rhetors.[78] Although these texts include rhetorical strategies used by women in the public arena, their relevance to my study is limited. Because my research is not focused on the discourse of one particular rhetor and I am not performing an analysis of persuasive public discourse in the traditional sense, only unconventional protest strategies discussed in these texts will be of significant value to my study.

Studies on specific protest rhetors—both male and female—their protest rhetoric, or other elements of the rhetorical situation are rooted in a definition of protest that traditionally has been acknowledged as aggressive—verbally and/or physically. For my study, I propose to question traditionally accepted assumptions; therefore, the value of such literature will be minimal. My purpose is not to validate theory; rather, I seek to generate new theory. Further, I do not intend to find a replacement or substitute theory for protest rhetoric; instead, I hope to add to existing knowledge by broadening the perspective of protest rhetoric to include that of women.

Feminist Perspectives on Rhetoric

In this review of the literature, I am distinguishing between feminist literature and literature that has as its subject matter women—women's rhetoric or women's issues. Although some feminist literature may focus on female rhetors and/or female-identified issues, the feminist researcher approaches scholarly inquiry from a perspective different from traditionally held perspectives.

The body of feminist literature that focuses on protest rhetoric is small and emphasizes two primary categories of topics: (1) Analyses of feminist events, speakers, and/or issues; and (2) Discussions of the need for and approach to analyses based on a feminist perspective.

Studies that address feminist rhetorical strategies include those by Kurs and Cathcart,[79] Campbell,[80] Gold,[81] and Conrad.[82] In these essays, the authors begin to identify strategies used by feminists throughout history in their efforts to achieve their goals. Karen Foss' study constitutes a useful supplement to these studies with its focus on the ideology of contemporary feminism.[83] A study that acknowledges women's rhetorical contributions in the private and public spheres from a feminist perspective is Sonja Foss' study of Judy Chicago's *The Dinner Party*.[84] Studies such as these that focus on feminist rhetoric and feminist studies of women's protest rhetoric comprise a relatively small number of essays on these subjects. These articles, however, provide a starting point for scholars who wish to address feminist rhetoric and may provide me with ideas for the rhetorical strategies that the creators of the quilts I will analyze may be using. They also lend support to my argument for the study of quilts as a protest form.

Articles about feminist protest events, speakers, and issues are, by their feminist nature, designed to focus on one aspect of the rhetorical situation. Thus, they serve as examples of the variety of approaches and conclusions scholars can reach through the study of feminist artifacts—especially when those artifacts are analyzed from a feminist perspective. Therefore, feminist studies of feminist rhetoric provide a body of scholarship with which I can compare my findings and draw conclusions that will more accurately represent feminist strategies of protest.

Of particular use to my study are articles that emphasize the need for a feminist research perspective in communication scholarship. Edson's study is particularly helpful in that she demonstrates the need for an expanded approach to the study of social movements and the rhetoric that occurs within them. In her discussion, Edson details the differences between males' and females' realities in order to support her claim that social movement studies have been conducted from a male-biased standpoint.[85] Edson's article includes discussions of women's conceptions of relationships, time, thought, and power that may be helpful to me as I search for features of quilts that function as protest artifacts.

The construct of power is relevant to protest rhetoric in that such rhetoric often is directed at individuals who are perceived as more powerful than the rhetors. Endress' essay provides a feminist methodological approach to power. She suggests that much of what is published in communication "does not adequately address or reflect a full under-standing of alternative conceptions of the communicative power of women."[86] Endress makes sound arguments for studies that are founded on women's perspectives and that include women's texts. She claims:

> In determining the correct method of analysis for the evaluation of rhetoric, we must consider the role and importance of the use of unconventional artifacts such as oral histories, diaries, and journal entries. And, we must be cautious in our use of methodologies based upon patriarchal principles. . . . Much of social movement analysis is based upon a concept of strategy, confrontation, and coercion.[87]

Unconventional artifacts that usually are not considered under the rubric of protest rhetoric—because they do not confront or they are not coercive—are necessary and valid texts for analysis, according to Endress.

Another article that emphasizes the need for a feminist approach in communication research is by Foss and Foss. They define the feminist perspective in research, explain its methodological assumptions, and provide a comparison/contrast of feminist versus old-paradigm methods of research.[88] This essay provides support for my study in that the authors make a strong case for using a feminist method to guide research—including the use of women's data such as quilts.

Essays that argue for a feminist approach to research provide justification for my study of the characteristics of quilts that protest. These articles also form a foundation upon which I can generate a theory of protest rhetoric that is not born of old-paradigm traditions.[3]

Notes

1. Adapted from the dissertation of Gail J. Chryslee, "The Construction of a Rhetorical Response to Visual Art: A Case Study of *Brushstrokes in Flight*" (PhD diss., Ohio State University, 1995).

2. Adapted from the dissertation of William Joseph Condon Waters, "The American Bloom: Did an American Language Birth American Literature?" (PhD diss., University of New Mexico, 2000).

3. Adapted from the dissertation of Mary Rose Williams, "A Reconceptualization of Protest Rhetoric: Characteristics of Quilts as Protest" (PhD diss., University of Oregon, 1990). Original footnote numbers were retained in this sample, but the references to which they refer were not.

CHAPTER SIX
GETTING THERE:
THE DISSERTATION PROPOSAL

When you travel, it's sometimes fun not to have a plan. You wander where your interests take you, find somewhere to stay when you come into a new place, and decide what you want to do according to how you feel on a particular day. At other times—usually when you have a limited amount of time—you want the kind of trip where you have figured out most things ahead of time—where to go, where to stay, and what to see—so that your trip will be easy and efficient and you don't spend large parts of every day figuring out the basics. You want to have key arrangements made so that you can get the most out of what you are experiencing and can do all the things you want to while you're there.

You want to do this second kind of traveling when you are writing a dissertation. Save the adventure for another time. You can't prearrange and know everything you're going to encounter, but some advance planning makes things go much more smoothly. In the dissertation process, the dissertation proposal constitutes this kind of planning. Just like tickets purchased for air travel and hotel reservations represent a commitment to particular travel plans, the dissertation proposal represents a major commitment on your part to doing a particular kind of study. It can be changed only at a price—a longer timetable for completing your dissertation.

You did the key planning for your dissertation, of course, when you created your preproposal. In that stage of the process, you created a one-page document that summarized the decisions you made about your research question, categories of your literature review, data, method of data collection, method of data analysis, significance of your study, and the outline of your study. In addition, if you've been following along with us in this book, you've completed your literature review, which is a major part of the proposal. Once you explain and elaborate on the decisions you made in your preproposal, you will have your dissertation proposal.

The first step in building on your preproposal to create your proposal is to find out what the expectations are for the format of a dissertation proposal in your department. Some proposals become the first chapter of the dissertation. These kinds of proposals are often used for qualitative dissertations and for dissertations composed of a series of publishable studies. They include as their basic sections an introduction, the research question, the literature review, the research design, significance of the study, and outline of the study.

A second common format for dissertation proposals is for the proposal to serve as the first three chapters of the dissertation. This is the kind of proposal that is expected when you are doing a five-chapter dissertation—usually the format for experimental studies—in which the first chapter of the dissertation is the introduction, the second chapter is the literature review, the third chapter is the research design, the fourth chapter is the findings or results, and the fifth chapter is the discussion. The proposal for this kind of study has three major sections, divided into the three chapters of introduction, literature review, and research design.

You also want to find out how long your dissertation proposal is expected to be. For some advisors and in some departments, your proposal is the same length as either your first chapter or your first three chapters, depending on the format you are using. In other departments, the proposal is considerably shorter than the corresponding chapters will be, and students are expected to fill in and elaborate on the ideas in the proposal for those chapters in the dissertation. If you have a choice, write your proposal as though it's going to be your actual chapter or chapters so that the proposal itself constitutes major progress on your dissertation. In such a case, the proposal is usually between 30 and 50 pages long. In our discussion of the proposal in the rest of this chapter, we're going to assume you have and are choosing this option for your dissertation proposal. In other words, what you write for your proposal becomes an actual chapter or chapters of your dissertation with only minor changes or additions. Let's turn now to the various sections of the proposal and what should be in them.

Introduction

The introduction section of the proposal constitutes an invitation into the dissertation. It invites the reader to consider the general problem your dissertation addresses and the theoretical conversation to which it will contribute. It provides context, in other words, for the question you are investigating—the reason for asking the question. You can issue this invitation in a number of ways. Begin with an anecdote that illustrates the problem with which you are dealing, explain how you became interested in it, or quote others who discuss the importance of the problem. Or lay out the key tenets of a debate on the problem that is taking place in the literature in your discipline. Perhaps you can feature proponents of key positions and suggest how your study is going to contribute to the debate among them. However you set up your introduction, make sure it flows easily into your discussion of your research question, which is the next section of your proposal.

In the introduction, as a general rule, stay away from discussing the data you'll be using to answer your research question. Stay focused on the theoretical debate to which your dissertation will be contributing. Your theoretical contribution—not your particular data—will be the significant part of your dissertation, so keep your readers' attention on the debate to which you will make this contribution. The introduction should be three to five pages long if your proposal will become your first chapter. Aim for 10 to 15 pages if your proposal turns into the first three chapters of your dissertation.

Introduction Sample #1

The impact of human problems on productivity and work performance has been and continues to be a concern of organizations. Occupational programs that offer employees assistance with a variety of problems were developed in response to this concern (Comstock, 1983, p. 46).

One of the assumptions underlying the rationale for such programs is that a person's psychological and physical well-being are reflected in his or her job performance. A decline in an employee's job performance is considered to be symptomatic of an underlying problem. Therefore, many businesspeople and mental health professionals believe that the workplace is a good environment for the early identification of problems (Egdahl et al., 1980, p. 86).

Traditionally, managers have responded to poor job performance with disciplinary action or threats of disciplinary action. Occupational programs are "more effective and efficient in altering the behavior of employees than purely disciplinary methods" (Shain and Groeneveld, 1980, p. 3). Thus, occupational programs provide employees with resources to help them resolve problems while remaining employed, offer managers an alternative to the "discipline-only" approach to management, and decrease the production costs of the organization (Scanlon, 1983; Shain and Groeneveld, 1980, pp. 19–20; Thoreson and Hosokawa, 1984, pp. 11–12).

The provision of occupational program benefits began in 1942, when DuPont and Eastman Kodak implemented Occupational Alcoholism Programs (OAPs). The establishment of OAPs within these organizations stemmed from the realization that alcoholic employees had a negative impact on productivity. The goals of the OAP included the identification and rehabilitation of the alcoholic employee with the subsequent restoration of the employee to a particular level of job performance (Archambault et al., 1982, pp. 11–12; Comstock, 1983, p. 46; Scanlon, 1983, p. 38).

In the 1970s, many OAPs dropped the word *alcohol* from their program titles and broadened their focus. These OAPs became Employee Assistance Programs (EAPs), and their treatment approach became known as the *broadbrush approach*. *Broadbrush* refers to the expansion of EAP-service provision to include a wide range of problems, not just alcohol problems (Archambault et al., 1982, pp. 12–13). The goal of the EAP changed from identifying the alcoholic worker to identifying the worker whose job performance had declined (Thoreson and Hosokawa, 1984).

As of 1979, over five thousand businesses, industries, and professional organizations were offering their employees and members OAP and EAP benefits, and the implementation of occupational programs within organizations is expected to continue to increase throughout the 1980s

(Roman, 1982, p. 141; Wrich, 1980). Although occupational programs reflect a diversity of approach, all share the following common goals:

> (1) To identify employees whose personal or health problems may be interfering with job performance; (2) To motivate those individuals to seek and accept appropriate help; (3) To address underlying stressors in the workplace through prevention, intervention, education, and evaluation strategies; and (4) To assist employees and employers in achieving their mutual aim: health and productivity. (Feinstein and Brown, 1982, p. 27)

Organizations evaluate their occupational programs by comparing the costs and benefits—both human and economic—of service provision (Egdahl et al., 1980, p. 104). Utilization rate, which refers to the percentage of an organization's total employee population who utilize occupational program services during any given year, is a primary indicator of program success (Egdahl et al., 1980, p. 104). The rate of employee utilization is determined by three types of referrals—formal supervisory referrals, informal supervisory referrals, and self-referrals.

A formal supervisory referral is a mandatory referral. The continued employment of the referred employee is dependent upon his or her participation in the program. These referrals usually are a response to a pattern of unsatisfactory job performance, which the employee has been unable or unwilling to reverse. Formal referrals often are preceded by informal referrals. An informal referral occurs when a supervisor suggests to an employee that she or he utilize the occupational assistance program. These suggestions are based upon observation of declining job performance or information that an employee is having problems. Self-referrals are voluntary referrals stemming from an employee's awareness of a problem and subsequent decision to seek help for that problem.

Most occupational program directors are aware of the utilization rate for their particular programs, and many strive to reach and maintain an identified goal for employee referrals. Directors attempt to accomplish this goal through various publicity techniques designed to inform employees of program services. The promotional techniques most commonly used by program directors are brochures, posters, orientation for new employees, supervisory training programs, newsletters, and home mailings (Archambault et al., 1982, pp. 57–61; Feinstein and Brown, 1982, p. 66; Braun and Novak, 1984, p. 18).

The vast majority of programs strive to achieve a high rate of self-referrals. Self-referrals indicate that the employee has taken the initiative to seek assistance before her or his job performance is affected. By resolving the difficulty in its early stages, the employee often avoids a supervisory confrontation and subsequent referral. Such confrontations may be time consuming and uncomfortable for all parties involved. In addition, self-referrals indicate that the program has attained a particular level of trust and is seen as viable by the employee population. Furthermore, many program directors argue that strict confidentiality only can be maintained through self-referral (Shain and Groeneveld, 1980, pp. 14–15). For these reasons, self-referrals are considered to be characteristic of program success (Archambault et al., 1982, p. 3; Thoreson and Hosokawa, 1984, pp. 213–215; Wrich, 1980, p. 29). Because of the desirability of encouraging self-referrals, increased efforts are being made to promote services to organizational employees.

Health-care marketing professionals maintain that effective promotional strategies take into account how the actual and potential client populations perceive the service, program, or product that is being marketed. If the clientele have negative perceptions about the occupational program, the staff should evaluate whether or not these perceptions stem from the services that are provided, the manner in which these services are offered, or inaccurate information about the program. Staff may be able to alter negative perceptions through program or promotional changes or communication of accurate information about the program (MacStravic, 1980, p. 12).

Literature in the area of occupational programming has not been concerned with the perceptions of or "visions" of employees about the occupational program, nor has there been any detailed discussion about the development of audience-tailored messages. In order to tailor messages to targeted audiences, researchers must understand, in addition to the visions of employees about the occupational program, how these visions contribute to program utilization and how these visions are supported by program-marketing strategies. This understanding will enable occupational program professionals to develop persuasive messages that challenge the visions that contribute to program non-utilization and support the visions that contribute to program utilization.[1]

Introduction Sample #2

"Communication is an embodied process" (Streeck & Knapp, 1992, p. 5) in that the human body is essential to virtually every communication act. Whether in the realms of interpersonal, organizational, cultural, or rhetorical communication, the importance of the human body is difficult to deny. Even in realms where the salience of the body may seem minimal—in textual and mediated communication forms, for example—the body is a vital, omnipresent force.

For instance, although you are now reading my seemingly disembodied written text, the fact that I am hungry, my back aches, and my cat is purring on my lap are all occurrences that undoubtedly affect my communication with you. My hunger involves impatience for anything but eating; thus, I am writing quickly with inattention to detail in anticipation of an upcoming meal. My ailing back causes irritability and lends a terseness to my expression. The sensation of the cat on my lap is comforting, hopefully tempering the irritation. These experiences are possible at all only because I "have" a body. Further, any combination of such embodied experiences can—and inevitably does—affect your process ofreceiving/decoding/interpreting my messages. Perhaps you are hungry, tense, or uncomfortable. Perhaps you are habituated to reading in a particular, patterned manner. Or maybe you are distracted from this reading by the varied sights, sounds, and sensations that comprise human experience.

Despite the empirical certainty of the role of the body in communication, the bulk of communication research, whether of humanistic, social scientific, or critical orientation, "has ignored for too long a significant part of the process" by predominantly focusing on verbal or written exchange often at the exclusion of the body (Knapp & Hall, 1992, p. 29). This lack of attention to the body is ironic because, as some nonverbal researchers insist, the act of speaking itself is accomplished by the gesturing of the tongue (Koechlin, 1992). Still, the underlying supposition in communication scholarship seems to be that somehow the product of a communication process (i.e., talk, words, the verbal code of formal language) is more important than the bodily processes from which it emanates. The relative absence of the body in communication scholarship may be because human experience and its vehicle—the body—are multifarious and seemingly resistant to scholarly theorizing.

In general, when the body is considered in communication research, it typically is situated within the category of nonverbal communication. Such labeling carries with it three underlying assumptions: First, because nonverbal communication is, by definition, nonverbal, it can be separated from its verbal counterpart; second, because verbal and nonverbal codes are distinct, verbal communication is primarily a cognitive process that occurs in the brain somehow separate from the body; and third, because nonverbal communication is defined according to what it is not (non-verbal), nonverbal communication is devalued.

One perspective that challenges these three assumptions is a somatic perspective. Somatics establishes the body as the theoretical entry point and makes the body central to every theoretical claim. The term *somatics* derives from the Greek *somatikos, soma,* and *somat,* which refer to the living body. More specifically, *soma* refers to "the biological body of functions by which and through which awareness and environment are mediated" (Hanna, 1983, p. 1). Conceptualizing the human as *soma* fuses the mind/body dichotomy so prevalent in European-American culture and in conventional communication scholarship by recognizing the embodied self in its wholeness. The term *somatics* describes the art and science of the inter-relational processes among awareness, biological functioning, and environment, with these three realms understood as a synergistic whole (Hanna, 1983).

Somatics is a relatively new arrival on the academic scene. Its origins can be traced to Hanna's book, *Bodies in Revolt: A Primer in Somatic Thinking,* published in 1970 by the American Council of Learned Societies. Responding to a nation in need of a "guide for the perplexed," Hanna, a philosopher, introduced somatic ways of conceptualizing the human race and the world by drawing on what he calls "somatic scientists and philosophers" (1970/1985, p. 3). In the book, he laid out the basic tenets of somatics and focused "the somatic attitude" on the present evolution of human culture (1985/1970, p. 3).

Since Hanna's introduction, somatics has grown into an interdisciplinary and multicultural field. Somatic knowledge and techniques derive from disciplines as varied as anatomy, physiology, chemistry, psychology, physics, electronics, kinesiology, education, and medicine, as well as Eastern philosophy, healing, and martial arts traditions and practices. Somatic institutes and educational facilities have sprung up throughout the United States and the world, and several American institutions, such as Ohio State University and the California Institute of Integral Studies, offer graduate programs in somatics.[2]

Research Question

In the second section of the dissertation proposal, state the research question you intend to answer in your study. You already developed your research question as part of your dissertation preproposal, so you just have to list the question (or questions, if you have more than one) here. If you have hypotheses for your study, they go in this section as well. Conventions in your field may dictate that you transform your research question into an objective, a purpose statement, or a thesis statement instead of stating it as a question. That's easy to do. Simply make a statement that you will explore a particular phenomenon instead of asking a question about it. For example, you could turn the research question, "What are the strategies that youth suggest for preventing youth violence?" into this purpose statement: "My purpose in this study is to discover the strategies that youth suggest for preventing youth violence." The section on your research question is usually no more than one page long, regardless of the kind of proposal you are writing.

Research Question Sample #1

Despite its impact on us, we know little about the process by which we come to assign particular meaning to architecture and how it affects us. This study is designed to provide a starting point for the understanding of this process. The ways in which architectural features guide viewers to construct a particular kind of message is the focus of this study. Thus, the research question directing this inquiry is: "How does a viewer formulate a message from a building?" I am assuming that architecture can function as a kind of argument in that a viewer can see a building as making a claim or an assertion of some kind. This study is an investigation of the process by which the viewer comes to see a claim as a result of interacting with a building.[3]

Research Question Sample #2

In both the scholarly and popular literature, *empowerment* as a term crosses many boundaries, but it is used largely as if all readers will understand its meaning. Empowerment as it relates to abused spouses, however, might mean something very different from the empowerment of students who would benefit from a choice in the learning mode they use. Not only is the definition of empowerment not clear, but no means of operationalizing it in a text exists. This study is designed to address both of these issues.

There are two primary purposes for this study: (1) To develop a schema that operationalizes empowerment in a text, and (2) To apply the schema to texts to discover the strategies involved in the rhetorical construction of empowerment.

I am interested in the process by which a text empowers because of my commitment to the democratization of public discourse. Despite the emergence of new technologies with the potential for such democratization, it often is not realized. A hierarchy most likely will continue to exist in public access to media, and those who currently are shut out of the dominant discourse—those who belong to ethnic minorities or those who lack economic clout—will continue to be excluded. Despite the emergence of the Internet, public access channels, proliferation of the camcorder, and fiber optics that can carry hundreds of channels of information to a single household, access to this extravagance of media will remain tightly controlled; market forces, not altruistic notions of democracy, will decree who gains access. The cost of electronic equipment to gain access to these channels also will continue to provide an economic disincentive to democratization. The difficulties in creating and disseminating empowering texts, then, are not likely to improve, and I envision this study as providing initial insights into how such texts can be constructed.

I also am interested in the analysis and construction of texts that empower because I have seen numerous instances in which efforts to create such texts fail to achieve the empowerment envisioned by their creators. Appropriation, commodification, and further marginalization are some of the fates that might befall a new voice in the public discourse. The question of appropriation, in particular, has significance for me as a result of my participation in video projects that attempted to document how some groups in Columbus, Ohio, were systematically excluded from representation in the mainstream media. The story was told, but instead of empowering anyone, our projects well might have appropriated others' voices or objectified the persons we attempted to help. This project is a theoretical extension of those video projects, then, in which I hope to be able to discover how texts of empowerment might be created that are more successful.[4]

Definition of Terms

There may be instances when you want to elaborate on your research question in the section in which you introduce it. One is when you need to define some of the terms in your research question. Define terms if many different definitions are available for the terms in your questions, if the terms are likely to be misunderstood, or if you are operationalizing a construct in a particular way. The definitions follow the formal statement of your research question, and you can define terms either in a list (if you have many terms to define) or in a paragraph (if you have relatively few).

Definition of Terms Sample #1

By *loneliness*, I mean a feeling of disconnection to self and/or to others that can manifest in a "sense of utter aloneness" (Weiss, 1973, p. 21). This definition of *loneliness* is a combination of ideas articulated by Weiss (1973) and Gaev (1976). I am combining the feelings associated with Weiss' definition of emotional isolation—a subjective response to a perceived lack of intimacy—with Gaev's vision of existential loneliness of the inner self to suggest that an individual's experience of loneliness may be connected to something other than a dearth of relationships or of "valid" intimacy.

The definition of *intimacy* that I use in this study is a combination of definitions of several communication scholars: Intimacy and intimate relationships are characterized by intense mutual influence between partners; the "generation of private cultures and shared systems of meaning" that help convince partners of the unique nature of their relationship (Stephen, 1992, p. 522); and the assumption of a long-term future that transcends particular incidents, feelings, or relational states (Wood, 1993).

By *relationship*, I mean any kind of committed, interdependent romantic intimate relationship between two persons. My definition of a *good relationship* is less important than my respondents' definitions, as they are the ones who will decide whether or not they are in "good" relationships. The purpose of this research is not to prove or disprove that individuals' relationships are healthy or good. Their perception is what will count them as eligible for the study.[5]

Definition of Terms Sample #2

An analysis of the communicative construction of empowerment in a text must be rooted in some definition of *empowerment*. To empower, according to the *Oxford English Dictionary*, is to "invest legally or formally with power or authority; to authorize, license" or to "impart or bestow power. . . ." *Empowerment* is either the "action of empowering" or "the state of being empowered" (1989, p. 192). Although *empowerment* and its variants seem to have come to prominence only recently, the first usage cited in the *Oxford English Dictionary* occurred in 1654 (published in 1655) in a description of a letter from the pope (L'Estrange, 1655); Thomas Jefferson's use of *empower* also has been documented in his *Writings*, penned in 1786 and published over seven decades later (1859).

These definitions are unsatisfactory for the purposes of this project primarily because of their implicit assumptions that empowerment can be bestowed from one person to another, an assumption that I do not share. For my purposes in this study, I define *empowerment* as a state of confidence in one's ability to affect positively one's environment, a state initiated by a text that presents options for action of which the audience previously was unaware.

Certainly, *empowerment* and *power* are linked. The definition of *power*, as I am conceptualizing it, means to gain power over or to influence a condition, another, or oneself. To be empowered under my definition is not necessarily to gain power over another, but such a situation could occur; in this situation, there must be no assumption made that power over another is necessarily negative. If power is not conceptualized as a zero-sum game, then a gain in power by one person does not inevitably result in a loss of power by another. A gain in power also could include power over conditions, rather than others, or power over oneself.

My definition of *empowerment* also contains assumptions relating to the use of *unaware, environment, positively*, and *text. Unaware*, in this case, does not necessarily mean the audience member has never thought about or come into contact with the options the text is presenting. Audience members quite likely are aware of the options presented but have not thought of those options in connection with themselves; for practical purposes, then, such audience members are being exposed to options of which they previously were unaware.

Environment, as used here, does not privilege the world outside one's own body. An audience member's environment certainly could include a household, a government, or some other setting, but the environment that is being addressed here also includes one's mental environment. A change in attitude would be construed, then, as an impact on one's environment.

A *positive* impact is one that is viewed as such by the audience member. The audience member's perspective is adopted in order to come to some judgment as to the positive or negative value of the impact being described. A positive impact is one that includes perceived advantages or benefits as seen from the point of view of the audience member.

A *text*, in the specific instances used here, assumes the intentional use of symbols by a rhetor to inform or persuade, but that limitation is not necessary; it is a function of the artifacts selected for analysis. Rhetoric, on the one hand, uses symbols with the intention to persuade, but a second purpose of these symbols is to create reality or to generate knowledge. A *text*, then, need not be discursive or intentionally persuasive; it can be either an act or an artifact. The artifacts selected for analysis are representations of prior acts, but the analysis easily could involve the acts themselves. A concert, for example, would be characterized as an act, while a videotape of a concert is deemed a rhetorical artifact; either could be a *text*.

My assumptions about and definition of *empowerment* also have implications for the concept of *disempowerment*. I interpret this term to mean a condition in which the persons affected are alienated—or perceive that they are alienated—from a set of conditions that would allow them to become empowered. There is no assumption that a person who is disempowered was at one time empowered; rather, my use of the term suggests that the potential for action on behalf of oneself has not been realized.

Literature Review

If you've been following the guidelines we've offered earlier in this book, you've already completed your literature review. You developed the categories for your literature review out of the key terms of your research question at the time you developed your preproposal. You then collected and coded the relevant literature and developed a schema for presenting it. You simply have to import that literature review into the proposal at this point. It becomes your third section if your proposal is your first chapter in your dissertation. It's your second chapter if your proposal turns into the first three chapters of your dissertation. The literature review should be in the range of 10 to 35 pages, depending on the amount of literature you have to cover. Because a sample review of literature is included at the end of chapter 5, we aren't including another one here. An additional sample is in the complete proposal at the end of this chapter.

Research Design

The section of the proposal on research design is typically divided into two sections—data and procedures. Sometimes, a section on context or history is included, and there can also be a section on assumptions about method. You made decisions about key aspects of your research design when you created your preproposal. Now you simply have to flesh them out and provide explanations for your choices. The section on research design is generally 5 to 10 pages long, depending on the methods you choose for data collection and analysis and how much explanation they require. (Note: This section can also be called the *Methods* section. Don't call it *Methodology*, though—*methodology* is the study of method, just as *biology* is the study of life. This section isn't a study of method but a description of the methods you'll be using.)

Data

In the data section, identify the data for your study. You figured out what your data will be earlier, so you simply have to provide a more detailed description of them here. The data section is also the place to provide basic information that readers might need to know to understand your data. This contextual information should be relatively brief. If you are analyzing films as your data, for example, tell the dates of the films, who the directors are, which actors play the major roles, and brief summaries of the plots. If you are studying an organization, provide details about the organization such as when it was formed, who its members are, how the organization is structured, its primary activities or products, and basic financial details about it. If you are doing the kind of study where it is required, describe the research variables you'll be using in this section as well. Identify them and describe the attributes or characteristics associated with the independent, dependent, and any confounding variables that are part of the study.

There's something else to do in this section besides identifying your data. Justify why they are appropriate for answering your research question. Theoretically, you could have chosen all kinds of data for answering your question, so readers want to know why you chose what you did. Two or three good reasons for your data will suffice.

What might such good reasons be? One is that the data exhibit the quality or phenomenon you want to study. If you are studying agency as it is enacted in popular culture, for example, you could argue that certain films are appropriate data because they exhibit different kinds of agency. If you are studying conflict resolution among stakeholders in public disputes, you could justify your selection of a conflict over the erection of a communications tower on the top of a mountain because it is a long-running public conflict and has many different kinds of stakeholders—environmentalists, hikers, nearby property owners, the city's chamber of commerce, and the communications company. Another reason for selecting your data is that they are easily accessible or available to you. You probably don't want this to be your only reason for selecting your data, but it is often a major reason and certainly an appropriate one. If you use this as a reason, explain why the data are accessible to you.

Data Sample #1

The rhetorical record of Abigail Scott Duniway is a rich and untapped resource for the study of women's communication strategies. Despite a limited formal education of less than a year and responsibility for a family of six children and a semi-invalid husband, Duniway was a prolific writer and an active lecturer for equal rights.

A number of historians and journalists have considered Duniway's extensive work as a regional and national advocate for the equal suffrage cause and as editor of the *New Northwest*, the "human rights" newspaper she published in Portland, Oregon, from 1871 to 1887, and the *Pacific Empire*, a Portland journal with which she was associated as editor from 1895 through 1897. (For citation purposes, the *New Northwest* will be designated as *NNW* and the *Pacific Empire* as *PE*.) In addition, several biographical works on Duniway have been made available for general adult and juvenile readership. Given the extent of Duniway's rhetorical record as a speaker, editor, equal rights organizer, and novelist, one would expect to find a number of studies of her rhetoric; however, only two articles with a focus on Duniway's rhetoric have been published. No scholar has focused on the communication strategies that Duniway recommended to other women through her novels, speeches, and essays.

In particular, Duniway's twenty-two novels, which spanned a publication period of forty-six years, invite exploration of the development of her theory of women's communication strategies. Her novels include *Captain Gray's Company; or, Crossing the Plains and Living in Oregon,*

---

published in 1859 and later serialized in her weekly newspaper, the *New Northwest*; seventeen other serialized novels that appeared in the *New Northwest* from 1871 to 1887; three serialized novels that appeared in the *Pacific Empire* from 1895 through 1897; and *From the West to the West; Across the Plains to Oregon*, published in 1905. Duniway's later revisions for three of the published serials also are available in the Duniway Papers. All twenty-two novels involve women's responses to male authority in a variety of Western frontier settings and circumstances. In addition to settings in the Middle West and the Far West, Duniway's readers are taken occasionally to settings in the East and even to Cuba, Australia, and England.

I have chosen Duniway's novels as primary data for four major reasons. First, the theme of women's responses to systems of male authority is central in all of Duniway's novels. Second, Duniway intended her novels to be realistic depictions of women's condition and options. In an early serialized novel, Duniway stated that the didactic and persuasive purpose of her novels was "to picture real life rather than fictitious life" (*The Happy Home*, ch. 19, *NNW*, 26 Mar. 1875). In published correspondence with one of her readers, Duniway wrote that she believed her novels did more to show women "their real status—social, religious, civic, pecuniary, and political—than all the preachers and all the lawyers in the land" accomplished for the same purpose ("An Hour with Correspondents," *NNW*, 22 Feb. 1878). In another serialized novel, Duniway explained that she sought "to reveal causes of human misery that need only to be generally seen and understood to be remedied and, in time uprooted" (*Madge Morrison*, ch. 10, *NNW*, 18 Feb. 1876).

My third reason for selecting Duniway's novels as texts is that published correspondence from readers of several of Duniway's serialized novels in the *New Northwest* attests to Duniway's success at realistic depictions in her novels. A correspondent from Boise City, Idaho, wrote: "Your paper has become daily food for me, and I would not be without it for ten times its costs. Your stories are marvelous, because they are so true" ("A Forenoon with Correspondents," *NNW*, 7 Sept. 1877). E. A. Case, writing from Williamstown, New York, observed:

> Allow me to congratulate you on the success of the stories that are from week to week published in the *New Northwest*. The stamp of truth which they bear wins for them a way to many hearts. Who, indeed, among us has not witnessed equally pitiful effects of one-sided government, which, while it claims to protect, so frequently oppresses woman? ("A Voice from the East," *NNW*, 31 Mar. 1876)

Although some correspondents—usually men—objected to "the stamp of truth" on the characters and circumstances in Duniway's novels, the vast majority indicated that the serials were realistic and effective in raising consciousness about the systems in which women found themselves.

My final reason for using Duniway's novels as the rhetorical texts for this study is that few scholars have noted the existence, let alone the rhetorical significance, of Duniway's fiction. In fact, to the best of my knowledge, no scholar has provided a complete list of Duniway's novels. Historian Ruth Barnes Moynihan provided the most complete listing in 1983 but was unaware of Duniway's publication of three novels in the *Pacific Empire* (*Rebel for Rights* 257–58).

Most frequently, Duniway's novels have been dismissed as "sentimental" and "flowery" and therefore of little consequence for serious scholarship. Although Moynihan recognizes the didactic purpose of Duniway's fiction and quotes from some of the novels as "a form of evidence" about Duniway's "personality and her society," her comment on the novels as rhetoric/literature is brief: "Familiar as she was with the dime novels of the day, she wrote for the same mass market and deliberately tried to articulate the 'reveries' of other women like herself" ("Abigail Scott Duniway of Oregon" 15–16). Journalist Roberta O. McKern provides a brief summary of one of Duniway's novels (*Ellen Dowd*) and concludes that, as Duniway "seldom used one adjective or adverb where three, four or five would do, the serials were superbly dreadful, but they served their purpose of reinforcing suffrage thought in the minds of their readers" (79–90). More appropriately, Duniway's novels should be considered as examples of what literary critic Nina Baym has identified as "woman's fiction" of the nineteenth century—fiction written by women, addressed to women, and intended to give readers something "that would help them in their lives" (*Woman's Fiction* 16).

Duniway's novels were agencies to communicate her equal rights arguments and complemented her nationally recognized work as an organizer and lecturer for equal suffrage. The serialized novels in the *New Northwest* and the *Pacific Empire* frequently held front-page prominence and drew considerable written response from readers across the country. Paid subscriptions to the *New Northwest* probably never exceeded about three thousand, but the paper was shared extensively with non-subscribers in Western frontier communities. Duniway also sent complimentary copies of the *New Northwest* to influential people throughout the country and exchanged with women's journals and newspapers in the East.

In addition to Duniway's twenty-two novels and published correspondence with readers of the serialized novels in the *New Northwest*, resources for this study will include a substantial collection of Duniway's other rhetoric—both private and public. Although the novels are the major texts for the study, Duniway's speeches, editorials, articles, and letters will be useful complementary data.

The Duniway Papers have been made available to me by David C. Duniway, Abigail Duniway's grandson and archivist emeritus for the state of Oregon. Included in the Duniway Papers are a variety of Abigail Duniway's public and private writings: "Journal of a Trip to Oregon," written by Duniway during her family's overland trip from Illinois in 1852; Duniway's scrapbooks of manuscript speeches, articles, news clippings, stories, poems, and letters; weekly letters from Duniway to her son, Clyde Duniway, 1890–1915; *My Musings*, a collection of Duniway's poetry published by the Duniway Publishing company, Portland, Oregon, 1875; and Duniway's articles in *The Coming Century*, Portland, Oregon, 1891.

Examples of Duniway's rhetoric are found in a variety of other sources. Her autobiography, *Path Breaking: An Autobiographical History of the Equal Suffrage Movement in Pacific Coast States*, includes several of Duniway's major speeches. *David and Anna Matson*, published as a book, is a lengthy narrative poem about a woman's struggles in New England. Her earliest newspaper articles were published in the Oregon City *Argus* and the *Oregon Farmer*. Duniway's editorials, speeches, and articles, published for sixteen years in the *New Northwest* and for three years in the *Pacific Empire*, provide even more examples of her rhetoric.

Finally, in addition to my four major reasons for selecting Duniway's novels as texts and her other writings as complementary primary data, I am aware that, in recent years, several communication scholars, particularly discourse analysts, have selected novels for the study of human communication. Although these scholars have focused on contemporary novels, their rationale for novels as rhetorical texts is persuasive. Not all communication scholars would agree about the legitimacy of using fiction as rhetorical texts for the study of interpersonal communication, but those engaged in the enterprise see fictional literature as "a rich storehouse" for analysis (Ragan and Hopper 312).

Kathleen Mary Kougl, who analyzed the interpersonal communication of main characters in three novels—one each by Doris Lessing, Saul Bellow, and Joseph Heller—argues that "a character's interpersonal relationships comprise a fictive case history," and the "novelist may penetrate to greater levels of subtlety about interpersonal relationships, suggesting possibilities not readily discernible in daily living" (282). Sandra L. Ragan and Robert Hopper agree with Kougl and conclude from their literature review that fiction represents a valid representation of behavior, that fictional talk and naturally occurring talk are more similar than disparate, and that reality and fiction—life and art—constitute a "co-construction" (312). As R. Fowler observes, fiction is a theory of reality constructed through a particular use of language, and a novel is "a linguistically constructed system of beliefs which bears some interesting, usually critical and defamiliarizing, relationship to the numerous ideologies current at the time" (35).[7]

Data Sample #2

The Health and Retirement Study (HRS) is ideal for examining how social, economic, and cultural capital mediate racial/ethnic and sex differences in physical activity (Survey Research Center, various years). The HRS contains data from individuals aged 51 to 61 who were interviewed in 1992 and re-interviewed in 1994, 1996, 1998, and 2000. In 1998, the HRS data were joined with data from its partner survey, the Assets and Health Dynamics among the Oldest Old (AHEAD), as well as two new cohorts, making the 1998 HRS a nationally representative survey of nearly 15,000 adults, aged 50 and older, as well as their spouses or domestic partners.

The 1998–2000 HRS data are well suited for my analysis for three reasons. First, panel data allow me to clearly specify causal relationships between physical activity and a variety of covariates. Indeed, they allow me to accurately assess the order of events that link income, wealth, social relationships, or cultural dispositions to health outcomes.

Second, because these data are longitudinal and include large numbers of individuals even into the oldest ages, I can distinguish between age-related changes and cohort differences in exercise. Cross-sectional data cannot fully distinguish between age- and cohort-related differences in physical activity, although some research suggests that both effects may be important. Indeed, changes in physical ability and norms for appropriate behavior change both by age and across cohorts (Bailey 2001; Campbell 2001; Riley 1973). Thus, the methodological advance of longitudinal data permits me to more accurately assess both age and cohort differences in physical activity than prior work has allowed (Grzywacz and Marks 2001; Hayes and Ross 1986; Idler and Kasl 1997; Ross 2000; Ross and Wu 1995; Wu and Porell 2000). Although these data will not permit an examination of physical activity at the younger ages, the surveyed individuals are at ideal ages for this analysis. They are young enough that many might undertake physical activity but old enough that physical activity might provide substantial advantages in future health.

The HRS data also are ideal because of the breadth and depth of the data collected. Indeed, few other data sets collect data on partner characteristics; time and money given to children, grandchildren, or parents; occupational characteristics for non-retired individuals; leisure-time activities, including exercise, volunteering, and religious participation; and a host of other socioeconomic, sociodemographic, and cultural factors. In addition, the HRS oversamples Blacks, Hispanics, and residents of Florida to ensure racial and ethnic diversity among the respondents. These advantages make the HRS better suited for this work than surveys that are cross-sectional, have fewer covariates, or are less current, including the National Health Interview Survey and the Longitudinal Study of Aging.

Variables

The 1998 and 2000 waves of the HRS ask about physical activity with this question: "On average over the past 12 months have you participated in vigorous physical activity or exercise three times a week or more? By *vigorous physical activity*, we mean things like sports, heavy housework, or a job that includes physical labor." This question allows only "yes" or "no" answers and will be coded dichotomously. Roughly 40% of the respondents were active in 2000, indicating substantial variation for the dependent variable, and this variable correlates positively with self-rated health ($r = 0.197$). Although this variable does not measure specific activities, such as running or swimming, it is advantageous because it assesses physical activity more broadly, prevents the exclusion of individuals who do not undertake specific activities, and allows respondents to interpret the questions within the context of their own lives. Notably, this variable also captures work-related activity. Some argue that work-related activity might lead to better health in the future (Cropper 1977), but others suggest that it may be repetitive and conducive to injury (Ehrenreich 2001). Thus, I will control, where appropriate, for how often the respondent's job requires "lots of physical effort," a separate variable in the HRS.

To evaluate differences among race/ethnic and sex groups in physical activity among aging individuals, I will include categorical variables for non-Hispanic Whites, non-Hispanic Blacks, and Hispanics. To insure confidentiality for survey respondents, the HRS collapses Asians and Native Americans into a single "other" category, thus prohibiting more detailed analyses of those racial/ethnic groups. Sex will be coded dichotomously into males and females. I will include age as a linear term to control for established decreases in physical activity with age but will also test for a curvilinear relationship.

Variables relevant to the social capital perspective include marital status, employment status, friends and neighbors, participation in religious activities, and volunteering in religious or charitable activities. Marital status will be coded as married or non-married, as this most closely relates to the theoretical argument above. Should numbers permit, non-married cohabiting relationships will be included separately, as they may confer some, but not all, of the benefits of marriage (Waite and Gallager 2001). The norms supported by marriage that might affect exercise behavior will be indicated by whether the spouse is physically active, a current smoker, or a moderate drinker. Further, the HRS asks questions about how enjoyable the respondent finds time spent with his or her spouse and which spouse has more power in the relationship—factors that might accentuate or diminish the effect of the household norms. Finally, I will examine potential costs associated with excessive time spent caring for children, grandchildren, parents, or sickly partners.

Employment status indicates whether individuals are currently employed. The costs and benefits of employment will be assessed with the number of hours worked, the number of hours spent working undesired overtime, and workplace-associated stress. When examining the hours worked or undesired overtime, I will test various functional forms, including categorical, linear, and curvilinear transformations. Integration into the neighborhood will be indicated by how often respondents stop to chat or socialize with their neighbors, how many of their neighbors' names they know, and their subjective satisfaction with their friendships. Although the HRS does not ask about the health behaviors of neighbors or friends or how they spend their time together, these variables allow some insight into social integration that takes place outside of the home, workplace, or religious communities. Participation in religious activities will include how often the individual attended religious services in the last year. An alternate variable asks how many hours the individual spent volunteering for religious or charitable organizations and will be coded to test whether very high or low amounts of participation predict less physical activity than moderate levels.

The variables relevant for the economic capital perspective include family income, wealth (or net worth, defined as assets minus debts), health insurance, and education. Both income and wealth will be measured as logged continuous variables. Kaufman et al. (1997) posit that residual confounding may bias estimates of the effect of economic factors on racial differences in health through problems associated with categorization, incommensurate indicators, and measurement error. Categorical SES indicators may bias results if they mask significant racial variation within groups. Thus, I will use logged, continuous measures of income and wealth to control for heteroscedasticity while minimizing problems associated with categorical coding (Berry and Feldman 1985).

The problem of incommensurate indicators suggests that a variable will be biased if Blacks, Hispanics, and Whites receive unequal benefits from the same level of income or wealth. Thus, I will test for interactions between race/ethnicity and the income and wealth measures to examine whether Blacks, Whites, and Hispanics receive the same returns in exercise for the same level of economic well-being. Finally, measurement error may bias results if it varies systematically by race. The HRS specifically attempts to minimize the effects of missing data for income and wealth by imputing values for the missing data with a "bracket technique." That is, respondents who "don't know" or "refuse" to answer questions about their income or wealth are asked whether they fit into broader amount categories (see Smith 1995 for a detailed discussion of this technique) and then are given imputed values accordingly. This technique introduces less bias in the imputation process so that some researchers find the HRS estimates of wealth to be more reliable than those in other surveys (Moon and Juster 1995).

Health insurance will include a series of categorical variables that include insurance from Medicare, Medicaid, private sources, other sources, or no insurance. Education will be coded categorically as 6 years of school or less, 6 years to less than a high school degree, a high school degree or graduate equivalence degree (GED), some college, an associate degree, a baccalaureate degree, or a post-baccalaureate degree. I will expand or collapse those categories as variation in the data permits.

Variables relevant to the cultural capital perspective include occupational status and religious denomination. Following Wu and Porell (2000), I will code occupational status using codes from the *Standard Occupational Classification Manual* (U.S. Department of Commerce 1980). White-collar status includes managerial, professional, technical, sales, and administrative support occupations; blue-collar status indicates workers in labor, manufacturing, industry, farming, forestry, construction, mechanics, transportation, and production-oriented tasks. Further, the HRS designates whether individuals are self-employed. Religious preference will be coded categorically as Protestant, Catholic, Jewish, other, or no religious preference, although I will explore smaller subdivisions as cell size permits.

The analyses will further control for other factors that are necessary for appropriately specified models. First, because poor health will make it difficult to participate in physical activity, I will control for baseline health status, with variables including subjective health status, the number of chronic conditions, and any activity limitations. Second, I will control for work-related physical activity, where appropriate, as some suggest that activity on the job may not confer the same health advantages as leisure-time exercise. Third, I will include dummy variables for different cohorts. The HRS includes a variable that locates individuals as part of the original AHEAD sample (born before 1924), children of the Depression era (born between 1924 and 1930), original HRS households (born between 1931 and 1941), and children born during the World War II era (born between 1942 and 1947). I will initially test for differences among these cohorts but will examine other combinations of birth years as well. Finally, I will test various functional forms of all the variables listed above as appropriate. The preliminary analyses suggest some modeling strategies that might be appropriate, but I will continue to test various categorical and linear transformations to insure that the findings are robust, the results are as clearly presented as possible, and the models represent the true relationships in the data as accurately as possible.[8]

History or Context

Sometimes, readers may need to know the history of a conflict or phenomenon to understand your data and analysis, and this history may require several pages of explanation. Labeled *history* or *context*, this section provides a descriptive and chronological report of the background without any analysis. This history or context is as neutral as you can make it and is factual rather than interpretive. If your study is about the resistance strategies used by antiwar protestors against the Vietnam War in the United States, for example, your history would be a history of the United States' involvement in Vietnam. If you are studying the conflict over the possible erection of a communications tower, provide in this section a history of the conflict in that city, the measures that have been passed in an effort to resolve the conflict over the years, the key participants in the conflict, and the current status of the conflict.

In some cases, the history or context discussion is long enough to make into a separate chapter of your dissertation. In this case, it's usually not part of your proposal and is something you prepare with your other chapters following the approval of your proposal. Such a chapter usually follows the introduction chapter (if your proposal will be the first chapter of your dissertation) or the research design chapter (if your proposal is the first three chapters of your dissertation). History or context sections are usually a few pages long if they are part of the proposal or the first chapter of the dissertation. As a separate chapter, the history or context discussion is usually somewhere in the range of 8 to 10 pages.

History or Context Sample #1

The following summary concentrates on the major events, dates, issues, and outcomes of the teachers' strike. Also included is information regarding the 4-J School District, the teachers and their union, major personalities, and a summary of possible causes of the strike.

On April 8, 1987, at 6:00 a.m., the teachers employed by the 4-J School District in Eugene, Oregon, went on strike. Since June 30, 1986 (for 10 months), the teachers had been working without the benefit of a contract, although bargaining talks prior to the strike had been in progress for over a year. On March 15, 1987, the District warned parents that a strike was possible, and the Eugene Education Association, the local teachers' union, formally notified the District that it intended to strike on March 17. Three days later, on March 30, Margaret Nichols, the District Superintendent, announced that she was beginning to recruit replacement teachers. The strike came on the heels of a 1979 strike and directly affected 17,000 students, 1,200 teachers, and other educational specialists.

On April 12, the first talks began following the walkout. As the negotiations continued to bog down, the teachers' role in the strike began to escalate. On April 24, they picketed the homes of Margaret Nichols and the school board members. Four days later, the first signs of violence erupted at Churchill High School in conjunction with the hiring of replacement teachers and the reopening of the schools on April 28, 1987. In this first serious confrontation, a picketer tried to prevent a police officer from using his baton on another picketer. The picketer stumbled when she was hit from behind by a police officer.

On April 29, after considerable encouragement, Nichols joined the bargaining team on behalf of the District. While the negotiating teams continued to struggle, the initial 80% student-return ratio, which occurred on April 28, dropped drastically by May 2, 1987. In fact, even the students who attended school protested, claiming that the classes were useless. While the bargaining teams debated over insurance issues, four teachers were arrested. The arrests occurred because striking teachers blocked the path of a replacement teachers' bus, breaking a public ordinance by blocking a public way. According to the police, they could not arrest everyone and so chose some, although several were involved in a blatant violation of the ordinance.

Seven major issues continued to stall contract talks: salary, insurance benefits, workload, assignment transfer, performance evaluation, and seniority. A settlement was reached on May 8 at 2:21 a.m., and the teachers unanimously voted on May 10 to accept the new contract. Resolution on most of the issues followed, although debate continued surrounding insurance and amnesty for the replacement teachers hired by the District. Sufficient resolution was attained, however, for the teachers to return to the classroom.

The cost of the strike to the typical teacher was approximately $3,100. Some claimed these financial losses, as well as other losses such as teacher credibility in the community, never would be regained. The events of the strike left some wondering if it was worthwhile. Even the final contract, enacted on May 8, would remain in force only until June 30, 1989.

The strike occurred in Eugene, Oregon, an educational environment that some described as a "Nirvana" or "Camelot."[107] The livability of Eugene and the surrounding communities is considered by the teachers who have chosen to work there to be among the highest in the country. The teachers generally applied to work in Eugene because of people involvement, open government, and an emphasis on process.[108]

Many parties were involved in the strike. The teachers, of course, were major participants. The 1,200 teachers and related educational specialists employed by the District implemented the overall objectives of the

District. They were concerned that people realize that teaching 25 to 30 students a day is hard work, draining them physically, mentally, and emotionally. In general, the teachers believed that they were underpaid, overworked, and unappreciated. They also believed that the District's spending priorities needed to be the teacher, the students, and the classroom. Thus, District money spent for paint, parking lots, and non-classroom personnel, they believed, warranted careful scrutiny.[109]

A second group involved in the strike were the District employees; representatives of the District involved in the teachers' strike were Superintendent Margaret Nichols and the District's negotiator, Steve Goldschmidt. The District maintained a staff of over 100, involved in various levels of management and management-support services. These personnel were distributed in the District's office, thirty-seven schools, and seven educational support centers, creating a decentralized structure that afforded a high degree of "building autonomy."[110]

In addition to the preceding personnel, the District had a seven-member school board. Members were elected as representatives of the 4-J District and were endorsed and encouraged to seek office by both the District and the union. The school board was chaired by Jack Billings, a Eugene attorney. The board was composed of another attorney, a business manager, a homemaker, a law student, the head of a computer-programming staff, and a campus minister at the University of Oregon.

The teachers' priorities were the major concern of the Eugene Education Association, headed by its president, Ray Gross, with Tom Doig serving as its chief negotiator. The union was a democratic organization that advanced the causes of its membership, the organization, and the instructional program of the students. One avenue through which the organization could achieve these objectives was collective bargaining, and each round of bargaining generally resulted in advances for the membership and the organization. A strike occurred when the collective bargaining process failed.

Several explanations have been offered regarding the cause of the strike. Contributing factors were summarized by Rudy Johnson, an independent consultant, hired to conduct a post-strike analysis. Johnson suggested the following eightfold explanation[111]

- The union entered collective bargaining with high expectations because Margaret Nichols, who was child centered and pro-teacher, was highly respected. In addition, the union believed there was adequate money available and that the District would be generous in recognizing teachers' contributions to the educational excellence of the 4-J District.

- Unresolved baggage from the 1979 strike provided a negative predisposition to the 1987 negotiating process.

- The board and the management team were inexperienced. Because many of them were new, they were anxious to avoid conflict and present an image of positive leadership to the community.

- The union's bargaining team had more experience than the District's team, and they both had a different sense of bargaining. Thus, when the District made an offer that amounted to its best and last offer, the experienced union did not believe the finality of the offer; it perceived the offer as bargaining. This difference in the perception of negotiating prolonged the strike.

- The union's initial proposal was perceived as "way out of line" and was reported as such by the local newspaper, the *Register-Guard*. Actually, the proposal was a "wish list," although coverage of the subsequent negotiation hardened the union's resolve. Thus, many teachers blamed the newspaper more than the District for the strike.

- The aspect of the negotiation process called "take-backs" frustrated the union. When the District took back items previously offered because of expense or other factors, the union expected something in their place.

- The 4-J principals played an ambiguous role. They made recommendations, yet they denied affiliation with either side, a stance that confused the teachers.

- The negotiators, specifically the District's Steve Goldschmidt and the union's Tom Doig and their respective teams' style of negotiating, were antithetical. The influence of their different styles was felt in their continual dogged commitment to their divergent bargaining positions. Both sides expressed confidence in their negotiators, although union representatives complained of the endless stalling techniques used by the District members.[9]

History or Context Sample #2

Natural Ties was founded at the University of Kansas in 1988 by Patrick Hughes, Jr. While walking through the lobby of his fraternity one day, Pat met a young man with a disability, J, and struck up a conversation with him. The two discovered that they shared the same taste in music. Pat called J's parents and explained how they had met and that he was interested in getting to know J. Pat and J began spending time together, and their friendship became the cornerstone for Natural Ties. Pat had the opportunity to get to know someone with a disability for the first time in his life, and J had the opportunity to develop a real friendship with someone who did not have a disability.

Eventually, the university newspaper wrote an article on Pat and J, detailing the new understanding and perspectives each of them had found as a result of their relationship. This relationship captured the interest and attention of others who wanted a similar experience. Pat received phone calls from both students on campus and the director of a residential facility for individuals with disabilities. With the guidance of J's parents and the facility director, in a three-week time span, Pat paired up 20 University of Kansas students with 20 individuals with disabilities. These students developed first a one-to-one friendship and then included their new friend in their everyday groups and activities.

During his remaining years at the University of Kansas, Pat developed and organized Natural Ties. He was invited to speak at several national disability conferences and received letters from all over the world indicating that what he was doing in Lawrence, Kansas, was unique and was needed everywhere. After graduating in 1991, Pat moved home to Evanston, Illinois, and formed Natural Ties as a nonprofit organization. Since 1991, Natural Ties has grown into a national organization with an office staff of 5 and a Board of Directors of 20 individuals. In 1992, President George Bush named Pat the 687th Point of Light in recognition of his work with National Ties. Natural Ties is currently active on 12 college campuses.

Natural Ties was founded on the belief that people with disabilities desire social contact with the mainstream community. The mission of Natural Ties is to increase awareness of the need for full participation in college communities by creating friendships between young adults with and without disabilities. Educating the mainstream community about the inclusion process is vital. Natural Ties increases community awareness not only by facilitating the development of relationships between people with and without disabilities but by opening existing recreational, social, and service organizations to people of all abilities and making buildings accessible.

Natural Ties chapters pair up individuals with and without disabilities to create "Ties" in which friendship is encouraged. Group events for all participants are organized, but the focus is on the individual friendship. Once the friendship is established, individuals are encouraged to invite their Ties to become involved in the groups to which they belong. The emphasis is on making the Natural Ties friendship exactly like any other friendship. The friendships are viewed as life-long commitments; participants are expected to handle them as they would any other friendship. They are expected to maintain contact over the summer, if that is what they usually would do, and to handle transition with their friends in whatever manner is most comfortable for them. It is hoped that individuals will invite their new friends to be involved in the groups or organizations to which they belong because these groups provide a consistent activity schedule, a place to meet other individuals, and a sense of belonging.

The basic vehicle for achieving the mission of Natural Ties is the establishment of student groups or chapters on college campuses that pair individuals with disabilities with students on campus. The college-age group is targeted because it is after graduation from high school that many individuals with disabilities lose all social contact with their peers who do not have disabilities. Through secondary school, social networks exist that allow integration. Once high school ends, if individuals with disabilities do not go on to college, chances are they will become fairly isolated. Whether they move into a group home, work in a sheltered workshop, or remain in the family home, they have limited opportunities for age-appropriate social interaction. The college campus has a wealth of social opportunities available if individuals with disabilities are invited to participate. Fraternities, sororities, clubs, athletics, volunteer groups, and residential programs all offer social networks that can open doors for individuals with disabilities.

The hope is that, by being included in the groups to which other students belong, individuals with disabilities will make other friends and have regularly occurring events in which to participate, such as Thursday-night dinner at a sorority house, Tuesday-evening meetings of the Circle K club, or Friday-night movies in a dorm. Such regular activity provides stability in the individuals' lives. It also helps with transition; undergraduates eventually complete their degrees and move on. If individuals are included in an organization, chances are they will meet many individuals, all at different stages in their undergraduate careers. If one graduates and moves away, there are other friends and regular activities to maintain the social network.[10]

Procedures

In the discussion of procedures in your section or chapter on research design, explain the procedures you are using for collecting and analyzing your data. The two subsections of the procedures section, then, are typically labeled *Data Collection* and *Data Analysis*.

Data Collection

In your discussion of the procedures for collecting your data, discuss how you plan to gather or obtain your data. Will you interview people? Conduct focus groups? Collect articles from certain newspapers? Request the documents you need from an organization? Videotape meetings? Distribute surveys? Gather documents from a historical archive? Engage in direct observation of behavior? Make use of an existing database? You might have multiple methods of data collection if you plan to use multiple kinds of data in your study.

Explain in detail exactly how you plan to collect your data using the method or methods you identify. If you plan to interview people, discuss who will be interviewed, the process you will use to select your participants, how you will locate interviewees for your study, the type of interview you plan to use, and the questions you plan to ask. Just as you did with your data, justify your choices for the methods you're using to collect the data. Explain, for example, why you believe the kinds of interviews you have selected are the most appropriate ones for getting the kinds of information you want from your participants. If you are using a research instrument such as a questionnaire or inventory to collect data, describe the instrument and its validity and reliability. If you are doing a pilot study—a small-scale version or trial run to test or assess a research instrument—describe the pilot study. (A copy of your questionnaire or instrument is typically included in an appendix at the end of the dissertation.)

Data Collection Sample #1

The data for this study will be gathered primarily from two sources: books about arts organizations and interviews with individuals involved in non-profit arts governance. These will be supplemented by journal articles, newspaper stories, miscellaneous papers and documents, and my personal experiences in arts organizations.

From the books that will be reviewed and coded, the data sought are any fragments about the governance process, especially the perspectives of participants involved in that process and descriptions of governance structure. Typical of the books that will be coded are Nathaniel Burt's *A Social History of the American Art Museum* and Ronald L. Davis' *Opera in Chicago*. In addition to these types of books, analytical works that contain commentaries on governance as well as examples that could be used as data also will be coded. Robert W. Crawford's *In Art We Trust: The Board of Trustees in the Performing Arts* and Joan Jeffri's *The Emerging Arts: Management, Survival and Growth* are two examples of this type of work. The coding of these written materials will allow me to expand the quantity and variety of arts-governance situations I am able to examine.

I also will conduct interviews with trustees and directors of non-profit arts organizations. I plan to interview 20 trustees and 20 directors for the study. Because this study deals with arts governance in America in general, interviews will be completed across the country and will not be confined to a single locale. The interviews also will be conducted in different parts of the country to determine whether there are any broad, geographical differences in the form and manner in which arts organizations are governed. I am planning to conduct interviews in the following cities: Chicago, Illinois; Reno, Nevada; Seattle, Washington; Eugene, Oregon; Portland, Oregon; Norfolk, Virginia; and Denver, Colorado. These are all places where I have contacts with arts organizations.

The sample from which the data will be drawn for this study is a judgmental sample. In such a sample, units to be examined are selected on the basis of the researcher's own judgment about which ones will be the most useful or representative. This type of sample is most useful for the exploratory nature of my study. Those interviewed will participate in a range of arts organizations, including performing arts organizations, visual arts organizations, and government-funded organizations serving the arts. The organizations the interviewees represent will be large, medium, and small organizations, with large organizations defined as those with budgets over $1 million, medium organizations as those with budgets between \$200,000 and \$1 million, and small organizations as those with budgets under \$200,000.

The interviews will not be tightly structured, thus allowing the interviewees to develop topics and raise issues concerning governance that they feel are important. Interviewees will be guided only in the following ways:

- After I greet the interviewee and introduce myself, I will provide a brief overview of the purpose of the research project, which is the development of a conceptual framework of governance in private, non-profit arts organizations.

- I will ask interviewees to provide a brief overview of their organizations and to provide any materials that would assist me in understanding the structure and programs of their organizations.

- I will ask the interviewees to detail the history of their involvement in their organizations.

- I will prompt the interviewees to talk about the governance process in their organizations.

- Later in the interviews, as issues and topic areas emerge, I will ask the interviewees to address specific areas if they have not covered them in their unstructured conversations. These questions will fill out any developing clusters of data around particular issues and will serve as a means of verifying or dismissing the presence of phenomena that emerge in earlier interviews. The questions will be asked in broad, non-directed terms such as, "Tell me about how you and the president work together" and "Is the founder of your organization still involved in it? If so, how does he or she function within it?"

To preserve utmost confidentiality, the interviews will be conducted without a tape recorder; I will take notes during each interview. Following the interviews, I will review my notes, correct them, and supplement them in order to make them as clear, comprehensive, accurate, and useful as possible. The primary reason for this confidentiality is that I believe the study will produce more useful data if those interviewed are totally candid in their statements about governance. In many cases, public revelation of their statements could cause embarrassment to the interviewees and, in some cases, perhaps even lead to their dismissal.[11]

Data Collection Sample #2

I will use ethnographic methods to collect my data. Ethnography is designed to generate understanding of behavior within a culture according to the meanings of its members and to describe that culture in its members' own terms. Ethnography as a method also allows the researcher to participate in the community in which she or he is working: "Ethnography is a process of exchange, whereby the researcher also reciprocates, with self-disclosure, with information needed by community members, with visits and gifts; the ethnographer necessarily has commitment to making a positive contribution in her relationships with those studied" (Kamphoefner, 1991, p. 41). Ethnography as a method of data collection is to be distinguished from producing an ethnography; ethnography as a form of research report depends on "thick description" to share experience with the reader. I will use ethnographic methods to collect my data; I am not writing an ethnography.

I became personally involved in the process of building shared vision first as an individual being brought into a shared vision and later as an individual facilitating shared vision. Ethnography not only allows this kind of personal participation on the part of the researcher but encourages it. The fact that I am looking at the process of building shared vision from a narrative perspective requires me to participate in the stories being told, constructed, and reconstructed. Simply being a passive, objective observer in this context is not possible. My presence at a meeting or in the office changes the stories being told and their impacts. The only option is to embrace this subjectivity and use it as an opportunity to gain valuable insight into the processes being examined (Conquergood, 1991).

There are several reasons why ethnographic methods are the most appropriate method of data collection for this study. First, I am interested in communication as the vehicle for the process of building shared vision; this communicative behavior is best captured by a participant. The meanings associated with the communication that occurs in context is understood fully only by individuals involved in the interaction.

Ethnographic methods are appropriate as well because the Natural Ties organization claims that the reason individuals with disabilities are excluded from community and isolated from individuals without disabilities is because relationships between individuals with and without disabilities never have been encouraged. Investigating this organization, which relies so heavily on relationships, through surveys or even one-time interviews violates the philosophy of Natural Ties. As a researcher, I need to engage the organization, the staff, the participants, the Board of Directors, and the participating communities in relationships. Furthermore, these relationships need to be sincere; a relationship established solely for the purpose of conducting research would not be appropriate. Ethnography engages the researcher in long-term relationships with the participants, and the participants are empowered as partners in the research process as a result.

The final reason I have chosen ethnography as the method for data collection for this research has to do with my own personal preferences, ethics, abilities, and style as a researcher. I have never felt comfortable conducting research that requires short-term "use" of individuals for information and distance between the researcher and the subjects. I have felt that this objectification of research subjects does nothing to develop an environment of trust and openness between the researcher and the research participants. I maintain that the discovery, development, and understanding for which researchers work must be done in partnership with the research participants. This partnership requires input from all research participants on all aspects of the research, including its purpose, design, implementation, and analysis. Because I view meaning as socially constructed, a researcher who does not participate in the construction of that meaning cannot approach full understanding. This partnership or dialogue is a collaborative effort that contributes to a greater richness of accountability.[12]

Data Analysis

After you describe how you plan to collect your data, explain how you plan to analyze those data. If you have to clean or process the data in some way to make them into usable data, begin by explaining that process. The most common method to create usable data in qualitative studies is to transcribe data from tape or video recordings. A note of caution here: Many students believe that if they conduct interviews or videotape sessions of some kind, they must transcribe them completely. This is a very tedious, time-consuming process if you do it yourself or expensive if you pay to have someone else do it. Unless your research question is an inquiry into the precise language that is used by participants, you don't need full transcripts of your data. Even a short, half-hour interview will have many irrelevant sections in it. A more efficient process is to listen to or view your tapes, listening and looking for those parts that are relevant for answering your question. Then transcribe just those sections.

The bulk of the discussion of your section on data analysis is a description of the method or methods of analysis you've chosen to apply to your data. Here is where you provide some explanation of or background about your method. This explanation can include literature about the method if there's discussion or controversy about the method. (A reminder: Literature about your method goes in this section on research design and not in your literature review.) If you have chosen to analyze your data using the grounded-theory method of analysis, for example, explain that it was developed by Barney Glaser and Anselm Strauss, lay out some of its basic features, and describe the major steps used to analyze data with the method. If appropriate for your study, here's the place to cite your use of statistical software programs such as SPSS and to provide a rationale for their use. There is no need to include histories or overviews of these software programs, though—just a rationale for using them.

Your discussion of your method of analysis also includes a justification of your method or methods. Because many options were available to use for your method of analysis, explain why the one(s) you chose best accomplish your objectives. For example, you might justify your use of grounded theory to analyze your data by stating that current research on your subject does not share a common conceptual framework. In an area where very little research has been completed, the grounded-theory method allows you to provide a comprehensive theoretical description of the phenomenon, offering the prospect of locating most of its significant features.

If your dissertation is the kind where you write a series of essays that you hope to be able to publish, with each major chapter a separate study, your section on research design is divided into the number of studies or potential articles you plan to complete. A dissertation on the impact of culture on consumer preferences using experimental economics might be composed, for example, of three studies—a hypothetical bias experiment, a risk-aversion experiment, and a time-preference experiment.[13] These become subheadings within the discussion of research design, and each one includes a discussion of the theory guiding that particular experiment, the hypotheses to be tested, and the methods that will be used to gather and analyze the data.

Data Analysis Sample #1

The method I will use to analyze the data is grounded theory. Grounded theory as a conceptual framework is presented by Barney Glaser and Anselm Strauss in *The Discovery of Grounded Theory*.[15] The grounded-theory method is rooted in the comparative analytic method, which has both anthropological and sociological sources. In sociology, the works of both Weber and Durkheim are cited as early examples of the use of the comparative method. Durkheim's work on suicide and Weber's study of bureaucracy both used the comparative method to generate theory.[16] In the field of anthropology, the comparative method has long been used to arrive at an understanding of societies. The nineteenth-century study of the Iroquois by Lewis Morgan is cited as an early and influential use of the method.[17] Later, in the mid–twentieth century, the comparative method was used in anthropology in such studies as *African Political Systems* by Forts and Evans-Pritchard[18] and *African Systems of Kinship and Marriage* by Radcliffe-Brown and Forde.[19]

Another source for the grounded-theory method is fieldwork, which has found its greatest development in the field of anthropology. Lewis Morgan's study of the Iroquois[20] and Franz Boas' study in British Columbia[21] were two of the first significant uses of the method. Sociologists such as Beatrice Potter Webb[22] and Charles Booth[23] also employed the method in their work, and perhaps its most widely known use was in the study that resulted in the book *Middletown* by Robert Lynd and Helen Lynd.[24]

The grounded-theory method has other historical roots as well. Discussion surrounding the book *The Polish Peasant in Poland and America* by W. I. Thomas and Florian Znaniecki, which was spearheaded by Herbert Blumer, centered on the adequacy of data to support theory, the amount of data needed for theory verification, and the degree to which researchers should approach data-based research with pre-conceived theoretical conceptions.[25] The work of Robert Merton in *Social Theory and Social Structure* also relates to the concept of generating theory grounded in data. Merton's comments in this area focused on the modification of theory through research feedback, which he called "grounded modification of theory."[26]

The grounded-theory method is defined by several characteristics. One is that the focus of the process is on theory generation rather than theory verification. The researcher focuses on the comprehensive and systematic review of data that will generate—rather than verify or reject—

hypotheses. Thus, the emphasis is on discovery and creation rather than empirical testing. Consequently, analysis using the grounded-theory method focuses on process rather than product. As the researcher discovers patterns in the data, they are viewed as indications of a phenomenon rather than a final statement about its nature. Absolute closure is ruled out because the array of interpretive possibilities afforded by the artifacts never can be exhausted.

A second characteristic of the grounded-theory method is the concept of grounding in data. The theory that emerges is formulated only after detailed review of the data through an inductive process. No theorizing occurs apart from the data. Rather than relying on pre-established propositions or hypotheses to test and interpret data, the researcher derives a structure from specific observations about the phenomenon. Developed directly from the data, the theory that results illustrates the patterns that are observed to constitute the phenomenon. Glaser and Strauss believe grounding a theory in the data has two major benefits: (1) The theory will fit the situation that was researched and will not contain artificial and forced aspects; and (2) The theory will be understandable and usable to those in the area under study because its basis is data with which they are familiar.[27]

The grounded-theory method features a particular kind of data. The data analyzed using the grounded-theory method are qualitative rather than quantitative. Narratives, novels, myths, interviews, music, film, paintings, sculpture, and other such artifacts are considered appropriate data from which to develop the theory. Quantitative data may serve as one of several arguments to support the presence of a particular proposition in the framework, but they seldom are the prime indicator of that proposition.

Using the grounded-theory method, I will proceed in the following steps: (1) I will code the interviews as to what aspect of governance the data segment might relate; (2) I will sort the codes into major variables in the process of governance and the characteristics evident of those variables; (3) I will compare and sort the codes in an inductive process until no further conceptual variables are generated and sufficient support has emerged for the existence of particular propositions that describe the qualities and functions of those variables and the relationships among the variables; (4) I will present the propositions derived from the categorization of the data, along with support for them from the data, to justify their identification as propositions or hypotheses; and (5) I will organize the propositions into a holistic conceptual framework that explains, in part, the process of governance.[14]

Data Analysis Sample #2

To examine the effects of social, economic, and cultural capital on physical activity and to take advantage of the panel data provided by the Health and Retirement Study (HRS), I will use logistic regression to predict physical activity at one time period with covariates from the prior period (Pampel 2000). That is, I will use bivariate logistic regression and covariates from 1998, including physical activity, to predict activity in 2000. The covariates, then, will be assessed prior to subsequent physical activity and essentially predict the change in physical activity from one time period to the next (Ross and Wu 1995).

The coefficient for physical activity in 1998 will likely be upwardly biased as it will control for unobservable characteristics that might lead a person to undertake exercise in the first place and that might correlate with social, cultural, and economic capital. But the upward bias of the coefficient for physical activity in 1998 is not problematic. The preliminary findings suggest that exercise between two time periods is highly correlated, although my focus is on whether covariates other than activity in 1998 are associated with activity in 2000. Further, by accounting for the unobserved factors that might associate with activity and employment, marriage, or other factors, this model will provide stringent and conservative estimates for the effects of the social, cultural, and economic factors on changes in future physical activity. Because the HRS uses a stratified, clustered, multi-stage sampling frame, I will run all final analyses in Stata 7.0 software (STATA 2001) to adjust the coefficients and standard errors for design effects.

Several modeling strategies will be followed to ensure that the findings will be clear and robust. First, following Mirowsky (1999), I will use progressive adjustment to model how social, cultural, and economic capital mediate race/ethnic and sex differences in physical activity by introducing the variables in a logical framework. In separate models, I will parse out the various dimensions of social, cultural, and economic capital that may impact health. For example, I will individually assess the social, cultural, and economic dimensions of employment and include them in a full model to determine how they relate to each other and mediate race/ethnic and sex differences in activity.

Second, I will examine each type of social, cultural, or economic capital in combination. Once I know how the various dimensions of marriage associate with health, I will examine how marriage and employment or religion and friend or neighborhood factors work together. This will allow me to understand the importance of each social institution in relation to others. Third, I will run separate models by marital status, employment status, race/ethnicity, sex, and other key dimensions to assess whether the findings are generally applicable or apply only to specific groups or for those in particular categories.

Fourth, I will run all analyses separately by retirement status. Some factors may change little; being married or living with a partner, for example, may promote exercise for all individuals. But other forms of capital, especially employment, may decline dramatically in importance after retirement (some retired individuals are also employed, but working may have a different impact on physical activity among retired than among non-retired individuals).

Finally, I will test for interactions among each form of capital. For example, perhaps social and cultural capital may provide norms and support for exercise but only if the individual has adequate economic resources. Alternately, low levels of social support or unhealthy cultural preferences may not be important if individuals have enough economic resources, and wealthy individuals may receive no advantages from social or cultural capital.[15]

Assumptions

Another topic sometimes included in the section on research design of a dissertation proposal is a discussion of the methodological assumptions that inform you as a researcher and guide your study. You don't need a section on assumptions unless yours are unusual or unconventional or need to be articulated so that readers can understand your rationale for your selection of your methods or how you will apply them.

Assumptions Sample #1

This study is built upon feminist assumptions, many of which overlap with assumptions of qualitative research in general. To better understand the methodological choices I make, I include in this section a discussion of the feminist assumptions that I bring to this qualitative study. These include a belief in a holistic perspective, an acknowledgment of the importance of self-reflexivity, a focus on process and the changing nature of any research study, a commitment to mutuality and reciprocity, and an acceptance of the notion that gender shapes epistemology.

Holistic Perspective

The feminist effort to bridge theory and practice in communication study necessitates viewing human communication within a larger context. Because the study of interpersonal communication tends to focus primarily on the communication that happens between people in particular relationships, it can be transformed by a feminist stance. Interpersonal scholarship does not often acknowledge the wider societal influences on the communicative relationships between and among people. Rubin (1983) asserts that

> society and personality live in a continuing reciprocal relationship with each other. The search for personal change without efforts to change the institutions within which we live and grow will, therefore, be met with only limited reward. And the changes we seek will not be fully ours unless and until we understand where the roots of our problems lie. (p. 206)

Rubin's prescription is built on feminist notions of changing institutional structures, and it troubles the kind of interpersonal communication study that does not often take societal structures into account in its study of human relationships.

In this study, I consciously place the particular relational phenomenon of loneliness within intimacy into a wider context. Although my main purpose concerns explicating individuals' definitions of loneliness in their relationships, I am aware that these individuals' social identities and roles affect their stances and must be acknowledged. Toward that end, I will ask participants to provide demographic information to help elucidate the positions from which they are participating. Also, I will actively seek out individuals in both heterosexual and gay/lesbian relationships. Because little research has addressed loneliness within social roles, I offer possibilities of connections and raise questions for future research.

Self-Reflexivity

Crucial to feminist scholarship is feminist researchers' awareness of our own positions and how those positions influence the questions we ask, the way we seek to address those questions, and the interpretations we gain from our study. Feminist scholars typically are invested in critiquing their own subject positions; they hold a belief that they "should locate themselves in the same critical plane as their overt subject matter; that is, researchers must take their own embeddedness in history, class, gender, and race as causal for their own investigations, rather than seeing only others as affected" (Steiner, 1989, p. 167). In so doing, feminist scholarship underlines the importance of the researcher inside the research process (Harding, 1991).

In the social science tradition, a recent advancement toward self-reflexivity is in the practice of researchers listing their own subject positions and thereby acknowledging on a basic level that their race/sex/class—all of their various identities—influence the research. Taking my subjectivity into account means taking responsibility for my own assumptions, for admitting them in the first place, and acknowledging that my various social positions have something to do with my research (c.f., Houston, 1002; Marty, 1996).

In this study, I will pay attention to the fact of my identities and positions—to my femaleness and whiteness and heterosexuality, for example—in the research design and in my interaction with the people I interview. My positions affect my interpretations and the questions I ask. For example, I begin this study with assumptions about commitment that includes a more closed relational stance. Heterosexuals are more likely to believe in and practice a more closed form of relating, where the intimate relationship is strictly boundaried, while gays and lesbians are more likely to believe in and practice a more open form of relating, where the intimate circle is broader. In acknowledging my own positionality, I have decided to ask the participants themselves to define for me what they mean by *commitment*.

Focus on Process

One of the key elements that distinguishes feminist scholarship is its insistence on focusing on the process of research. I view a focus on process as strongly tied to self-reflexivity. In the research process, for instance, feminist methods are supposed to allow for intersubjectivity of researcher and researched: This intersubjectivity "will permit the [feminist] researcher constantly to compare her work with her own experiences as a woman and a scientist and to share it with the researched, who then will add their opinions to her research, which in turn might change it again" (Duelli-Klein, 1980, p. 56). The process itself is as important as the end result, and it can be, in fact, the end in itself.

In this study, I predict, some participants will attempt to negotiate the interview and perhaps some of their own dissonance by asking me questions about my personal life and about the study. I plan to respond to their questions—and in fact, invite them at the beginning of the interview to ask me whatever they want to know. This mutual self-disclosure, common especially in interviews influenced by traditional feminist thought (Minister, 1991), will provide a break from the spotlight for the interviewees and perhaps will give them a chance to test me out, to get more of a handle on how I am perceiving their responses, and to figure out if I will apply negative judgments to those who admit loneliness.

Some tenets of feminist thought emphasize the particular need to focus on the affective element of process. Reason and emotion have been split apart in traditional Western notions of science, and credibility in academe has largely rested on (ostensibly emotionless) reason (Jaggar, 1989). Part of the reason that other kinds of research are not very process oriented is that emotion is inherently part of the process of research; according to many notions of objectivity, however, emotion is not supposed to be there. We do not typically address emotionality in any part of our research, particularly in the explication of the findings:

> Notably missing, or at least reduced to virtual silence, is the passion that obviously drives our choices to write about particular topics in particular ways. Our writings suppress our convictions, our enthusiasm, our anger, in the interest of achieving an impersonal, "expert" distance and tone. . . . Masked also are the mistakes we inevitably make in the process of research and writing. (Blair, Baxter & Brown, 1994, p. 383)

We like or dislike the people we interview. We can empathize with some people we interview but not others (see Reinharz, 1992, ch. 1). We are happy or unhappy with how our research is going. We are moved to study something that has touched our lives. How does that affect our interpretations? Essentially, focusing on our own affective states highlights the possibility that we are influencing our own results. Feminist research suggests that emotion always plays a part in our research process, no matter what methods we use.

Mutuality and Reciprocity

Philosophical underpinnings of much qualitative research include the idea that knowledge is co-created between the interviewer and interviewee. These ideas reflect a worldview that respects interaction and the importance of mutuality, ideas that are far from the mainstream approach to research:

> A more traditional research stance would see . . . reciprocal perspective-taking on the part of interviewers and interviewees as

a problem, in that what is said by a respondent is supposed to be a reflection of what is "out there" rather than as an interpretation that is jointly produced by interviewer and respondent (Briffs, 1986). What is needed, however, is a heightened awareness of the research interview as a context in which meanings ("findings") are cooperatively constructed (Jorgenson, 1989, p. 38).

An acknowledgment of the cooperative symbolic construction of meaning influences the whole research process tremendously. One way that valuing mutuality or interdependence changes the research process is in how it necessitates a different view of interviewees from that in traditional scientific approaches.

One way I will attempt to enact the principle of mutuality and reciprocity is by offering a follow-up meeting to interested participants in which I will share the results of this research. It is important for me to offer everyone the possibility of finding out what I have done with their words because that commitment serves as a reminder to me to treat their interviews with care and as a reminder to them, I hope, that I value their participation.

Mutuality and reciprocity are also emphasized in feminist interviewing. Feminist researchers have problematized what it means to conduct an academic interview. The traditional approach, for instance, is one built on distance and an assumed hierarchy between the untouchable and unaffected interviewer and the emotional interviewee. Oakley (1981) suggests:

"Proper" interviews in the methodology textbooks owe a great deal more to a masculine social and sociological vantage point than to a feminine one. For example, the paradigm of the "proper" interview appeals to such values as objectivity, detachment, hierarchy and "science" as an important cultural activity which takes priority over people's more individualised concerns. (p. 38)

In feminist research (in the ideal), there is no "artificial object/subject split between researcher and researched (which is by definition inherent in an approach to knowledge that praises its distant 'neutrality')" (Duelli-Klein, 1980, p. 57). It is interactive and participatory (Minister, 1991; Oakley, 1980).

I will attempt to enact the principles of feminist interviewing. The goals of feminist interviewing, however, are idealized and difficult to attain. Feminist researchers, suggest Reinharz (1992), expect a "'deep identification' that breathes life into that which is studied and into the woman doing the study" (cited in Kleinman & Copp, 1993, p. 34). This expectation places tremendous pressure on interviewers to establish a perfect feminist rapport that will facilitate the kind of sharing they hope to induce. I have yet to build a perfect rapport in any interview, but I do hold feminist interviewing as a goal.

Gender Shapes Epistemology

Most feminist research is predicated on the belief that our gender "serves as a lens through which all experience is filtered" and therefore does more than affect our viewpoints (Foss & Foss, 1991, p. 20). It also affects, on a basic level, how we know; it affects our way of being in the world and how we experience the world. Belenky, Clinchy, Goldberger, and Tarule (1986), among others, have been instrumental in developing the idea that how we know is inherently connected to our gender.

The feminist belief that one's gender affects one's epistemological assumptions is a tremendous challenge to established notions of science. At the same time, feminist research (in the ideal) does not suggest that our gender *determines* how we know the world. We simply must be aware that our gender is not a variable, it is not something that can be parceled out of our lives. It inherently affects every part of our being. I believe we cannot "turn off" parts of ourselves. We can acknowledge, however, that what we do know is affected by our gender. In this study, I attempt to address how gender interacts with assumptions about and experiences of relating and loneliness.[16]

Assumptions Sample #2

I adopt a somatic perspective on communication in this study. Such a perspective is grounded in certain epistemological and ontological assumptions that provide a unique framework from which to view communication. Three interconnected assumptions contribute to the perspective.

First, the human is conceptualized as *soma*. This means the human is understood in its wholeness as an embodied living organism. A somatic perspective on communication takes the *soma*, the embodied self, as the theoretical entry point. Somatics is "a field which studies the *soma*; namely, the body as perceived from within by first-person perception" (Hanna, 1986, p. 4). A somatic perspective advocates increasing proprioception—awareness of the myriad stimuli produced within our bodies. Thus, a somatic perspective conceptualizes living human experience from the inside out. The perspective is self-focused and legitimizes the internal realm where inner awareness and proprioceptive communication are central foci. This is a radical departure from the conventionally accepted scholarly perspective of observing communication phenomena from an external, third-person standpoint.

A second assumption of a somatic perspective is that of holism. As the site of the synergistic interrelated processes of awareness, biological functioning, and environment, the embodied self is conceptualized in its complete multidimensionality. A somatic perspective recognizes four simultaneous and interconnected dimensions of human existence: the physical, emotional, mental, and transpersonal. The body is understood as the site and location of the convergence of these dimensions. The result is an alternative somatic ontology that conceptualizes the human in integrated wholeness as embodied self.

Somatics also assumes human interdependence. Within this framework, human beings cannot be reduced to isolated entities but must be understood as part of a mutually interrelated web. None of the constituents of this network is discrete or fundamental in that each component reflects the properties of the other parts. In essence, embodied selves have no meaning as isolated entities and must be understood as interconnections and potential interconnections. Thus, a "social" concern, a concern for the interrelationship between self and others, is implicit in somatics. The potentiality of interconnectedness is located within the embodied self.[17]

Significance of the Study

In the section of the proposal concerned with the significance of the study, discuss the importance of your study and the contributions it will make. You already identified at least some reasons why your study will be significant in your preproposal, so you simply have to elaborate on them to have a good start on this section for your proposal. Now that you've actually written your literature review, which you hadn't done at the time you created your preproposal, you probably have more ideas about why your study is significant. Aim for three or four reasons as to why your study is significant, and take a paragraph to talk about each one. The discussion of significance goes in your first chapter, whichever form your proposal assumes.

Significance of the Study Sample #1

Although the notion of empowerment has been a topic of interest and study in academe for several years, its shift into popular usage reflects an expansion, presumably of its definition and certainly of its impact on public life. This study will contribute to an understanding of the term by sorting out existing definitions to arrive at a more coherent, comprehensive definition than those that currently exist.

In addition, the schema developed will provide an initial way to conceptualize empowerment as rhetorically constructed in texts. Such a conceptualization contains the potential for others to construct empowering texts more easily. This project, then, is an extension of my commitment to the process of allowing those who are disempowered to gain voice in the public discourse.

This project also will offer a glimpse into three major trends in American life: Citizen outrage at an unresponsive government, a form of feminism that has been integrated into mainstream entertainment, and a revival of militant civil rights activism in a commodified form that pays homage to the struggle of the 1960s and suggests both continuing and altering the direction of that struggle. An examination of the artifacts and what they seem to offer will suggest commonalities within the dynamic of the movements themselves and reasons for the important position that empowerment has achieved in the national dialogue.[18]

Significance of the Study Sample #2

My study of aesthetic communication will help to bridge a gap between the aesthetics and the communication literature. The literature in aesthetics expresses an ill-defined connection between aesthetics and human experience but rarely deals with its communicative dimensions. Communication literature focuses indirectly on aesthetics in two ways. First, traditional communication studies explore the phenomenon of aesthetics under the rubric of style. These studies tend to focus on word choice and placement or on techniques for the delivery of public speeches. Second, scholars of nonverbal communication come closer to what I want to study, but although they recognize that aesthetic dimensions of communication affect others, they have done little to explicate the process by which the effects occur. My work will extend the literature in aesthetics and communication in an effort to understand the communicative dimensions of aesthetics.

My work also will contribute to the conversation concerning feminism and aesthetics. Many feminist scholars have focused on how aesthetic communication functions in women's cultures. For example, Hein notes that feminist theory is linked fundamentally to the aesthetic because of similar values: Both feminism and aesthetics are theoretically grounded in experience and pluralism. Hein argues that feminist theory is hindered, at present, by the lack of an adequate aesthetic theory. She suggests, in fact, that feminist "aesthetics may well be the prologue to feminist theory understood more broadly because aesthetic theorizing has an intrinsic adherence to the immediate and the experiential on the one hand, and is dedicated to the communion of form on the other."[117]

In contrast, Devereaux sees the relationship between feminism and aesthetics as one of challenge. As a body of theory, feminism has succeeded in making gender a central issue of contemporary literary and artistic theory, and this new agenda has unsettling consequences for traditional aesthetics. Devereaux calls special attention to the formal concept of disinterested contemplation as a requirement for an aesthetic experience. She equates this concept with the idea of the male gaze, a notion originating from film criticism and referring to a way of looking that dehumanizes the object of perception and inscribes the patriarchal unconscious of the culture at large. Devereaux argues that aesthetic contemplation need not involve dehumanizing someone.[118]

Some scholars argue for a distinctive feminist aesthetic. They recognize that women's communication is characterized by unique features due to women's oppressed position, which means they must communicate using a patriarchal language. This view is expressed, for example, by Penelope and Wolfe:

A feminist aesthetic, as it emerges out of women's evolution, grounds itself in a woman's consciousness and in the unrelenting language of process and change. A feminist aesthetic encompasses the cultural and social attempts to cripple women, to bind us, to strip us of our self-awareness, and it also traces the unwinding of the patriarchal bonds that have limited our perceptions and descriptions of our experience. As women strain to break through the limits of English, certain patterns begin to emerge, recurrences of similar syntactic ways of ordering perception that is always moving and often contradictory.[119]

Felski, in contrast, represents the rejection of the notion of a universal feminine aesthetic, choosing instead to provide a model of communication, a feminist public sphere, that allows for the analysis of diverse forms of women's aesthetic communication. Felski's model of a feminist public sphere is similar to Habermas' concept of the public sphere, but Felski's model balances the particular with the universal.[120] Bovenschen also rejects the idea of a feminine aesthetic characterized as an unusual variant of artistic production or expression, but she does so ambivalently: "We ought to rid ourselves of the notion of a historically ever-present female counter-culture. And yet, on the other hand, the very different way in which women experience things, their very different experiences of themselves, enable us to anticipate different imaginations and means of expression."[121] Because I believe that aesthetic communication is a distinguishing feature of traditional women's cultures, I hope to contribute to the conversation concerning the relationship among feminism, the feminine, and aesthetics.

In addition, my study of aesthetic communication in traditional women's cultures may reveal significant insights into previous interpretations of nondiscursive aspects of women's communicative styles. While generally accepted that fundamental differences exist between the way men and women communicate,[122] few studies question the interpretation of power that undergirds the operational definitions of these differences. Women's communication strategies often have been labeled as *powerless* when examined as a traditional construct that features a hierarchy of power, with some strategies ranking high in perceived power and others ranking low.

Traditional women's cultures, in particular, are judged poorly because of their emphasis on aesthetics. The attention to form as played out in traditional women's cultures is not valued as a serious or legitimate means of communication in our society. Women who exhibit a concern for aesthetics are often seen as superficial, materialistic, or suffering from false consciousness. One study, for example, reported that individuals who show particular interest in their dress (in this case, sorority women) are often labeled "conventional, conscientious, compliant before authority, stereotyped in thinking, persistent, suspicious, insecure, and tense— i.e., uncomplicated and socially conscientious, with indications of adjustment problems."[123] My study may suggest that women's communication may not be characterized simply as *powerful* or *powerless* in the traditional use of those terms. Examination of women's communication through the lens of aesthetic communication may provide alternative interpretations of women's ways of communicating.

The significance of my study, then, lies in its potential to bridge a gap between aesthetics and communication, to contribute to the discussion concerning the relationship between feminism and aesthetics, and to provide a reinterpretation of the evaluation typically accorded to women's nonverbal communication.[19]

Outline of the Study

You decided how to organize your study in your dissertation preproposal, so you have nothing new to work out for this last section. Turn the outline of the study that is in your preproposal into a narrative paragraph that tells how many chapters your study will have and what each one will contain. Include in this summary chapter 1, even if the proposal itself will turn into that chapter and you've already completed it. In referencing the first chapter, you might say something like, "Chapter 1 has been an introduction to the study, including the research question, the literature review, the research design, and the significance of the study." The discussion of how the study is organized should take between one paragraph and one page of your proposal. It goes in your first chapter, whatever form your proposal assumes.

Outline of the Study Sample #1

Chapter 1 introduces the project and lays out the relevant context for it. Chapter 2 is a description of the foundations for a feminist-rhetorical-schizoanalytic perspective, with those foundations translated into tools for reading. The tools for reading then will be applied to the artifacts created by Madonna, with each analyzed in a separate chapter. Chapter 3 is an analysis of *The Immaculate Collection*, Chapter 4 of *Truth or Dare*, and Chapter 5 of *Sex*. Chapter 6 deals with insights developed about feminism and Madonna and the transformative potential of schizoanalysis for feminist rhetorical theory.[20]

Outline of the Study Sample #2

My primary goal in Chapter 1 is to situate my topic within the literature of public memory, rhetoric, and history museums, demonstrating the significance of the National Civil Rights Museum (NCRM) as a site of memory and the benefits a rhetorical perspective yields to appreciating its textual features. The studies reviewed, particularly those of Katriel, Prosise, and Taylor, should illustrate that history museums, though rhetoricians have largely overlooked them, are institutions worthy of sustained critical analysis.

In Chapter 2, I will trace the historical and political circumstances surrounding the transformation of Martin Luther King, Jr.'s assassination site from the Lorraine Motel to the NCRM. In this chapter, I will contextualize the study by describing the history of the NCRM and the exhibits it houses. I will conclude this chapter with a descriptive walking tour of the interior exhibits to provide a reference point for readers who have not visited the NCRM.

The purpose of Chapter 3 is to examine the rhetorical interplay of space and agency within the NCRM. Bennett (1995) argues that the narrative structure employed by museums enables certain people to "recognize themselves as fully addressed by that narrative and thus be able to carry out its performative routines" (p. 193). I will use the museum's mission statement as a criterion against which to evaluate the museum's permanent exhibits to discover whether they encourage or discourage agency.

Chapter 4 of the study will be an examination of what I argue are the crowning features of the museum: the King shrine at rooms 306 and 307 (including the balcony where his assassination took place) and Jacqueline Smith's counter-memorial situated across the street. Although I will touch upon these two places earlier in the dissertation, I believe their significance to the overall museum experience merits a close analysis. My inquiry will focus on the symbolic tension created between these two very different manifestations of King's legacy.

The main objective of the concluding chapter will be to summarize the study and highlight its primary contributions to rhetorical theory and criticism. I will underscore the importance of the NCRM as a rhetorical text and offer suggestions for additional ways in which scholars may take up notions of race, identity, agency, and space as they relate to collective memory.[21]

Recap: Sections of a Dissertation Proposal

To review, these are the sections in your dissertation proposal:

- Introduction
- Research question(s)
- Literature review
- Research design
  - Data
  - Context or history (if necessary)
  - Procedures
    - Data collection
    - Data analysis
  - Assumptions (if necessary)
- Significance of the study
- Outline of the study

If your proposal will become the first chapter of your dissertation, all of these sections will be together in that proposal/chapter. If your proposal will become the first three chapters of your proposal, the introduction, research question(s), significance of the study, and outline of the study will form your first chapter. The literature review will become the second chapter, and the research design will become the third. You can see a sample proposal in which all the sections have been put together into a complete proposal at the end of this chapter (the sample is one for a proposal that becomes the first chapter of the dissertation).

Approval of the Proposal

Different universities and departments have different methods for approving dissertation proposals. In some departments, approval is simply a matter of your advisor's signature on a form. In other departments, the advisor and all of the committee members read the proposal and approve it with their signatures. The most common means is with an oral defense, in which the members of your committee meet with you in a formal session to ask you questions about your proposal.

Typically, if you defend your proposal orally, there's a set procedure to follow prior to the defense. It typically begins with your advisor approving the proposal, working with you to get the proposal where she thinks it needs to be. You distribute it to the other committee members two weeks ahead of the defense to give them plenty of time to read it. You might ask your advisor to attach a note endorsing the proposal as it is distributed to the committee members. In this note, she can tell the other members that she believes your proposal is well done and ready to defend. This kind of endorsement gives your credibility a boost as your proposal goes out to your committee.

Faculty members' primary objective in your defense of your proposal is not to test your knowledge or to try to trip you up but to help you eliminate potential obstacles to the smooth completion of your dissertation. Because of their greater experience with research design, they might be able to identify some areas where you might get slowed down or stuck and can propose some ways to eliminate those pitfalls from the start. If you're trying to do too much in your dissertation, they can help you cut back on the project. Another purpose of the proposal defense is for you and your committee to agree on a "contract" concerning what you will do so that the committee members can't come back later and ask for something additional or different from what you produced. Because your proposal is based on your preproposal, which your advisor already approved (and which you might have shared with your other committee members earlier), you shouldn't encounter any major resistance to your proposal at this stage.

The strategies for preparing for a defense of your proposal are exactly the same as those for preparing for the defense of your dissertation at the end of the process. For ideas about strategies for preparing for the proposal defense, what to expect in it, and possible strategies for dealing with what might come up, take a look at chapter 10.

You have worked out your preproposal, completed your literature review, written your dissertation proposal, and had it approved. Now you want to secure the approval of your university's human subjects review committee. This committee evaluates research involving human subjects, and you typically need written approval from this committee before you can begin to collect your data. At most universities, all research must receive the written approval of the committee, but a full committee review is not required for exempt research—research that is of minimal risk to participants in the study. Exempt research typically involves surveys or interviews of subjects when the data are recorded without an identifiable link to the participants, surveys or interviews of public officials, and archival or secondary data. At most universities, the human subjects review committee requires that you submit an approved dissertation proposal with your application, so with the approval of your proposal, you're ready to submit your application. If you need human subjects approval, get advice from your advisor or other faculty members on the committee so that your application meets the committee's requirements as precisely as possible. You want to do everything you can to facilitate this process.

Because it can take a while to receive approval from the human subjects committee, while you are waiting for the committee's approval, see what you can be doing on your dissertation (other than data collection) that will move you ahead. Can you begin identifying participants who might be appropriate to interview? Can you write the history or context chapter of your dissertation? Can you set up the proper formatting of your dissertation so that all of the chapters you write are in that format? Can you put your bibliography or works cited in the correct form? Once you secure approval from the human subjects review committee, you're ready to act on all of the decisions and arrangements you've made for your study, and you can begin collecting your data. Full speed ahead!

Dissertation Proposal Sample #1
A Generic Analysis of the Rhetoric of Incivility in Popular Culture
<u>Introduction</u>
Cultural commentators claim, "We are in a culture war. And one of the first casualties of war is civility" (Himmelfarb in DeMott 15). In this war, no

> one respects anyone and anything anymore because there are no one and nothing left to be held in high regard. . . . Decency has been dethroned. We have become nothing more than a nation of selfish, whining complainers, and every time we open our mouths, the cavities are there for all to see. We are all conniving to get ahead in the Age of Irrelevance, a time in which respect is breaking down on all levels of society. Vulgarity, malaise, off-color entertainment, lack of civility and decorum, and a penchant for sensationalism are all typical of the modern age. (Barrett 11)

Civility has become a popular rallying cry for, among others, national politicians and small-town government officials. President Bill Clinton, for example, encouraged more civility and less partisanship in his 1995 commencement speech to his alma mater, Georgetown University. Clinton explained that the

> national conversation had suffered at the hands of more and more and more sharply defined organized groups [that] communicate more and more in extreme rhetoric through mass mailings . . . or 30 second ads designed far more to inflame than to inform. [Thus] Americans' future has been clouded, and their doubts about their leaders and their institutions are profound. (Elving 2114)

He also attempted to "seize the high moral ground from his critics" and claimed that "we need more conversation and less verbal combat" ("Clinton" 74).

In the spring of 1997, members of Congress met in Hershey, Pennsylvania, for more than the kisses. The retreat in which they participated came about because of a proposal by David Skaggs (D-Colo) and Ray LaHood (R-Ill), who believed civility could be enhanced if members of Congress and their spouses spent a few days socializing and getting to know one another. Over 200 Congressional members and approximately 100 spouses and children attended the three-day event. Before the retreat, members were given a report, "Civility in the House of Representatives," prepared by the University of Pennsylvania's Annenberg School of Communications. The report, which traced the rise of rude language on the House floor, claimed that the words "damn, whore, stupid, weirdo, nerd, bozo, idiot, fatso, scum, and nitwit" have increasingly littered the Congressional discourse (McCarthy 8). According to Kathleen Hall Jamieson, Dean of the Annenburg School, "It's a sign of the general coarsening of our culture. Things we used to say in private we now say in public. Congress may simply be reflecting a social norm" (McCarthy 8). Although the motivation for the retreat was to restore a deeply divided Congress and a sense of civility, both parties held independent retreats prior to Hershey. While "attendance was encouraged by the leadership of both parties . . . , as one Republican Congressman said, it was not clear they really wanted it" (McCarthy 8).

Concern with an apparent increase in uncivil behavior is being manifest in non-political arenas as well. Many communities across the country are spending thousands of dollars bringing in consultants to restore a sense of civility. One town in particular, Raritan, New Jersey, has gone so far as to pass a law that prohibits the use of rude language in public ("In the Front Line" 22). Corporations and schools "are sending peer groups for training in conflict management" (Lyttle 38). Former Ohio State University president E. Gordon Gee explains, "Civility is a notion whose time has come. There's been a lot of deterioration in the way we conduct ourselves as people over the last 20–25 years. Without civility, we'll never be able to ultimately solve the problems of the social community" (Lyttle 38).

In his 1996 presidential address to the International Communication Association, Charles Berger articulated what he believed to be the potential big questions that communication scholars should be asking and how the communication field can contribute to public policy discussions. It is Berger's third question that is of interest and relevance here: "Why do we believe that we as a people are speaking and treating each other less civilly" (Berger 114)?

While the words *civil* and *civility* conjure up a diversity of positive images—participatory government, citizens working side by side for a common cause, colleagues problem solving together, peace, an environment of mutual respect—just what is civility? What constitutes a rhetoric of civility or a civil rhetoric? Definitions of civility range from "civility means cultivating personal humility rather than indulging in self-righteousness" (Pappano 44) to "civility is inclusive of individuals: an awareness of the commonness of us all" (Benson 361) to "the kinds of behavior persons can rightfully expect from one another" (Sinopoli 613). These definitions are generic and imprecise and do little to illustrate what a civil or uncivil act may look like. Incivility is assumed and implied to be the simple opposite of civility. But is it?

Research Question

As a feminist scholar, I am committed to disrupting the ideology of oppression that pervades Western culture—an ideology that values and supports the enactment of competition, hierarchy, dichotomy, otherness, and incivility. According to hooks, "to be a 'feminist' in any authentic sense of the term is to want for all people, female and male, liberation from sexist role patterns, domination, and oppression (hooks, *Ain't* 195). A liberatory goal, then, "directs our attention to systems of domination and the interrelatedness of sex, race, and class oppression" (hooks, *Feminist* 31). Thus, a feminism movement becomes a struggle "to eradicate the underlying cultural basis and causes of sexism and other forms of group oppression" and a challenge to "an entire structure of domination of which patriarchy is one part" (hooks, *Feminist* 31; hooks, *Talking* 25).

In addition to challenging and disrupting an ideology of oppression and domination, feminism has a creative, proactive component, too: "it can transform relationships so that the alienation, competition, and dehumanization that characterize human interaction can be replaced with feelings of intimacy, mutuality, and camaraderie" (hooks, *Feminist* 34). While feminism begins with a struggle to end sexist oppression, it is a movement for all people because it "challenges each of us to alter our person, our personal engagement (either as victims or perpetrators or both) in a system of domination" (hooks, *Talking* 22).

As a rhetorician, I believe that criticism has the potential to assist in the disruption of an ideology of oppression. Equipped with rhetorical tools, scholars can identify the forms and sites of domination and oppression in popular culture and create a culture that is less elitist, hierarchical, uncivil, and disrespectful. Foss identifies this kind of criticism as feminist and suggests that it "is rooted in the same commitment to the elimination of oppression that characterizes feminism, but its focus is on the rhetorical forms and processes through which oppression is maintained and transformed" (168).

As a media consumer, I cannot help noticing the abundance, popularity, and prevalence of texts that are antithetical to my professed feminist beliefs—texts that create hierarchies, are uncivil and disrespectful, and do not value the perspectives of those who are different from oneself. Yet, I must admit that I am amused and entertained by some of these texts, an admission that feels uncomfortable given my commitment to feminism. The tension between my feminism and my laughter at these texts, then, draws me to this research on incivility. My own tension is an important starting place because critics should

> begin the search for things worth writing about as critics by reflecting on their own experiences, curiosity, and commitments— with what they care about, and think would be worth understanding. Critics should judge finished criticism, in part, by the extent to which its conclusions are useful or insightful for them, and relevant to their own experiences, curiosity, and commitments. (Nothstine, Blair, and Copeland 10)

I intend to discover just what is going on rhetorically in uncivil texts to make sense of the tension. Specifically, I will examine the notion and expression of uncivil discourse as it is enacted rhetorically. Is this uncivil discourse really a problem? Does it serve a positive function for the audience and the larger society? Is our society just going downhill, as Jamieson suggests, with uncivil discourse the norm and acceptable to increasing numbers of individuals? Or is something more complex going on? My research question is: "What are the rhetorical features of the genre of popular incivility?" The discovery of the rhetorical features or characteristics of uncivil discourse will better enable scholars and media audiences to recognize its presence in rhetorical texts, understand how it operates, and the purpose it serves for the audience.

Literature Review

Understanding the role of incivility in the three artifacts I have chosen to study requires a familiarity with the relevant literature. The literature pertinent to this research will be drawn from three primary areas: research in civility and/or incivility in communication and other disciplines; work focusing on the rhetoric of incivility; and scholarly studies on *Beavis and Butt-Head*, *The Howard Stern Show*, and *Seinfeld*. I am aware of the literature that exists concerning the relationship between a civic society and democracy as it relates to the state, originating primarily from the disciplines of political science and history. This body of work will not be reviewed here because it falls beyond the scope of this research: To define and describe a rhetoric of incivility. The relevant literature was approached and discussed by answering the following questions: (1) How have civility and incivility been defined? and (2) What are the causes of uncivil rhetoric?

Definitions of Civility and Incivility

Civility is an old idea, similar in meaning to the ancient Greek term *sophrosyne*, meaning self-control and moderation. Its opposite was "hubris: excessive pride, insolence and arrogance" (Barrett 146). For the ancient Greeks, civility was characterized by courage, temperance, justice, and wisdom (Barrett 146). Speaking for both historical and contemporary contexts, Barrett explains that civility is "at the heart of rhetorical maturity, [it] is a social good—an ethical value—and a rich source of ethos" (147).

In one of the few communication studies of incivility, Benson studied political discourse as expressed on computer bulletin boards to offer scholars "a provisional rhetorical criticism of the discussions, asking how, if at all, networked political debate meets, fails, or challenges the standards of civility and community implied by rhetoric as a mode of human action" (359). Benson defines *civility* as

> welcoming all parties to the debate and foster[ing] the dignity of all participants; for an ongoing sense that all participants share a common humanity and fate; for an acceptance to submit arguments, broadly defined to general consideration, and to accept victory or defeat in debate while protecting minority rights. (361)

The implication is that incivility is the absence of such features. Incivility, then, can be defined as an interaction with others that denies respect and consideration of diverse opinions and perspectives. In such interactions, victory, at whatever cost, is the goal of communication, and domination is the prevailing philosophy.

A theme consistent within the sparse incivility literature is the notion of the individual as self-absorbed and isolated. Explicitly connecting the uncivil rhetor with qualities of selfishness and isolation, Barrett claims, "a person with no conception of being an integral part of society whose proper operation depends significantly on his behavior or of having responsibilities to others is not a civil being" (147). The uncivil individual engages in such "unsocial or antisocial" behaviors as "coercing, confronting, deceiving, and manipulating," presumably as a means to his or her own ends (147). He is careful to note the distinction between individuality and individualism: the former is a socially necessary quality to distinguish one person from another and is "even a mark of civility" (152). The latter, a "doctrine or personal aberration enforcing the assumption that the individual and not society is the dominant consideration or end," results in rampant incivility that threatens community interest (152). In our daily life, individualism appears as "ordinary incivilities": "the behaviors of difficult people, inane and deleterious television programming, monopolistic pursuit of attention, inauthenticity, and interpersonal insensitivity" (153). Individualism, then, is the "parent of incivility" (Barrett 154). Benson concurs: "the debates [on the Usenet] appear to emphasize the radical individuality of each participant, who achieves connection to a collective through identification with high level ideological affiliations" (368). The rhetor is therefore isolated and separated from others in a perceived community.

Causes of Incivility

To date, there has been little scholarly inquiry into the causes of incivility. One study that addresses this question received national attention when President Clinton invited its author, Robert Putnam, to participate in White House discussions. In "Bowling Alone," Putnam traces America's declining social capital—those "features of social organization such as networks, norms, and social trust that facilitate coordination and cooperation for mutual benefit"—through the nation's declining membership and participation in civic organizations (67).

Putnam's cleverly titled article comes from his discovery that, while "more Americans are bowling today than ever before, . . . bowling in organized leagues has plummeted in the last decade or so. [Specifically], between 1980 and 1993 the total number of bowlers in America increased by 10 percent, while league bowling decreased by 40 percent" (70). He explains:

> Lest this be thought a wholly trivial example, I should note that nearly 80 million Americans went bowling at least once during 1993, nearly a third more than voted in the 1994 congressional elections. . . . The rise of solo bowling threatens the livelihood of bowling-lane proprietors because those who bowl as members of leagues consume three times as much beer and pizza as solo bowlers, and the money in bowling is in the beer and pizza, not the balls and shoes. The broader social significance, however, lies in the social interaction and even occasionally civic conversations over beer and pizza that solo bowlers forgo. (70)

Chronicling the decline in associational membership, Putnam concludes, "more Americans than ever before are in social circumstances that foster associational involvement (higher education, middle age, and so on), but nevertheless aggregate associational membership appears to be stagnant or declining" (72). While he cites four possible explanations for this trend—the movement of women into the labor force, mobility (the re-potting hypothesis), other demographic transformations, and the technological transformation of leisure—the first three factors explain why participation in civil organizations has lessened (74–75).

As women have moved from work in the home to paid employment over the past few decades, there has been a seemingly related decline in civic participation. For women, the demands of working leave them with less leisure time to devote to the PTA, the League of Women Voters, the Red Cross, and other similar organizations. Similarly, as their wives or girlfriends spend more time at the office and less time taking care of the house and children, men, in turn, devote more time to these tasks, thus leaving them with less leisure time to spend at the lodge. The re-potting hypothesis suggests that because there is less residential stability among Americans due to the automobile, suburbanization, and the migration to the Sun Belt, they have fewer roots to put down in civic organizations. Similarly, other demographic transformations in our society include fewer marriages and children, more divorces, and lower real wages. All of these changes may affect civic participation "since married, middle-class parents are generally more socially involved than other people" (Putnam 75).

While these three phenomena are all factors in explaining a declining social capital, recent technological advances in leisure also account for a greater lack of civility. Technological advances have privatized and individualized leisure time and, as a result, have disrupted "many opportunities for social capital formation" (Putnam 75). For Putnam, the "most obvious and probably the most powerful instrument of this revolution is television" (75). Television has made what Americans experience as communities "wider and shallower" in that they can have access to a wide variety of experiences via the experiences of television characters, but their understanding of such an experience is limited and dictated by the television character itself (75). By watching television as the primary form of leisure, Americans' access to and membership in civic organizations is limited and thus reduced.

Although the literature on incivility is sparse, it does suggest two common themes: (1) Incivility is believed to be highly correlated to individualism; and (2) When incivility is present in a culture, people are less likely to become involved with civic, religious, or associational groups. Taken together, these two features suggest an interdependent relationship: Incivility is related to an individual's isolation from a community. However, the need to understand the rhetorical features of incivility as enacted in popular culture arises from: (1) Absence of understanding of the rhetorical characteristics and strategies of uncivil discourse; and (2) Lack of understanding about the purpose that uncivil discourse may serve for the audience. This research, then, is a necessary contribution to the scholarly discussion about uncivil discourse in our culture.

Research Design

Data

In selecting rhetorical texts to be included in this research, I applied a number of criteria. First, I wanted to select artifacts of popular culture.

According to Brummett, "popular culture refers to those systems or artifacts that most people share and that most people know about " (21). He explains, for example, that

> television is an immensely rich world of popular culture, as nearly everyone watches television and, even if not everyone sees the same shows, they are likely to know in general about the shows that they do not see. In speaking of popular culture, then, we are concerned with things, like television, that are part of the everyday experience of most people. (21)

Because I am interested in our culture at large and the charges of incivility upon it, I wanted to select artifacts that many members of our culture share and have in common, assuming, as Garvey does, that "our only common culture is made up of law and television" (599). I selected media texts because the entertainment industry often is blamed for the ills of society and often is charged with generating incivility. Barrett, for example, argues that "the entertainment media has become a major contributor to the Age of Irreverence, setting the tone for impressionable audiences, especially American youth" (12). In fact, Senator Ernest Hollings opened hearings before the Senate Commerce Committee on the Television Improvement Act by citing the violence contained in *Beavis and Butt-Head* (Cooper 127). I chose popular culture generally and media texts in particular as my area of focus because they provide me with sites of shared rhetorical meanings in which to ascertain the presence of incivility, define its characteristics, and describe the substantive and stylistic features.

A second criterion I applied in the selection of artifacts was variety: I wanted variety among my artifacts in verbal and visual forms. Variety among my artifacts will enable me to make stronger claims about a rhetoric of incivility. If I do find that there is, indeed, a genre of uncivil rhetoric, I want to understand how it is manifest and enacted in a multitude of rhetorical forms. By selecting a variety of forms, I also hope to avoid mistaking characteristics of this genre with characteristics of specific program types.

Finally, I wanted to select artifacts that are popular and are watched or listened to by a substantial segment of the television and radio audience. If there is a direct correlation between the entertainment industry and the level of incivility in our culture, as some critics suggest, then it is necessary to analyze widely viewed shows. The more popular the program, the greater the impact it may have on the culture at large.

In keeping with all three criteria, I selected *Beavis and Butt-Head, The Howard Stern Show*, and *Seinfeld* for inclusion in this study. All meet Brummett's definition of popular culture, all are different from one another in form and type (animated cartoon, live-action situation comedy, and radio and television program), and all are very popular and earn high ratings in their respective categories. Moreover, all seem to structure their discourse in both form and content in ways that violate standards of civility. The rhetors involved place utmost importance on the self or individual and do not locate themselves in any broad social or political context. Their circle of friends is small, and few, if any, are allowed into the "inner circle"; otherness and diversity appear to be features to be avoided at all cost.

Beavis and Butt-Head. Beavis and Butt-Head was the brainchild of creator Mike Judge and appears on the Music Television Network (MTV). The show first premiered on MTV on March 8, 1993, and was an instant success. The on-screen promotional clip read, "Beavis and Butt-Head are dumb, crude, thoughtless, ugly, sexist, self-destructive fools. But for some reason the little weinerheads make us laugh" (Mc-Neil 83). The target audience for the show was 12- to 34-year-olds, and the premise of the show was simple: "Beavis and Butt-Head are the cartoon representations of everything that can possibly go wrong with an adolescent boy. The half-hour episode shows the pair at their underdeveloped best: telling very stupid jokes, behaving like idiots in the back of their high school classes and masturbating while they watch rock video[s] on MTV" (Zagano 6).

The audience never sees or hears from Beavis' and Butt-Head's parents, although Beavis' mother is sometimes referred to as a *slut*, and Butt-Head claims to have seen her naked. Minor characters include a few of the kids' teachers—Mr. Buzzcut, The Principal, and Mr. Van Dreissen. Beavis and Butt-Head do not have any real friends, but other classmates include Todd, a senior who drives and is cool because he knows how to "pick up chicks and party," and Stewart. Todd sees Beavis and Butt-Head as annoying and stupid kids and likes to torment them. Because Beavis and Butt-Head worship Todd and are themselves a bit slow, they fail to see his torment as dislike and think it's cool to be in his company; negative attention is better than no attention. Stewart is the same age as Beavis and Butt-Head and wants to hang out with them and be like them; however, Beavis and Butt-Head think Stewart is a baby and only hang out with him when it is in their best interest. For example, they go over to Stewart's house because Stewart has a satellite dish, which allows them to watch violent movies.

For this study, I will review the Beavis and Butt-Head movie, *Beavis and Butt-Head Do America*, released in December, 1996, and 12 episodes that aired on television. Each half-hour episode contains two vignettes, interspersed with the boys sitting on the couch and critiquing music videos on MTV (MTV made its entire video collection available to Mike Judge to create the series).

The Howard Stern Show. Like *Beavis and Butt-Head*, disk jockey Howard Stern has received his fair share of criticism and blame for contributing to an uncivil society. In an article titled, "One More Ounce of Civility," Budiansky reports that Stern is faced with $2 million in Federal Communications Commission fines as a result of his uncivil tongue (122). The fines result from behaviors such as his discussions of vaginas and sex-related jokes on the air (McConnell and Fleming 24). Stern's sidekick since 1980, Robin Quivers, explains the appeal of the show: "We are the high wire act. We're working without a net so you have to tune in everyday just to see what will happen" (Stark 80). Stern has earned the nickname *shock jock* for his ability to say the unexpected and amaze his listeners.

His shocking style has secured Stern a large and loyal following. As of March 31, 1997, Stern could claim to his credit a number-one movie; a number-one album; the fastest selling book in Simon-Schuster history; cover stories in *Penthouse, Rolling Stone, Entertainment Weekly, Movieline, Time Out New York, Los Angeles,* and *TV Guide*; major features in *The New Yorker, Playboy, Vanity Fair, Esquire, Cosmopolitan, Time, Newsweek,* and *Billboard*; and guest spots on *Letterman, Dateline, Today,* and *World News Tonight* (Alterman 6).

The Howard Stern Show is broadcast live every morning from New York to syndicated stations all across the country. His show runs four hours and is totally unscripted and spontaneous. Sometimes he has celebrity guests, sometimes local eccentric personalities, and sometimes no guests at all. On these days, he and his cohorts pick up on a topic and just "go with it," taking calls from the audience. Quivers is responsible for reading the daily news that often provides the impetus for a day's topic and antics. His other two on-air playmates are Jackie and Fred, who back up Stern's jokes and support his humor.

Quivers has received her own share of criticism for her role in *The Howard Stern Show.* An African-American woman, Quivers has been called a "self-hating black woman" for her part of what some African-Americans and women perceive as a "misogynistic and racist show" (Stark 80). Quivers seems unflustered by the critics and rationalizes the criticism by explaining, "we do an entertainment show. People want to make it into some social commentary. I feel sorry for them" (Stark 80). Besides being the news reporter, Quivers' other on-air roles are listening to Stern and articulating "the voice of reason on the show" (Stark 80).

For this research, I will analyze five radio shows, which are four hours each, and four segments of *The Howard Stern Show* on E! TV. Stern's two books, *Private Parts* and *Miss America*, and the film, *Private Parts*, also will be included as supplementary and supporting material for the broadcast discourse.

Seinfeld. The comedy *Seinfeld* is the third artifact under study in this research. *Seinfeld* first aired July 5, 1989, and was co-created and written by Jerry Seinfeld, a stand-up comic, and Larry David. It is a half-hour situation comedy that aired weekly on Thursday nights at 9:00 p.m. and was a crucial program of NBC's "Must See TV" night. "Must See TV" is a programming device used to entice viewers to watch TV from 8:00 to 11:00 p.m. on Thursday evenings. NBC placed three of its top-ratings draws—*Friends*, *Seinfeld*, and *ER*—in this time slot.

The show ended after its ninth season and had "evolved into something as close to a religion as pop culture allows" (Flaherty and Schilling 24). The show was a top-five Nielson show for the past four years, thanks to the loyal 30 million who tuned in every Thursday night. Likewise, the millions who faithfully tune into the reruns have made it number five in national syndication (Flaherty and Schilling 24).

On the surface, *Seinfeld* is about the daily lives of four friends—Jerry Seinfeld, Elaine Benes, George Costanza, and Cosmo Kramer—who live and work in New York City. There are no major—or even minor—social or political issues dealt with by these four characters; in fact, they are so self-centered that they would fail to see a socio-political issue if it were right in front of them. All of the characters embody the narcissistic individuality that captures Barrett's notion of incivility: Elaine calls herself the "Queen of Confrontation," George and Jerry continuously manipulate women, and Kramer is always scheming to make an easy buck.

In one of the later episodes, for example, George failed to swerve his car in time and ran over and killed a pigeon. He turned to his date, shrugged, and asked, "So, what do you want to do for dinner?" On the same episode, Jerry dated a woman who had an incredible toy collection but would not let him play with the toys because of their economic value. After a series of unsuccessful attempts to gain access to the toys, Jerry drugged the woman so she would pass out and he would have free reign among the collection. When George and Elaine heard about the toys, they, too, came over and drugged the woman in order to play.

For this study, I will analyze 12 episodes of *Seinfeld* from the current 1997 season and the previous eight seasons. As supporting material, I will draw from the book, *Sein Language*, by Jerry Seinfeld.

<u>Data Analysis</u>

To define and describe a rhetoric of incivility in the discourse of *Beavis and Butt-Head*, *Howard Stern*, and *Seinfeld*, I will use genre or generic criticism. Generic criticism "is rooted in the assumption that certain types of situations provoke similar needs and expectations among audiences and thus call for particular kinds of rhetoric" (Foss 225). The goal of the rhetorical critic using this method is to discover rhetorical trends that occur throughout similar rhetorical situations. Doing so allows the critic to "understand rhetorical practices in different time periods and in different places by discovering the similarities in rhetorical situations and the rhetoric constructed in response to them" (Foss 225). Generic criticism provides the critic with "an angle of vision, a window, that reveals the . . . dynamic within the rhetorical acts of human beings . . . , responding in similar ways as they attempt to encompass certain rhetorical problems" (Campbell and Jamieson 21).

When a critic is engaged in generic criticism, the artifacts are grouped according to similarities so that a rhetorical genre is a clustering of three different kinds of elements—situational requirements, substantive and stylistic features, and the organizing principle. Situational requirements are those situations that provoke a particular type of rhetoric. The substantive and stylistic features of the rhetoric are the rhetorical choices made by the rhetor concerning how to respond to the requirements of a given situation. *Organizing principle* is the label for the internal schematic formed by the situational, substantive, and stylistic features of the genre. According to Campbell and Jamieson, "a genre is a group of acts unified by a constellation of forms that recurs in each of its members. These forms, in isolation, appear in other discourses. What is distinctive about the acts in a genre is the recurrence of the forms together in a constellation" (335). Thus, the features of the genre must be interdependent.

The concept of a rhetorical genre first appeared in Aristotle's *Rhetoric*; Fisher claims that genres "are an Aristotelian construct . . . [because] they are constituted through actual examinations of discourse. They are inductive" (291). Contemporary scholars have made important contributions to the study and practice of what Black first labeled *generic criticism* in 1965. In this work, Black outlines the assumptions of his method:

> First, we must assume that there is a limited number of situations in which a rhetor can find himself. . . . Second, we must assume that there is a limited number of ways in which a rhetor can and will respond rhetorically to any given situational type. . . . Third, we must assume that the recurrence of a given situational type through history will provide the critic with information on the rhetorical responses available in that situation, and with this information the critic can better understand and evaluate any specific rhetorical discourse in which he may be interested. (133)

Bitzer's development of the concept of the situation in 1968 contributed significantly to the theoretical advancement of this critical model. He reasserts and reinforces Black's first and second assumptions, described above: "Rhetorical discourse is called into existence by situation; the situation that the rhetor perceives amounts to an invitation to create and present discourse" (306). Bitzer offers the following definition of a rhetorical situation: "a complex of persons, events, objects, and relations presenting an actual or potential exigence that can be completely or partially removed if discourse, introduced into the situation, can so constrain human decision or action as to bring about the significant modification of the exigence" (304). His position thus assumes that rhetoric is persuasive in that a rhetorical response to a situation has the potential to somehow alter it. As he explains, "The rhetor alters reality by bringing into existence a discourse of such a character that the audience, in thought and action, is so engaged that it becomes a mediator of change. In this sense rhetoric is always persuasive" (302).

An additional contribution to the study of generic criticism is provided by Campbell and Jamieson. Their book, *Form and Genre: Shaping Rhetorical Action*, was the result of a conference held in Lawrence, Kansas. Entitled "Significant Form in Rhetorical Criticism," the proceedings of the conference provide both theoretical discussions and sample essays of generic criticism. According to Foss, the book "brought into one volume the best thinking that had been done on generic criticism and served as a catalyst for further work in the area" (228).

Some contemporary communication scholars are cautious of generic criticism and wary of the "difficulties and critical deficiencies genre approaches confront us with" (Conley 47). Conley reminds scholars that, in Aristotle's *Rhetoric*, genres constitute a way a problem is solved as interpreted by the audience rather than "anything distinctive about the work itself" (48). He warns the generic critic that

> (1) seeing acts of discourse through the prism of genre theory guarantees a blindness to a good deal of what is going on in them . . . [because] one of the worst aspects of genre criticism is precisely that it detaches us from our experience of the work and (2) the tendency of generic classifications to proliferate into tiresome and useless taxonomies. (52–53)

Although Miller agrees with Conley that "rhetorical criticism has not provided firm guidance on what constitutes a genre," she does not concur that it yields no useful information or should not be used by rhetorical critics (151). By drawing from Campbell and Jamieson's argument that genre criticism is important because it attempts to place and understand rhetorical discourse through its social and historical connections, Miller asserts that "classification is necessary to language and learning" (151). Methodologically, genre criticism embodies the importance of context, as Campbell and Jamieson claim:

> Generic rhetorical criticism aims at understanding rhetorical practice over time by discerning recurrent patterns that reflect the rules practitioners follow. Such rules reflect culturally recognized motives, they define rhetorical situations, and they mark audience expectations. In other words, genres are jointly constructed by rhetors and audiences out of shared cultural knowledge. (*Introduction*, 1986, 295)

Despite the above criticisms, I believe that generic criticism is a valuable tool for this study. Given that little scholarly inquiry exists into the rhetoric of incivility, genre criticism is appropriate because it provides definitions and descriptions of this rhetoric that can be used as starting places for additional research. Moreover, the concept of definition is important to a rhetor's understanding of the rhetorical choices available to him or her in a given situation because "situations are social constructs that are the result, not of 'perception,' but of 'definition.' Because human action is based on and guided by meaning . . . at the center of action is a process of interpretation. Before we can act, we must interpret the indeterminate material environment; we define, or 'determine' a situation" (Miller 156). To ascertain appropriate rhetorical choices, then, the critic must be able to define the given rhetorical situation, and genre criticism provides such a definition.

There are three types of generic criticism the critic can perform—generic participation, generic application, and generic description—all leading the critic to different observations and conclusions. Both generic participation and generic application are deductive processes. With the first option, the critic moves from a general rhetorical classification to a specific text or artifact. The critic's goal is to determine if the specific artifact is a member of a particular genre. Generic application requires the critic to apply a generic model to specific rhetorical artifacts to assess them. Campbell and Jamieson note that most generic studies are deductive and thus carry two potential limitations. First, "the critic may fail to delineate the essential characteristics of the model so that the basis for comparison is faulty" (22). Second, "a generic fit" may be "asserted although certain essential characteristics are absent or significant dissimilarities exist" (22).

The third type of generic criticism is generic description, an inductive process in which the critic investigates several artifacts to ascertain if a genre exists. Broadly, generic description requires the critic to examine various rhetorical artifacts to determine if a genre exists and to "formulate theoretical constructs about its characteristics" (Foss 229). The risk for inductive criticism, according to Campbell and Jamieson, is that it must transcend the problems "inherent in any procedure that draws inductive generalizations" (22).

Given that minimal scholarly inquiry exists on the rhetoric of incivility, a necessary and logical starting point for me for this initial inquiry into the rhetoric of incivility is generic description. To conduct such an inquiry, the critic must proceed through the following four steps: "(1) observation of similarities in rhetorical responses to particular situations; (2) collection of rhetorical artifacts occurring in similar situations; (3) analysis of the artifacts to discover if they share characteristics; and (4) formulation of the organizing principle of the genre" (Foss 229).

The first step, observing "similarities in rhetorical responses to particular situations," was the original impetus for the study. I noticed many striking similarities between *Beavis and Butt-Head* and *Howard Stern*. Focusing on the similarities, I began to search and inquire as to the specific situations to which these rhetors were responding. I noticed that all the texts and rhetors in them, although their target audience is primarily adults, were speaking from contexts and situations that are reminiscent of boyhood adolescence. Their discourse exhibits a preoccupation with sex, the objectification of girls and women, the absence of any socio-political awareness, and explicit selfishness. Through their discourse, they seem to be implicitly commenting on the demand for political correctness in our public discourse; their discourse appears to be a backlash against the women's and civil rights movements. The talk across the rhetorical situations appears to be self-centered, disrespectful, rude, and often sexist and racist. In short, their communication violates all Western social rules and norms for polite and proper discourse.

Once I figured out the specific situation that initially seemed to unite these two texts, I began looking for a "collection of rhetorical artifacts occurring in similar situations." For reasons discussed later, I selected the television show *Seinfeld* to be included in this study. The third step, "analysis of the artifacts to discover if they share characteristics," will be accomplished by a close textual analysis of these artifacts. The analysis will focus on the specific substantive and stylistic features used by each rhetor to enable him to respond to the demand for political correctness and effectively produce uncivil discourse. Ultimately, I will organize my analysis to define and describe the organizing principle—if one can be identified—for the genre.

Significance of the Study

This study into the rhetorical genre of incivility is important for three primary reasons: (1) It constitutes a starting place from which to determine if a rhetorical genre exists and, if so, its rhetorical features and organizing principle; (2) Understanding the rhetorical features of this genre will help scholars and public policy makers restore civility in our cultural discourse; and (3) Restoring a sense of civility is important for disrupting the ideology of domination of our current culture.

Given that the talk and concern over a current lack of civility are increasing and may be serving as a scapegoat for other social problems, this research is important because it will offer a clear definition and description of a rhetoric of incivility. While examples of incivility abound—such as road rage, impoliteness, and rudeness—no research has offered a

thorough rhetorical definition or description of the rhetorical characteristics of such discourse as a whole. Defining and describing this rhetorical phenomenon is a crucial first step in determining the prevalence and
location of such discourse in our culture.

By attempting to discover the rhetorical features of incivility, communication scholars can contribute to public policy discussions and decisions concerning incivility. Not until scholars and public policy makers
know exactly what constitutes a rhetoric of incivility can we assess if incivility is something that needs to be eradicated from our cultural discourse. The alliance with public policy makers is important for two
primary reasons. One, communication in general and rhetoric specifically is directly related to the enactment of incivility. Ideas and feelings
are communicated though symbols that others read and interpret as uncivil. A rhetorical analysis yields a more comprehensive understanding of
the form, content, and power of such symbols. Second, an alliance with
public policy makers is beneficial to our field. In recent years, an increasing number of communication departments have come under at-
tack because universities and the general public fail to see how
communication as a discipline is related to "real world" issues. Wider
recognition of the discipline's contribution to the social problem of incivility may deter some critics and enhance the discipline's standing.

Finally, this research is important because of the significant role civility plays in eradicating an ideology of oppression. When alienation,
competition, and individualism are the status quo, it is difficult to
achieve the goals of a feminist movement—the feminist goals of elimi-
nating alienation and dehumanization seem antithetical in a climate of
incivility. Restoring a sense of civility, then, contributes to the creation of
an environment characterized by respect and value of diverse perspectives, immanent value, self-determination, safety, and mutuality.

Outline of the Study

In the first chapter, I identify the purpose of the study, the research design, the relevant literature on rhetoric and incivility, the significance of
the study, and an outline of the study. Chapters 2, 3, and 4 are a generic
analysis of the discourse of each of the three artifacts of popular culture
selected for inclusion is this research: Chapter 2 focuses on the rhetoric
of *Seinfeld*, Chapter 3 on *Beavis and Butt-Head*, and Chapter 4 on the
rhetoric of *The Howard Stern Show*. In the final chapter, I will construct
the rhetorical genre of incivility—its substantive and stylistic features—

by synthesizing the analyses from the previous three chapters. In this chapter, I also will define and describe the organizing principle of this genre, discuss the implications for rhetorical criticism, and suggest paths for future research.[22]

Notes

1. Adapted from the proposal of Abby Leverett Braun, "The Impact of Rhetorical Visions on Employee Assistance Program Utilization" (PhD diss., University of Denver, 1986). Original parenthetical citations and footnote numbers were retained in the samples in this chapter, but the references to which they refer were not.

2. Adapted from the proposal of Debra Greene, "Embodying Holism: A Somatic Perspective on Communication" (PhD diss., Ohio State University, 1995).

3. Adapted from the proposal of Marla R. Kanengieter, "Message Formation from Architecture: A Rhetorical Analysis" (PhD diss., University of Oregon, 1990).

4. Adapted from the proposal of Arthur Lytle Ranney, "A Schema for the Construction and Assessment of Messages of Empowerment" (PhD diss., Ohio State University, 1994).

5. Adapted from the proposal of Sharon M. Varallo, "Communication, Loneliness, and Intimacy" (PhD diss., Ohio State University, 1996).

6. Ranney.

7. Adapted from the proposal of Jean Mary Guske Ward, "Women's Responses to Systems of Male Authority: Communication Strategies in the Novels of Abigail Scott Duniway" (PhD diss., University of Oregon, 1989).

8. Adapted from the proposal of Patrick M. Krueger, "Social, Cultural, and Economic Capital, and Behavioral Investments in Health" (PhD diss., University of Colorado, 2004); and proposals, "Race/Ethnic and Sex Disparities in Physical Activity," submitted to and funded by the Agency for Healthcare Research and Quality, National Institutes of Health (1 R03 HS013996-01), 2003, and "Doctoral Dissertation Research: Physical Activity and Aging in the U.S.," submitted to and funded by the National Science Foundation (SES 0221093), 2002.

9. Adapted from the proposal of Daniel Dwight Gross, "Narrative Agreement Surrounding Contractual Agreement" (PhD diss., University of Oregon, 1989).

10. Adapted from the proposal of Michelle Fabian Simmons, "The Functions of Narrative in the Process of Building Shared Vision" (PhD diss., University of Iowa, 1998).

11. Adapted from the proposal of Anthony John Radich, "Governance in Non-Profit Arts Organizations: A Grounded-Theory Perspective" (DPA diss., University of Colorado, 1986).

12. Simmons.

13. Mariah Dolsen Tanner Ehmke, "Identifying the Impact of Culture on Economic Behavior with Applications to Food and the Environment" (PhD diss., Purdue University, 2005).

14. Radich.

15. Krueger.

16. Varallo.

17. Greene.

18. Ranney.

19. Adapted from the proposal of Catherine Egley Waggoner, "The Nature and Function of Aesthetic Communication: A Case Study of Traditional Women's Cultures" (PhD diss., Ohio State University, 1994).

20. Adapted from the proposal of D. Lynn O'Brien Hallstein, "Transforming Feminist Rhetorical Criticism and Schizoanalysis: A Collaboration Between Feminist Rhetorical Theory and Schizoanalytic Theory" (PhD diss., Ohio State University, 1994).

21. Adapted from the proposal of Bernard John Armada, "'The Fierce Urgency of Now': Public Memory and Civic Transformation at the National Civil Rights Museum" (PhD diss., Pennsylvania State University, 1999).

22. Adapted from the proposal of Laura K. Hahn, "A Generic Analysis of the Rhetoric of Humorous Incivility in Popular Culture" (PhD diss., Ohio State University, 1999).

THINGS TO SEE AND DO:
DATA COLLECTION AND ANALYSIS

Steps 12–18 (247–447 hours)

You've put a lot of planning into your trip. You've talked to previous travelers and have studied the guidebooks about what to see and do. Now you've arrived at your destination and are ready to see and do the things you've heard and read about. You might even discover some new things that were unknown to previous travelers. In the dissertation, this is the point in your trip where you are collecting and analyzing your data. This is what you came for—the experience of your trip, the discovery of what will answer the question that started you on your journey.

Collecting Your Data

You made a decision in your preproposal—that you carried through into your proposal—about how to collect your data. Perhaps you are interviewing or surveying people or are locating and gathering articles from newspapers. Maybe you are collecting episodes of a television program. You might be using a database that already exists and simply have to gain access to it. Perhaps you are using an ethnographic method and are taking notes on what you are observing. Whatever your method of data collection, now is the time to do what you said you would do: Question, survey, gather, collect, access, or observe. You'll have great fun doing the actual research after all of your planning.

Because methods of data collection are so varied and you're likely to have been well trained in whatever method you have chosen, we're not going to discuss specific procedures for collecting data here. We do want to remind you, though, to be as efficient as you can in your data collection and not to over-collect your data. (If you followed our earlier guidelines for selecting your data, this won't be a problem for you.)

Creating Codable Data

Depending on the form your data take, you may have to transform your data into codable form. Transcribe your interviews or type up your observations or do whatever is required to get your data into a form that you can work with and analyze. Remember, though: You don't need to transcribe every word and pause of interviews or focus groups you have recorded. Listen to the recording for ideas relevant to your research question, identify the beginning and end of those sections, and transcribe only those sections. Don't forget, too, that you can save a lot of time by paying someone to transcribe for you. Transcribing even five minutes of a taped interview, especially if you aren't used to it, can take 40 to 50 minutes. People who are experienced transcribers can do it much faster than you can, and this is one way to pick up speed in your dissertation schedule—a lot of speed, in fact.

Even if you don't have to transform your data in any way—say it's qualitative data already in hard copy, ready to be coded, as with newspaper articles or completed transcriptions—there's one more step to take before you begin coding: Make a second copy of each page of your data and set the pages aside. You'll see why shortly.

Identifying Your Unit(s) of Analysis

Just as you collect a lot of experiences when you travel, your method of data collection is likely to yield plenty of data. But how do you make sense of all your experiences and all those data? That's where the crucial step of coding comes in. You chose to do your study for a reason: to answer your research question. You are now at the step in the process where you pick out those aspects of your data that are most relevant to answering that research question. This involves identifying the unit or units of analysis. A unit of analysis will help you know which aspects of the data to focus on in your coding. It's a fancy way of saying a specific kind of example, and it serves as a scanning device for coding your data in order to answer your research question.

You don't have to invent your unit of analysis because it comes from your research question. The unit of analysis should be a concept, idea, or action that illuminates the significant features of your data so that the question you asked can be answered. If your research question is about the kinds of questions teachers ask in classrooms that stimulate the greatest amount of discussion among students, your unit of analysis is the types of questions asked by teachers. If you are studying methods by which parents transmit political beliefs to their children, your unit of analysis is methods of transmission of political beliefs, whatever form those might assume. If you are studying means by which dance companies balance economic viability and artistic vision, your unit of analysis is any mechanism or strategy where there is evidence of balancing between survivability and artistic vision.

In some instances, you will have a greater range of options about the unit of analysis to use in coding the data. This is when your unit of analysis can be operationalized in a number of ways. For example, if your research question deals with the strategies communicators use to regain their credibility, units of analysis could be metaphors, word choice, or types of evidence, to name a few. You could use all of these as your units of analysis, or you could select one or two for particular reasons.

If you can't figure out what your unit of analysis is from your research question, your research question might not be sufficiently refined. In particular, it might not meet that criterion of recognizability that we talked about in chapter 4. If you're having difficulty identifying the units of analysis from your research question, you might need to tweak your research question so that it clearly points you to particular units of analysis.

Once you know your unit of analysis or have decided the form it will take if you have a choice, it's the only thing you'll look for when you code your data. Knowing your unit of analysis, then, is the first step to unpacking the wealth of data before you. Next you're going to find examples of your unit of analysis in your data and code them so that you can assemble the examples into an answer to your question.

Coding Your Data

Because the coding of qualitative data tends to trip students up the most, we're going to focus on how to code those kinds of data. Plus, there are well-established procedures for running and analyzing quantitative data, and if you're using such data, you're undoubtedly familiar with them. Whether you are coding transcripts of interviews, field notes, ethnographic observations, speeches, or newspaper articles, the principles are the same, so we're going to offer a generic method of coding that applies to most qualitative research.

The task ahead might seem daunting as you look at all those pages of data in front of you. This feeling is understandable and, in fact, because of it, this is the stage where many otherwise fully operational dissertations come to a crashing halt. Without a clear method for reviewing and analyzing the data, you might feel like you'll never be able to turn your data into an answer for your research question. Once again, though, we're going to divide the process into discrete units that are concrete and manageable. You'll be able to make progress step by step.

Your first step is to find examples of your unit of analysis in your data. Don't worry—they'll be there. You have designed your research question and your methods so that you collected appropriate data. Now you simply have to isolate the units of analysis so that you can see and work with them easily. To do this, go through your pages of data and, when you come to a unit of analysis, mark the beginning and the end of the excerpt that constitutes or contains that unit.

For example, if you are looking for the unit of analysis of mechanisms by which parents transmit political beliefs to their children, every time you see in your transcripts what seems to you to be a transmission mechanism, mark the beginning and end of the description of that mechanism. It might be, for example, a parent's description of how she makes a regular practice of sitting down with her children to watch Fox news and discussing with them what they heard and saw. Or perhaps she talks about how she introduces political topics into the family's conversation at dinner. Each of these would be a unit of analysis—a transmission mechanism—that you would mark in your transcript. Keep enough information in your marked excerpt so that you are clear on what is happening in it. But don't get carried away with giving yourself context around a relevant excerpt. Keep the focus on the relevant quote that constitutes an example of your unit of analysis.

After you locate an excerpt that you see as a unit of analysis, write a code next to the excerpt in the margin. Come up with a term or phrase that captures what you're are seeing there. A code for the mechanism of watching and discussing Fox news, for example, might be "watches and discusses Fox news." Don't agonize over the wording of this code. It's just something that describes what you see as relevant in the excerpt. Don't stray too far from what you are seeing when you construct this code—don't try, for example, to come up with a more abstract word as your code. For example, if you are coding classroom interactions and a teacher yells at a student, code that excerpt as "teacher yells at student." Don't code it as "violence" or "irrational response." Those are too abstract. You'll be doing that kind of transcendence and abstraction later, but now isn't the time. Capturing what you are literally seeing will also help you go much faster with your coding.

Go through all of your pages of data, marking units of analysis and devising a code that captures what you are seeing in them. Look for excerpts that contain units of analysis, mark them, and give them a code in the margin. Yes, this will take some time—it may take the most time of any part of your dissertation. Finding the excerpts that constitute units of analysis is relatively easy. What takes the time is coming up with the code for an excerpt you have marked. Although you'll code slowly at first, as you get more practiced at it, you'll get faster. A double-spaced page of data should take no more than two or three minutes to code. To keep yourself moving along as you code, you might set a kitchen timer for 15 minutes and set yourself a goal of coding eight or nine pages in that amount of time. When the timer goes off, if you find that you've only done three or four pages, see if you can move faster.

As you code, code with naïveté. What we mean by this is that you should code trying to forget what you know about your subject. Try not to use background and accumulated knowledge to decide what is going on in the data. Let's say that you know the reason why the teacher yelled at the student—because he had a migraine headache that day. Code "teacher yells at student" and not "teacher lashes out because of migraine." The migraine headache is not something that others would be able to get from the videotape or the transcript of the interaction. Staying at the surface level of the text as you code prevents you from coding for what you want to find or for what you think you will find. It also makes using the coded examples as support in your analysis much easier because there will be less that you need to explain.

A good test for whether you are bringing too much of your previous knowledge into your coding is to ask yourself if you would be able to explain to someone else how you came up with a particular code using only the excerpt in a transcript or article. This is the standard of reasonable inference. You must be able to show how you moved from the unit of analysis to the code you have given it. Would you be able to point to the excerpt and explain to someone how, from that alone, you came up with the code "teacher lashes out because of migraine"? No. There's nothing in the excerpt itself that points to pain on the part of the teacher. You would, however, be able to point to the excerpt and explain how you came up with the code "teacher yells at student." That behavior on the part of the teacher would be evident to anyone who reads the transcript or views the videotape.

You might find yourself in situations in which you resist using the standard of reasonable inference—you want to code so that your data give you particular results. If you are tempted to do this, it's probably because you already have an idea of what you want the data to say. This, of course, leads to a lopsided analysis of the data. Remember: When you code in this way, you are no longer conducting research but are simply confirming a position you already hold. You are capable of doing better research than that.

As you move through your data, you might discover that one excerpt requires more than one code because it contains several units of analysis. This happens most often if you have a long excerpt. Perhaps a parent is discussing how she tries to transmit her political beliefs to her children, and she names three such mechanisms within one excerpt. That's OK. Just give that one excerpt three different codes—one for each mechanism. But don't code the same incident in more than one way. In other words, you wouldn't want to code the teacher yelling at the student as both "teacher yells at student" and "teacher goads student." You have to decide, at the moment you attach a code to a unit of analysis, what one code you will give it.

It's also important to keep track of where the coded excerpts come from in your data. You are soon going to be cutting the coded excerpts apart and using them as support in your findings chapter(s), so you'll need to be able to cite your sources. If you have transcripts of interviews from 10 people, for example, you want to be able to tell where a particular excerpt came from—from which page of which transcript linked to which interviewee. If you are coding newspaper articles, you'll want to be able to tell the newspaper, date, and page from which a coded excerpt came. One way to keep track of the origins of your excerpts is to make a shorthand citation at the end of each excerpt that you code. For example, you could put something like *2-9* by the excerpt to indicate that it is from interview #2 and is on page 9.

Another system for keeping track of your data is to color code each separate transcript or data set. If you have transcripts from ten interviewees, for example, you can take a crayon or colored pencil from a set of ten different colored pencils and draw a line in one color vertically down each page of one transcript in the margin. Do the same with the second transcript, except use a different color. If you have more than ten interviews, just repeat the colors but as multiple lines. For example, if transcript #1 has red lines and transcript #2 has green lines, then transcript #11 might have two red lines and transcript #12 a red and a green line. Keep a list, of course, of which color goes with which transcript: Transcript #1 is red, transcript #2 is green, and so on. If you use this system, you'll only have to put the page number of the transcript next to each coded excerpt because the colored lines reference the transcript.

Whatever system you use for keeping track of your data, you'll end up with pages and pages and pages of coded data. Each excerpt that constitutes an example of your unit of analysis is marked for where it starts and ends and is coded with a word or phrase that captures what you are seeing in it. Also on the excerpt is a citation that notes the page and source from which it comes. The sample on the next page shows what a coded page of data might look like. Nicki's research question is, "What is the nature of the resistance identity constructed by the residents of the San Luis Valley in Colorado between 1960 and 2002?"[1]

Sorting Your Codes

Remember how you made good use of your scissors to complete your literature review? It's time to bring those scissors out again. After coding all of your data, cut out each excerpt you coded from your pages of data. If you coded transcripts of interviews, cut out the coded excerpts from those pages. If you coded newspaper articles, cut out the coded excerpts

N: Was your data involved in that early group, the La Associación?

GM: Yes, he was.

N: What did he do with them?

GM: Well, at the time, La Associación was established by people so that they could keep control of how many sheep and how many cattle could be taken there. And they watched the overgrazing so it didn't happen. Things like that. They patrolled; that was their purpose. And from there came the land Rights Council. Land Rights Council grew right from that. But that was the idea. It was a management of sorts. But among themselves because they respected each other's life. If anyone brought more cows to a certain area than they were supposed to, they'd tell them, "OK, you've got 100 cows too many in there. You've got to take them out, take them somewhere else. And leave the rest, but you've got too many, you are not allowed that many. They never went to court, they never had arguments of any sort. If someone was stepping out of line and they'd take too many sheep up there . . . because sheep will clean up a place, they graze differently . . . so that was the purpose of the Associación. (#2, p. 9)

N: And they were still grazing on Taylor's land at that point?

GM: Yeah, the Associación de Derechos Cívicos was established. But even before they established the Associación, they were already keeping everything under control.

N: Informal? Yeah. And who were the founders of that Associación?

GM: I really don't know. I know that he was involved. He may have been one of them. But I couldn't tell you who the founders really were. I don't know.

N: Were there any women? What always strikes me is the involvement of you, Marianne, Glenda, and Shirley. You are like leaders within the whole movement. And you don't see that in a lot of these movements—women taking charge.

GM: Well, back, then, you didn't see it, either.

N: You didn't?

GM: No. The women were to stay at home and keep their mouths shut.,

N: Really!

GM: Yeah. That was their upbringing, I guess. The women were at home; they were the family caretakers. They took care of the family and the family needs and so on and so forth.

N: So what changed?

GM: I don't know. I know my dad got us involved. And my brothers were in the service, so the only ones he could involve were me and my sisters.

N: What did he do to get you involved?

GM: Well, he would tell us, "This is what's taking place. If you do not become interested, if you do not show that you are aware of all these things, you're going to lose everything. Protect what you have. Protect the rights of the people." He would lecture us that way. And that's how we got involved.

from the articles. This is why you made a second copy of your data. You are cutting one copy up, but you still have another one intact. You might find that some of your coded excerpts go over more than one page. If that's the case, tape them together as you are cutting them out. If you have any excerpts that have more than one code, make multiple copies of those excerpts—one for each code.

Just as you did after you cut out the notes for your literature review, you now have a huge pile of excerpts in front of you, each containing an example of your unit of analysis that has a code and a citation on it. Just as you did to get the schema for your literature review, you're now going to sort the coded excerpts. A big open space is useful here—a large table, a bed, the floor—someplace where you can keep things spread out for a while.

One by one, take an excerpt and put it into a pile according to which codes seem to go together. Use your codes, not the quotes themselves, to decide how to categorize your excerpts. Don't think about patterns in the codes or wonder about what you are going to do with them. Simply put together codes that seem similar. Don't worry about whether you're doing the sorting right or not—you'll get a chance to check and revise your sorting later. Simply pick up one excerpt after another and put it into a pile, or start a new pile if it doesn't fit into the ones that are already out there. Do it again. And again. Remember those excerpts with multiple codes—the ones you copied? Sort each of those different codes into their proper piles.

As your piles start to take shape and have three or four excerpts in them, use sticky notes to label your piles with terms that express succinctly what all the codes in that one pile have in common. That will help you continue to sort quickly. You might label one pile, for example, *EXPLICIT DISCUSSIONS* to capture any mechanisms parents describe that involve explicit discussions with their children about what to think about politics. This pile might contain both the mechanisms of deliberately introducing political topics into dinner conversations and discussing the nightly news following a broadcast.

If you discover that you have one pile that is becoming much larger than your other piles, you probably have codes on different topics in that pile. Pause for a minute and sort the excerpts in that pile, making several smaller piles out of that big one. Don't worry if you have lots of small piles. That's better than a few large piles. You'll review the piles later to see if you can combine them. If you have only a few large piles, though, you probably are doing too much abstracting as you sort to make many different codes fit under one label. If that's the case, stop and sort all of your piles into smaller ones, making finer distinctions among your codes than you did earlier.

Keep going until all of the excerpts are in piles. As you sort, you'll probably come across a number of excerpts that don't seem to belong anywhere. Either these excerpts don't seem relevant anymore or are about things other than your units of analysis. Or maybe you can't quite remember why you coded them. Don't worry. This happens. Make a *DON'T KNOW* pile—a pile that contains excerpts that you can't fit into any existing pile and that don't seem as relevant as you earlier thought they would be to answering your research question. You'll come back to these later.

When you've finished sorting your excerpts, your piles and their labels will look something like the figure on the next page, although you'll have many more piles of coded data than this. These are from Nicki's dissertation dealing with the nature of resistance identity in a particular area of Colorado.

Checking Your Codes

You now have many different piles in front of you, and each one has a sticky notes label describing what characteristic, attribute, or mechanism the codes in the pile share. Now check your piles to be sure that all of the codes on the excerpts in each pile are relevant to the label you've given it. Take each pile in turn and look at the excerpts it contains, checking to be sure that all the codes deal with the topic summarized by the label you've given to that pile. You might find that some excerpts don't belong in one pile but belong to another. Move them. You'll gradually refine the piles until you are satisfied that the codes on the excerpts in each pile share significant characteristics.

Now is also the time to look through that *DON'T KNOW* pile. Can any of the excerpts in this pile go into other piles? Perhaps there is an excerpt about self-disciplining on the part of a student that you could not place before that might fit in the disciplining category you just created. There are likely to be some excerpts in this pile, though, that you can't convince yourself belong in another pile or are important enough to sort. Don't worry about them. Set them aside in a *NOT USED* pile. You will

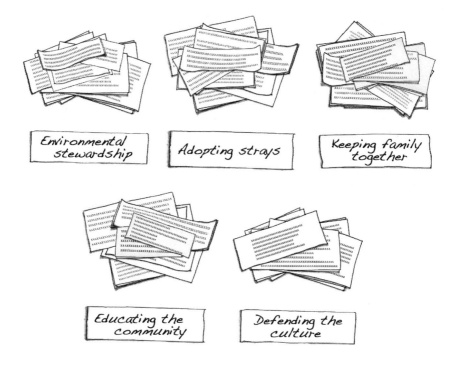

have sufficient evidence to make a claim about your data without them, and, if they truly don't fit in any pile, they're probably outliers—not important enough to be considered as you interpret your data.

How many piles should you have after you've coded and sorted your data? The answer, of course, is however many piles your data suggest. About 40 or 50 piles is typical for coding data for a dissertation. In some cases, though, you might have as few as 10 or 20. Can you have too many piles? If you have a hundred or so, you probably do have too many. That many piles will make it very hard to find an explanatory schema and to write up your findings chapter(s). If you find yourself in this situation, go back through your piles and try to combine some of them. Move up one or two levels of abstraction in how you think about your codes so that some of the piles can be put together. You want to be able to work with your data in categories, so do enough abstracting so that you have categories of data and not simply individual pieces of data. Too many piles make it as difficult to come up with insightful findings as too few. Here is where you might begin to combine the earlier example of a teacher yelling at a student with excerpts such as "teacher sends student to office" and "teacher puts student in time out" under a label of *DISCIPLINING*.

Once you are convinced that your piles all contain excerpts dealing with the same codes, put the piles into envelopes so that they don't get mixed up or rearranged by a family pet or young helper. Put the *NOT USED* excerpts into an envelope as well. While it is unlikely that you'll be using them in this project, you might have occasion to return to them in some future project. Then give the envelopes labels that represent the category of code they contain. These labels will probably be the same as those on the sticky notes that you used while sorting the codes. If one of your piles was labeled *DISCIPLINING*, that's the label that you'll probably want to put on the envelope containing the excerpts from that pile.

Creating Your Explanatory Schema

You have before you many different envelopes with labels on them containing coded excerpts. What you really have, of course, is the beginning of an explanatory schema for your findings. An explanatory schema is an explanation for what you see across your piles of coded data. It is the conceptual, organizing principle that allows you to tell the story of your data in an interesting and insightful way. Your coded excerpts haven't been organized yet or connected to one another, but they represent a good start on coming up with an explanatory schema for your findings. Now you are going to imaginatively piece that schema or skeleton together so that you can flesh it out into your data chapter(s). The envelopes represent major ideas—pieces of a whole—that, when combined together, will become the answer to your research question. They will also become the supporting quotes and examples for your chapter(s).

To turn your envelopes into an explanatory schema, return to your computer and type the labels that are on your envelopes. Type each label on a separate line and in a large font size—something like 26 point—and leave a space between each label. There is no need to worry about the order in which you type these labels into your computer. Nor is there any need to worry about grammar or spelling. When you have finished typing in all the labels, print them out and cut them apart. Take the labels back to your flat surface, and lay them out in any order. Nicki, the student writing the dissertation on the resistance identity in the San Luis Valley, had labels like those shown on the next page.

Now you're going to use the labels to find relationships among the piles of coded excerpts that are inside your envelopes. Once you have the labels laid out, play around with the relationships you see among the topics they represent. Put topics together that seem to go together, making piles out of the labels that seem connected in some way. Move them around, seeing if you can make them into an explanatory schema. Keep moving them, putting labels together that seem to go together, looking for relationships. As you sort the labels into piles, you might use a kind of outline form, placing some topics under others. Or you might use a kind of pairing, placing one set of topics on the left and another set that relates to them on the right. Perhaps you see a chronological or cause-and-effect relationship. In whatever way seems to make sense, lay out the labels so that you have your labels in piles and see a pattern across them or relationships among them.

Your first layout is likely to be an obvious one, and you'll typically find yourself sorting, grouping, and arranging the labels in topical, chronological, or other conventional ways. For example, if you are trying to discover the ethical system by which state legislators operate, you might sort your labels into standard ethical categories like honesty, fairness, and trustworthiness. You might describe the relationship among the three concepts in this way: Being fair leads to the need to be honest, which in turn leads to being perceived as trustworthy. This is fine, but it's an obvious and expected schema. Don't be surprised if you come up with such a schema on your first attempt. Often, this first layout is a schema of what you want to find, so it will tend to reflect the story you already know about your data. While this explanatory schema will be serviceable, we believe there is always a more original and useful pattern to be discovered if you keep sorting and arranging your labels.

When you're done with your first sort and have some piles of labels that make sense to you and you see some relationships among them, label the piles with sticky notes and jot down some notes about the basic relationships you are seeing among the labels. For example, for the explanatory schema above, you would have sticky notes for *HONESTY*, *FAIRNESS*, and *TRUSTWORTHINESS*, and you would quickly map out

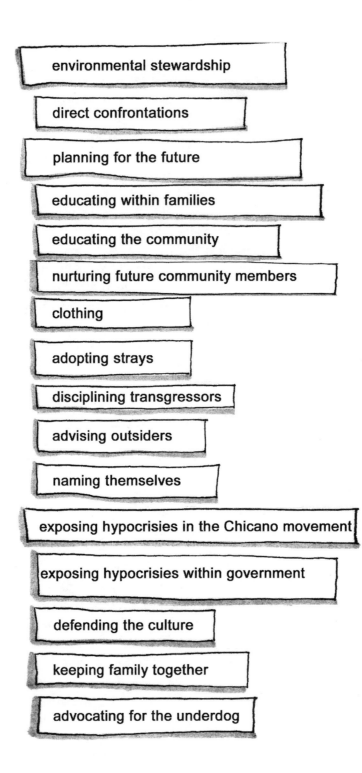

environmental stewardship

direct confrontations

planning for the future

educating within families

educating the community

nurturing future community members

clothing

adopting strays

disciplining transgressors

advising outsiders

naming themselves

exposing hypocrisies in the Chicano movement

exposing hypocrisies within government

defending the culture

keeping family together

advocating for the underdog

on a sheet of paper the cause-and-effect relationship you are seeing in the labels. Then mark the backs of the labels in each pile with the same mark so that you'll be able to reconstruct each pile if you want to at a later time. For example, put a green X on the backs of all the excerpts in the *FAIRNESS* pile, a red X on the backs of the excerpts in the *HONESTY* pile, a blue X on the backs of the excerpts in the *TRUSTWORTHINESS* pile, and so on. In this way, you can easily and quickly recreate the piles if something were to happen to them. And something is going to happen to them.

Now comes the scary—but exciting—part. Remove your sticky note headings from the piles of labels and set them aside. Then mix your labels up. In other words, dismantle all your piles of labels and whatever layout you had of how they relate to one another. Shuffle them all around. Sort them again, making yourself sort differently from how you did before. The goal is to find completely different piles for the labels and entirely new relationships among the labels from what you found the first time. You might have a couple of labels that stay in the same relationship as they were in your earlier sort, but the general rule guiding you here should be to force yourself to think of new relationships among the labels and new ways in which they connect to one another. Make yourself come up with categories that aren't so literal, for example. Look for patterns other than traditional ones.

After you find a second explanatory relationship or schema, we recommend that, just as you did before, you mark your labels and jot down that schema and then mix the labels up again, resorting and rearranging yet another time. What you are doing is forcing yourself to look beyond the obvious as you try to create an explanatory schema for your data. We've found that the second or third sort is likely to birth a truly exciting, original explanatory schema.

As you are playing around with the labels and trying to come up with a schema that explains your data, you might find it helpful to try out some methods designed to prompt you to think creatively. One of our favorite ways to formulate an explanatory schema from data is to talk out loud about the labels, the piles, and any relationships that seem evident. Explain what you are thinking about or what you are trying to figure out to someone. Articulate the key ideas of your labels. Talk about the relationships among the labels. You don't have to do this talking to your advisor or a fellow student or anyone who knows anything about academia or your field. Your spouse or partner will do just fine. As you work to explain your labels and ask for ideas about an explanatory schema that holds them together, you will probably articulate things you had been thinking about that you didn't know you understood. Your explanation of the relationships of the labels and the questions from your conversational partner often can lead to an insightful explanatory schema.

Formal brainstorming techniques can also help you come up with an explanatory schema from your data. These are formal techniques designed to facilitate creative and original thinking, and if you apply them to your thinking about your labels and the relationships among them, new ideas for an explanatory schema might emerge. One of these techniques is random stimulation. Using this technique, you deliberately introduce apparently irrelevant and unconnected information into your thinking about your schema. You can open a dictionary, point to a word, and then relate that word to your topic in as many ways as you can. Or you might look around the room and select an object. Create as many connections as you can between that object and the topics of your labels.

Sonja used this technique to construct an explanatory schema for a group of artworks she was studying known as *body art*. These were popular in the 1970s and involved artists using their physical bodies as their medium of expression in unusual and often painful ways. As she was trying to devise an explanatory schema for her coded data, she looked up and saw a picture of a clown on the wall. She began connecting the clown to her labels about various aspects of body art in as many ways as she could. After just a few minutes, she had her explanatory schema. The clown wasn't the explanation she was seeking, but the insane person was. She constructed a schema around the notion of insanity, in which the viewer adopts the role of a therapist to make sense of the works of art. She never would have developed that schema without the image of the clown as a prompt.

Shifting focus is a second brainstorming technique that might help you think in more creative ways about how to organize your labels. Human beings can pay only limited attention to things in their environment, which means we must choose where to focus our attention. Because our attention usually settles over the most obvious areas, a slight shift in attention by itself might suggest a new explanation for your data. In shifting focus, you deliberately turn away from your natural attention areas to see what happens if you pay attention to something else. If you are studying George W. Bush's appeals to Latino/a voters at the Republican convention, for example, you undoubtedly coded your data (and thus attended to) the kinds of appeals the campaign made to these specific voters. Your labels are probably organized around that focus. If you deliberately select a different, less obvious point of attention—the real intended audience for the appeals—you might discover an explanation for your data you had not thought about before. Perhaps the appeals were really directed at White voters who were listening to the appeals in approval and not at Latino/a voters at all. This insight could provide the organizing principle for your explanatory schema.

A third brainstorming technique that might help you think in creative ways about the labels laid out before you is Aristotle's *topoi* or topics. In his book *Rhetoric*, Aristotle suggests various topics or places to go to discover ideas for arguments, including definition, comparison, contrast, cause and effect, opposites, relation of parts to a whole, and conflicting facts. Three of the topics are used below to illustrate how they might generate ideas for an explanatory schema that deals with the rhetoric of Arnold Schwarzenegger as he campaigned for the governorship of California prior to the recall election of Governor Gray Davis in 2003:

- **Definition**: How can Schwarzenegger's rhetoric be defined? Can it be defined as an effort to achieve credibility—an effort to diminish his careers of bodybuilding and acting? Can it be defined as acting? Can it be defined as building a political body? Can it be defined as a sequel?

- **Comparison and contrast**: How was Schwarzenegger's rhetoric like or unlike that of Ronald Reagan, another actor who began his political career by winning the governorship of California? Were the similarities and differences significant? How was his rhetoric like or unlike that of Gray Davis and the other 132 candidates running in the election?

- **Cause and effect**: What effects might Schwarzenegger's rhetoric have on the perceptions of politics by Americans and others? Did the election of wrestler Jesse Ventura as governor of

Minnesota a few years earlier create an environment in which Schwarzenegger's candidacy was taken more seriously? Is Schwarzenegger an effect of Ventura's success? What might the effects of Schwarzenegger's governorship be on the Republican Party?

Any of these might encourage you to look at your labels in new ways to develop an explanatory schema for your findings.

Reversing is another brainstorming technique that can prod you to creative thinking as you are trying to come up with an explanatory schema. Using the reversal technique, you deliberately move away from what you know or believe you have figured out from the relationships among your labels and pursue an opposite direction or opposite qualities. Simply take the ideas encoded in your labels and the relationships you see and turn them around, inside out, upside down, and back to front to see if the reversal generates ideas for an explanatory schema. Let's say you are analyzing the film *Run Lola Run* and are trying to develop an explanatory schema from labels derived from coding the film. Reversal would encourage you to ask questions such as these:

- Lola is running to save Manni's life. Is there a way in which Manni is saving Lola's life?

- The security guard stands at the entrance to the bank where Lola goes to ask her banker father for money. Is there something that Lola guards? What does her father guard?

- Manni's boss demands money by noon. What does the money demand that the boss do?

- Manni is killed by an ambulance. If the ambulance doesn't save Manni, who or what does it save?

Applying various metaphors to your labels is another way to push you to think in new ways about relationships among your labels and to come up with an insightful explanatory schema. See if you can come up with a metaphor that captures most of the relationships among the labels or the essence of the idea they represent. Try out different metaphors, suggesting different kinds of relationships that might explain what is going on in the labels. So, for example, you might ask metaphoric questions of your labels such as these: Is what is going on here the frontier West, with cowboys and shoot-outs and lawlessness? Is the proper metaphor that captures my labels a three-ring circus, with lots of kinds of activities going on at once, all trying to capture people's attention? Is it the Olympic Games, with people from diverse backgrounds competing in lots of different events before audiences? If you try a metaphor that doesn't work, it will help you say what it was about the relationship that was overstated by the metaphor or what was missing from the metaphor. As a result, you clarify the groupings of the labels and the relationships among them.

There are two ways in which you can make use of a metaphor in connection with an explanatory schema. One is to use it simply to help you think about and develop your schema. In this case, you use a metaphor to isolate and clarify the connections among the labels, but it doesn't become part of your actual schema. If you decide that the image of the frontier West helps you clarify your thinking about your labels, for example, play around with all of the things you know about the frontier West to help you develop the explanatory schema. In your schema, think about who or what functions as the sheriff. Who are the outlaws? Who are the townspeople? What are the laws that are being followed and broken? Are some people deputized by others? What constitutes the saloon in your data? Is the railroad coming through town? What's the railroad in your data, and what is it bringing? Who is building the railroad? You get the idea. The elements of the metaphor help you think about the relationships among your labels and push you to think in new ways about how various labels and the coded excerpts they represent are functioning.

When you use a metaphor in this way as a prompt to help you think, the metaphor disappears before you write up your data. You won't talk about your findings in terms of sheriffs, outlaws, and saloons. You'll talk about your findings using the labels you formulated from your coding process. No one reading your analysis would have a clue that you ever thought about your data in terms of the frontier, but thinking about them in that way may have been key to constructing your explanatory schema. It helped you find the underlying organizational principle for your schema.

Another way to use a metaphor to develop an explanatory schema is to make it an explicit organizing principle for your schema. In this option, the metaphor is obvious in your presentation of your findings, and the various elements of your schema are titled according to the parts of the metaphor. For example, as Nicki played around with her labels, she discovered that the means of resistance her codes revealed were activities typically associated with mothering. She used the metaphor to test the relationships she was seeing and to push her thinking: What do mothers do? They're pregnant. What's the pregnancy in this identity? When do they give birth? What do they birth? What are the qualities of mothers? The metaphor of the typical role of a mother seemed to apply perfectly to what Nicki was seeing in her data, so she decided to use it explicitly and organized her labels using it. The metaphor itself became her explanatory schema, and she answered her research question using aspects of mothering.

The concepts of Nicki's explanatory schema, then, were primary activities associated with mothers—protecting, cleaning, clothing, and educating. The nature of the resistance identity, she suggested, involves conventional motherly roles, whether they're assumed by women or men. In fact, she argued, by adopting a motherly role in their resistance identity, the residents of the San Luis Valley birthed a new generation of metaphorical children who themselves adopted this mothering behavior. Over time, this led to the preservation of community identity despite continuous environmental and social challenges. Nicki, then, ended up with the explanatory schema shown on the next page.

You have another example of a metaphor functioning as an explanatory schema right in front of you—this book. When we first began writing this book, we knew the things we wanted to talk about—having a conceptual conversation, writing the literature review, collecting and coding data, and so on. We tried to find an explanatory schema that held all of these general categories together—something that would be more insightful and interesting than simply saying they were all parts of the dissertation process. That would be one of those obvious schemas we talked about. We were trying to account for the process of going somewhere, collecting a whole bunch of little pieces, coming back, and getting something at the end. We tried out several metaphors, including one of a scavenger hunt. We played around with that metaphor for a while, but we rejected it

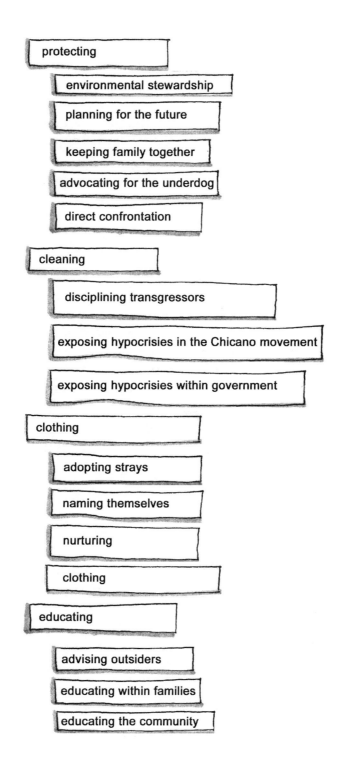

- protecting
  - environmental stewardship
  - planning for the future
  - keeping family together
  - advocating for the underdog
  - direct confrontation
- cleaning
  - disciplining transgressors
  - exposing hypocrisies in the Chicano movement
  - exposing hypocrisies within government
- clothing
  - adopting strays
  - naming themselves
  - nurturing
  - clothing
- educating
  - advising outsiders
  - educating within families
  - educating the community

for a couple of reasons. Although some aspects of scavenger hunts fit the dissertation—the participants follow a list, assemble parts, and win—other things don't. For example, what about the losers? In scavenger hunts, there are lots of players and only one or two winners. Also, someone besides the hunters organizes the hunt, which means that the participants don't have much agency in the process or control over what happens. That didn't fit with our perspective on writing a dissertation. Then we hit on using the travel metaphor you see in this book. After testing this metaphor, we found it nicely explains the key relationships among our processes and introduces into those processes entailments we like such as fun, an aberration from normal life, a limited period of time, and a confidence that any obstacles can be readily overcome.

What determines how many times you sort and rearrange labels before you decide you have your explanatory schema? You can stop when the schema you propose meets several criteria. One is that it must *encompass all of the major categories of your data*. All of the labels that represent your data should have a clear role in this schema. If the schema leaves out or omits several key labels that represent envelopes of coded data, you don't have your schema yet. Keep re-sorting, rearranging, and thinking.

A second criterion for an explanatory schema is that it should be marked by an *organic and coherent relationship among the labels*. All of the labels should function together, without undue strain, to answer your research question. The schema should clearly show connections among labels and contributing relations among the piles.

A third criterion is *reasonable inference*—the same criterion you used for coding your data. Just as you want to be able to explain how a code you are using to capture what you see in an excerpt comes from the data, you want to be able to explain how the explanatory schema you are proposing fits your labels. There has to be a clear and plausible fit between your schema and your coded data (represented by the labels) that is evident to others.

Another criterion you should be trying for as you develop your schema is *insightfulness*. You don't want your schema to be an obvious one—one that almost anyone would derive from a quick review of your data. You want to produce new insights and new understandings as a result of your analysis of the data. The obvious schema is likely to have been the first one you developed. That's why we encourage you to keep sorting and rearranging so that you'll come up with an original one.

The final criterion a schema should meet is a strange one, we know, but it's the one that really tells you that it's time to stop sorting and mixing labels and that you have your schema. It's an *ah-ha feeling* you get when the schema you see before you really does explain your data. You really will get the feeling that you've got it. This feeling doesn't tell you that your schema is the right schema because there is no right or wrong schema that explains your data. Any number of different schemas could be developed to explain the same data. What you should feel, though, is that, from your perspective, the schema captures what you are seeing in the data.

That's what happened with Nicki. She saw that the concept of mothering created a very strong schema that explained what was unique in the resistance strategies used in the San Luis Valley. The concept explained both how the resistance persisted even when it didn't accomplish its stated goals and how women, in an otherwise typically patriarchal society, played prominent roles in the resistance. The schema resonated strongly with Nicki's sense of what was going on, even though it was a total surprise to her when she first found it. When you get this ah-ha feeling, it's quite exciting, and our experience is that the feeling will reinvigorate you at a critical time in the dissertation process.

When you do have a working explanatory schema, document it. Put the labels that you've been working with that go together in envelopes and label those envelopes. Sketch out the relationships you see among your labels, just like you did with your first obvious schema. Write down enough so that you won't forget the schema you've seen—the roadmap, in effect, of the decisions and insights you've come to about your data. Note what leads to what among the labels. What starts the process the schema describes? What is the chain of events or actions or ideas that holds the process you are describing together?

When you have your explanatory schema fully developed, create the actual names or terms you will use for the various concepts and relationships of your schema. Choose these explanatory terms carefully because they are both the concepts of your schema and the headings in the write-up of your schema in your findings chapter(s). If possible, give the concepts and the relationships among them terms that are original and not conventional—terms that don't come from existing literature. Certainly, if some part of your schema is a well-known process with a known term, you want to use that term, but not everything in your schema should repeat what is already known. If you have new observations and insights, they should produce new terms. You might come up with terms such as *Victim*, *Supplicant*, and *Director*, for example, for the three major concepts in an explanatory schema about the enactment of agency. Although common words, they have not been used before to describe options concerning agency. Thus, they are new in that no previous theory puts them together in this way.

Also be sure that the terms you devise are parallel in form and abstractness. For example, if you have four strategies of some kind, you might name them all using the gerund form—*Asking, Asserting, Enacting*, and *Appreciating*, for example. You wouldn't want one of these strategies to have the label of *Ask* and another *Appreciating* because the language isn't parallel. Likewise, you don't want to label one concept with something that is very abstract—such as *Asserting*—and another that is very concrete—such as *Enacting the Housekeeper Role*. These two are not at the same level of abstraction. Aim for originality, consistency, and parallelism, then, in the terms of your schema—that will make your theory more sophisticated as well as easy for others to understand and use.

Explanatory Schema Sample #1

Research question: "Why do people continue to tune into local television news broadcasts that cannot compete with the more in-depth war coverage provided by international and national news?"

Viewers feel physical helplessness

    Helplessness associated with inability to physically assist soldiers or war effort

    Helplessness associated with inability to control decision making and outcomes

    Helplessness associated with physical separation from loved one

Local news creates subject positions that address physical

    helplessness

    Booster

    American patriot

Practicing Christian
Family/friend of absent soldier
Viewers feel intellectual helplessness
Helplessness associated with behavioral uncertainty
Helplessness associated with cognitive uncertainty
Local news creates subject positions that address intellectual
helplessness
Responsible viewer
Business (as usual) person
Student
Practicing Christian
Viewers feel emotional helplessness
Helplessness associated with feelings of anger
Helplessness associated with feelings of disappointment
Helplessness associated with feelings of isolation
Helplessness associated with feelings of hopelessness
Helplessness associated with feelings of grief
Helplessness associated with fear of loss of local identity
Local news creates subject positions that address emotional
helplessness
American patriot
(Vicarious) proud parent
Friend/family of absent soldier
Practicing Christian
Communal mourner
Community member[2]

Explanatory Schema Sample #2

Research questions: (1) "How does race shape the ways in which
White teachers conceptualize urban schools, students, and
teaching?" (2) "What role can teacher education play in impact-
ing some of these conceptualizations?"[3]

The Unexamined Whiteness of Teaching

I. BIOGRAPHY

Identity
Religion
Class
White ethnic experience

Experiences
Family influence
Media influence
Sameness
"Help" of color
Early diversity experience

Defining racial incident
Peer influence
Don't know history
Cafeteria/segregation

2. HEGEMONIC UNDERSTANDINGS

Fear	**Deficit schools**	**Stereotypes**	**Whites as victims**
Fear of people of color	Fear of students	Assumptions	Whites: victim of racism
Fear of urban setting	Public/city vs. private/suburban	Stereotypes	Anti-affirmative action
Fear of being minority	Role of parents	Blackness	Americanism/patriotism

3. THE COURSE

Challenge   **Syllabus**

4. TOOLS OF WHITENESS

Emotional	**Ideological**	**Performative**
Anger	Progress	White silence
Defensiveness	Personal vs. institutional	White protection
Guilt	Colorblindness	"I want to help"
Discomfort	Denial of race	Sexualizing
	"Out of my control"	Strategic use of people of color
	"Just be nice"	
	Can't relate	

5. WILL THE CYCLE BE UNBROKEN?

Remain Complicit
Thought it over—feel same
Out of my control
Resistance to multicultural perspectives
Fear of multicultural education
Confronted with racism—do nothing

Act as Agent
"Never thought about it"
"I question"
Reconceptualization of color, race, privilege
Moving toward antiracism
Rethinking parents' attitudes
Transformed educational philosophy
Transform practice: students, social studies

Explanatory Schema Sample #3

Research question: "How do social workers negotiate group purpose in compulsory treatment groups for adolescents with emotional disturbances in therapeutic day schools?"[4]

Impediment of student problems   Impediment of student interactions

Setting
Dealing with Requirement

Students' Purpose for Group   **Social Workers Objectives**
Relationships   Create safety
Positive Regard for group   Create comfort

Facilitators   **Obstacles**   **Facilitators**   **Obstacles**
Sharing leadership Tensions between   Food   Individual students
Student input   clinical and academics   Play   Time demands
    Changing membership   Humor
    Focus on positives
    Social work theories

SKILLS
Self-Management
Coping
Interpersonal

OUTCOMES
Improved self-esteem
Reduced isolation

Writing It Up

You now have an explanatory schema that explains your data and answers your research question. It's summarized on a piece of paper and is represented in envelopes that contain the labels you've been working with to develop the schema. You're almost ready to begin writing up your analysis. But there's one more thing to do first—something that will help make the writing go quickly. Figure out about how long your findings chapter(s) should be. Divide your chapter up according to the categories of your explanatory schema. If your chapter is expected to be 40 pages long, for example, and you have eight major concepts in your explanatory schema, that means you have five pages to write about each concept. Keep that in mind as you figure out how in-depth to go in explaining and supporting the various aspects of your explanatory schema.

You are now ready to write, and you'll be surprised at how easy it is and how quickly it goes. Pick any concept of the schema that you feel like writing about first. You can start anywhere in writing up your schema because you know the whole picture. That's because you know each concept you want to develop and each relationship you want to explain.

Whatever concept you pick is represented by an envelope that contains some of those labels you were playing around with. Let's say the envelope is labeled *PROTECTING* and contains the labels of *ENVIRONMENTAL STEWARDSHIP, PLANNING FOR THE FUTURE, KEEPING THE FAMILY TOGETHER, ADVOCATING FOR THE UNDERDOG,* and *DIRECT CONFRONTATION.* Remember that each of these is the label on an envelope that contains excerpts of coded data. Pick one of the labels—let's say *ENVIRONMENTAL STEWARD-SHIP.* Find that corresponding envelope. Take all the excerpts from that envelope, and lay them out in front of you. Move the excerpts around to play with different ways of arranging them. You are creating a miniexplanatory schema that presents the major ideas you see among the coded data related to that one topic. In other words, do the same thing you did with the labels earlier but on a smaller scale. Arrange the excerpts about environmental stewardship so that they make the argument you want to make about what the data say about that concept.

As you develop the miniexplanatory schema for this one concept of your explanatory schema, you'll discover that some excerpts say the same thing. Group those together and then choose the excerpt that says the idea the best. You'll also discover that some excerpts aren't as relevant or are weak examples of the concept you're discussing. Take those out. What is left when you are done arranging the excerpts from the *ENVIRONMEN-TAL STEWARDSHIP* envelope is a layout in front of you of your coded excerpts on that concept and the order in which you want to talk about them. The example you want to discuss first is at the top of your workspace, the second one next, and so on down through the entire pile of excerpts in the envelope. You have in front of you something that looks like the example below.

When some in the community decided it might be a good idea to have the county open a road through La Sierra: "Why don't we have the county open up a road here and take us all the way to Trinidad?" My dad would say, "You've got to be crazy. You've got to be crazy. We cannot have—we cannot join Trinidad from this side of the mountain. We have to go around." My dad didn't want the county opening up roads to go across those mountains, you know, because it was for pasturing, for the people to enjoy the mountain. It wasn't to be opened up as a major highway, you know. (#6, p. 4)

Sheep were taken up to the mountain only after the cattle. Move the sheep after about three or four days or a week, then they would start another camp and then move it a little bit more. (#3, p. 7)

No fires, no overgrazing. (#9, p. 16)

This message of caring for the natural environment was instilled in the youth. We had to take care of our mountain if we were to have enough food and water in the future. (#3, p. 10)

We were always very, very careful not to—like our trash, we always burned it in a controlled fire. Cans—we used to bury them because a can or bottle, if the sun hits it a certain way, it could start a fire. Like the older bottles, the bottom of the glass, if it heats up, could start a fire. People were always very protective, and they always—even now, they don't like to trash the mountains or any place. They always kept the place very clean. (#3, p. 6)

The mountain has meant a lot to us. We would not destroy any part of it. We took care of it at the same time we used it. (#5, p. 18)

When you have all of the best-coded excerpts arranged in front of you, use the number of pages you have to discuss a concept of your schema to decide roughly how many data excerpts you want to include as evidence for that concept. If you have 10 pages to discuss a concept and 100 excerpts of coded data, that means, first of all, that you can't use all of the pieces of evidence you have to discuss that concept. You'd have to cover 10 pieces of evidence or 10 of the excerpts of coded data per page. You can't do that and do an analysis of the data at the same time. Your analysis of your coded data and not the amount of data you cite is what produces an insightful analysis. Too much support for a claim about a concept makes it easy for readers to lose track of your argument. Select the appropriate number of the coded excerpts that best tell the story of your concept. This means you'll pull some of the excerpts out of your line-up so you have the best ones that make your argument in the space that you have.

Now comes the magical part because your explanatory schema almost writes itself. Begin by writing a one-paragraph introduction that talks about the function or significance of all the data excerpts together that support or explain a concept. Then introduce your first excerpt and quote it. Follow this with an analysis that relates the excerpt back to what you said its function in the section is. Give a couple more examples using the next excerpts in your line-up. Follow those with analysis as well.

Don't just list several of your data excerpts in a row and leave them at that with nothing of yourself and your analysis inserted. You've seen this done in some dissertations and articles—where the data are floating out in the middle of the text in a column. The quotes are just plopped into the text with no discussion of how the author sees them functioning to make the argument that is the explanatory schema. You want to drive the analysis, so feature what *you* are doing with the excerpts as you write them up. The excerpts are examples of or evidence to support the story that you are telling about the data, but they aren't the story itself. That has to come from you.

Repeat the process until you've told the story—presented your claims about and evidence for all of the concepts and relationships of your schema. You might even want to include a diagram that summarizes visually the various elements of your explanatory schema—your concepts and the relationships among them.

You'll notice how easy it is to organize your findings chapter(s) using this system. The major concepts and relationships of your explanatory schema become the headings of your chapters. Subtopics within the concepts become the subheadings of your chapters. Each heading and subheading is followed by a short introduction to that section, which is followed by a claim about how the excerpts that follow are functioning. This is followed by quoted examples from the excerpts, which in turn are followed by analysis that relates those quoted excerpts back to the first claim. You have to do very little thinking during the writing process because you've worked out everything in the various levels of sorting you've just completed. The writing is simply reporting and supporting the explanatory schema you developed.

Are you beginning to see how easily and quickly you can write up your findings chapter(s) using this system? You always know exactly where you are in a section of the chapter. The next data slip with which you want to deal is right there in front of you, physical and tactile, prompting you to keep writing. You can carry an envelope of coded excerpts with you and write through that envelope when you have even just a few minutes of free time. Starting and stopping aren't problems either because you have the big picture. When you've written through the excerpts in all of your envelopes, you're done with a draft of the findings or analysis chapter(s). As you work your way through your data and your schema—as you explain the major sites you visited on your journey—your awareness that you have something new to say propels you forward with anticipation to the next stage of your trip.

Notes

1. Constructed from conversations with Nicki M. Gonzales about her dissertation, as yet untitled (PhD diss., University of Colorado, forthcoming).

2. Wendy Hilton-Morrow, "Local News, National Story: Television's Construction of Viewer Subject Positions during the Iraq War" (PhD diss., University of Iowa, 2005).

3. Constructed from the dissertation of Bree Picower, "The Unexamined Whiteness of Teaching: Will the Cycle Be Unbroken?" (EdD diss., New York University, 2007).

4. Constructed from conversations with Francis S. Bartolomeo about his dissertation, tentatively titled "Group Work with Adolescents in Therapeutic Day Schools: Negotiating Group Purpose with Nonvoluntary Clients" (PhD diss., Simmons College, forthcoming).

CHAPTER EIGHT
MAKING THE MOST OF YOUR TRAVELS: THE LAST CHAPTER PLUS

Steps 19–20 (25 hours)

Your trip is nearing its end. You begin to look homeward, anticipating your return to a familiar routine but a bit disappointed, too, that the journey is coming to a close. You begin to reflect on what you enjoyed most, what you learned, and what you plan to do differently in future travels. These kinds of reflections mark the final chapter of the dissertation.

If you're like most students, when you get to the last chapter, you're completely spent. You feel like you have no new ideas to offer and that you simply can't muster up the brain power to write another word. You're probably also thinking, "After reading the dissertation, won't readers know what the conclusion is? Can't they figure that out for themselves?" We know that this last chapter can be tough when you're so ready to be done. But you know how we're going to respond to your pleas: Regardless of your current condition, you do indeed have to write one more chapter, and you want to make good use of it to direct readers to *your* conclusions—to offer them the insights *you* are seeing.

There are two things about this last chapter that might motivate you to get going on it: It's a very important chapter, and it's short. Why is this last chapter so important? For a couple of reasons. One is that many readers will only read the last chapter of your dissertation because it provides them with the answer to your research question and the implications that follow from that answer. This last chapter, then, is your chance to present the key details of your study in a way that is useful to these readers. It's also the place where you make your contribution to a conversation in your discipline using your findings. What you do with your findings here is really the reason you undertook your study, so you want to showcase your insights. But just because it's important doesn't mean this chapter has to be long. You presented and discussed the nuances of your key findings earlier. Now you have to interpret them or do something with them, but this doesn't require all that many pages.

There are four sections of your final chapter: summary, interpretation, limitations, and suggestions for future research. Final chapters are usually about 15 pages long, which means that none of these sections takes that long to write. We think you can write the whole chapter in 20 hours—a weekend. And once you dive in, you'll get energized and will be surprised at how quickly you finish this final reflection on your journey. Ready to get started? Let's take a look at what should happen in each section.

Summary

Begin your last chapter with a summary of your study. Because some people are only going to read this chapter, you want to summarize your study here. Tell readers what your research question was, the data you chose for your study, how you collected and analyzed the data, and what your major findings were. You can probably summarize your study in three or four pages.

Summary Sample #1

The purpose of this study was to discover how a viewer formulates a message from a building. Stephen Toulmin's model of argument was used as the starting point for the formulation of a method to discover how this process occurs. The model includes two components relevant to the assessment of architecture—the grounds (physical or presented elements of the building) and a claim (a message a viewer could derive from the physical structure of the building). To discover the movement or process between viewers' observations of the physical features of a building and the claim they might infer from those features—what Toulmin labels the *warrant*—three buildings designed by Michael

Graves were analyzed. The buildings analyzed were: the Portland Public Service Building in Portland, Oregon; the San Juan Capistrano Regional Library in San Juan Capistrano, California; and the Humana Building in Louisville, Kentucky. For each building, I noted the presented or physical elements of the building, identified where those elements could lead the viewer in terms of themes and references, and formulated a claim that might be reached as a result.

In my analysis of the Portland Public Service Building, I discovered the following major presented elements: columns, ceramic tiles, colors, concrete, gypsum board, geometric shapes, windows, square cut-out spaces, lighting, security station, information booth and concession stand, seal of Portland, layering of spaces, molding, stenciled wall patterns, models of Portlandia and the Portland Building, and the lounge area. I determined that the presented elements, in turn, suggested the following ideas, concepts, and themes: order, strength, regularity, informality, sensuality, romance, delicateness, permanence and stability, flatness, ribbons and garlands, uniformity, monotony, welcome, enduring qualities of government, theatre gallery boxes, a stage, portraits of city officials, ticket sellers, bounty, infinite regression of space, animation, decoration, gaiety, vision, an ideal, stage lighting, theatre lighting, and smoked-filled rooms of crooked politicians.

I then sought patterns in those qualities and found that the suggested elements grouped into categories of theatricality, celebration, anthropomorphism, routinization, dysfunction, and inconsistency. These categories were classified into two broader groups. The categories of theatricality, celebration, and anthropomorphism seemed to indicate qualities that were lively and creative, while the categories of routinization, dysfunction, and inconsistency evidenced boring and habitual qualities. Once a viewer recognizes these groups, the formulation of the message—the contrast between actual and real city government, the bureaucratization of the imaginative—is likely to follow.

In chapter two, which was my exploration of the San Juan Capistrano Library, I discovered the following presented elements: color, columns and pillars, diagonal lines, windows, geometric shapes, towers, stucco, gazebos, flora, courtyard, wood, layering of spaces, small spaces, large spaces, furniture, and lighting. The suggested elements inferred from the presented physical features included: sensuality, relaxation, romance, uniformity, order, formality, Christian symbols in the cross and water, seclusion and remoteness, sun porches, garden rooms, ethereal qualities, animation, playfulness, whimsy, enduring qualities, celebrations, intimacy and privacy, quiet repose, Spanish monasteries, artistry, endless regression of spaces, intrigue, community, church-like qualities, informality, and softness.

After reviewing the list of suggested elements, I found that they organized into the following categories: contemplation, ceremony, spirituality, mystery, fantasy, romance, and homeyness. In an effort to formulate a message from these contradictory themes, the viewer may apply a metaphorical framework that structures the themes as genres or narrative plot lines. Seen in this context, the elements are no longer paradoxical but complementary of one another. A possible message the viewer may formulate is that library patrons are encouraged to discover alternative "life stories" or plot lines for their lives.

The final building I analyzed was the Humana Building. I identified the following as the major presented elements: granite, scale, building shape, top of building, rounded shaft, columns, water, glass panels, vertical lines, crossed lines, truss, parking garage, lobby rotunda, information station, art works, wood, and various elements found on the 25th floor. The suggested elements inferred from the presented elements were: permanence, durability, wealth, grandeur, tombstones, cash register, ziggurat, Greek and Roman burial temples, memorial column, order, ceremony, decorum, sustenance, purification, flags hung in mourning, crosses, hidden and secretive entrances, cathedral qualities, the Pantheon, grave markings, burial grounds or cemeteries, tombs, mausoleum, caretakers, treasures, coffins, stately home or mansion, outdoor plaza, ballroom, and a church.

As in the previous analyses, I sought patterns and relationships among the suggested elements and discovered that they grouped into the categories of death and wealth. To move from the organization of the suggested elements to the construction of a message, the viewer is likely to transfer the suggested elements that cluster around the categories of death and wealth back to the Humana Corporation, linking Humana to those qualities by way of metaphor. The interaction between the metaphors of death and wealth encourages the viewer to formulate a message that characterizes the Humana Building as a memorial to those who have suffered or died because of a system of health care that emphasizes profit over charity.

As a result of my analyses of the buildings, using Toulmin's layout of argument as a starting point, I created a three-step procedure for discovering how a viewer formulates a message from a building. In the first step, a viewer discovers the various presented elements that characterize a building. The presented elements are the major physical features observed by the viewer.

The second step involves processing or orchestrating the elements observed and occurs in two stages. In the first stage, the viewer makes inferences about what the presented elements suggest. The suggested elements reveal a variety of themes, ideas, concepts, images, qualities, and references a viewer might make from the presented elements. In the second stage, the viewer organizes the various suggested elements. Here, viewers look for the similarities, differences, and interactive possibilities among the suggested elements. These categories then become bridges to clues that allow the viewer to proceed to the naming of a message from the building. The third step of the method involves identification of a message a viewer may formulate from a building as a result of the previous two steps.[1]

Summary Sample #2

Given the fervent cries for civility from politicians, religious leaders, and social critics and the seemingly increasing popularity of this discourse within popular culture, I became interested in learning more about the nature and function of uncivil discourse, particularly as it occurs in popular humorous texts. I wondered if uncivil discourse provides some sort of benefit to its audience not obvious through casual observation. Therefore, my specific purpose within this study was to discover, describe, and understand a rhetoric of incivility, particularly as it occurs in contexts of humor.

To answer my research question, I used the method of generic criticism because it allows the critic ways of looking at texts to discover rhetorical trends that occur through similar rhetorical situations. Generic criticism allows the critic to understand the "dynamic within the rhetorical acts of human beings" and how rhetors respond "in similar ways as they attempt to encompass certain rhetorical problems . . ." (Campbell and Jamieson *Form* 21). To practice generic criticism, the critic groups the artifacts according to similarities so that a rhetorical genre is a clustering of three different kinds of elements—the rhetorical situation, substantive and stylistic features, and the organizing principle. Situational requirements are those situations that provoke a particular type of rhetoric. The substantive and stylistic features of the rhetoric are the rhetorical choices made by the rhetor concerning how to respond to the requirements of a given situation. The organizing principle is the label for the internal schematic formed by the situational, substantive, and stylistic features of the genre.

In selecting rhetorical texts to be included in this research, I applied four criteria. All the texts were situated within the broad category of popular culture, were humorous, represented a variety of verbal and visual forms, and were popular. Based on these criteria, I selected the television shows *Seinfeld* and *Beavis and Butt-Head* and the radio and television versions of *The Howard Stern Show* as the data for this study. Specifically, I analyzed 13 episodes of *Seinfeld*, 12 of *Beavis and Butt-Head*, and five radio broadcasts of *The Howard Stern Show* and four episodes of the television version. For each text, I examined and analyzed the rhetorical situation or exigence for the discourse, its substantive and stylistic features, and its organizing principle.

In this final chapter, I synthesize and analyze the data discussed in the previous three chapters and use the analysis to develop a theory of the genre of humorous incivility to answer my research question. Before proceeding, however, I briefly will summarize the analysis of the shows, identifying their rhetorical situations, substantive and stylistic features, and organizing principles.

The exigence for *Seinfeld* was that of smart comedy. The show was trying to appeal to an educated and sophisticated segment of the baby-boom generation. This audience, presumably tired of and too sophisticated for the more predictable comedic formulas of traditional sitcoms, wanted something new to reflect its lifestyle. Given the demand for advertising dollars, its desire was met. *Seinfeld* responded and situated itself as a smart comedy through the creation of characters to which the audience could relate and through humor that arose from mundane situations. This was a radical departure from the traditional sitcom that inserts one-line jokes into a basic situation that is repeated weekly.

The substantive and stylistic characteristics of this show are lack of employment of the main characters; application of childhood logic, concerns, and communication styles; children's food; the blurring of fantasy and reality; bodily functions; joking about adult concerns and lives; lack of adult relationships; prominence of childhood games; prominence of toys; use of adult technology for play; lack of meaning accorded to prices of goods; insider expressions; and the idealized childhood home. Together, these features suggest that the organizing principle for *Seinfeld* is children's play.

The organizing principle of children's play on *Seinfeld* is exemplified in the multiple ways in which the four main characters—Jerry, George, Kramer, and Elaine—react to the mundane situations in which they find themselves weekly. All of the male characters, for example, demonstrate an aversion to conventional adult employment: Jerry avoids it by being a stand-up comedian, George frequently changes careers and selects jobs requiring minimal effort, and Kramer avoids employment altogether. The characters make numerous references to superheroes and often apply childhood experiences and logic to solving adult problems. Technology is rarely used for its original intent but is adapted instead for the purpose of play. By creating this playground complete with toys, games, and children's food, the audience is drawn into a world where life was less work and less complicated.

The exigence for *Beavis and Butt-Head* reflects a transition in both the music-video business and the television network built on this industry—notably, MTV's transition from an all-video channel to one where few videos are played. Moreover, the main role assumed by Beavis and Butt-Head is to offer a tired and blasé critique of the videos—also a reflection of the public's attitude toward videos and their declining popularity.

The substantive and stylistic features specific to this show are the prominence of television; cultural references; references to violence; dumb, obvious, or wrong statements; images of women as sexual objects; bodily functions; references to unlawful behavior; men as caricatures; insider expressions; children's food; and work as play. All of these characteristics suggest an organizing principle of the anti-family for *Beavis and Butt-Head*.

The anti-family is created through the use of two strategies: oppositional characterization and symbolic orphans. Oppositional characterization allows the construction of these characters as a direct inversion to characters within the traditional family television genre. For example, the name *Beavis* recalls for viewers a similarly named character, *Beaver*—featured on a show that was the prototype of the family genre. By creating the characters as symbolic orphans, free from parental or adult guidance, a space is created where the characters and, by extension, the audience are freed from control, rules, or limitations.

The final text I studied was *The Howard Stern Show*, both in its radio and television versions. The exigence for Stern's show is the need to stand out among the competition. The plethora of current talk shows and news shows in the present market makes success difficult to achieve.

Therefore, the host or the show needs to be unique in some fashion. Stern's brand of uniqueness is manifest in his name *shock jock*.

Analyzing Stern's discourse, I discovered the following substantive and stylistic characteristics: violation of norms of civility; exertion of power and dominance; encouraging illegal acts; humiliation of others; images of women as sex objects; contradictions; and a rough, raw appearance. Together, these characteristics create the organizing principle of men in beer groups.

Stern, his crew, the guests on his show, and the callers talk as if they were in the context of a bar. The talk is crude, rough, and unpolished and often violates the norms of civility found in more public, institutional settings. Women are kept outside of the groups and are referenced in sexual or derogatory terms. The men within the groups are privileged, and those outside are ridiculed, teased, or humiliated. The type of power that characterizes this group is that of dominance and power-over. This perspective on Stern suggests the presence of a separate space—a space away from the rules and norms of mainstream, professional, or institutional discourse. By creating the context as men in beer groups, Stern provides his audience with an alternative space for discourse. I now will explain the genre of humorous incivility and how it can be utilized to explain the appeal of these three shows.[2]

Interpretation of Findings

The second section of your final chapter is the most important. This is where you interpret your findings to make a contribution to your discipline. You want to answer the question "so what?" about your earlier analysis of your data. In this section, you're supposed to "do something" with or transcend your findings. What exactly does that mean?

One way to conceptualize the function of this section is to think of it as a place where you move from the specific to the general. Until now, your dissertation has been moving from the general to the specific. You began by asking an abstract research question about a general concept or phenomenon and ended with specific findings. If you asked a question, for example, about how parents transmit political beliefs to their children, your analysis produced some ideas about the specific mechanisms that parents use. That's what you talked about in your analysis chapter or chapters.

Now you want to reverse direction and move from the specific to the general—from your specific data set and your particular findings to something larger. You want to transcend the specifics of the answer that is rooted in your findings.

What might this "something larger" be? A number of possibilities are available for interpreting your findings. One is to lay out a theory that results from your findings. If your dissertation was one where you analyzed different artifacts, each in a different chapter, the easiest way to create a theory is to put all your analyses together and to develop a theory across them. Look for patterns of similarity or difference across your findings about the different artifacts, and make those patterns into a theory that conceptualizes a process or a phenomenon as a whole.

You can also come up with a theory if you used only one data set or one artifact in your study. Your presentation of your findings in your analysis chapter(s) was a schema about your particular data. One option in your last chapter is to make that schema into a theory by laying out the concepts and relationship in more abstract terms. Let's say you analyzed a film to discover the conception of agency it offers. In your schema of the findings, you laid out what you found out about different ways of enacting agency in the film. In your last chapter, theorize ways of enacting agency in general that may apply to contexts other than that one film. In other words, transcend your specific data and talk more generally and more theoretically about the phenomenon you have been studying.

You can also develop a theory by creating a list of theoretical propositions or hypotheses from your findings that need to be tested. This is a particularly effective way to interpret your findings if you used grounded theory as your method of data analysis. This method is designed to generate propositions that function as hypotheses that can be tested in future research projects. Clearly laying out what the theoretical propositions are that derive from your findings can be an easy route to interpretation.

Perhaps we should pause here for a moment and talk about that word *theory*. Yes, you really are qualified to create and present a theory in this last chapter. If you're like many students, when you hear that you can or should formulate a theory at this point, you get a bit skeptical or even fearful. You might be thinking that you're not at the stage of your career where you have the right to generate a new theory.

A couple of things might change your mind about this. One is that a theory isn't something that has to be complex and at such a high level of sophistication that you can't create one. It has just two elements—concepts (or variables) and relationships among the concepts (or axioms). In other words, a theory identifies some things that it's about, and it also says something about the relationships among those things. A second thing to remember is that you generate theories all the time. Let's say you call a friend five days in a row and leave messages for her to call you back, but she never does. You develop a theory as a result of these data and your analysis of them. You might theorize that she isn't interested in being your friend anymore, for example. The same is true for your dissertation. You know some things as a result of your analysis that can become the tenets of a theory, so identify them and create a theory out of them.

But creating a theory isn't your only option for interpreting your findings. Another is to relate the schema of your findings to the previous literature. Remember that literature review you did at the start of the dissertation process? Referring back to it will generate ideas for interpreting your findings. How do your findings align with that literature? Did you confirm that earlier literature? Extend it in some way? Contradict it? Can you use your findings to propose a new theoretical explanation that differs from what earlier studies proposed? Can you explain why your findings are different from previous ones? When referring back to the literature, remember to begin with your insights and then make the connections from your ideas to the literature, rather than the other way around. If you begin by emphasizing what the literature says and then follow that with some kind of agreement or disagreement with your findings, you diminish the impact of your findings and weaken your voice. Begin by restating and featuring your findings and then allow the literature to support or challenge them.

You have other options, too, for interpreting your findings. Review why you said your study would be significant. Can you transform those reasons into an interpretation of your findings? In other words, can you use a rationale for significance as a prompt to use your findings in some way? For example, if you said in your first chapter that your dissertation would help sort out the relationship among feminism, the feminine, and aesthetics, you can discuss the relationship among these that is suggested by your findings. In other words, show your readers that your study contributes what you said it would.

Another way to interpret your findings is to discuss the implications of your findings for one or more major conversations in your discipline. Perhaps your findings encourage a new way of conceptualizing a construct or a phenomenon. Maybe they challenge conventional understandings of a phenomenon. Or they might suggest new directions for theorizing. In this option, you suggest some ways in which your findings might have an impact on theorizing in your field.

And don't forget about application as an option for the interpretation of your findings. Are there ways you can suggest that your findings be applied? Can they help solve a particular problem or create a best practice? Use your expertise about the phenomenon and your knowledge of real world problems to propose some ways in which how what you discovered might be applied. Make recommendations for ways to do something better.

The interpretation section of the last chapter is the most important one. It's what enables you to enter the conversation in your field around your topic, and it allows your findings to become relevant to more than just the participants, organizations, or data of your particular study. This section is usually in the range of 7 to 15 pages long, depending on which option for interpretation you select and the nature of your data and findings.

Interpretation of Findings Sample #1

Several contributions to rhetorical theory grow out of Hannah Arendt's speech perspective. Some of these are readily placed within debates on issues that traditionally have been associated with the study of rhetoric. Others augment rhetorical theory by offering new constructs or new perspectives on traditional constructs. Arendt's primary contributions to rhetorical theory lie in the areas of speech vs. writing, rhetoric as epistemic, the rhetorical situation, the rehabilitation of public discourse, the essence of humanness, and the focus of her theory.

Speech vs. Writing

One of the ancient debates in rhetorical theory is over the supremacy of orality or literacy. With her notion of reification, Arendt offers the basis for a rapprochement between speech and writing, between orality and literacy. Although reification is necessary for a thought to become a thing, in her view, it is inferior to speech mainly because there is a price to be paid for it: "it is always the 'dead letter' in which the 'living spirit' must survive."[2]

At the same time, however, Arendt sees writing as vital to memory "because remembrance and the gift of recollection, from which all desire for imperishability springs, need tangible things to remind them, lest they perish themselves."[3] She cites the example of poetry, which, because it takes its form so much from the rhythm of language, has a closeness "to living recollection that enables the poem to remain, to retain its durability, outside the printed or the written page, and though the 'quality' of a poem may be subject to a variety of standards, its 'memorability' will inevitably determine its durability, that is, its chance to be permanently fixed in the recollection of humanity."[4]

In poetic language, speaking and writing appear to be interdependent or complementary in their relationship. But the larger principle here pertains to more than just the endurance of a pattern of words. Arendt shows how the interdependency of speaking and writing provides the sustenance for the endurance of culture.

Rhetoric as Epistemic

A second debate to which Arendt's speech perspective contributes is that concerning the nature of rhetoric as epistemic. Arendt's contribution to the debate on rhetoric as epistemic focuses on the role of human mental experience and its link to the presentation of the human in speech and action.[5] She does not deal with the actual process of symbolization as it is involved in the creation of reality.[6] Her potential contribution to the debate rests on her notion of intersubjectivity, which is not the sharing by humans of the same perspective on an object but the same object being sensed and the "same sensual equipment" being used by humans to sense it.

Another of Arendt's notions that has pertinence to the idea of intersubjectivity is her view of language. She views language as a bridge between the world of appearances—objective reality—and the world of being—subjective reality: "Language, by lending itself to metaphorical usage, enables us to think, that is, to have traffic with non-sensory matters, because it permits a carrying-over, *metapherein*, of our sense experiences."[7] The connection of the inner and outer world through language suggests, for Arendt, that "no speechless thought can exist" and that the mind is "geared to the world of appearances."[8] Because of the function of language in thought and its constitution as a system of symbols that we all use, the meaning of our world is shared.

Arendt's notions of intersubjectivity and language clearly place her in the discussion about the relationship between rhetoric and knowledge. But she seems to have a foot on both sides of the rhetoric-as-epistemic question. On the one hand, she seems to side with those scholars in the debate, such as Robert Scott and Barry Brummett, who argue that humans apprehend sense data by symbolic processes; hence, "reality" is constructed by humans, in concert, as they transform sense data into symbolic, intelligible experience. Her similarity to the view of Scott and others can be seen in the contention that our individual assurance that such a reality exists is confirmed in the communication we have with others.

On the other hand, Arendt seems also to side with those scholars, such as Richard Cherwitz, James Hikins, and Earl Croasmun, who suggest that reality exists independently of human experience but is accessible to humans; truth is correspondence to reality. Arendt suggests that an independent tangible reality obviously exists and that our knowledge of it arises through the senses and is transformed with the aid of language into images that become the substance of thought.

Through Arendt's interpretation of the existentialist perspective, with which she seems to agree, the two sides of the rhetoric-as-epistemic debate are combined. The existentialist perspective, as advocated by Gotthold Ephraim Lessing and Karl Jaspers, insists on the inseparability of truth and communication: "[T]ruth can exist only where it is humanized by discourse."[9] By this they mean that the dogmatic claims of any view would be dissolved by the criterion of what is "universally communicative."[10] The kind of truth conceived of here is a truth that binds us together rather than one that splits us apart. However, the additional qualification Arendt emphasizes with regard to this concept of truth is not the obliteration of differences among individuals and cultures in uniformity but the recognition and allowance of such differences, combined with a "will to limitless communication": "The unity of mankind and its solidarity cannot consist in a universal agreement upon one religion, or one philosophy, or one form of government, but in the faith that the manifold points to a Oneness which diversity conceals and reveals at the same time."[11]

In short, Arendt agrees with one view that the world of human affairs is contingent and that speech is necessary in order for truth to exist. She also agrees with the other view that there exists a reality that is knowable. Given the complexity of the issues in the epistemic debate, a more detailed examination of Arendt's ideas and how they might extend, resolve, or integrate the various positions would be appropriate.

The Rhetorical Situation

Another debate among rhetorical theorists for which Arendt has relevance is that regarding the rhetorical situation. Much of the debate surrounding this theory seems to be concerned with the nature of the rhetorical situation and particularly the issue of who or what controls meaning. Richard Vatz interprets Lloyd Bitzer to say that meaning resides in objects, people, and events themselves. Vatz disagrees, claiming that, in most cases, we learn of facts and events when a rhetor communicates them to us, thereby creating meaning. Scott Consigny attempts to take a middle ground between Bitzer and Vatz by arguing that meaning is partly created by the rhetor and partly determined by the situational constraints.[12]

Arendt's speech perspective, as it incorporates the notion of *sensus communis*, adds clarity and insight to this debate. Her perspective features the community rather than the situation or the individual rhetor as the ground of meaning. All three authors—Bitzer, Vatz, and Consigny—place emphasis on the individual rhetor in assessing and acting in a particular situation.

Arendt might say that the interpretation of the meaning of situations arises in a *sensus communis*, the community sense, that puts one's sensate perceptions into the context of one's community. *Sensus communis*, then, functions as a kind of community hermeneutic for interpreting the meaning of various phenomena. Arendt's view would allow for individuals to have differing perspectives about the meaning of an object, person, or event; the difference, in Bitzer's terms, would "invite utterance."[13]

In Arendt's public realm, individuals manifest their unique distinctness to each other in speech and action. She argues that individuals are called out of their plurality by mutual interests—the tangible things that exist between them, such as the environment—as well as by the intangible aspects of human life, such as freedom and justice. The recognition of their paradoxical existence as different and yet the same evokes the activity of speech from individuals as they engage in discourse about the meaning of their world.

The Rehabilitation of Public Discourse

Arendt also offers a view that helps us reexamine public discourse to assess its value and viability in contemporary mass society. Arendt offers two ways in which political rhetoric can and should be improved. The first is by combining speech and action; for her, problems arise primarily when action is performed without speech. To claim that public discourse can be rehabilitated is to imply that something is wrong with it. One of the main problems Arendt addresses is the separation of speech and action in public discourse. The term *rhetoric*, in popular usage, carries with it a great deal of negative baggage. One of the most common assumptions is that rhetoric is all talk and no action. Arendt argues that speech and action, as the two supreme human capacities, are meant to be together. She often reads one into the other. From her book on the human condition, one easily could get the idea that her main concern is with action because she subsumes speech under that division. However, such a conclusion is inaccurate because she clearly states that action and speech are coeval and coequal. An even stronger statement appears later when she states that action is meaningless without speech.

Arendt offers suggestions, then, about how public discourse should be improved by describing how speech and action ought to be united. Her view also has implications for how we think of speech and its role in our age. If it is the definitive characteristic of politics, much more emphasis should be placed upon its responsible development.

A second way in which public discourse should be rehabilitated concerns the education and development of those who participate in the public realm. Her focus is on the cultivation of speech in those who will be a part of the public discourse. In *Eloquence in an Electronic Age*, Kathleen Hall Jamieson points out that speech cannot flourish in a society in which it cannot be practiced. [14] Thus, more focus needs to be placed on the development of the individual not only to speak up but to become more involved. Jamieson provides, then, a rationale and theory for speech education as well as argumentation theory. The relevance of political speech for most individuals is minimal in a mass society like our own. Arendt advocates the necessity of viable and relevant speech by a greater number of people about affairs that have an impact on their lives; without such participation, individuals are alienated.

The Essence of Humanness

Another contribution to rhetorical theory is that Arendt adds to the meaning of the essence of humanness. She does this in two ways. First, she argues that instead of taking a view of life that features the end of humans, she suggests we take a view of life that features the beginnings of which humans are capable. In other words, rather than focusing on our mortality, she suggests we focus on natality as one of the distinctive features of humans. Because we are unique beings by virtue of our birth, she argues, we are capable of creating new beginnings. Her focus complements the work of other scholars, such as Kenneth Burke, who are interested in the human being as rhetor.

A second way in which Arendt contributes to our understanding of the essence of humanness is through her explanation of speech as finding its highest value not in its function as a tool or an instrument that is used to achieve another purpose but in its function in the manifestation of an individual's identity. Thus, the end of speech lies in the very act of speaking itself because it is the revelation of the individual. In singling out "speech as the decisive distinction between human and animal life,"[15] Arendt is not saying simply that it is merely the tool of a more advanced animal; rather, speech is the ontological characteristic that distinguishes humans from other animals.

The combination of these two characteristics of human essence, the notion of natality and speech as an end in itself, has obvious implications for the area of ethics. What is said or left unsaid, as the manifestation of a person's character, can trigger chains of consequences that last for decades, if not centuries. For example, one might quip "And Brutus is an honorable man"—a statement that, for some time to come, will carry the meaning that someone's will to power may have no ethical bounds. These characteristics of the essence of humanness also add more depth and detail to the ontological study of rhetorical theory.

Focus of Arendt's Theory

One of the unusual features of Arendt's speech perspective is that, while the ultimate goal of her theory carries the common political implications of people held together in a community, it places uncommon emphasis on the mental processes of the individual in that community. Most rhetorical theory seems to deal with external dimensions of the communication situation—symbol, message, audience, and situation. Arendt, in contrast, explains how humans function mentally in such a way as to anticipate and prepare for speaking and acting. Her work thus represents a complement to work on the manifestations of mental processes in rhetoric by focusing on the mental processes themselves.[3]

Interpretation of Findings Sample #2

Five years ago, as I was reading Ywahoo's *Voices of Our Ancestors*, I began to think that the rhetorical theory that I was studying at the time was not helping me to understand how the rituals in the text were working as rhetorical artifacts. I remember feeling very moved and very disturbed that I could not explain those feelings. Five years later, as I am writing this concluding chapter, I am beginning to understand how the rituals created by Dhyani—and now Starhawk and Shakti—work and why they affected me. Through this analysis, I have discovered several insights into the functioning of these rituals.

Although I had recognized each rhetor as seeking a type of cultural change, through genre analysis, I discovered the nature of that change. I came to recognize each rhetor as seeking a physically and spiritually nonviolent, intrapersonal, and interpersonal rhetoric that would enable individuals to dissolve internal and external barriers to an integrated, harmonious consciousness of body, spirit, self, world outside of self, and power. Thus, I came to realize that, although they were seeking cultural transformation, the transformation they sought was a *process* of transformation rather than any specific product.

In examining the rhetorical elements that the rhetors employed, I found that each woman uses both objects and concepts from the personal, cosmic, and symbolic realms in embodied, dramatic, ludic, mystical, interrogative, and non-oppositional ways. Moreover, I realized that, in doing so, each rhetor has created rituals that enable her participants to enact a reorientation in their consciousness—to create or remember different understandings of symbolic elements, embrace a multidimensional reality, and achieve transformation within their bodies.

Finally, through writing this analysis, I also have discovered that I was correct five years ago in my assessment that the rhetorical theory I was studying at that time could not account for the functioning of these rituals. To account for the symbolic effectiveness of the rituals of this study, several rhetorical constructs had to be reconceptualized. I turn now to examine those constructs and to suggest the implications that these reconceptualizations have for rhetorical theory.

As a result of this study, I see at least six aspects of rhetorical theory that are challenged by these rituals and that need to be reconceptualized to account for the symbolic effectiveness of the rhetoric of reorientation. First and perhaps most obvious, this study reconceptualizes notions of social change that traditionally have been accepted in rhetorical theory.

In contrast to conceptions of social change rhetoric as violent, confrontational, or agitational, the non-confrontational, non-engaging, intrapersonal, and enacted or embodied strategies that Starhawk, Shakti, and Dhyani employ in their rituals were previously unrecognized in rhetorical theory. As a result, such strategies were unaccounted for by previous conceptions of how the rhetoric of social change works. Within this study, then, I have suggested alternative strategies for engendering cultural transformation through personal transformation—physically and spiritually non-violent intrapersonal strategies that allow transformation within the consciousness of the participant.

A second aspect of rhetorical theory reconceptualized by this study is the previously dichotomous categorization of rhetorical texts as either sacred or profane. Insofar as they enact secular personal and cultural transformation through spiritual praxis, the rituals studied here seem to function as both at the same time. As a result, spirituality is reintroduced into the study of secular rhetoric, a reintroduction that, in turn, reconceptualizes understandings of artistic proofs. For example, religious studies scholar Charlene Spretnak has argued that "consciousness can be fed from arational as well as rational sources, and women's rituals have emerged as a channel for that nourishment" (162). Given such a realization, *logos* must be reconceptualized to include arational proofs such as multivocal symbols, *ethos* must be expanded to include immanent value, and *pathos* must be stretched to incorporate mystery. Ultimately, such reconceptualizations may lead us to question even these very categories of proofs.

Once spirituality is reintroduced into the study of secular rhetoric, we must ask how the spiritual dimensions of this rhetoric are working—or not working—to enable the world that feminist rhetors are seeking to create. Anthropologist Mary Catherine Bateson has addressed this issue in *Composing a Life*, where she argues that "millennia of monotheism have made us idealize" a single conception of "the good" (166). Bateson asks, however, "what if we were to recognize the capacity for distraction, the divided will, as representing a higher wisdom" (166)? "Instead of concentration on a transcendent ideal," she suggests that "sustained attention to diversity and interdependence may offer a different clarity of vision, one that is sensitive to ecological complexity, to the multiple rather than the singular" (166). Again, then, reconceptualizing secular rhetoric to include an awareness of its spiritual or sacred dimension and suggesting some of the implications of this dimension are important contributions of this study to rhetorical theory.

A third implication of this study relates to the assumptions that traditionally have served as the theoretical framework upon which studies using genre criticism have been built. In my previous discussion of method, I noted that both Lloyd Bitzer and Edwin Black had written important theoretical works that lent support to this method early in the history of its use. Both Bitzer and Black, however, hold an assumption called into question by this study. Both assume that "there is a limited number of situations in which a rhetor can find himself" and that "there is a limited number of ways in which a rhetor can and will respond rhetorically to any given situational type" (Black 133). This study challenges that assumption by recognizing the power of the rhetor to define and redefine any situation in new and previously unconceived ways. Perhaps under certain circumstances, both the number of rhetorical situations and the number of possible responses to those situations may explode such that an infinite number of situations and responses are possible.

The possibility of an unlimited number of rhetorical situations does not undercut the rationale for using genre criticism in this study, however, because situations still may recur. Recognizing that an unlimited number of rhetorical situations is possible in no way implies that every situation is unique. Consequently, a study of a recurrent rhetorical situation still would "provide the critic with information on the rhetorical responses available in that situation" (Black 133). Moreover, this information still would allow the critic "to better understand and evaluate any specific rhetorical discourse in which he may be interested" (Black 133). The implication, then, is that the assumptions supporting the use of genre criticism need to be reconceptualized—not that genre criticism should be abandoned as a method of rhetorical analysis.

A fourth potential reconceptualization suggested as a result of this study involves the divisions that traditionally have existed within the field of communication among the study of intrapersonal communication, interpersonal communication, small group communication, and rhetoric. The rituals within this study seem to dissolve those boundaries and, in fact, suggest that the boundaries are unnecessarily limiting and prevent us from studying certain types of communication that fall between the divisions.

A fifth area of rhetorical theory that I have begun to question as a result of this study is the rhetorical canons. For example, arrangement, as it traditionally has been conceptualized as fixed or pregiven, is nearly nonexistent in these rituals because all steps of reorientation occur virtually simultaneously. Memory, on the other hand, becomes far more important than it has been recognized as being in the rhetorics that are traditionally studied. In fact, if multivocal symbols enable the multidimensional reasoning that is an essential step of reorientation and if memory is essential for the functioning of those symbols, memory, in effect, becomes the essential ingredient of reorientation.

The importance of the process of listening also is suggested by this study, a process mentioned but typically ignored and undertheorized in rhetorical theory. Expanded to include intrapersonal listening or proprioception, listening becomes the primary and privileged function of communication in the rhetoric of reorientation—it is not simply a passive process that facilitates better exchange of messages.

Finally, this study contributes to a reconceptualization of women's communication. Spretnak explains that ritual empowers and sustains women "in our beliefs and commitments. It is an area in which women have moved beyond myriad patriarchal conscriptions of mind and body. We declare what is meaningful to us, and we honor it in our own ways" (162). Thus, through the enactment of these rituals of reorientation, women are giving voice to their lives and their bodies as they have experienced them—not as they fit into the structure of the dominant discourse. Because the rituals are both interrogative and embodied, the participant herself is an essential component of the enactment; her voice cannot be silenced. As a result, the enacted rituals constitute an authentic text of women's intrapersonal communication, unencumbered by the stylistic and substantive structures of the dominant culture and, as such, contribute to our knowledge of such communication.

Although scholars of rhetoric traditionally have been most interested in public communication, Karen Foss and Sonja Foss have argued that the communication that affects human beings much more often than discourse at the national and international level is the communication experienced close up. This is the case, they argue, because these "messages do matter in terms of how our lives are lived," "the friendships we form," the organizations in which we work," and "the nature of the communities in which we live" (*Women Speak* 14). Consequently, the insight that this study provides into the intrapersonal communication of women suggests significant revisions for our understanding of women's communication.[4]

Limitations

The third section of your final chapter should be about the limitations of your study. Discuss the restrictions or qualifications concerning the study. Don't worry that having limitations somehow invalidates what you have done—every study, to be practical, has some limitations. This section, then, is where you head off potential critics by acknowledging yourself some of the shortcomings of the study you designed and conducted. Common limitations cited for studies include:

- The study's design was flawed.

- Limited data were available.

- The scope of the study was limited.

- The purposive sampling procedure decreased the generalizability of the findings.

- The sample size was small.

- The sampling procedures used college students, who are not representative of the larger population.

- Only one case was studied, and the study of more cases might produce different results.

- Only one type of data or one artifact was analyzed; other types or artifacts might have produced different results.

- The self-report method may have produced findings different from what participants actually do in situations.

- The controlled environment encouraged participants to act in abnormal ways and may have produced artificial results.

- The tasks the participants were asked to perform may not be ones they are accustomed to doing, and their processes thus may have been distorted.

- The data analyzed represent a Western perspective, and other perspectives might have generated different results.

- Because of limited background or training in certain areas, I may have misinterpreted the data.

- The study did not take into account a body of work that might have enriched the analysis.

- Certain criteria were used to evaluate the artifact, and the application of different criteria might have resulted in a different evaluation.

Usually, the limitations section includes three or four limitations, with at least one paragraph devoted to each. In addition to identifying the limitation, you can discuss why the limitation is not as problematic as it might initially seem or justify your methodological choices that resulted in the limitation. You don't want your discussion of limitations to be so extensive that the entire study comes to seem problematic to your readers. Your discussion of limitations should be two to five pages long.

Limitations Sample #1

The National Civil Rights Museum (NCRM) is an unconventional and challenging text for rhetorical analysis. As a memorial site layered with both discursive and non-discursive dimensions, the museum presents the rhetorical critic with a number of challenging responsibilities, the least of which is to describe coherently the visual experience for readers who have not visited the museum. Although I have attempted to explain the museum's rhetorical dynamics to the best of my ability, there are still a number of critical gaps that merit attention.

The insights yielded from this dissertation have come from the perspective of a non-African American rhetorical critic. Consequently, this study is limited to the extent that it reflects the biases of someone whose personal investments in African American identity and community could not be as deep as those of some African American critics. To those who believe that a given African American perspective would be better suited to interpreting the NCRM, this study will seem limited.

On the other hand, I believe that analyses of the museum from a variety of perspectives can yield additional insights that may or may not otherwise have been uncovered. On this point, I agree with bell hooks, who expresses my point with eloquence:

> I did not think that I needed to be a white man to understand
> Hemingway's *The Sun Also Rises* nor did I think I needed to be in

---

> a classroom with white men to study this novel [. . .] [However,]
> as a black woman reading this white male writer I might have in-
> sights and interpretations that would be quite different from those
> of white male readers who might approach the text with the as-
> sumption that the novel's depiction of white male social reality was
> one they shared. (47)

Like hooks, I, too, believe that I have something to offer not only to "dis-
tanced" critics but also to those with deep personal investments in
African American communities. It may be in the latter's interest to understand additional ways in which the NCRM is received by audiences
without these ties.

At the same time, I have to acknowledge that an interpretation of the
museum from the perspective of someone with deeper ties to African
American communities—or even to Memphis, for that matter—would
be valuable. Such an interpretation probably would exhibit a different
quality of sensitivity to issues related to white racism, the emotional impact of the King shrine, and especially reactions to Jacqueline Smith's
counter-memorial. An African American perspective filtered through a
lifetime of culture-specific narratives, for example, might enable another
critic to see things in the museum that have been invisible to my own
critical sensibilities.

Another area of concern has to do with the limits of my expertise in
subject areas that are pertinent to this study. Although I have been
trained as an expert in rhetorical criticism, my analysis of the NCRM
has relied heavily upon literature from the disciplines of history, sociology, art, architecture, museum studies, and geography. I have read the literature extensively to become reasonably familiar with the vocabularies
and critical perspectives of each area in order to enhance my interpretation of the museum. Ultimately, however, I relied most heavily on my
training in rhetorical studies to uncover the rhetorical dynamics of the
museum—training that encouraged me to be as open and receptive as
possible to dimensions such as design layout, the spatial positioning of
visitors' bodies, identity formation, and agency. Although I have uncovered much in my examination of the museum, I know that critics with
more formal training in the areas mentioned above—particularly in architecture and museum studies—would be able to bring a host of fresh
insights to a study of this nature. Simply to articulate the ways in which
space and material objects function to shape visitors' experience of the
museum has been a great challenge. A critic better versed in this vocabulary

might be able to elaborate my own points with more sophisticated insights, clarity, and eloquence.

Another limitation of this study is that most of the insights generated here have resulted from my own critical abilities without any reliance on visitors' reactions to the museum. That is, I did not interview any visitors to determine whether my conclusions about the museum fit with visitors' interpretations. There are two reasons for this. First, time constraints dictated that some things be relinquished in order to place greater emphasis on others. Logistical concerns meant that some sacrifices simply had to be made.

Second, visitors' reactions to the museum are a helpful piece of the criticism puzzle, but they are not, in my opinion, absolutely essential for determining the validity of my arguments. Jennifer Stromer-Galley and Edward Schiappa argue that "many rhetorical criticisms of popular texts do not stipulate a specific conceptualization of audience even though [...] explicit references to audiences are often made" (29). Upon reviewing the literature of rhetorical criticism, the authors then observe that "audience conjectures are being advanced without adequate evidence" (30).

If I agreed with Stromer-Galley and Schiappa's argument, then I would have to concede that the present study leaves much to be desired. However, although I do believe that audience feedback can add some face validity to claims advanced in critical essays—particularly in convincing some social scientists who believe that the only good criticism is the kind that presents some empirical, quantifiable data in support of its claims—I also believe that it has its limitations. Part of the value of criticism is that it is an act of interpretation by individuals trained with a heightened sensitivity to the persuasive power of symbolic behavior. Such training means that a good critic should be able to discover and articulate the persuasive dimensions of texts of which most laypersons are unaware, just as a good auto mechanic should be able to pinpoint the problem preventing an engine from starting in ways that laypersons who simply drive cars cannot. In my opinion, audience feedback can be helpful, but it is not a lynchpin on which to base the validity of one's critical insights.

A final area to be noted pertains to the evaluative criterion by which I have judged the rhetoric of the NCRM. My critique of the museum—especially in Chapter Three—is rather pessimistic. This is because I have judged its rhetoric according to the criterion of intent or, in other words, its thesis, which the visitor encounters upon entering the museum. This criterion seems particularly appropriate given the museum's mission statement and other related discourses that quite overtly express a desire to mobilize new generations of civil rights sympathizers. For this reason, I do not believe that I am holding the museum and its founders to an unfair standard. Furthermore, I do not believe I am exaggerating that standard to gain argumentative leverage. The notion of active agency is communicated quite clearly by the interpretive caption under Pavlovsky's lobby sculpture, *Movement to Overcome*, and the introductory film, *Cornerstone of Freedom*. The sculpture and the film are clearly meant to frame visitors' introduction to the museum and to filter the rest of their experience. Therefore, much of my experience has focused on the ways in which the museum fails to constitute an audience of active agents of change.

Another critic, however, might abandon my chosen criterion and evaluate the museum more positively based on completely different criteria. One possibility might be to judge the museum using the criteria that are applied to rhetorical biography. Despite its faults regarding human agency, the NCRM provides visitors with a thorough rhetorical biography of King's public life. Although it does filter visitors' perceptions of King to a degree by presenting him as a near-perfect individual, this narrative might be overlooked in favor of the enormity of information available throughout the museum—documentary footage, photographs, primary and secondary source documents, and material artifacts. Judged from this perspective, the NCRM could be evaluated favorably for using these materials, as well as the King shrine, to capture an essence of King and his contributions to both African American civil rights and humanity in general.

Another set of criteria also would warrant a more favorable evaluation of the museum—that of community building inspired through its "extra-museum" activities, such as the annual celebrations held there on the anniversaries of King's birth and death. In terms of community building, the museum does function to bring people together in ways that they previously were not. For instance, the museum maintains an active role in the Memphis community by presenting its annual Freedom Awards to two outstanding individuals—regardless of whether they are black or white, male or female, American or foreign—who embody the spirit of King in their role as public advocates for human rights. Some past recipients have been Barbara Jordan, Rosa Parks, Jimmy Carter, and Archbishop Desmond Tutu. By bringing people together to honor King and others like him, the museum plays a role in strengthening Memphis' identity and encouraging activism in the larger community.[5]

Limitations Sample #2

There are several limitations to this study, most of which are limitations of the data I used to develop Arendt's speech perspective. One limitation was in the number of sources used from which to develop her theory. My reading has encompassed nearly all her works, but because my primary objective was to lay out the general framework of her perspective, I focused mainly on those works in which she attempts to articulate her view and which, through my reading, seem to contain the most ideas that have direct relevance for the development of her speech perspective—*The Human Condition*, *The Life of the Mind*, "Lectures on Kant's Political Philosophy," and *Between Past and Future*. Greater clarification or elaboration might have occurred had I included insights and observations gleaned from those works in which she devotes attention to specific events or people rather than restricting myself to her philosophical treatises. My conclusions also might have been affected had I included in my investigation those scholars who had a direct influence on her thinking—Martin Heidegger, Karl Jaspers, St. Augustine, and Immanuel Kant, to name a few of the more significant of such influences.

My conclusions also might have been expanded had I used as data works by commentators on Arendt. I did not use secondary sources in the formulation of her speech perspective. Perhaps the most important unexplored resource for clarifying, elaborating, or correcting my interpretation, of course, would have been Hannah Arendt herself. Because she died in 1975, however, that resource was not available to me.

Another limitation with respect to the data from which I developed Arendt's speech perspective is that Arendt did not view herself as a rhetorical theorist or her work as situated in the discipline of rhetoric. Despite my best attempts to read her in her own context, I may have altered some of her concepts simply by choosing to interpret them as a rhetorical theory. My goal, to present her speech perspective, means that I have put her ideas together differently from what she intended, which may or may not have done justice to her larger theoretical perspective.

One possible limitation of the study does not pertain to the data as much as it does to me as the researcher. My background is not in political theory or philosophy, two of the fields in which most of Arendt's concepts naturally are situated. However, while my lack of background could be viewed as a limitation, it also could be seen as advantageous by al-lowing for fresh insights into the data and issues of a different discipline.[6]

Suggestions for Future Research

You're almost there. This is the last section of your last chapter. It's an easy one to write because it flows easily and logically out of the previous limitations section. You can simply take each of the limitations you iden-tified in the previous section—or at least the most important ones and the ones that can be remedied—and turn them into suggestions for future re-search. If you analyzed the films of only one director, for example, you can suggest that future research should be done on films by other directors in order to gain a more comprehensive understanding of whatever it is you are studying. If your data were limited by a Western perspective, you can suggest that future research be done on data that encode more diverse per-spectives. You get the idea.

And, of course, you don't need to be limited by the limitations you identified to formulate suggestions for future research. There may be things you want to suggest should be done next that have nothing to do with the limitations of your study. Perhaps the next step is to test the propositions or hypotheses you developed in this study, for example, or to fill out the theory you developed by investigating aspects of it that are un-dertheorized. This last section of your last chapter is actually a good place to begin thinking about your own research program. What would you want to do next in terms of research to build on what you've done here? Planning for your next study in the last pages of your current one keeps you going on a research trajectory that is programmatic and unified—both good things for a research program.

Suggestions for Future Research Sample #1

The results of this study have several implications for future research. This section will detail recommendations for research in the following areas: (1) The relationship between the visions in which employees par-ticipate and program utilization; (2) The relationship between the vi-sions in which employees participate and demographic variables; (3) The relationship between the visions in which supervisors participate regarding their organization's Employee Assistance Program (EAP) and whether or not they refer employees who have job-performance problems to the program; (4) Use of the Q-technique in program development and expansion; and (5) Exploration of the effectiveness of promotional messages in changing the visions in which employees participate regarding their EAP.

Examination of the relationship between the visions in which employees participate regarding their organization's EAP and whether or not they have or have not used program services entails studying a sample population that is representative of program utilizers and non-utilizers. One way to ensure that the sample is representative of both populations would be to conduct a purposive sample, selecting participants from each of the two populations—the population of program utilizers and non-utilizers. Because program policy of all EAPs guarantees the confidentiality of program clients, a study using this type of sampling plan would have to be conducted by an EAP counselor. Counselors are likely to have access to a list of employees who represent both populations; therefore, program confidentiality would not be violated.

Another way to ensure that the sample is representative of program utilizers and non-utilizers would be to increase the number of employees who are randomly selected to sort the structured Q-deck. The organization to which EAP-1 provided services employed over 13,000 employees in the Denver metropolitan area. Thus, the fact that the sample included only one program utilizer is surprising. A significant increase in the size of the sample would increase the probability that both program utilizers and non-utilizers would be represented by the sample.

If the sample size were increased, employees would have to be placed randomly in groups of 30 and a separate Q-analysis conducted for each group. This would ensure that the number of observations or Q-cards exceeds the number of variables, or respondents, by a ratio of 2:1 (Cragan and Shields, 1981, p. 244). The increase in the sample size also would enable the use of a chi square statistic to determine whether or not there is a significant relationship between typal groupings and program utilization.

To explore the relationship between employees' perceptions toward the EAP and program utilization, then, selecting a sample that is representative of program utilizers and non-utilizers would be necessary. The sorting behavior of the respondents would be analyzed to determine whether or not program utilizers participate in visions that are different from the visions in which non-program utilizers participate. This research would add to an understanding of the relationship between the beliefs and behavior of organizational employees.

In the present study, a frequency count was conducted using the responses to the questionnaire given by the persons who represent each type. The frequency count explored whether or not any of the demographic variables appear to identify persons who represent each type. The frequency count indicated that there was a trend across both organizations that suggests that certain variables—age, marital status, and education—do distinguish the typal groupings.

Due to the absence of findings that indicate that the relationship between the types and these three variables is significant, conclusions cannot be drawn or interpretations made. However, based on the trend evidenced across both organizations, the need for further research on the relationship between age, marital status, and education and employees' perceptions about their organization's EAP is indicated.

A third recommendation for future research is to explore the relationship between the visions in which supervisors participate regarding their organization's EAP and whether or not they refer employees who have job-performance problems to the program. The rate of employee utilization of an EAP is determined by three types of referrals—formal supervisory referrals, informal supervisory referrals, and self-referrals. Self-referrals have been the focus of the present study and occur when an employee is aware of a problem and takes the initiative to seek help from the EAP for that problem. Supervisory referrals, whether formal or informal, occur when a supervisor suggests to an employee that he or she use the EAP. These suggestions are based upon observation of poor job performance or information that an employee is having problems. Thus, supervisors are an important source of referrals to an EAP.

Previous research has attempted to distinguish between supervisors who refer and supervisors who do not refer employees to the EAP and to identify differences between referring and non-referring supervisors' attitudes toward the EAP (Kurtz, Googins, and Williams, 1980; Googins and Kurtz, 1981; Googins, 1979). A research design that is similar to that used in the present study could be employed to gain a greater understanding about the relationship between the visions in which supervisors participate regarding their organization's EAP and whether or not they refer employees to the program.

Specifically, an understanding of the rhetoric used to train supervisors to make supervisory referrals could be gained through a rhetorical analysis of the training literature and workshops. Focus-group interviews could elicit information from supervisors about their perceptions of the EAP and the role and responsibilities of the supervisor in referring employees to the program. The results of the rhetorical analysis and the content analysis could be used to develop a structured Q-deck, which would measure the attitudinal differences between referring and non-referring supervisors. The results could be used to develop training messages for supervisors who do not refer employees with job-performance problems to the EAP.

A fourth recommendation for future research is to explore the use of Q-technique as an aid in program expansion and development. Structured Q-decks typically are used to measure people's current perceptions toward a particular phenomenon. The structured Q-deck that was developed for the purpose of this study can be used to measure the discrepancy between how employees currently perceive their EAP and their idealized vision of the program. Specifically, participants would be asked to sort the deck along the forced-choice continuum from most reflective to least reflective of their view of the program as it currently is. Participants then would be asked to re-sort the deck according to their "idealized" view of the EAP. The data obtained from the "as-is" sort would be analyzed separately from the data obtained from the "ideal" sort. The results of the two separate analyses could be used by program professionals to gain an understanding of how employees currently perceive the program and how they would like the program to change. This information would be useful as a guide for service development and expansion.

The final recommendation for further research is to explore the effectiveness of promotional messages in changing the visions in which employees participate regarding their EAP. Research that explores this issue might utilize a research design similar to that used in this study. However, the study would be expanded and new promotional messages would be developed using the results of the Q-analysis. After exposure to the new marketing messages, the employee sample would be re-administered the Q-deck, and the data obtained from the two different Q-sortings could be used to measure attitudinal changes.[7]

Suggestions for Future Research Sample #2

By reconceptualizing popular music as inter-textual and, if the reader will allow, as inter-contextual, I have developed a schema that assists critics in going beyond the interpretation of musical texts. Beginning with a text, a critic employing this schema can understand the response to the text as a process that connects the listening experience to a number of patterns of experience that govern it.

The most obvious need for future research in terms of the schema is for further testing and refining. In the evaluation section above, I noted several aspects of the schema that require further work. Continued use of the schema by rhetorical critics would provide further tests of its usefulness and refinement of elements that are not effective. The most obvious refinements could come in the area of connecting the schema to other approaches to music. For example, by connecting the schema more explicitly to Frith's discursive formations, critics can develop complex understanding of how individual texts and genres are articulated to listeners within the framework of a given formation. Continuing my research of the Pixies' music, for example, I might emphasize how the Pixies' avant-garde impulses connect the pop and the bourgeois discursive formations. Other refinements to the schema could include a more explicit connection of its concepts to constructs such as taste cultures or musemes.

Continued use of the schema also would help to enhance understanding of popular music as rhetorical. Studies of several songs by one artist, songs by different artists within the same musical style, or comparison of songs across musical styles would lead to more precise and meaningful explanations of music's power to influence. Such studies also would help to develop understanding of the ways musical styles, genres, and performers are articulated to audiences at given historical junctures.

An alternative approach to using the schema would be not to begin with a text but to end with one. As Becker and McGee suggest, listeners construct texts and messages from a mosaic of possible influences. A fan of punk rock, for example, may listen to hundreds of punk songs and non-punk songs in a given time period, may read dozens of books on punk rock in a lifetime, may attend many concerts in a year, and may be engaged daily in conversation about music and culture, replete with taste judgments that Frith argues are the common currency of popular music. Studying punk music as rhetoric in this case may proceed not from the reading of a single punk text but from the treatment of the collected texts and experiences with music that inform an individual's understanding of what punk is, why he or she values it, and how its creators employ fragments of rock and roll and other cultural discourses in producing it.

Taking McGee's notion to heart—that a postmodern shift in contemporary culture means audiences' and critics' most vital practice has become text construction and rhetors' most vital practice has become interpretation—critics of rhetoric and popular music could use the schema to examine how culture has been interpreted by given performers, styles, and institutions and how audiences may formulate the meaning of music based on their experiences with it. From this approach, critics would investigate, say, how the Rock and Roll Hall of Fame uses bourgeois cultural practices to legitimize rock and roll and how this affects visitors' construction of rock and roll as an ideological form. Using my proposed schema, critics would investigate how the myriad bits of the mosaic that constitute the Hall add up to a message about rock and roll—how the Hall constitutes a text that tells the visitor what rock and roll is.

Alternatively, critics may begin with a musical style, asking, for example, why swing music is emerging at this point among fans of punk music—in other words, asking against and within what musical and social contexts must swing be read. Using the schema, critics would actually construct (or illustrate how fans construct) swing style as a text—explainable only in terms of the fragments of context that inform it. Similarly, critics may investigate the messages communicated by musical styles by addressing the various fragments of context that may be observed by a given fan of the style. Using the schema would lead critics to focus not only on the music itself but also on the discourse that surrounds the music—such as arguments made in fanzines, expressions of musical taste in Internet groups, or perhaps interviews with fans themselves. This approach would mirror the ways fans construct their musical taste preferences on an everyday basis.

Whether or not such research on popular music is framed in terms of the schema I developed in this thesis, the contribution I hope to make is in convincing critics to avoid moving more deeply into the musical text in order to understand how the text works in consumption. Musical form itself harbors no inherent meaning; its cultural and social significance derive from what situated listeners put into it—conceptions of taste, affective involvement, and personal beliefs. Understanding music's rhetorical power requires a critical move into the social, aesthetic, and cultural contexts that inform it.[8]

Finishing Up

Your last chapter is done. That wasn't so bad, was it? There are just a few small things left to do to complete a draft of your entire dissertation. These revisions will be minor. They're not hard and won't take you long, so they aren't anything that will hold you up.

One of these finishing-up tasks is to return to your proposal and revise it to turn it into the first chapter or the first three chapters of your dissertation. Go back through your proposal, paying attention to and revising it in two ways. One is to change your discussion of any elements of your research design that you might have altered in the actual execution of your study. At the proposal stage, did you think you were going to be interviewing people in three cities, but you ended up doing the interviews in only two cities for some reason? Or maybe you expected to hold five focus groups, and you ended up conducting seven. These are the kinds of things to watch for and to revise to turn your proposal into your first chapter or chapters of your dissertation.

A second act in the revision process is to change the tense of the language you used in your proposal. There, you talked about what you would do in the future using phrases such as "My data will be" and "I will analyze the data by. . . ." At the point at which your dissertation is done, of course, you've already completed the things you said you would do, so change your language to reflect the fact that they're completed. You can either write in the present tense or the past tense: "My data are . . ." and "I analyze the data by . . ." or "My data were . . ." and "I analyzed the data by. . . ."

Next comes the abstract. Writing the abstract last makes sense because you now know definitively what your dissertation includes. The abstract is what will be published in *Dissertation Abstracts International* so that other scholars can determine if your dissertation is relevant to their own research. The abstract, which is typically limited to 350 words, summarizes the study and generally contains three items: purpose of the study, basics of the research design, and major results. The purpose of the study is a statement that summarizes your research question, so simply turn your research question into a purpose statement. Then explain the key aspects of your research design—the data you analyzed and how you collected and analyzed them. Wind up the abstract by summarizing the key findings of your study.

Abstract Sample #1

The purpose of the study was to define the rhetorical strategies—both discursive (verbal) and non-discursive (nonverbal)—that women use in working for peace and to formulate a theory of rhetorical strategies that might prove useful to those engaged in the peacemaking process. Ecofeminism constituted the framework for studying women's strategies of peacemaking.

Qualitative data were drawn from four artifacts representative of the ecofeminist perspective and focused on a range of human symbolic activity. The artifacts were rituals performed by Starhawk; Ursula LeGuin's novel *Always Coming Home*; the film *Goddess Remembered*, produced by Studio D of the National Film Board of Canada; and three paintings by Meinred Craighead. The method of analysis was grounded theory, developed by Glaser and Strauss. Patterns that emerged from the data were sorted, categorized, and identified as rhetorical strategies, with each major rhetorical strategy supported by one or more specific sub-strategies.

An analysis of Starhawk's rituals revealed the following major strategies: (1) Use of natural elements, (2) Self-affirmation, and (3) Development of interconnection. Analysis of LeGuin's novel *Always Coming Home* revealed the following major strategies: (1) Use of metaphors, (2) Creation of new realities, (3) Use of contrast, (4) Violation of conventional form, and (5) Enactment of content through form. Analysis of the Studio D film *Goddess Remembered* revealed the following major strategies: (1) Provision of legitimacy, (2) Factual presentation, (3) Discontinuity, (4) Wholeness, and (5) Slow pace. Analysis of Craighead's paintings revealed the following major strategies: (1) Use of conventional metaphors, (2) Presentation of dual perspectives, and (3) Evidence of historical origins.

The rhetorical strategies discovered were organized into a framework that explains how they function to persuade audiences to engage in peacemaking. The framework involves two major categories of strategies—facilitating the audience's break with the current world order and providing positive depictions for the audience of ways of being in a new and peaceful world. This framework is applied to two instances of peacemaking efforts to demonstrate how it may be implemented by others.[9]

Abstract Sample #2

This research examined the rhetoric of humorous incivility as it is enacted in popular culture, specifically in the television programs *Seinfeld* and *Beavis and Butt-Head* and the radio and television program *The Howard Stern Show.* The purpose was to identify, describe, and understand the features and functions of a rhetoric of humorous incivility. The method of genre criticism was used to identify and explain the rhetorical situation, the substantive and stylistic features, and the organizing principle of each program.

The analysis of the shows suggested that they may be read as both civil and uncivil, depending on the frame from which the audience views them. If the audience focuses on how these shows treat issues of difference and otherness, they appear uncivil. In a second reading of the shows, the themes of sex, family, technology, and bodily functions act as strategic diversions to focus attention away from the closed-mindedness and incivility of the characters and the dialogue and toward the novelty factor of each show. They thus create a frame in which to read the shows as open, new, playful, and creative. When dealing with self-focused topics, the shows are civil; when dealing with other-focused topics, they are uncivil.[10]

There are just a few more things to do now. Prepare the front matter of your dissertation. This includes: the title page, the copyright page, the approval (signature page), the dedication page (if you want to have one), the acknowledgments page, the table of contents, the list of figures and the list of tables (if you have them), the bibliography or works cited, and any appendices you have. Your university will provide specific guidelines for all of these. Follow them carefully—they often are given the greatest scrutiny by the person who does the format checking in the graduate school. This is also a good time to check all of the quotes in your dissertation against the original sources. Look up each passage to be sure you quoted it accurately.

Some of these finishing-up tasks are tedious, but none of them takes very long, especially because you're quite likely to have been working on them earlier in the process of the dissertation. You probably aren't starting from scratch on most of them. And when you're this close to having a complete draft done of your dissertation, you're certainly not going to let anything stop you now!

The hard part is done. You have your ideas down on paper, and your task now is to turn to the process of revising and editing your work. How to go about refining, shaping, and sculpting the words that express your ideas is the topic of the next chapter. After one of those quick breaks to celebrate the achievement of a major goal—the completion of the entire draft of your dissertation—sit down again with your manuscript and get back to work.

Conclusion Chapter Sample #1

CHAPTER VI
CONCLUSION: PROTEST
RHETORIC RE-CONCEPTUALIZED

For centuries, women have struggled—individually and collectively—to piece their lives together with the bits of choice and freedom men have allotted them. The pattern of life into which women have arranged these remnants is testimony to women's fortitude and ingenuity. Unable to accept fully their suppressed and muted status, women have devised creative outlets for their thoughts, feelings, and desires. One such strategy is the use of quilts to communicate their ideas about social and political issues and their own lives and experiences. Through the analyses performed for my study of quilts as protest artifacts, the complex nature of quilts has been illuminated.

In this chapter, I will summarize my analyses of four quilts by reviewing the method of analysis and the protest characteristics and conclusions I drew about each of the quilts. Then, drawing from the conclusions of the analyses, I will formulate a theory of protest rhetoric and compare this theory to traditional notions of protest rhetoric. The third section of this chapter will contain a discussion of the limitations of my study. Finally, I will conclude with suggestions for future research.

Summary of Analyses

The purpose of my study was to formulate a theory of protest rhetoric derived from an analysis of protest quilts. This study was designed to address two research questions:

1. What are the characteristics of quilts that protest?
2. Does the study of protest quilts change traditional notions about protest rhetoric?

I employed an inductive method of analysis to study the protest characteristics of four quilts: the *Secession Quilt*, the *Crusade Quilt*, the *AIDS Memorial Quilt*, and the *Eugene Peace Quilt*. I began my analysis of the quilts without preconceived ideas of the protest characteristics of quilts that I might discover and instead delineated the characteristics of quilts that protest following a systematic collection of observations from my artifacts. I did begin, however, with a definition of the phenomenon to be studied. *Quilt* was defined as an eclectic amalgamation of materials—such as fabric, thread, and paint—for the end result of function and expression.

The quilts were coded to discover core categories and properties. To accomplish this coding, I listed the primary observable elements and properties of the quilts. Then, I compared the elements and properties to one another, placing those that had similar characteristics in a common category. When all of the data had been coded, I generated categories that helped to explain how quilts function as symbols of protest. The conclusions I drew are summarized below.

The Secession Quilt

There are a relatively small number of elements and properties observable in the *Secession Quilt*. Such features as base materials, needlework, images, aesthetic elements, and themes were coded. From these groups, I determined two primary categories that help to explain how the quilt functions as a protest artifact: references to the world represented by the Union and references to the break-up of the Union.

Cook's support of the Union is demonstrated through references she makes to the history of the Union and common symbols used to represent it. There are three primary ways that Cook communicates her lack of enthusiasm for the break-up of the Union: through the names on the quilt and their placement; reference to war; and the elements she does *not* include in the quilt.

Upon first viewing the *Secession Quilt*, the viewer's impression is that Cook supported secession. Dominant references to the Union, however, led me to conclude that Cook wanted to keep the Union intact. Given her position as the wife of a plantation owner, Cook could not express her support for unity openly; therefore, she used her quilt as a covert expression of her thoughts. Professing the desire for one course of action, while covertly indicating preference for another, provided Cook with an official front of protection. This veil of protection allowed Cook to express her feelings without fear of offending the dominant group. A strategy of expressing a preferred policy without really expressing it seems to be viable for a rhetor such as Cook, who holds little power to affect political policies and whose position is radically different from that of the majority.

The Crusade Quilt

In the course of my analysis of this quilt, major elements and properties I discovered included visual images, verbal text, organization of blocks, sparseness of decoration, use of machines in the quilt's construction, and institutional themes. From these elements, I determined one major protest characteristic of this quilt. The *Crusade Quilt* functions as a protest symbol by featuring women as participants in the public realm. The quilt's properties seem to deny or omit virtually all references to femininity and to depict the WCTU women embracing behaviors traditionally attributed to the public sphere. Thus, in the process of denying femininity and embracing public behaviors, woman's realm is transformed from the private to the public sphere.

Contradictions that became apparent through the analysis of this quilt led me to conclude that the *Crusade Quilt* is a sophisticated response designed to meet the contradictory features of the exigence. Five pairs of contrasting messages were identified through which the women seem to claim an allegiance with the public over the private while maintaining women's connection to the private: alliance with women's sphere/denial of women's sphere; protest/denial of protest; engaging in public activity/not engaging in public activity; personal persuasion/public persuasion; and support for the system/challenge of the system. The five pairs of contrasting messages contain both a denial of women's sphere and an emphasis on that sphere. This contradiction seems to be intentionally devised and fostered by the women. While straddling the fence between the private and public domains, the women could maintain ambiguity—affording them the latitude they needed to operate legitimately in both spheres.

The AIDS Memorial Quilt

Major elements and properties of this quilt fell within three main categories of items: media, aesthetic elements, and relation of elements to the deceased. From these categories, I determined that the protest function of the *AIDS Memorial Quilt* is achieved through three primary characteristics: development of victims' credibility, demonstration of the magnitude of the AIDS crisis, and creation of identification between the victim and the audience.

Characteristics of both content and form distinguish the *Quilt* from traditional protest symbols. The content of the *Quilt*—characteristics relating to the content of the message communicated—functions to polarize the audience and victims by establishing the victims as special individuals who deserve more respect and admiration than most people. At the same time, viewers are encouraged to identify with the victims. Thus, feeling both in awe of victims and a kinship with them, viewers begin to understand the magnitude of what is being lost as a result of AIDS.

The form of the *Quilt*—characteristics associated with its configuration as a quilt—suggests several concepts that distinguish it from other protest symbols. Many of the concepts represented by the form are not parallel, such as death, illness, comfort, protection, and love. In addition, the context in which the *Quilt* appears is limited. Finally, the *Quilt* is not a symbol that is readily displayed; its size, however, demands that it not be ignored.

The Eugene Peace Quilt

When listing the physical, observable elements and properties of this quilt, I discovered that they fell within four groups or categories: media—the processes by which the quilt and blocks were created; aesthetic elements; verbal text; and nature themes. From these groups, three characteristics of the quilt emerged: depiction of a state of peace; absence of strategies for achieving peace; and labeling of peace advocates. The three characteristics suggest a strategy of protest that involves creating an alternate discourse for peace. Thus, the quilt constitutes a strategy for peacemaking that challenges the dominant social order by creating an alternative discourse to that of the mainstream world.

A Theory of Protest Rhetoric

Through a systematic analysis of four quilts that function as channels for voicing change, I discovered four protest characteristics shared by the four quilts I analyzed. They all have in common depiction of the system as positive, establishment of common ground, lack of credibility of rhetors, and ambiguity—features that suggest alternative views of protest rhetoric. In the following section, I discuss each feature as it is manifest in the four quilts and conclude with a summary of the theory constituted by these elements. Then, I will compare this theory with traditional features of protest rhetoric.

Depiction of the System as Positive

In all of the quilts studied, the dominant power structure does not receive blame for the ills of the non-dominant group. Either the system is not directly discussed, or its contribution to the subordinate power's dissatisfaction is muted. In the *Secession Quilt*, the Union—the dominant power group—is not depicted as evil or blameworthy. The propensity of Union symbols that appear on the quilt, coupled with an absence of Southern symbols, led me to conclude that Cook is not displeased with the Union. She does not blame the Union for the dissension within the country, even though her quilt ostensibly supports a breaking away from the Union. My analysis, of course, showed that Cook may have been a Union supporter or at least nostalgic for a unified country. Even viewed from such a perspective, however, her quilt does not blame or disparage the system against which she protests. The depictions of the Southerners breaking apart the Union are neutral; nothing negative is associated with them, except for their secessionist stance.

The Woman's Christian Temperance Union, through the *Crusade Quilt*, evidences support for the system the WCTU members desire to change in that the political and social institutions—the government and religious systems—receive positive recognition in the quilt. The WCTU women do not hold these institutions to be responsible for instituting policies that encouraged the social ills the women were trying to correct.

In the *AIDS Memorial Quilt*, panel makers and victims rarely use the *Quilt* as a forum to assign blame to "mainstream" society. Although there are a few panels that are overtly politically oriented and that suggest that the system, in its indifference, may have hastened a victim's death, the bulk of the panels are not; they focus on the victim.

The discourse of peace articulated by the Eugene women in the *Eugene Peace Quilt* does not include references to policies of the dominant power group that have stymied progress toward peace. There are no references at all—and thus no negative evaluations made—to the United States government, missiles, war, or the Pentagon, for example. In addition, the references to making peace with nature as a step toward attaining world peace do not include depictions of the state of non-peace the dominant order now maintains with nature. Thus, the Eugene women's discourse of peace is not based on finding fault with or placing blame on the dominant system.

Establishment of Common Ground

Through each of the quilts, the non-dominant person or members of the subordinate group seek to establish what they have in common with members of the dominant system. Rather than emphasizing the differences between them, the rhetors focus on similarities between the protesters and the system. The focus on commonalities is less prevalent in some quilts than in others; however, the feature appears in all of the quilts. In the *Secession Quilt*, Cook identifies herself as a supporter, to some extent, of both the North and the South—both dominant political systems. Of course, because she is not explicit about the side she identifies herself as supporting, the common ground she seeks to establish is somewhat obscure.

In the *Crusade Quilt*, the WCTU women identify themselves as legitimate participants in the public arena. Seeking to empower themselves in order to effect changes in public policies and private attitudes about alcohol consumption, the women represent themselves, in the quilt, as enfranchised members of the system. They sign the quilt; it becomes their petition and their ballot. Blocks are made by county and township organs, representing the women's membership in governmentally organized and designated regions. They show themselves as active participants in the very system they seek to challenge.

Through the *AIDS Memorial Quilt*, victims are presented as legitimate members of the dominant system who have much in common with non-victims. Common ground between the system and the victims is established by depictions of events, careers, and organizational affiliations that victims share with non-victims; universally owned objects and experiences; and common concerns and beliefs.

The *Eugene Peace Quilt* is the one quilt of the four that stresses common ground more than any other protest feature. In their discourse of peace, the Eugene women speak of the need for all people to find a common ground—a common unity. They specify that the common ground shared by all is nature.

Lack of Credibility of Rhetors

Through their quilts, the rhetors depict themselves as lacking mainstream credibility. The quilt makers acknowledge, in their quilts, that they are operating from a low-power position. Cook's *Secession Quilt* exemplifies her acceptance of her lack of credibility in that she cloaks her opinion of the Union within the design of her quilt. Recognizing her position as a woman and a Southern woman, Cook could not and did not overtly express her views.

The rhetoric of the *Crusade Quilt* indicates that the WCTU women recognize their status as one of low credibility. As members of the private sphere, they realize they have little power to persuade; therefore, they seek to transform their realm to include the public. Still, they do not attempt to gain complete credibility by identifying themselves as full members of the public sphere. By maintaining their membership in the private realm, they seek to assure the dominant group that they are not trying to usurp power, further reinforcing their low credibility.

Panel makers of the *AIDS Memorial Quilt* recognize the lack of credibility that is afforded AIDS victims. In the panels they make, they attempt to build victims' credibility by depicting them as people with strong moral character, as valued members of society, and as inspirations for the living.

Makers of the *Eugene Peace Quilt* identify themselves as having low credibility with the dominant power group in two ways. First, the women choose to create their own language with which to speak about peace. Whether consciously or unconsciously, the women understand that they have little input into the development of a language that talks about peace in terms of war. Because they have no power or credibility to change the dominant discourse, they choose to create their own discourse. The second way in which the Eugene women acknowledge their low credibility is through the people they choose to depict on their quilt. The dominant group is not represented in this quilt; instead, there are children, minority groups, and members of the counter culture. These low-power, low-status groups are the groups with which the women identify.

<u>Ambiguity</u>

Each of the four quilts contains ambiguous features—the messages they present are complex, difficult to identify and define, and sometimes contradictory. Ambiguity is particularly evident in the *Secession Quilt*. At first glance, the quilt appears to be Cook's vote in favor of secession. A closer look, however, causes the viewer to become less sure of her position. Although Cook seems to be advocating secession—she embroiders the word opposite the name of a leading secessionist—her reliance on Union symbols causes the viewer to wonder about the true nature of Cook's message.

In the *Crusade Quilt*, ambiguity abounds as the women communicate contradictory messages. For example, they present themselves as members of the private sphere and public sphere. They seem to be protesting, yet they are not protesting. As they deny their femininity, they also embrace femininity. While they seem to support the system, they challenge the system. Finally, although the quilt facilitates public protest, it also is a symbol for personal persuasion—encouraging the fainthearted crusader to continue the fight.

The *AIDS Memorial Quilt* is characterized by ambiguity as well. For instance, the *Quilt* stands as a memorial to victims at the same time that it is a call for help for future victims. While the rhetoric of the *Quilt* seems to polarize victims and viewers by establishing the victims as special individuals who deserve more respect and admiration than most people, the arguments advanced by the *Quilt* also encourage viewers to identify themselves with the victims.

There is a great deal of ambiguity in the *Eugene Peace Quilt*. Slogans that leave the reader wondering what is meant are common on the quilt. The relationship between the image of peace and the individual rhetor's definition of peace often is difficult to determine. How the unity that is necessary to achieve peace can be attained is left to the viewer to determine, creating an ambiguous message concerning means to use to achieve peace.

<u>Summary of the Theory and Comparison to</u>
<u>Traditional Notions of Protest Rhetoric</u>

In the four quilts studied, the feature of ambiguity—the last common characteristic identified—serves as the base from which a theory of protest rhetoric can be developed. Ambiguity is the element that connects and makes sense of the other three features. All of the rhetors attempt to make use of a system in which they lack credibility through a strategy of ambiguity. By remaining noncommittal about the system that subsumes their power—they do not blame the system—these muted, low-status rhetors are able to possess some credibility because the dominant group is not able to identify them as for or against it. By establishing common ground with the dominant group, the protesters are able to be both part of and against the system simultaneously.

A strategy of ambiguity helps the protesters work within a system that affords them little or no credibility by establishing and maintaining mystery around them. According to Kenneth Burke, those who hold positions high on the social hierarchy are anomalies to those who are lower on the hierarchy; the mystery that surrounds the dominant group keeps the non-dominant groups in awe. Similarly, those lower on the hierarchy are unknown to those at the top.[1]

This mystery serves an important function, however, as Burke explains: "Mystery allows for the transcending of the differences among members—whether real or imagined—by hiding some of the differences that do exist and allowing them to believe that they share some substance with one another."[2] By maintaining mystery, the divisions among groups of people become obscured—the dominant group has difficulty recognizing how they differ from non-dominant groups. Therefore, when protesters bring inequalities in the system to light, the dominant group is more inclined to identify with the protesters. With this identification comes a greater possibility that the system will be changed. Thus, ambiguity enables rhetors who lack credibility to establish common ground with the social order that perpetuates their non-dominant position through the maintenance of mystery.

The theory of protest rhetoric developed from the four quilts, then, identifies four primary features of protest: depiction of the system as positive, establishment of common ground, lack of credibility of rhetors, and ambiguity. Ambiguity is the connecting and root strategy and facilitates the development of mystery around the protesters. This theory differs from traditional notions of protest rhetoric identified as rhetoric intended to effect change in the status quo by members of non-dominant groups who challenge the dominant system through confrontational means.

The four major elements of the traditional definition of protest rhetoric can be contrasted with the view of protest I have formulated. First, the women, through their quilts, do not always want to effect change. The *Secession Quilt*, for example, appears to be a vehicle through which Cook expresses her views. Although the Eugene women advocate peace, their visualizations of peace do not include images that encourage a change in the current system.

Efforts of the quilters are not always directed at the status quo—the second element of the traditional definition of protest rhetoric. In the *AIDS Memorial Quilt*, for instance, the efforts of the panel makers are directed toward the victims, who are remembered, mourned, and memorialized. Also, the *Crusade Quilt* was—in addition to a protest symbol—a symbol of unity and motivation for the members of the WCTU.

The third element of the traditional definition of protest is challenging the dominant system. Rather than challenging the system, the quilt makers often identify themselves with it. The women of the WCTU represent themselves as participants in both the public and private spheres. Panel makers of the *AIDS Memorial Quilt* present the victims as people with whom the viewer can identify. Sometimes, because of ambiguity, there is difficulty determining what side the quilter is on, as is the case with the *Secession Quilt*.

Finally, the fourth element of the traditional notion of protest—confrontational means—can be contrasted with the view of protest offered in this study. The quilt makers' means are not usually confrontational. They acknowledge their lack of power to confront and are accommodating to the system that deprives them of this power. The *Crusade Quilt*, for instance, through its support of government and religious institutions, is an acknowledgment of the system's authority. Cook's acceptance of her position as a low-credibility source is evidenced by the fact that she does not overtly express her views in the *Secession Quilt*. The *AIDS Memorial Quilt* does not resist the system; instead, the *Quilt's* makers are accommodating of it—depicting the victims as legitimate members of the system.

Limitations of the Study

There are several limitations to this study. First, only four artifacts were used as data from which to develop a feminist theory of protest rhetoric. As a consequence of the small number of quilts used in the study, the explanations of protest formulated apply to those quilts alone. Second, the protest nature of the quilts varied. In particular, the *Secession Quilt* and the *Eugene Peace Quilt* did not function as protest symbols in the same way that the *Crusade Quilt* and the *AIDS Memorial Quilt* did. Formulation of a theory of protest rhetoric that relates to all the quilts required greater generalization as a result; a less detailed theory of protest rhetoric thus was generated.

The third limitation of this study is that the quilts used as data were drawn from different time periods. I chose to study both historical and contemporary data in an effort to develop a theory of protest using data from dissimilar contexts. While using a variety of data had some advantages—consistent characteristics could be documented and changes in the quilts over time could be discovered—data derived from different time periods present some disadvantages. Given the different contexts in which the quilters worked, comparisons made among strategies of communication that were discovered in the quilts were sometimes strained. For instance, relating Jemima Cook's method of couching one message within the folds of another to the Eugene women's efforts to create an alternative discourse results in comparing an implicit to an explicit strategy of resistance. The approaches are so different that a valid relationship between the two is difficult to develop. Such comparisons might have been easier with the contexts of time periods consistent.

A fourth limitation of this study is its lack of generalizability to other protest artifacts created by women and other non-dominant groups. Because I used only one alternate protest form as data—quilts—I was not able to identify other means of protest that might be evident in other forms.

261

The fact that I could not personally view the *Secession Quilt* was a fifth limitation of the study. This was the one quilt that I was not able to see in person and analyzed from photographs alone. Details of the quilt that I missed by viewing only photographs of the quilt might have caused me to draw conclusions about the quilt that are not accurate.

Problems inherent in the re-conceptualization of a construct is another limitation of this study. Where to draw the definitional limits is difficult to know. At what point am I no longer dealing with protest but with another construct entirely? Have I discovered a new view of protest rhetoric as a result of this study, or have I simply rediscovered, for example, the notion of identification so well elaborated by Kenneth Burke?[4] The problem becomes more acute when comparing my "new" notion of protest to traditional definitions that are not clearly outlined. Because there is no agreement on a definition of protest rhetoric, the difficulty of comparing traditional definitions with alternative definitions is compounded.

Suggestions for Future Research

The limitations of this study provide some threads from which future studies may be woven. First, the small number of quilts used in this study provided the beginnings of a theory of the protest rhetoric that is articulated through quilts. More quilts need to be analyzed for their protest characteristics in order to validate the theory identified in this study and to elaborate on that theory.

From this theory of protest rhetoric derived from quilts, a second thread of inquiry needed is to test the theory on other forms of women's rhetoric. For example, women's protest through art, music, poetry, and discourse might be analyzed to discover whether the theory articulated in this study is evident in those as well.

Given the re-conceptualized theory of protest rhetoric discussed in this study, a third area of future inquiry should involve a reassessment of the theory and literature of social movements from a feminist perspective. Feminist scholars now need to review past theories of movements and assess and re-vision them, sorting out those that seem to incorporate the perspectives of women from those that do not.

A final thread of inquiry could involve designing a study in which the theory developed in this study could be used and thus tested by a protest group. An experimental study of this nature would afford the opportunity to discover whether the strategies of protest identified provide effective, alternative means for creating change.[11]

Notes

1. Adapted from the dissertation of Marla R. Kanengieter, "Message Formation from Architecture: A Rhetorical Analysis" (PhD diss., University of Oregon, 1990). Original parenthetical citations and footnote numbers were retained in the samples in this chapter, but the references to which they refer were not.

2. Adapted from the dissertation of Laura K. Hahn, "A Generic Analysis of the Rhetoric of Humorous Incivility in Popular Culture" (PhD diss., Ohio State University, 1999).

3. Adapted from the dissertation of Daniel L. Wildeson, "The Speech Perspective of Hannah Arendt and Its Implications for Rhetorical Theory" (PhD diss., University of Oregon, 1990).

4. Adapted from the dissertation of Kimberly Denise Barnett Gibson, "Weaving a New World: The Rhetoric of Reorientation in Contemporary Women's Spirituality Rituals" (PhD diss., Ohio State University, 1993).

5. Adapted from the dissertation of Bernard John Armada, "'The Fierce Urgency of Now': Public Memory and Civic Transformation at the National Civil Rights Museum" (PhD diss., Pennsylvania State University, 1999).

6. Wildeson.

7. Adapted from the dissertation of Abby Leverett Braun, "The Impact of Rhetorical Visions on Employee Assistance Program Utilization" (PhD diss., University of Denver, 1986).

8. Adapted from the dissertation of Theodore Matula, "A Rhetorical Schema for Studying Popular Music" (PhD diss., Ohio State University, 1998).

9. Adapted from the dissertation of Diana Brown Sheridan, "Ecofeminist Strategies of Peacemaking" (PhD diss., University of Oregon, 1990).

10. Hahn.

11. Adapted from the dissertation of Mary Rose Williams, "A Re-Conceptualization of Protest Rhetoric: Characteristics of Quilts as Protest" (PhD diss., University of Oregon, 1990).

CHAPTER NINE
USEFUL PHRASES: WRITING AND EDITING

Your experience as a traveler is always enhanced when you know the local language. You understand more of what you're seeing, and you're able to get around more easily. Most important, you're able to share your ideas with others. Even if you aren't fluent in the language of the place you are visiting, your experience is enriched if you're able to use some words and phrases and understand some basic conventions as you interact with those you meet. The same is true for dissertation writers. You want to share your ideas in the clearest, most effective form with those who can make use of them, but if you don't know the idioms of writing and revising, you'll find yourself stammering and unable to express your ideas.

We don't intend to teach you how to write in this chapter. What we want to do is to help you make the processes of writing and revising easier and more effective if they are difficult for you. Our focus here is on those places where students tend to get stuck or slowed down while writing. If you write easily and quickly and are happy with what you produce, there's no need for you to read this chapter. Just get back to writing and revising!

Our assumption in this chapter is that you are clear about what you want to say—you know the ideas you want to communicate. Whether you are working on your proposal or one of your chapters, if you have been following along with us in this book, you should have a general idea about what to write. Now you want to put your ideas into print. You want to turn them into prose as quickly as possible and then polish that prose into a well-written dissertation.

There are two key processes you need to know in order to write effectively—fast writing and slow revising. We want to begin by separating the two processes because many students think they are one and the same. Although some students try to go faster by combining these two steps, it's much more efficient to keep them separate because they rely on different parts of the brain. Writing is capturing your ideas on paper, while revising is sculpting to express your ideas effectively and perhaps even eloquently. Writing is about adding materials, while revising is about scrutinizing, moving, removing, and transforming materials.

Fast Writing

When it's time for you to write, *only* write. Don't do any revising as you write. What this means is that you'll be writing a "spew draft"—a draft in which you write as fast as you can until you have a complete rough draft of a chapter. Write without concern for full sentences, proper spelling, or correct grammar. Don't stop to correct typos, add citations, figure out the nuances of an argument you are making, or reread what you just wrote. Just keep going, typing as fast as you can in a state of uninhibited invention. We're talking about writing so fast that you're producing as many as six or seven pages an hour. The pages should literally be flying out from your printer. You'll revise later, but right now, your task is to get your ideas on paper in any form.

We're very committed to fast writing as one of the major ways to become a productive writer for several reasons. One is that it's much faster than the typical alternative, which is to write perfect first drafts. If you write perfect first drafts, you know how agonizingly slow writing can be. It's slow in part because you spend your time making perfect prose that you later end up having to cut when you discover that it doesn't fit. You might have spent hours on a particular piece of text, and then, in the editing process, you find yourself cutting large sections of a paragraph, a section, or even a chapter. As a result, you've lost precious dissertation time. Our guess is, too, that when you write perfect first drafts, the writing process is painful and not a lot of fun. We think writing should and can be fun, and one of the ways to make it so is to write as fast as you can, delightfully watching those pages mound up.

A second reason why we encourage you to do fast writing is that it's a method that works for big projects like the dissertation. Sure, the perfect-first-draft method might work fine if you're trying to write a 20-page paper. You can keep all your ideas in your head for 20 pages' worth. A dissertation or any kind of longer writing project, though, is something entirely different. You can't possibly work out and keep in your head what you want to say for 200 or 300 pages. The method will fail you if you try to write that many pages as a perfect first draft. You're likely to get stuck, then, when the writing method you've always used doesn't work.

We're also big fans of fast writing because, when you're beginning to write your proposal or a chapter, you have no criteria to use to decide whether a sentence should be in a particular spot or whether a word is the precise one you want to use. You can't make those decisions until you see the whole product and can see how that sentence and that word fit into the whole. No wonder you agonize over which word to use or how to sculpt a particular sentence. There's no way you can make the decision at this point, but that's exactly what you're trying to do. This kind of debate, of course, slows you way down.

Editing as you write is not unlike moving into a new house or apartment and trying to arrange the furniture by focusing on one or two pieces. It's like moving a single table and a lamp here and there until you get it in just the right place. The problem is that you've ignored the couch and the chairs and the coffee table that may need to go in the exact place you positioned the table and the lamp. The perfect place is no longer so perfect when the other pieces of furniture fill the room, and you probably won't be able to keep the perfect placement of the table and the lamp. Imagine instead placing all the furniture in a rough, workable arrangement and then making smaller and smaller adjustments until the room is perfect. When you work from that rough arrangement, all of your adjustments take into account the whole, and there aren't any major surprises or changes along the way. Fast writing, then, gives you the arrangement of the whole room before you begin to make smaller adjustments.

Writing a perfect first draft instead of writing fast can also contribute to a weaker overall text. The longer you spend thinking about and wording an example or producing the perfect sentence or picking the perfect word, the more attached you become to it. Consequently, the more you'll resist putting it aside in favor of making a stronger argument. Imagine that you have five perfect pages of prose, complete with exceptional wording, exquisite examples, and carefully documented citations. Then imagine that you discover that you no longer really believe what you worked out in those pages or that you find some holes in your argument that make you uncomfortable. Maybe you decide that what you wrote is really irrelevant to your topic.

Having spent the time to create this perfect piece of text, you are less likely to want to dispense with it altogether. You are more likely to spend time trying to patch it up, trying to make it fit. Then you limp forward, dragging with you something you know doesn't work but that you can't bear to cut. In fast writing, in contrast, you try to work out the argument first, and you may find yourself moving back and forth across several sides of a point before coming to grips with the nuanced perspective that is going to create your argument. You do this before any polishing of your prose takes place.

If fast writing isn't something you've done before, we encourage you to give it a try. The following strategies might help—they're all designed to keep you writing and to stop you from editing. They are: turning off the screen, making notes to yourself, writing with headings, skipping around, and keeping the ideas flowing.

Turning Off the Screen

One of the most fun and dramatic ways to get yourself to write fast is to turn off the screen on your computer. Yes, turn it off so you can't see what you are writing. The same effect can be achieved if you have one of those wireless keyboards. Sit with your back to your screen or sit far from your desk and type away. It's scary at first, and, of course, you have to be careful that your hands are on the right keys because you won't be able to tell that from the screen. But what turning off the screen does is force you to keep moving. You can't go back and reread the sentence you just wrote. You can't go back and correct typos. There's nothing to do but keep writing. We use this strategy a lot at our Scholars' Retreats. Students who try it usually enjoy the feeling of freedom it generates, and they often have fun writing for the first time in their lives.

Making Notes to Self

You're writing along, and you can't think of the word you want to use. Or maybe you know you need an example of something, but you can't think of one. Perhaps you need a citation, but you don't have the source at hand. Maybe you know that a theorist in your field said something about an idea you are developing, and you wonder if that concept would help you elaborate your idea. Most students, when they find themselves in one of these situations, stop and go find what they need. That, of course, stops the fast writing. You interrupt the flow you have going, and, once you leave your computer to take care of these things, you'll find it much harder to get writing again.

When you hit one of these places and are tempted to wander away from your desk to find what you need, don't. Instead, type a note to yourself in the text about what to insert there and keep writing. There are lots of ways you can do this: Type the note in all capital letters or type it in bold text or put it in a different color font. (Don't choose a system that just allows you to waste time, though. The system you choose should be one you can do quickly.) Anything that you can't write right now should simply be noted in one of these ways in your text. For example: *NEED EXAMPLE, SUPPLY CITATION, DOES FOUCAULT FIT HERE? CHECK HEADINGS FOR PARALLEL LANGUAGE.* It will be easy for you to fill in the missing information or to make these decisions when you revise.

In the example below, Wendy knows that she needs some details about what scholars have written about the connection between local news and a sense of community. Then she discovers that she needs to locate a citation for a set-off quote. Notice how she simply makes notes to herself and keeps writing.

Communication and journalism scholars have written widely about the connection between local news, both print and broadcast, and a sense of community. (BRIEFLY REVIEW SOME LITERATURE HERE) Many broadcast journalism scholars contend that economic incentive drives local news organizations' larger efforts to create a sense of community within their viewing audience (Hallin & Gitlin, 1993; Kaniss, 1991; Reese & Buckalew, 1995). Phyllis Kaniss (1991), whose book-length study examines the processes involved in creating local news, explains:

> The major focus of local news coverage in media markets throughout the country has come to be placed on issues with the symbolic capital necessary to unite the fragmented suburban audience. In other words, in order to sell their product—a set of messages the hallmark of which is their uniquely local character—the metropolitan news media have had to produce local identity as much as they produce news and entertainment. (FIND CITATION)[1]

By inserting a note to yourself in such places instead of stopping to supply details or to find a citation, you are able to keep writing. You can then insert these items later when you have a small amount of time or are feeling tired. If you find yourself with 10 or 15 minutes free to work on your dissertation, you can use that time to find a citation and fill it in. Perhaps several missing pieces come from the same book, and you also save time when you are finding the materials to fill in several holes at once.

Writing with Headings

Headings are single words, short phrases, or complete sentences that cover all of the material under them until the next heading. You're used to using headings to divide ideas in a paper as guideposts to help your readers understand your content more easily. You can use them in another way, too—a way that helps you keep writing fast.

Start by identifying how many parts your chapter or section will require. For each chapter, you know exactly what job that chapter has. Given the specific function of a chapter, ask yourself what the parts of that chapter need to be. Those parts become your sections.

You'll also find it helpful to give your sections titles. Descriptive headings that explain a bit more about the section are likely to make it easier for you to write fast because they clearly indicate to you what the function of the section is. Descriptive headings describe in more detail the information they are previewing. Consider these headings within a dissertation chapter about disciplining students at a school for special education: (1) Problems, (2) Techniques, and (3) Alternatives. They don't tell much of a story, do they? They certainly won't help you expand the sections, either. Consider these alternative descriptive headings: (1) Adolescent

Discipline Problems in Special Education, (2) Common Techniques for Disciplining Emotionally Challenged Students, and (3) Alternative Methods of Disciplining with Respect and Rigor. By being descriptive, filling in the sections of the chapter by fast writing becomes easier.

Type all your headings into your document when you first sit down to work on a chapter. You can see in front of you the sections you have to fill. What you are doing is turning a seemingly overwhelming project into many small steps. When the size of what you have to write is small enough, you can deal with it more effectively emotionally. Telling yourself "I only have to fill in this small section" weighs very differently from "I have to write a chapter now." When you are fast writing to fill in a section, you see a very doable, concrete task ahead of you that will take perhaps 25 minutes (something that you've done hundreds of times before).

After you set up all of your sections with their titles, use the complexity and importance of the ideas in each section to get an idea of how long it should be. For example, if you want to have a 30-page findings chapter and you have five equally important sections, you know that each of these sections needs to be about six pages long. Once you know you have six pages to use for explaining an idea, you can look at that idea to see what smaller parts are included. If there are three other parts, assign each of those parts a page count—perhaps a page or a page and a half. You might also have half a page for an introduction and another half a page for a conclusion to this section. Now that you know how long the section is going to be, you can effectively limit the amount of information you have to write to fill that section. This helps you pace out the project and tells you how in-depth you can go on a particular topic as you are doing your fast writing.

There's yet another way to make use of headings to encourage yourself to write fast. Put in more headings than you'll keep in your final document. This allows you to break the writing down into even smaller sections—even smaller doable pieces. Make a heading for each idea or even each paragraph you want to write if that helps you write fast because you are very clear about what you need to write for that paragraph and how it should function. It will be easy to remove the extra headings at revising time.

Skipping Around

Something else that might encourage you to keep writing fast is that you can jump around. In contrast to the method of writing a perfect first draft, where you typically have to start at the beginning and develop the essay chronologically because you develop each idea from the previous one, with fast writing, you aren't bound to writing in order. Because you know the sections you want to write and know what you want to say in each section, you can start writing in whichever section you choose. If you feel like starting with the justification of your data in your proposal, start there. If you're in the mood to explain your research question, start with that section. When you can write on whichever section appeals to you at the moment, writing becomes much more fun. If you do get stuck, you can leave a section for a while and come back to it later.

Keeping the Ideas Flowing

Even though you've figured out the content of your chapters and sections before you start to write, you'll still get stuck sometimes. You won't have a clear idea of what you should say about something or where you should go next as you try to develop an idea. A few strategies can be useful for helping you unfreeze from these kinds of temporary writer's block during fast writing: free writing, making lists, and talking out loud.

Sometimes, free writing about the ideas in a section where you're stuck will give you enough energy and clarity to find your way again. Free writing is short, nonstop, timed writing designed to generate ideas, but it isn't anything you'll keep in your actual draft. To use free writing to encourage your ideas to flow, try setting up some questions about the section that you think are important to answer: Who am I talking to? What am I trying to tell them? Why is this important? You might even try free writing to answer these questions: Why am I stuck? What's keeping me from figuring out this idea? By writing for five minutes about these questions, you'll often find your way back into the ideas of the section.

Something else that can help you figure out what you want to say as you develop your ideas is to make a list of all the points that you think need to be in the section. This is a version of outlining and offers you the freedom of figuring out ideas without getting caught up in exact wording. After you develop a list of points, organize them so you know the order in which you want to write about them. Then flesh out the points in the list into sentences and paragraphs using fast writing.

Here's something else to try if you're temporarily at a loss for ideas while you're fast writing. Talk through ideas out loud—to a friend, to a nearby stuffed animal, or to yourself. If you're a teacher, you might imagine yourself in front of a classroom. A student has just asked you to explain the idea on which you're stuck. You wouldn't just stand there and not respond, would you? Of course not. You would open your mouth, and something would come out. So open your mouth and see what comes out. You're likely to discover that you know more about what you want to say than you thought you did. You might even try this with a tape recorder so you can capture your points easily when you're ready to write.

The first part of the process of getting your ideas on paper is writing. Writing fast gets a complete first draft done in a short amount of time. You know what your entire draft says before you begin the process of revising.

Slow Revising

Only after you have a complete spew draft as a result of fast writing should you begin to revise. This is a slower, more systematic process than writing, and it includes two different kinds of acts—editing and proofreading. Although they are often considered identical, they are really two very different stages with different functions. Both demand close and careful reading, but they focus on different levels of the writing and make use of different techniques to make different kinds of changes. Because editing decisions demand a large scope of vision and proofreading demands a very small scope of vision, combining the two tasks is like trying to focus on both the forest and the trees at the same time. Very difficult! Begin with the editing and then move on to proofreading.

Editing

Editing involves higher level concerns and larger changes than proofreading does. When editing, you want to see, for example, if your ideas are in the correct order, if your evidence backs up your argument, if you have effective transitions between paragraphs, and if you are stylistically consistent. Don't try to edit for everything at once. Make a number of passes through your chapter, each time editing for just one thing. Look first at the highest level of the argument and then move progressively to lower levels of organization, style, and word choice.

Make a pass through the chapter first to remove unnecessary information or text where you got off track and developed an idea that doesn't belong. Having a clear sense of your research question and the purpose of your chapter will help you determine any information that doesn't fit. Only include information that is pertinent to making the argument you are making in this chapter. All other information will only cloud your presentation and make it weaker. Ask yourself, when editing to remove extra information, if you really need a section or a sentence to make your case. Repeat as necessary.

Edit a second time to rearrange the essential pieces of the remaining information so that you have the clearest presentation of your argument. Here you are asking yourself if the major ideas included in your chapter follow one from another. Because you've already removed any extra information, you might need to rearrange some of the ideas to get the most out of your argument. When you have finished with this step, you want to see a pattern of connections among all the major pieces of your chapter. Repeat as necessary.

Make a third pass through your chapter to find places where you need to add new information to fill in gaps in your argument. Here you are beginning to pay attention to missing examples or underdeveloped arguments. One way to do this is to check the thesis sentences of your paragraphs to see if and how they connect to one another. Type out the thesis sentence of each paragraph in a section—only the thesis statement and nothing else from the paragraph. Then read down the list. You will be able to tell whether you have all the key pieces you need to make your argument or to tell the story you want to tell. You'll see where you need to add paragraphs, cut paragraphs, or rework thesis sentences so they make a link in your argument more clearly. At the end of this step, you should be confident that your chapter does what you want it to do and reads smoothly for argument and organization. Repeat as necessary.

You're on your fourth time through your draft, and your focus is now on your paragraphs themselves. Read each paragraph to see if what is in the paragraph fits with the thesis sentence of the paragraph. Make sure you assess the content against what the thesis sentence actually says, not what you intended it to say. Note all the details, examples, and explanations in the paragraph. Do these materials develop the thesis sentence? Do you need more examples? More explanation? Are the materials related enough to be in the same paragraph? You may discover that you have more than one idea in a paragraph and that it needs to be made into two paragraphs.

Your fifth time through your document, review for the transitions between paragraphs. Transitions are words, phrases, or sentences that connect ideas. Because they summarize or restate the point you just discussed and preview your next idea, they let your reader know where you've been and where you're going. Decide if you need to make a transition more explicit, to rearrange the order of your paragraphs to make a transition possible, or to create new transitions where yours are missing. Also check to see if your transitions are all the same kind. Repeated use of *also, as well,* and *in addition* suggests that you're simply making a list—and not a very creative one at that. In such a case, your draft needs more development so that you can highlight the hierarchical or subordinating connections you see among the ideas. Repeat as necessary.

Edit your draft a sixth time to review your sentences. Do you have complete sentences? Do you have variety in the types of sentences you've written? Repeat as necessary.

Make a seventh pass through the draft to review your word choices. Have you used the best words to capture the ideas you want to express? Repeat as necessary.

The eighth time through is to review your spelling and punctuation. Repeat as necessary.

Proofreading

Proofreading is concerned with lower order concerns such as mechanical errors and formatting requirements. You only begin proofreading after you are convinced that your draft is conceptually complete and stylistically sound. This is the final step in polishing a chapter and is crucial for a professional presentation of your ideas. You finish proofreading when you are absolutely convinced that there are no errors in your text. You may not need all of the proofreading strategies we suggest here, but taking advantage of several of them will increase your confidence that your final version of your proposal or chapter is error free.

As with editing, you want to proofread a chapter several times. Each time, make use of a different technique for proofreading so you'll be able to catch all of your errors. Proofread for only one kind of error at a time.

For example, if you know that you have a difficult time with commas, go through the chapter once looking just for commas. If you try to identify too many things at once, you risk losing focus, and your proofreading becomes less effective. In addition, some of the techniques that work well for catching one kind of mistake won't catch others.

As the basis for effective proofreading, we encourage you to develop a style sheet of your own most common errors. When you notice errors that you make frequently, write them down alphabetically on a piece of paper to create your own personal style sheet. Using this style sheet, you can easily look for the errors you make most frequently. Maybe you tend to confuse *affect* and *effect* or you find that you usually put a period after instead of before the citation in a set-off quote. Your list of such errors becomes an excellent starting point for proofreading because you can check each item on the list.

Two proofreading techniques are available for catching the errors on your personal style sheet as well as other mistakes: computer-aided and hard-copy proofreading. Be sure to apply techniques from each category as you're proofing. After completing computer-aided techniques, you should always proofread a hard copy of your chapter because it's very easy to miss errors when reading on a computer screen.

Computer-Aided Proofreading

One kind of proofreading makes use of the tools available on your computer. These techniques are only a beginning point, though, and while helpful in many ways, they have several shortcomings that make them inadequate for use by themselves. These tools are your spell checker and the find-and-replace function.

Before printing out a hard copy of your text to proofread, run your spell checker. Spell checkers can be useful tools, but don't rely on them solely to identify misspellings. They are literal and limited. Because a spell checker can only compare a typed word to its own databank of correctly spelled words, if a word that you have correctly spelled isn't in that spell checker's data bank, that word will be flagged as misspelled. Likewise, if you have mistyped a word like *their* as *they're*, because both words are correctly spelled, your spell checker will not flag this misspelling. Run the spell checker and check each flagged misspelling carefully. It's a start for catching spelling errors. And remember, if you habitually misspell or misuse a word, write it down on your style sheet so that you can make sure you check for it in the future.

Many computer programs have a find-and-replace function. Use this option to catch the errors you have on your personal style sheet. Search for *–ing* if dangling modifiers are a problem for you, for *it* if you confuse *its* and *it's*, or for opening quote marks if you tend to leave out the closing ones. As your style sheet grows, this option becomes more expedient.

Hard-Copy Proofreading

After using the proofreading options on your computer, print out your chapter and read through it slowly, reading every word. Try reading out loud, which forces you to say each word and also lets you hear how the words sound together. This is especially helpful for spotting run-on sentences, but you'll also hear other problems that you may not see when reading silently. When you read silently or too quickly, you can skip over errors or make unconscious corrections. Another technique is to point with your finger or a pen as you read one word at a time. This will slow you down, but, of course, that's the idea.

If you have trouble with sentence punctuation, try separating the text into individual sentences, which will help you read each sentence carefully. When you're working with a printed copy, you might use two highlighters of different colors to alternately mark sentences. This will help you isolate and evaluate your sentences as well as identify and assess beginning and ending punctuation marks.

Perhaps you tend to miss things in your footnotes, endnotes, or citations. If that's the case, circle or highlight every note or citation in your text and then review only those items. This forces you to look at each one so that you can see if anything is missing or incorrect. After you highlight each citation, you can quickly review each one to make sure it matches the style expectations for your discipline. Highlighting your footnotes or endnotes and the numbers in the text also lets you quickly check to see that you have a note—and the correct one—for each reference.

Don't stop to fix your errors on the computer at the moment that you identify them. When you identify an error or a potential error, mark it on the hard copy and continue looking for more errors. If you have a question, write your question on a sticky note and place it on the page beside the item in question. If you need to use a reference book to look up one error, you can look up several at a time. Marking your errors like this allows you to find answers to all of them at once, so you don't have to interrupt your proofing multiple times throughout the document.

Writing and revising your dissertation can look overwhelming in the beginning. You can find yourself looking at a blank computer screen and wondering how you are going to communicate all of your ideas effectively—or even how you're going to generate the amount of text you're going to need to turn that blank screen into a dissertation. You might also fear that you don't know the right words to use or that you aren't very good at expressing yourself. That's kind of how you feel when you travel and don't know any of the local language, isn't it? Once you learn some useful phrases, you find you are able to accomplish what you want to do and begin to enjoy the journey more. Try out some of these ideas for writing and editing if these processes cause you difficulties. We suspect that you'll be delighted with how quickly you pick up the local lingo and begin to develop effective writing and editing skills.

Notes

1. Constructed from the dissertation of Wendy Hilton-Morrow, "Local News, National Story: Television's Construction of Viewer Subject Positions during the Iraq War" (PhD diss., University of Iowa, 2005).

TRAVELOGUE: THE DISSERTATION DEFENSE

Steps 26–29 (124 hours)

W hen you return home from your travels, you are eager to share your experiences with others. You might create a blog, e-mail pictures and accounts of your journey to friends and family, or create a video or CD of your photographs to share with others. For dissertation writers, sharing takes the form of explaining and justifying your ideas in conversations with interested and educated others. Of course, you are sharing your ideas in written form in your dissertation itself, but discussing your ideas orally is another way in which this sharing takes place.

When you think about a defense, you're probably thinking about the final defense—the defense with your chair and committee members that happens after you've completed the writing of your dissertation. But that's not the only defense in which you're engaged in the dissertation process. There's also an ongoing defense that begins as soon as you start working on your dissertation. In this defense, you'll be defending and supporting any number of aspects of your project—perhaps your topic, the categories of your literature review, your methods, how to present your findings, and your writing style—in conversations with your advisor and other committee members.

We aren't suggesting that you go into defense mode every time your advisor asks for revisions or questions something you want to do. He will have many excellent suggestions for revision that you'll be happy to follow because you can see how they make your dissertation better. But there will be times when you have an idea that is really important to you or when you have a strong commitment to a particular way of presenting something in your dissertation, and you'll want to defend your ideas in an effort to gain your advisor's support.

There are several functions, then, that your ongoing defense performs. It helps you retain control of your dissertation so that you're able to do a study that excites and interests you. It also helps you develop the skills of presenting, supporting, and scrutinizing ideas in scholarly conversations. Equally important, the ongoing defense builds your confidence in your ability to use these skills. In other chapters, we've suggested some of the critical times when you'll want to engage in an ongoing defense of your dissertation, so our focus in this chapter is on the final defense—the one you'll do after you have completed your travels.

The functions of your final formal defense are different from those of your ongoing defense. The final defense is designed to allow you to disseminate the findings of your study. This is the first time you'll have a chance to talk formally about your findings, sharing new scholarship that contributes to your discipline. You are also publicly showcasing and celebrating the skills you developed and the confidence you gained through your work on the dissertation. Because your defense marks the end of your research apprenticeship, it has another function, too: It is your formal welcome into the community of scholars.

Defenses vary substantially from department to department and from university to university. The steps we outline below are true of most defenses, but you'll want to augment our description with specific information about how defenses are conducted in your department.

Preparing for Your Defense

The first step of preparation begins long before you enter the seminar room for your own defense. Attend the defenses of some other students in your department. Attending others' defenses will give you an idea of the kinds of questions that faculty members ask, the tone of the proceedings, and any skills you might need to practice to ensure a successful defense for yourself. If defenses aren't open to the public in your own department, attend some in other departments and ask students who have been through the process in your department what the experience was like.

As you are finishing up the writing of your dissertation, schedule your defense. Graduate schools have rules about what the latest date is when a defense can be held each quarter or semester if you want to graduate that term. Find out what that date is and schedule your defense accordingly. Scheduling can take some work given faculty members' busy schedules, so begin working on figuring out a time when everyone can get together well ahead of when you want your defense to take place. One way of finding a time that everyone can meet is to ask for available times and days from each faculty member for a particular period of time—say, the last week in March. When you get these dates back, see if you can find a common time.

At most universities, in addition to your advisor and committee members, an outside person is likely to be present at your defense—a representative of the graduate school. She sits in on your defense to be sure it is conducted properly and to protect you from conflicts among committee members that they might try to take out on you. Sometimes, when you schedule your defense, you can designate whom you would like this person to be. If you have a choice, you can select a professor from whom you've taken courses and whose research specialty is relevant to your study.

You may have a choice about whether your defense will be open to other students, faculty, friends, and family. If you do have a choice, think carefully about the decision. How comfortable do you feel defending your ideas orally? Does having a large audience make you more nervous? If you don't defend your dissertation as well as you would like or if committee members identify serious flaws in your project, do you want lots of people watching? If you decide you want to invite others to attend, create invitations or develop a flier to advertise your defense.

Now is the time to package your dissertation effectively. At some point in the process of completing your dissertation, you are required to have the format reviewed by someone in the graduate school. This person will check your dissertation for things like the size of your margins and the format of your headings. At most universities, you have a choice about when to have this checking done. It can be done now or after your defense. We suggest you do it now so that the dissertation is in the proper form when you submit it to your committee members. Having it checked at this point in the process will also leave you less to do following your defense, when you'll really be ready to be done.

After you've made any revisions the graduate school requires in terms of formatting, make your manuscript as clean and as perfect as you can make it. Put it in a box (copy shops have manuscript boxes that are perfect for this), or bind it with one of those coil bindings so the pages stay together. All of these presentational strategies encourage a positive response to what you have written because they communicate to your committee members that your dissertation is of high quality.

Give your committee members your dissertation two weeks ahead of your defense date. This will give them time to read the dissertation before your defense, and there's also enough time so that, if a committee member thinks there's a major problem with the dissertation, the defense can be rescheduled. (Don't worry: This doesn't happen very often, but you would rather have your defense delayed and revise your dissertation than go into a defense when your committee members don't believe your dissertation is ready to defend.) When you distribute your dissertation to your committee members, you might want to do again what we recommended with your proposal: Ask your advisor to include a note with the dissertation endorsing it and stating that it is ready for defense.

If your advisor agrees and if the practice doesn't violate norms in your department, call or e-mail your committee members a few days before your defense to see if they have any questions or comments to share with you. Faculty members are usually willing to share concerns they have or to preview some of the questions they'll ask you at the defense. At the very least, you will have a sense of how they are likely to respond to your dissertation at the defense. An alternative to contacting your committee members yourself is for your chair to contact them. Either way, such conversations reduce surprises at the defense.

Now is a good time to have a conversation with your advisor about the role he will play in your defense. Some advisors adopt a role of mediator, clarifier, and cheerleader. This might involve clarifying confusing questions, asking you questions to which he knows you know the answer, and interrupting trains of hostile questioning. Other advisors assume the role of harsh critic, expecting you to rise to the challenge and display how much you know. An advisor who adopts this role often may surprise you with criticism that he hasn't given you before—perhaps about the need to reorganize your study or about the inadequacy of your findings. Knowing what you can expect about the role your advisor will assume will help you be prepared.

Before your defense begins, ask your advisor something else: To write down the questions that you are asked and by whom. There are several reasons for this. Your advisor wants a record of the questions so she can talk with the committee members about which ones require revisions in your dissertation. The record also gives you a sense of the kind of responses you're likely to get to your study when you revise it for publication as an article or a book. There's another reason, too: You are likely, at the end of your defense, to remember very few of the questions you were asked because you were nervous and concentrating on your own performance, and it's useful and fun to have a record of them. But you don't want to be writing the questions down yourself because you want to focus on giving good answers to the questions. That's why it's a good idea to establish with your advisor ahead of your defense that she'll keep a record of the questions for you.

Also ask your advisor to prepare a list of possible questions you might be asked at your defense—questions that cover the range of types of questions you'll be asked at varying levels of difficulty. Here's where those conversations with committee members will be very helpful. But even if such conversations aren't possible, your advisor is probably familiar enough with your study and the committee members that he can make some pretty good guesses about the kinds of questions they'll ask.

Then hold a mock defense and answer out loud the questions your advisor has given you. If possible, do this practice defense with your advisor, who can critique your responses and help you develop strategies for responding to questions. If this isn't something your advisor is willing to do, you can have a mock defense with a fellow student or students or even your partner or spouse. Pretend you are actually at the defense, and answer the questions as you actually would in the real situation. You will get used to presenting complete answers and articulating ideas out loud, and some of your nervousness should dissipate because of your increased comfort level with the process.

If your advisor is not willing to suggest some questions you might be asked, we recommend that you do another kind of preparation: Prepare 10 basic answers. Some of these answers should be about major aspects of your study—an answer about your method, an answer about your data, and an answer about your findings, for example. Some should be more global answers about the history of trends in your field and about the literature on which you drew for your study. At a minimum, you will have 10 solid, articulate, rehearsed "speaking modules" on which you can draw to formulate the answers to the questions you are asked.

Your next step should be to prepare your presentation for the defense. Departments differ as to how long and how formal your presentation should be, so be sure to find out what is expected in yours. In some departments, you are asked to give a five-minute summary of your project while you are sitting down at the table with your committee members. With these kinds of presentations, the attitude of the faculty is that they've all read the dissertation and don't need a lengthy summary, but they want to be sure you can give one. This short summary is also useful for anyone in the room who hasn't read your dissertation. In other departments, you are expected to give a 30-minute formal presentation, often with PowerPoint or transparencies, summarizing your project in detail. With this format, of course, there will be less time for questions by your committee members. Regardless of the length of the presentation, you want these items to be included in it: (1) Research question, (2) Literature that sets up the theoretical conversation for your study and that you found most helpful, (3) Methods for gathering and analyzing your data, (4) Major findings, and (5) Recommendations for future research.

There's still more preparation to be done. If you are doing a Power-Point presentation or using overhead transparencies, get them ready. In some departments, the custom is to have a one-page handout that summarizes your dissertation prepared for guests who have not read the dissertation in advance. If this is the case in your department, get it ready. Then practice and practice and practice your presentation until it flows easily and eloquently. There are other things you'll want to pull together to bring to your defense: A copy of your dissertation, a legal pad on which to take notes, a pen, water, and a handkerchief or Kleenex if you tend to sweat or cry during such events. Also bring along copies on the required bond paper of any of the dissertation pages that have to be signed by your committee if you'll be submitting your dissertation in hard copy.

The Defense Itself

You can expect your defense to be two hours long. It will probably be held in a conference or seminar room in your department, where the standard arrangement is a rectangular table, where you sit at the head. Your advisor will introduce the proceedings, usually explaining that everyone is gathered for your defense, and she'll also summarize the procedures that will be followed. In some departments, defenses begin by having the student leave the room so that the committee members can determine the order of questioning and discuss any major concerns they might have, so don't be surprised if you are asked to leave the room immediately when your defense begins.

Then it's your turn. You probably want to begin your opening presentation by thanking your advisor and your committee members for their assistance with your project. Then you'll give the oral presentation or summary of your project that you've been practicing. Following your presentation, you are likely to be asked to talk about any changes you would want to make in your study. Come prepared to talk about a few. Avoid two common mistakes students make in discussing such changes. One is to point out such major flaws that the committee members begin to question whether they should pass you. Another is to pick out piddling revisions you would like to make, including typos. Remember that you want to exude confidence about your project, so your explanation of changes you would make should be ones that other scholars might readily identify but that don't substantially diminish the value of your study (the sample consisted of college students and thus lacked heterogeneity, for example). Your final defense has begun, so make even your suggested changes be part of your effort to justify your choices and demonstrate your familiarity with conventions of scholarship.

The major part of the defense consists of the professors on your committee asking you questions. They will do this in one of two ways. They might choose to take turns, going around the table, one by one, with each person asking you the questions he wants to ask. Or the defense may take the form of a conversation, where one person will begin the questioning, others jump in, and the committee members ask their questions at the point in the conversation where they seem to fit. Even if the procedure is a turn-taking one, you'll find that the question asking often turns into a conversation. Others may ask follow-up questions or respond to your answer after one professor asks a question before the turn-taking format is restored. Sometimes, too, you'll find that the professors will start talking and debating an idea among themselves. Faculty members enjoy talking with their peers about ideas, but they don't get the chance to very often. A defense provides them with this opportunity. Don't worry if that happens. You're out of the hot seat temporarily, so take a deep breath and get ready for the next question when your committee members discover that they ought to refocus their attention back onto you.

So what kinds of questions are you likely to be asked at your defense? Some will be narrow questions focused on a sentence you wrote on a certain page. A committee member perhaps doesn't understand what you mean or takes issue with what you've said or how you've expressed an idea. In these cases, the questioner will ask all the committee members to turn to that page of your dissertation, and you'll be asked to explain the statement. A question in this category might be something like this: "On page 27 of your dissertation, in the first sentence of the second paragraph, you make a statement about truth. This suggests that you believe there is an objective reality out there that can be discovered. Is this what you mean to be implying here?"

A second type of question will have to do with the logistics of your study. Questions may be asked about why you chose the data or methods you did or why you organized your dissertation in a particular way. Likewise, you might be asked to explain how you applied a particular method in your study or to explain some aspect of your statistical procedures. A question of this type would be something like: "Can you explain in more detail the process you used to code the television programs?" or "Why did you use grounded theory as your method instead of content analysis?"

Other questions will focus on your findings or the results of your analysis. These questions might be about the schema you developed to present your findings, the implications of your findings, or the connection between your findings and previous literature. Here are two questions of this type: "The theory of humor you developed in your last chapter provides an explanation for humor that is very different from previous theories of humor. How do you reconcile your findings with past studies that provide different causal explanations for humor?" or "Did anything surprise you about your findings?"

Some questions will be asked about topics related to but not directly concerned with the subject of your dissertation. Your committee members will assume that you are familiar with related theories and bodies of literature and may ask you questions about them. They also might want to ask you questions about related theories or concepts because they seem useful for developing an explanation of your findings. An example of such a question is: "Do you remember Kenneth Burke's notion of perspective by incongruity? Can this idea be used to enrich your analysis of your data?"

Other questions will ask you to reflect on the dissertation process and move you forward into a professional life. These questions are things like: "Now that you have finished this study, what have you learned about doing research?" or "What are your plans for research following completion of your dissertation?"

The questions you are asked by the graduate school representative or outside reader at your defense are likely to be different still. Unless this person has a vendetta against you for some reason (as we saw once when the assigned outside person happened to be the best friend of the man with whom the student had just broken off a relationship), the outside person will be supportive and interested. Because of a lack of knowledge of your discipline, though, she will tend to ask questions from an educated outsider's perspective. Her questions typically will be of general interest, application questions, or questions that allow her to learn more about a subject and methods that are new to her. Although the external reader may see herself as the final gatekeeper who must validate your expertise through rigorous inquiry, such a stance is rare, and the external person rarely disagrees with your committee on the final evaluation.

If your committee members complete their questioning and there's still some time left, any other people present at your defense may be invited to ask questions. Fellow students, friends, and family members will be genuinely interested in understanding your dissertation, so their questions will be fun and easy for you to answer. They might even ask you questions they know you can answer readily just to be supportive and to try to decrease your anxiety.

Let's turn now to some strategies for answering questions. Your strategy for answering any question you are asked should be the same: Answer it confidently but not arrogantly and explain yourself as articulately and clearly as you can. Be assertive about your knowledge—remember that you know more about your study than your committee members do. Provide expansive responses to questions. Be in command of the literature that informs your dissertation. Your committee members may not agree with some of the choices you made in your dissertation and might not have done your study in exactly the same way you did, but your job is to show them that you can justify your choices in ways that make sense.

First be sure that you understand a question. Some questions will be poorly worded, and you'll miss parts of some questions simply because you're nervous. Don't answer a question if you're not sure what it is. Get clarity first. It's all right to pause for 10 seconds or so to think. One way to create a pause is to jot notes on your legal pad while a faculty member is asking a question. Then you can look back at what you've written to try to understand the question. You can also ask a faculty member to ask a question again or to elaborate on it if you don't understand it. Don't be afraid to engage in the practice of active listening to be sure you've understood a question: "Let me see if I have this right. You're asking me to explain the methodological assumptions that led me to do interviews for my study?"

You may be asked some questions that are difficult to answer for various reasons. Strategizing about how you might answer them will help you feel more at ease if you get asked these kinds of questions. For example, what if you get asked a question to which you truly don't know the answer? Such questions are often questions about subjects you didn't deal with in your dissertation, theories with which you aren't familiar, or issues that you haven't thought about in conjunction with your study. Don't respond to such a question by saying "I don't know." Instead, you want to demonstrate that you know how to respond professionally in such situations. You might simply say, "I'm not prepared to discuss that because it's beyond the scope of my study." Another option is to say, "That's an interesting question. I hadn't thought about that connection before. Let me talk through some possible connections I can come up with off the top of my head so you can see how I might begin to approach this." Now might also be the time to bring in one of those 10 answers you prepared and to try to make a connection between the answer and the subject of the question.

Another kind of question you might be asked is also likely to confuse you. This is a question that doesn't make sense to you because the answer is clearly in your dissertation—in fact, you might have dealt extensively in the dissertation with what the questioner is asking you to explain. In such cases, you'll be tempted to try to figure out the motive of the questioner for asking the question or will wonder if the questioner is asking you for a deep and profound answer that goes beyond what is in your dissertation.

Probably not. When these kinds of questions are asked, it's usually because the questioner hasn't read your dissertation very well or at all. (Yes, this happens. In fact, we just heard of a case where a student was quite certain her advisor hadn't read her dissertation by the time she defended it.) Your first effort to answer these kinds of questions should be to answer them as you did in your dissertation, perhaps pointing out graciously that you dealt with this issue in a particular section of the dissertation but that you are happy to reiterate the information contained there.

You also might be asked questions that are designed to allow faculty members to demonstrate their knowledge in front of their colleagues. These questions might be quite lengthy and seem more like sermonettes than questions. They're difficult to answer because they aren't really questions. If you get one of these questions, see if you can find something in the statement/question with which you agree and that's relevant to your dissertation. Affirm the questioner by restating the so-called question, agreeing with it, and relating it to your dissertation. Here's an example: "You make an excellent point, Dr. Freyer, about the abuses of the ethnographic method as it is being used today. I tried to avoid those in my dissertation by. . . ."

You also might be asked questions about why you did not do something in your dissertation, with the implication that your study should have been bigger than it is, encompassed other subjects, employed other methods, or generally been a different study. Your answer to such questions can be something along the lines of: "That's a fine idea, and expanding my data certainly would enhance my findings. But that's really a different study, and I hope others will do that in the future to build on the work I've begun. It might even be something I'll want to do myself because it would fit nicely into my research program."

After everyone is done asking questions, you'll be asked to leave the room. If there are visitors sitting in on the defense, they'll be asked to leave with you. Don't take your things with you as you leave because you'll be asked to come back in again fairly soon. Hang around not too far from the door so that your advisor can find you easily when your committee members are ready to bring you back again.

While you are out of the room, your committee members will be making several decisions. They'll first decide whether to pass you on your defense and your dissertation. Voting processes and requirements vary across universities, so be sure to find out what they are before you go into your defense. At some universities, you can receive one negative vote on your defense or dissertation and still pass. At other universities, you can have one negative vote on one but not the other, or you must have all positive votes on both the defense and the dissertation in order to pass. If you don't pass, the options are likely to be to redo the dissertation and the defense, schedule a second oral defense, or terminate matriculation. At some universities, your committee also has an option of choosing to pass you "with distinction." This means you have done an exemplary job on your dissertation.

If you pass—certainly the most likely option—a second decision your committee members will be making concerns the nature of the revisions they want you to make. The choices often are "pass with no revisions," "pass with minor revisions," or "pass with major revisions." "No revisions" rarely means absolutely no revisions. It can mean correcting tables, correcting typos, or adding a few sentences of clarification. "Minor revisions" means explanation or clarification of several paragraphs at various places in your dissertation. "Major revisions" are those that involve a substantial rewriting of sections of your dissertation.

A third decision the committee members will make is about who will be accountable for making sure the revisions they ask for are completed satisfactorily. In some cases, some or all members of your committee will want to see the revisions, but typically, the committee members agree that your advisor will be the final arbiter about whether you have successfully made the revisions they requested. To help with these revisions, committee members often return their copies of the dissertation with margin notes and editing suggestions.

When the committee's deliberations are done, you will be called back into the room. In many departments, you know right away how well you've done. The convention is for your advisor to greet you outside of the door, if you've passed, with "Congratulations, Dr. ___." You can breathe a sigh of relief then—you may have revisions left to do, but you've made it through the defense, and your committee has passed your dissertation.

Following Your Defense

The final stage, of course, is your celebration. In some departments, a reception takes place immediately after the defense—perhaps in the same room in which the defense was held or somewhere else in the department. There might be a norm that your faculty advisor brings champagne (if alcohol is allowed on your campus), which is then shared among you, your committee members, and any friends and family members who have gathered. In some departments, the norm is for the student to supply food at the defense for the committee members and/or a reception immediately following. Be sure to find out what the norms are in your department.

For some students, gift giving follows the defense. Again, this practice varies across departments, so check on the conventions. Some students give gifts to all of their committee members immediately after the defense or at a later time. These gifts might be things like bookmarks, gift certificates to a bookstore, mugs, or pens. If your committee members have not been very involved in your dissertation, gifts can seem excessive, in which case you might want to give a small gift only to your advisor and perhaps write thank-you notes to your committee members. If you want to give your advisor a gift, those gift certificates, mugs, or pens work well, as does something a bit more personal, such as a scarf, a piece of pottery, desk accessories, or flowers. Some advisors give their advisees a gift following the defense, so don't be surprised if you receive such a congratulatory item from yours.

The defense is the moment you've been planning and preparing for over the course of months and even years. It might feel anticlimactic when it's over—like it wasn't such a big deal after all. To counter the possibility that you might feel a bit let down, plan a small celebration for that day—perhaps go out to lunch with friends or family after your defense. You might not want your big party to be that night, though, because you are likely to feel utterly drained after the defense and more like taking a nap than partying.

The day after the defense, begin to attend to any revisions your committee members have asked you to make. You're not likely to feel much like making revisions to the dissertation at this moment, but tackle them quickly. Make a list for yourself of all the revisions you need to do, breaking each one down into discrete, doable units. This is the same process that you did innumerable times to get your dissertation done, and you just have to do it one more time. Take each item on your list one by one and make the revision. When you've done all of them, read the entire dissertation through to make sure your revisions don't require changes in other parts of the dissertation and that there is alignment throughout.

A note about revisions: If the revisions seem major and designed not to correct flaws in your study but to make it into a substantially more sophisticated work, chances are you are being asked to make the kinds of revisions that would be needed to turn your dissertation into a book. If you think this is what's happening to you, you'll need to engage in that ongoing defense one more time. Remind your advisor and committee members that this is a dissertation, and the revisions required should be ones required to make the dissertation satisfactory. You might have to assert that you will be happy to make book-type revisions if you decide to turn your dissertation into a book.

When your advisor (and any committee members who have asked to be involved) sign off on your revisions, you're almost done. Make the required number of copies on the required bond of paper. (If you are allowed to submit your dissertation electronically, of course, this won't be necessary.) You'll also probably want to give your advisor a copy and perhaps your committee members, although these copies don't have to be bound in any fancy way. Now is the time, too, to make copies for family members and close friends. Be sure to have extra money in your budget or on your credit card at submission time because the submission fees and copying and binding costs can be substantial.

Both your ongoing defense and your final defense help you develop the skills involved in sharing and defending ideas in conversation. In contrast to those situations in which you impose a travelogue on friends and relatives who may be less than interested, at the defense, those in the conversation are interested in the ideas you've developed and want to explore them with you. They also want you to succeed and aren't deliberately trying to harass or block you. Relax as much as you can, feel good about what you have done, try to have some fun, and remember that you know more about your dissertation than anyone else. As Peters rightly notes, "Remember that not only is the defense an open-book examination but you wrote the book!"[1]

Notes

1. Robert L. Peters, *Getting What You Came For: The Smart Student's Guide to Earning a Master's or Ph.D.* (New York: Noonday/Farrar, Straus & Giroux, 1997), 245.

CHAPTER ELEVEN
MAKING THE BEST USE OF YOUR GUIDE: ADVISOR ADVISING

Sometimes, when you travel, you are fortunate to be accompanied by a guide who shows you the way, shares knowledge and expertise with you, frames your experience of a site in a useful way, answers your questions, and generally enhances your traveling experience. Your advisor has the potential to serve in this same way for you. Just as a guide can have a major impact on your experience while traveling, your relationship with your advisor affects the kind of dissertation you write, your experience of doing the dissertation, the time it takes to complete it, and your career options once the dissertation is done.

Because advisors have the greater power in the advising situation, you might expect them to take the lead in initiating communication that facilitates effective relationships. Ideally, you'd like your advisor to engage in communication such as inviting interaction between the two of you, offering assistance, creating a safe environment in which to explore ideas, and adapting his communication to you and your needs. Not all advisors, though, engage in these kinds of communication. They don't always have or make use of the kinds of communication skills required to create an effective mentoring relationship.

Does your advisor's lack of skill in communicating mean she doesn't want to help you? Definitely not. Most advisors are well-intentioned and want to be helpful. Faculty members generally don't take on graduate advisees unless they want to work with them and help them succeed. Many, however, simply don't know what to do to be good advisors. They also aren't likely to get much support in helping them learn how to improve their advising skills. What this means is that they're likely to be using as an advising script their own experience as an advisee—what their relationship with their own graduate advisor was like—and that can be a limiting and often dysfunctional model.

If your advisor seems to lack the skills of a good advisor, does this mean you're doomed to have a troubled relationship that may slow you down? Again, no. The advising relationship is, at its core, a communication relationship. It is initiated, developed, and maintained through communication, which means that, by using skillful communication, you can exert some influence in the relationship. Engaging in particular kinds of communication can help you make your advisor into the best possible advisor for you—someone who will allow you to complete your dissertation and flourish as a professional. There's another reason for you to employ effective communication skills: Such skills can help reduce the power differential between you and your advisor and can dramatically affect your advisor's perception of you. By using good communication skills, you can transform yourself from a groveling graduate student into a proactive, capable, committed, potential colleague.

Five communication skills are particularly important in helping you create an effective advisor: Asking a faculty member to be your advisor appropriately, agreeing on a vision, articulating your needs, enacting professionalism, and assessing your relationship.

Asking Appropriately

Asking appropriately has to do with asking a faculty member to be your advisor. If you are reading this book because you are in the throes of the dissertation process, you already have your advisor. If that's the case, skip this discussion of the skill of asking and go on to the next skill—agreeing on a vision. If you are reading this at the beginning of your program, haven't yet begun to think about your dissertation, and don't have an advisor, keep reading.

The first step is something you know a lot about as a graduate student—doing research. Now, though, you want to do research on the faculty members you are considering for your advisor. How do you go about this? Talk with other students who have the faculty members as advisors. Take classes from potential advisors. Read their books and articles. Serve on committees in your department that have student members so you'll be able to see various faculty members in action. When you're getting close to making a decision, interview the faculty members you're considering. They might be surprised that you are being so thorough and systematic in picking an advisor, but they'll be pleased, too. You have already begun to demonstrate your professionalism and competence in the relationship with your future advisor.

What should you find out about the potential advisors from your research? All sorts of things:

- What reputations do they have as advisors?

- How many advisees do they have?

- How many students have they graduated?

- How do they treat their advisees?

- What percentage of their students finish?

- How long do their students take to finish?

- Where do their students get jobs?

- Do they favor certain kinds of students over others and give them more time and attention?

- How rigorous are they?

- How famous are they? Does their fame impact the time and energy they give to advising, or does their fame provide access to valuable resources?

- What are their schedules like for the next few years? Are they working on books? Planning sabbaticals? Getting divorced?

- Does your working style mesh with theirs?

- Are they consistent in what they demand?

- Do they give credit for work or will they be first author on articles from your dissertation?

There's one more thing to find out, and it's a big one. Find out whether the potential advisors have directed dissertations before. If they haven't, use caution. Sure, there may be advantages to being a young faculty member's first advisee. He is likely to be energetic and enthusiastic and to remember how it felt to be a graduate student. How many students he graduates could factor into his own tenure decision, so he also might be eager to perform well. But being someone's first advisee can delay your progress on your dissertation. He may simply not know what to do and won't be able to provide you with the guidance you need.

A first-time advisor also can delay you because she wants to prove her brilliance to her faculty colleagues using your dissertation. Jackson worked for five years on his dissertation, going through draft after draft. No version was good enough for his advisor, though. She was a new faculty member who wanted a perfect dissertation for her first student to defend to demonstrate her own competence. Jackson ended up not getting tenure himself because his dissertation wasn't finished on time.

There are other advantages to a more seasoned advisor. She won't be focused on trying to get tenure at the expense of helping you. She will be less likely to steal your ideas (unfortunately, not an uncommon practice in academia), and she'll be more able to protect you in academic conflicts. A tenured professor is also more likely to remain at your university and to see you through your dissertation instead of leaving for a better position somewhere else.

Let's assume you've done your research and have decided on the faculty member you want to have as your advisor. Don't ask yet. Remember the onus your request to be an advisor places on a faculty member. He may have many advisees, and if you become his advisee, you'll be taking a great deal of his time. If this is the person you really want to be your advisor, you don't want to ask before he's had a chance to get to know you, thus increasing the likelihood that he'll say "yes." Getting to know him means going through the process people usually go through to get to know someone.

Interpersonal relationships typically go through five stages, starting with when people first meet someone and ending with a fully developed relationship. The stages are: initiating, experimenting, intensifying, integrating, and bonding. In the initiating stage, two people meet each other for the first time and engage in polite, safe, and superficial conversation, trying to make a positive impression on one another. In the experimenting stage, they begin to express their likes and dislikes, values, attitudes, personal opinions, and common interests. The third stage is the intensifying stage, and it's characterized by more breadth and depth of self-disclosure. In other words, the people involved will talk about more topics in more in-depth ways. The next stage, the integrating stage, is marked by a high degree of intimacy and is the stage at which the tastes, attitudes, and opinions of the two people begin to merge. They begin to present themselves as a team or a couple, and others begin to see them that way. In the last stage, the bonding stage, two people publicly declare their commitment to each other. This happens through marriage or a commitment ceremony in romantic relationships. In advising relationships, of course, this is when a faculty member commits to serve as a student's advisor.[1]

When two people develop a relationship through these five stages, it's on solid footing because the relationship has been built gradually on shared information. What's important about these relationship stages for you is that they suggest the appropriate time for you to ask a faculty member to be your advisor. Asking is a move to a committed relationship, and asking too early in the relationship can result in a rejection of your invitation just because the faculty member you've selected doesn't know you. Initiate and develop that relationship in the ways people normally do, going through at least most of the stages of initiating, experimenting, intensifying, and integrating before you pop the question.

Knowing about the stages of a relationship can also be helpful for you if you've been assigned an advisor or don't have a choice about an advisor because there's only one person in your department who is qualified to direct your dissertation. In these instances, your advising relationship isn't beginning at the initiating stage but at the integrating or even the bonding stage. Relationships don't typically begin with a request to the proposed friend to be a friend, but that's the way your advising relationship is beginning if you're in this situation. You are starting your relationship late in the steps of relationship building without the benefit of mutual interests, shared enthusiasm, and the reciprocal exchange of information.

So how do you develop a relationship with your potential advisor? Take advantage of any opportunities that are available to exchange the kind of information that typically would be shared at the early stages of a relationship. Join her research team, attend a workshop she's conducting, attend the business meeting of an interest group at a conference in which she participates, attend social events in your department, take classes from her, and perhaps even work out an independent study with her. Don't forget the option of inviting her to tea or lunch. Another strategy is to ask your potential advisor for advice on a paper for another class or that you want to submit to a convention. After several such interactions, ask the targeted faculty member to be your advisor.[2] If she says "no," you'll begin the process over again with another potential advisor. If she says "yes," you're ready to go on to applying the next skill—agreeing on a vision.

Agreeing on a Vision

Something that can cause major difficulties between students and advisors is lack of a shared vision for the dissertation. You and your advisor each have a view of the dissertation and the process you'll be using to create it, but these views might not match up. What's more, you're not likely to be aware that the other has a dramatically different view from yours. As a result, all sorts of problems are likely to arise as the two of you try to work together. Where can things go wrong? Three common misalignments make sharing a vision difficult—lack of agreement on your roles, the advising model you'll be using, and what the dissertation is supposed to be.

Expectations about Roles

You and your advisor need to agree on the roles you expect to adopt during the dissertation process. Roles are sets of behaviors that reflect your view of what is appropriate. Both you and your advisor bring characteristics, identities, commitments, and experiences of various kinds to the advising relationship that affect how each of you thinks you both should act. Let's look at a couple of examples of how this can work.

You and your advisor each bring physical characteristics to the relationship. You may see yourselves in particular ways and try to live up to particular expectations because of these characteristics. It's not the characteristics themselves but how you interpret them that's important here. They can serve as obstacles to shared expectations about roles when they create different expectations for behavior.

Sex is an obvious example. What we're talking about here is a situation in which the characteristic of sex encourages the adoption of particular roles either by you or your advisor, and the two of you disagree on what those should be. You might believe, for example, that because you're a woman, you must adopt a particular role—perhaps being deferential, putting yourself down, or being unassertive. Your advisor, however, doesn't see that as an appropriate role for you. Or perhaps you're a young woman who has an older man as an advisor. You may see him in a fatherly role and expect him to guide, support, and protect you. But he might not be viewing your relationship in those terms at all. Similarly, when you and your advisor are of the same sex and relatively close in age, you may find that one of you sees the relationship as a friendship, while the other doesn't. In all of these cases, your interpretation of a physical characteristic creates expectations that are different between you and your advisor.

How you and your advisor interpret race also might disrupt the potential for sharing a vision of role expectations. If you and your advisor are both persons of color, you might see your advisor's role as supporting you and compensating for the discrimination you might have experienced in the past. Perhaps you believe that he should give you a break and hold you to less rigorous standards than other students. Your advisor, though, might see his job as toughening you up and insisting that you meet the highest standards so you'll be able to succeed in academia. If the perceptions that you and your advisor have don't match up, you'll have a difficult time figuring out how to work together.

Expectations about Advising

Different expectations between advisors and advisees also occur around advising models. You and your advisor might not be approaching the work of the dissertation using the same advising model. An advising model is the basic approach to mentoring that the two of you will use to do the work of the dissertation. Because this model has a lot to do with how the dissertation is created and developed, lack of agreement here is a big problem.

There are three major advising models—replication, apprenticeship, and cocreation. They are all legitimate and appropriate to use. All three can result in a good or a poor relationship between you and your advisor.

All three can enable you to finish your dissertation efficiently or not. And all three can produce high- or low-quality dissertations. What's important about the models is not which one you're using but whether you and your advisor are working from the same one. Let's take a look at the differences among the three models.

Replication Model

Just like the name sounds, in the replication model, you recreate a model supplied by your advisor. She gives you the formula, outline, or basic plan for your dissertation. This might mean that your dissertation is on a topic of her choosing, that you ask a research question she's interested in answering, or that you use research methods she dictates. You might also be asked to use her data set. When your advisor supplies the basic plan for your dissertation, you still have choices, but they're made within a prescribed set of options.

Different kinds of communication by the advisor and student characterize the advising models. In the replication model, your advisor's communication is focused on establishing clear boundaries within which you can work. He provides explicit instructions about what you should do and gives you a lot of information about how to accomplish his view of the dissertation. Your primary communication behaviors, in response, are to listen to the instructions of your advisor, ask questions when you don't understand something, and perform as close to his ideal as you can.

Apprenticeship Model

A second option is the apprenticeship model of advising. Here you have some freedom in how to accomplish the tasks involved in the dissertation, but they're assigned and directed by your advisor. Your advisor guides and models for you, much as a master artist would for an apprentice. You select the plan for your dissertation from a range of options that your advisor offers you, and your primary job is to perform an insightful and credible interpretation of whatever option you choose.

In the apprenticeship model, your advisor supervises and monitors your work. She tries to prevent you from making errors, often by giving you what amount to mini-lectures on best practices. She responds to the work you produce and lets you know how far you can deviate from the boundaries she has established. For your part, you are trying out the processes she recommends, listening to her critiques and responding to them, and negotiating places where your own vision for your study can come through.

Cocreation Model

There's a third option for an advising model, and that's the cocreation model. Here is where you and your advisor both contribute in substantial ways to the plan for your dissertation. Together, you create something that neither of you would have created alone and, in fact, what you create might be quite different from the kind of work your advisor usually does because of your input. You drive the research agenda and process in this model. If your advisor has greater input into the process at some points, it's simply because he has more experience than you do with the research process.

In the cocreation model of advising, communication is reciprocal and symmetrical, so you and your advisor are communicating almost equally. There are times, in fact, when your advisor is likely to deliberately hold back and keep from making suggestions to encourage you to come up with your own answers and ideas. Conversations in which the two of you explore ideas are a primary form that communication takes in this model. And, of course, conversation can't take place without question asking, so that's a major kind of communication in this model of advising, too.

The advising model determines how your dissertation project is planned and developed, the kinds of communication you and your advisor will use, and the standards by which your dissertation will be judged. Thus, it's one of the most important things on which to reach agreement with your advisor.

Expectations about Dissertations

Another stumbling block to a shared vision is widely disparate expectations of what a dissertation is. The two of you might disagree, for example, about the function of a dissertation. Some see it as a test to be passed. Others believe that if students have passed their comprehensive exams, they are qualified to write a dissertation. Some believe a dissertation is the culmination of an individual's scholarly work and is the best research a student will ever produce. Others see it as something that simply demonstrates that a student can do research. If you have one idea of its function and your advisor has another, the kind of dissertation you each envision will be substantially different.

Conception of the scope of the dissertation is another potential source of disagreement. Scope has to do with magnitude and significance and usually translates into the level of difficulty of doing a dissertation and the length of time it takes to write it. Your advisor might think a dissertation is supposed to be a major struggle that takes years to complete, while you see it as a doable project you can accomplish in seven or eight months. Or it can work the other way around. Many students see the dissertation as a project of such enormity and intellectual sophistication that they blow it all out of proportion. They believe it must be incredibly difficult and time consuming to complete. If you are one of these students and your advisor tells you the dissertation is not unlike writing a series of papers, which you've done quite successfully for classes in the past, you aren't likely to believe her. Misalignment on the nature of the product, then, is likely to be the result.

Your career goals have a lot to do with the kind of dissertation you'll produce, and, again, if you and your advisor have different ideas about your future career, misalignment can result in what you see as appropriate for a dissertation. Perhaps you want to be a renowned scholar. Or maybe you want to teach at a community college or a teaching-oriented university. You might be getting a doctorate just because you've always wanted to and not for anything it will give you in terms of a career. Maybe you're getting a PhD simply to advance in a career in which you're already well established. These different career goals translate into different ideas about what a dissertation should be. Again, if you and your advisor don't agree, you won't have a shared vision of your dissertation.

Different visions of your dissertation can result, then, if you and your advisor don't agree on the roles you'll adopt in the relationship, the advising model you'll be using, and the nature of a dissertation. An effective advising relationship and completion of your dissertation depend on getting your view and your advisor's view on these issues to line up. This doesn't mean, though, that you have to completely share the same view as your advisor on all three of these factors to have an effective relationship. But you do want to develop agreement on as many as possible. If you identify some areas in which you and your advisor don't agree, we encourage you to have a conversation with your advisor about those differences. Such a conversation can go a long way toward making your advisor into a good advisor for you. If both of you are aware that there may be some difficulty in working together as a result of your differences, those differences are less likely to turn into significant obstacles.

Articulating Needs

There's another way to make your advisor into a good advisor and that's to articulate your needs. It's perfectly appropriate to ask for what you need and want from your advisor. In fact, asking your advisor for explicit assistance around your needs is most likely to encourage him to view you as a committed and engaged professional. Let's take a look at what some of these areas are.

Conceptual Conversation

Ask your advisor to engage in a conceptual conversation to develop your dissertation preproposal. As we explained in chapter 3, we think a conceptual conversation, which results in a preproposal, is the best way to get your dissertation off to a good start because it's a way for you and your advisor to work out and agree on the basic elements of your study. We know that engaging in a conceptual conversation with your advisor may not be possible for a number of reasons, though, so don't worry if you don't feel comfortable asking your advisor to have this kind of conversation with you. There are others things for which you can ask.

Ground Rules

Ask for a discussion with your advisor to lay out ground rules for your interaction around the dissertation. We suggest that you cover some key topics in this meeting:

- How often will you and your advisor communicate? What form will the communication take? In-person meetings? E-mail exchanges? Phone calls? Are there rules you want to adopt in terms of how these are conducted? For example, perhaps you'll agree that you can call one another at home but not before 8:00 a.m. and not after 10:00 p.m.

- How will you and your advisor keep track of the decisions you make about your dissertation? Will you send an e-mail to your advisor documenting the meeting? Will your advisor type a brief note at the end of a meeting and make a copy for both of you?

- Does your advisor want you to notify her in advance that you'll be giving her a chapter to read?

- How quickly will your advisor respond when you give her something to read? You might establish a guideline that your advisor will read a chapter within two weeks, for example, unless there are extenuating circumstances.

- What kind of advising model will the two of you be using as you work together to produce the dissertation? Replication? Apprenticeship? Cocreation?

- How do you learn best? How can your advisor facilitate your learning?

- What coaching techniques work well with you? Does guilt work? How about deadlines? Rewards? What doesn't work? What should your advisor never say to you if she wants to motivate you?

- What expectations does your advisor have for your behavior? Not avoiding her when you are having problems with your dissertation? Telling her when you don't understand something? Meeting deadlines?

What you and your advisor are doing here is creating a system under which you will work together to get your dissertation done. Some advisors have written, well-articulated statements of the ground rules under which they prefer to work, so ask your advisor if she has such a statement. Here are samples of two of these statements. If you're a graduate student, they'll give you ideas about what to work out in terms of ground rules with your advisor. If you're a faculty member, they're good models if you'd like to write such a statement for your advisees.

Ground Rules Sample #1

<u>Working Together</u>

As we get started working on the working and writing process together, let me stress that I am committed to your success! You also need to be aware that I will need your help and cooperation as your advisor. I normally have several people in various stages of the coursework, comps, and writing process—some times are heavier than others. Here are three things to think about, followed by practices I am asking us to follow to guide our working together:

First, it is important that we work together—we are a team. Make me the first person to know what is going on with you, and please keep me apprised of your progress. It is important that I be your first line of communication. Please do not zoom ahead without me. Except for small questions, please do not contact your committee members, send out chapters, discuss orals dates, or do anything major without you and me being on the same page and me giving you the go-ahead. My goal is to follow a workable protocol and to help and protect you.

Similarly, if you are struggling and/or stuck, I want to know that, too, so I can help you through it. Silence is the hardest thing for me to interpret, and you likely know me well enough now to know that I do not deal well with this kind of ambiguity. Of course, everyone has short periods of being stuck or frustrated—that is normal. But at some point, if it persists, let me help you.

When dealing with policy-related issues (e.g., paperwork, deadlines), please try to handle your questions internally first. Check the department's graduate handbook and the graduate college's Web site or bulletin first. Talk with me if necessary and please call Graduate Studies last—I want to save questions and contact with them for when we really need it.

Second, I encourage you to seek support from your own networks and especially your student and/or alumni colleagues. Read one another's drafts, interview protocols, do practice interviews with one another, proofread for one another. This really helped me, and I ask my advisees to have one or more colleagues who are reading their work before it ever comes before me. It makes a difference. I suggest that you set up your

---

own comps, thesis/dissertation network—have someone to report into weekly and hold one another to deadlines. Sometimes, recent graduates you know are very helpful as they just went through all this (and successfully!). So, when you send me something it should not be a first draft but should have the benefit of several drafts from you and other scholars. The version you are sending to me is at its best, then. Think of everything you send me as a version rather than a draft (see below).

Third, try as I might to sequence students so I am not handling everyone at once, it rarely works. What often happens is that multiple people send their stuff at once or I will set aside time for one student who says something is coming on this date or that, and then the student does not meet the deadline he or she promised. Believe me, I understand completely how this works from your end. I often have big plans for writing that get moved back. This is not a critique, but it is a plea for help, understanding, and action as we start this process.

This is how we will proceed together:

1. *Advance warning, please!* I need at least one week (preferably more) warning that a document or chapter is coming. Please do remind me even if you are meeting a deadline that you set and told me about earlier. Understand that it takes planning on my part to queue up this work to be able to devote the time to read your work. It can take me the better part of a day to read a single chapter. For example, I recently spent three hours and wrote four pages of comments on just the first 11 pages of text of a chapter I was seeing for the first time. This is not atypical. In turn, I will keep you posted on my progress getting things back to you.

2. *Title and date each version and attachment*: Be sure to title and date *each* item you give me each time (do this on top of the first page of a document and copy and on the document title): Gonzalez Prospectus Ch. 1—Version #1, 11/27/04. Title the electronic document title similarly: GonzProspecCh1_11/27/04.doc.

3. *What you need to do: The learning curve*: Of course, you can reduce the time it takes for me to respond to your chapter by turning in work that is the best that you can do. In other words, I should never be reading an early draft. In the end, that will slow us both down. Remember, one major purpose of this dissertation process is to launch your career as an independent scholar. This is your last opportunity for this level of support and feedback. Make the most of it.

Expect to write multiple versions of any document. It will not be unusual for us to pass three or more versions back and forth, and that would represent several drafts each round on your part before I see it. Note that I am not calling these *drafts* because that implies work in progress. Whatever you send me should be the best version you can send me at the time.

It is very important to me that you learn from previous feedback and implement the suggestions. Each subsequent version should demonstrate growth. If I do not see that, I will send the chapter back to you. I keep your earlier papers and each version you send of a chapter. As I have suggested elsewhere, keep a writing journal—keep noting things you are learning and working on so you do not forget them the next time you sit down to write, especially post dissertation. I do expect that you will correct errors and incorporate suggestions from earlier papers (and remember I have all your papers electronically and, yes, I do check when frustrated and believe I have made comment X before. I am sure you can understand that). So, do read over your old papers and comments before starting to write a prospectus and dissertation or thesis. If there is a previous comment that you do not agree with, talk with me or write me a note rather than just going about your business and sending back what I will perceive to be an error.

What I am saying is, "Hit me with your best stuff." Don't float something to see how I will react. You may certainly ask me questions as you write, rather than wondering if you should do this or that. What you hand to me, then, is the best you can do at the time. I would rather move a deadline forward than have you rush and send me something that is not ready for me to read. Finally, of course, we do need to balance this against becoming paralyzed and trying for some level of perfection not possible either, right? Again, keep me in the loop—talk with me!

4. *Promises, promises*: Please do not promise me a deadline you cannot deliver. It may make you feel better to set a goal, but you feel terrible when you do not reach it, and I am left juggling my schedule. If you need to move a deadline, give me as much warning as you can. I do need you to set realistic deadlines and do your best to meet them. This is also part of the learning process for your future success.

5. *Turn-around time*: While sometimes I can work quickly, my general rule of thumb is a minimum of one-week turnaround; my valiant attempt is one to two weeks unless there is something big going on or an emergency. This quick turn-around time applies to those who are making good progress. Generally, my rule of thumb is that I have as long to return things to you as you took to get them to me. So, if you take a long writing hiatus, realize that it unlikely that I will return your work quickly, and I will be prioritizing students who are making rapid progress.

   My one-to-two-week time frame grows when you give me items right before conferences, finals time, or holidays (just as would be true for you, right?). Working yourself to the end of deadlines is a very risky thing to do. This will be your emergency, but it is not an emergency that can be imposed on your advisor, committee members, or graduate school. I am sure you can understand all this, and do plan accordingly. I will let you know as I make progress and prepare to send things back to you.

6. *Scheduling*: I reserve holiday breaks and summers for my own work, and I will protect that right for your other committee members as well. I may choose to work with you over breaks or the summer, but I am sure you can understand that this is not to be an expectation. Except in dire emergencies, the department does not hold orals after classes have ended (finals week), and we generally try not to hold orals the last week of classes. Do plan accordingly.

7. *Always, always, write from an outline*: First, send me the outline to check over before you write the chapter. I cannot catch everything from looking at an outline, but, hopefully, I can start helping you before you write. Second, when you revise a chapter or part of a chapter, start with a revision of the outline. I cannot tell you how many times I have received revisions, and it is obvious that the revision was not written from an outline. All of a sudden, the structure goes out the window. So, revise the outline first, and be sure to send along a copy of the revised outline with your revision, highlighting for me where the main revisions are.

8. *Logistics*: Unless I request otherwise, send your document as a Word attachment. Be sure to date and label the top of the first

page as well as the attachment title. I will return comments using Word Track Changes. Know how to use it (it is easy).

I hope this helps! I want to do the best I can by each of my students. It is my desire to be open about this process and also to teach you about faculty life at the same time. Each student is important to me, and your work is important. And I can only do so much. I want to help you understand what is going on so that we can work together the best we can toward our ultimate goal—your success![3]

Ground Rules Sample #2
<u>Expectations for Working Together</u>
<u>Professional Relationship</u>

Our relationship—as advisor and student—will be a long-term one. In most cases, it will last for the duration of our academic careers. Furthermore, your advisor is extremely important to your career in terms of writing letters of recommendation throughout your career. Finally, my reputation is on the line almost as much as yours is in this process; if I direct your project poorly, that affects me. For these reasons, I like to spell out my expectations so we can make our decision to work together based on as much information as possible.

When you first ask me to be your advisor, I will ask why you would like me to serve in that capacity. Whatever your answer is—whether it's an interest in the same content, in rhetorical criticism as a method, in a perspective on the world, an approach to the discipline, or something else—I believe it will give me a sense of your interests, expectations, and concerns. If I choose to serve in this capacity, we will be embarking on the co-creation of a relationship that can be one of the most rewarding of your life. I will expect a sense of professionalism from both of us throughout this relationship. For me, the professional relationship is built on trust and respect. While we may not be best buddies, I hope to enjoy your company, appreciate your abilities and interests, and know that we share a commitment to the community that is the Communication & Journalism Department. We have both chosen to be at this institution, and I want us to contribute in positive ways to the overall climate by how we work together, relate to our colleagues, and undertake the process of research. And if our relationship, for whatever reason, fails to work, either one of us can choose to terminate it—and I hope we can do so without hard feelings.

Comprehensive Exam

For doctoral students, the comprehensive exam is a requirement to be completed before writing the dissertation. From my perspective, the comprehensive exam fulfills two functions: (1) It is an opportunity for you to synthesize material—material often closely related to the subject of your dissertation, and (2) It is an opportunity for us as faculty to see how you think. Comprehensive exams are less about spewing out all of the information you know on a given subject and more about stating a claim and making a coherent argument about something.

To begin the process of studying for comps, you will meet with each of your committee members and get a reading list from them after talking with them about the areas they represent for you. At that point, I suggest you take general notes on the computer for each source on the list. Know the gist of the argument being made, any particular nuances, and perhaps memorize a quote or two. Then turn the book back into the library—don't look at it again. Once you have prepared these notes, get up every morning and read through them. Don't try to memorize them, don't panic about them, just read them. When it comes time to write, you will have specific material in your head without having had to work hard to get it there.

If you feel you need to spend more than half an hour a day studying for comps, give yourself practice questions and spend your time at the computer, formulating an answer. Concentrate on coherence, creativity, and making a contribution of your own in the process. Don't simply regurgitate what others have said; use what others say to offer your own argument.

Keep in mind throughout this entire process that you are a student first and a teacher second. If you need to be a good teacher instead of an excellent or outstanding teacher for a few weeks because of your scholarly commitments, your students probably will not be able to tell the difference.

Basic Procedures for the Thesis/Dissertation

Check in with the graduate administrative assistant to make sure you are familiar with all deadlines. You will need to submit paperwork throughout the process, and I do not know all of the deadlines or requirements. That's what the staff are there for. If you are confused about something, do come and talk to me, but you are primarily responsible for knowing and meeting these deadlines.

In terms of the thesis, project, or dissertation itself, I will be your primary reader. You will give me drafts of the project first—prospectus, chapters, etc.—and once we have worked through them to our satisfaction, you will distribute them to other committee members. I try to make myself available so that you can progress in a timely fashion toward your degree. To this end, you may email me or call me between 7:00 a.m. and 9:00 p.m., seven days a week. I will return chapters to you within a day or two.

I expect you to attend my writing groups on a regular basis and to make appointments with me as needed to make sufficient progress. This is a learning process, so you need to let me know what you don't know and what you need my help with. Furthermore, keep in mind that there are an almost infinite number of ways to approach a topic. You are not looking for the "correct" one; you are looking for one that provides useful and interesting insights into some communication phenomenon. I will do everything I can to help you come up with a topic and method that works for you, overcome writing blocks, and the like, but ultimately, you are the expert on your topic and are responsible for putting the work together. And while I have my own biases as a researcher, just because I suggest something doesn't mean you have to do it. Often, my suggestions are designed to get you thinking in new ways, so use my ideas in whatever ways they work for you. That is the point of this task: to become, by the end, an independent scholar/researcher, capable of making contributions to our discipline.

You will do multiple drafts of everything you write—writing one draft will not be sufficient. I often write 10 to 20 drafts of things I write. Rewriting is fundamental to the process of conceptualization, organization, and style that go into a polished piece of writing. I expect you to do the best you can on each draft, but I do not expect it to be perfect. Don't be discouraged when every draft has comments; I can always find more to ask about. But there will come a time when we both stop the process and say it's good and that it's time to turn it in. This also means that writing a thesis or dissertation will take time. A good thesis or dissertation is not written and polished in a week.

From the beginning, set your margins to correspond to the regulations of the Office of Graduate Studies; this will save your having to reformat at the end. Left: 1.5 inches; all other margins: 1 inch.

In terms of the writing process, I expect you to make timely progress. Remember, this project is not the culmination of your life's work—it is merely the beginning of it. And if you do not finish this, you cannot get to your life's work. Think of this as simply writing five papers (each chapter is equivalent to a paper)—something you've done virtually every semester, so this is nothing new. I am here to help with whatever obstacles seem to be in the way of making progress, whether that is difficulty conceptualizing, writing, or whatever. I always remember my friend Cindy, who used to have a ritual before she wrote: She would sharpen three pencils and make a cup of tea. Now, she just writes. While you may have writing rituals, make sure they are not ones designed primarily for procrastination, and remember that even 15 minutes is long enough to write a paragraph. So just do it! Or, as one of my students once said, "Don't whine, write!"

Many students get stuck on the literature review. This is the place where you report what has been done in your chosen area of investigation so we can see that (1) you are not repeating what has been done, and (2) how your study builds on existing scholarship. If you are not familiar with the *Index to Journals in Communication Studies* (ed. Matlon and Ortiz), it's an excellent place to begin to do a literature review. It lists the tables of contents for all of the major journals in the communication discipline. I have found it much easier to use this than to depend on what an Internet search produces in terms of scholarly work in the discipline. Our library has a copy. You do not need to read every article or book in depth to do a literature review. You read to get the gist and to be able to summarize that work in a few sentences and to organize what you've read into some broad categories.

The approval of the thesis or dissertation involves two formal meetings: a prospectus meeting and the defense. The prospectus typically involves Chapter 1 (introduction and background), Chapter 2 (literature review), and Chapter 3 (research design). If these chapters are written carefully, they can become part of the thesis or dissertation itself. (There are sample theses and dissertations in the Communication & Journalism conference room that you can check out and use as models.) The prospectus is a contract between your committee and you about what you will and won't do in the thesis/dissertation. Once we have approved the prospectus, your committee cannot come back and ask you to add another major component to your study, for example.

The prospectus must be approved in a different semester from the one in which you defend your thesis or dissertation; it can occur between semesters as well, with the defense in the upcoming semester. Many committees expect to have the prospectus two weeks before your prospectus meeting. If you are under a tight timetable, check with all of your committee members about a shorter reading time. I would like to have the final version a month before the defense so you and I are not rushed in pulling together the final version. Remember, I may not be available for around-the-clock help when you are trying to finish—I might be attending a conference, on vacation, or finishing a project of my own with a deadline. Let's work together to set a realistic timetable.

At the prospectus meeting, I will ask you to speak for about 10 minutes to give us an overview of your project. Yes, we will all have just read it, but it gets us thinking together about the project and also helps out those committee members who may not have read it that carefully. Often, candidates begin by talking about how they came to study this topic. Once your presentation is over, the committee members can ask questions. I will ask the other committee members to ask questions first because you will have heard most of mine throughout the process. This really is an opportunity for the committee to work out any kinks in the project, so this is usually more a conversation among everyone than any formal questioning about it.

The defense occurs after your committee has read what you believe to be a completed and polished version of your thesis/dissertation. The format is similar to the prospectus meeting in that you will be asked to make a presentation about your project, and each committee member will have a chance to ask questions. Sometimes, these questions are purely for information's sake: The committee member wants clarification about something. More often than not, the questions have to do with implications, insights, and extensions of your work. This is because, by this point, we should all have had input into the thesis/dissertation, most kinks will have been worked out, and we can have an interesting conversation with you.

There usually are no right or wrong answers—so don't try to figure out what the right answer is as you answer questions at your defense. Rather, there are good answers—interesting, thoughtful, creative answers versus not-so-good answers—answers where you don't commit to a position, can't seem to think through a situation, or have no idea of the overall significance of your project. I will take notes throughout the process so you don't have to try to remember what changes committee members want you to make.

When no one has any more questions, we will ask you to leave the room so we can make a judgment about the project. Our options are: "pass," "pass with distinction," or "fail." Virtually everyone is asked to make some changes after the defense, so don't get upset if we ask this of you.

Please bring the red-bordered signature pages to your defense. Bring at least three of these sheets so that both of the required copies have these original pages in them. If you would like your own copies to have original signature pages, bring as many copies as you like. These pages can be purchased in the bookstore or downloaded off of the Web.

The prospectus meeting is for the candidate and the committee, but the defense is open to the public. You may invite family and friends, and the defense is advertised in the department. You may find it helpful to attend a defense before you go through the process yourself.

Graduation

Communication & Journalism has a separate graduation each spring that typically is held on the Friday of finals' week. I encourage you to attend. All graduate students are "hooded" by their advisors, and the ceremony is quite nice. I would like the opportunity to hood you at the end of our formal advising relationship.[4]

Information about the Dissertation Process

Ask your advisor for information about the dissertation process itself. Be sure you find out, near the beginning of your project, answers to questions like these:

- What goes into a proposal? Does the proposal become the first chapter of your dissertation? The first three chapters?

- How long is the proposal expected to be? How long is the dissertation supposed to be?

- What is the procedure for having your dissertation proposal approved? Is there an oral defense of the proposal as part of the process?

- What is the system of approval your advisor and committee members will use for your dissertation? Will your advisor read and approve all chapters before your committee members see them? Do some or all committee members want to read drafts along with your advisor?

- Is there an oral defense of your dissertation?

- How will you be required to submit your dissertation? In hard copy? Electronically?

- Can your advisor recommend some dissertations that can serve as good models for you to follow?

Information about Research and Writing

Ask your advisor to share with you his perspectives on the processes involved in research and writing. Some of the information you might want to gather includes:

- Is there a particular format your advisor wants you to use in writing your literature review?

- Are there particular ways in which your advisor wants you to code your data? Ask him to code some of your data with you so you can see the coding process he'll be expecting you to use.

- Does your advisor have tips for you on writing that he's found particularly useful?

- Does your advisor have helpful ideas for dealing with writer's block?

- Does your university require a particular style sheet? If not, what style sheet does your advisor want you to use?

Information about the Dissertation Defense

The dissertation defense is often a mysterious event to students, but if you specifically ask your advisor to talk about it with you, you'll be prepared for what happens there. Ask your advisor to clarify things such as:

- How long do defenses in your department usually take?

- What kinds of questions are faculty likely to ask at a defense?

- Is the defense open to the public?

- Will you be asked to give a presentation summarizing your study at the defense? If so, how long is it expected to be?

You'll find more on what you need to know about the defense in chapter 10.

We've suggested a number of areas in which to ask for the kinds of information you need from your advisor. But you want to do this asking in particular ways. You want to choose ways of communicating both verbally and nonverbally that suggest a peer relationship and self-confidence. Clearly, you don't want to go overboard here so that you aren't respectful of your advisor and don't communicate that you acknowledge and appreciate the status she has earned. But, at the same time, you want to communicate that you have ideas to offer that are worthwhile and that you are interested in adopting the role of competent scholar.

We associate some kinds of communication with high-status, powerful people and other kinds with low-status, less powerful people. To communicate as a peer with your advisor, choose your behaviors from your repertoire of behaviors that suggest high status. This means, for example, being direct in your speech and avoiding qualifiers and hedges as in, "I guess my draft of the chapter is sorta done" or "This may not be a good idea but. . . ." Don't denigrate your abilities and your ideas—advisors get tired of students who constantly need propping up. Communicate equal status through your nonverbal behavior as well. Assume a relaxed position as you sit in your advisor's office, use direct eye contact, and avoid those approval-seeking kinds of smiles.

Tillie discovered what a difference direct communication could make with her advisor. She had written 14 preproposals for her dissertation in response to her advisor's requests, and her communication through all of these drafts was deferential and unassertive. After several years of being ABD, she stopped writing preproposals for her advisor and completed a draft of her entire—and very defensible—dissertation. When she gave it to her advisor, he asked her to write yet another preproposal before he would read the completed dissertation. Tillie responded assertively to her advisor for the first time in their relationship: "I've written 14 preproposals for you, and I'm not going to write another one. I'd like you to read my dissertation, and I think you'll see that it's a good, defensible dissertation." Her advisor did indeed read the dissertation, and Tillie defended it a month later.

Advisors often forget what you don't know. Asking for the information you need from your advisor not only generates the information but helps you polish your image with your advisor as a concerned and committed professional. When you communicate confidently and assertively in your interactions, you enhance your image even more.

Enacting Professionalism

There's another communication behavior you can use to help make your advisor into a good one and that's to enact professionalism. Certainly, all of the advice we're giving you in this chapter helps you do that, but there are some things you can do that are particularly effective in developing a professional image. You want to demonstrate to your advisor that you are becoming the professional he is mentoring you to be, and you can do this in a number of ways.

Start by keeping appointments and showing up on time for meetings with your advisor. Don't forget, too, to respect the ground rules you established together. Cultivate a professional image by getting your work done on time and appearing serious about your work. Don't make statements that might hurt your image with your advisor or other faculty by, for example, refusing to cut your hair or wearing shorts all year-round regardless of the weather.

An equally important way to assert professionalism is to only give your advisor polished work. Whether research support for a project she is doing, papers for her classes, or dissertation chapters, don't give your advisor spew drafts or drafts you've only edited once or twice. Even better, ask some fellow graduate students or other friends whose opinions you respect to read your drafts before you submit them to your advisor. When you give your advisor an unpolished draft to read, you leave a bad residue in her mind about the nature of the work that you do. And if your advisor has to read drafts that you both know aren't complete or fully edited, she is likely to become frustrated and irritated. She knows she's going to have to read another draft of the same thing in the not-too-distant future.

Asking for and accepting feedback also involves professionalism. When you submit papers or program proposals for presentation at professional conventions, essays to journals, or proposals to book publishers, you will be receiving feedback. How you handle that feedback often determines how quickly you advance in your career. At the dissertation stage, it can determine how quickly you progress on your dissertation and how much of a professional you appear to your advisor. There's no doubt about it: Accepting feedback is difficult, and it's especially so when it comes from someone you respect and really want to impress. By keeping a few guidelines in mind, you'll be able to respond gracefully and professionally to feedback and to make the best use of it as you revise your proposal and the chapters of your dissertation.

First, see feedback for what it is—something that helps you learn and grow as a scholar. Feedback doesn't mean you have a terribly flawed project that can't be repaired, and it isn't a commentary on your worth or value. Your advisor has spent a lot of time giving you feedback, so appreciate his efforts to help you be successful. Remember, too, to focus on those sections where he hasn't made comments on your chapter—these are places he believes are solid.

We highly recommend that you get feedback from your advisor in writing. Some advisors like to meet with students and give feedback orally as they go through a dissertation chapter. This is difficult for you because you can't take notes fast enough to capture everything your advisor is saying. Plus, your advisor can easily forget what she tells you orally, and you'll have no written record of her comments. What can happen, then, is that your advisor might respond quite differently to your next draft, and there's no way either one of you can tell if you've made the revisions asked of you. So ask your advisor to give you feedback in writing—either on the pages of the chapter themselves or typed in separate notes (easier to read than some advisors' handwriting).

If negative feedback from your advisor comes as a surprise to you, use silence as a technique for response. Silence allows your advisor to rephrase or clarify his meaning. Try not to respond with the emotions you're feeling at that moment. Waiting longer before you respond gives you time to be in greater control of your response. And, of course, if you can't figure out what your advisor wants you to do, ask questions and ask for examples.

Accepting feedback, though, doesn't mean that you have to acquiesce to every suggestion your advisor makes. Scholars often must defend their ideas, so begin even now to engage in this scholarly behavior with your advisor. As we've suggested throughout this book, the defense of your dissertation is an ongoing process, and responding to feedback from your advisor is a place where you'll want to defend. If you have a clear and coherent preproposal that both you and your advisor approved, you have the right to confidently assert that a revision your advisor is suggesting will take you away from the preproposal.

You can also ask questions about how your advisor's suggestions for revision can be tweaked to fit with your ideas. You can explain, for example, that you're excited about the schema you developed to explain your findings and ask him something like, "What do I need to do to be able to use this schema to present my findings?" "How can my schema be made to work with what you're suggesting?" "Can you help me fit your ideas into the preproposal we created for my dissertation?" Rather than acquiescing to changes that radically change the nature of your work or your vision for it, ask your advisor to help you make what you want to do satisfactory.

Although academics don't do it as often as they should, enacting professionalism also involves appreciating—appreciating others' support, their reading of manuscript drafts, their construction of theories useful to you, and the research they've done on which you can build. You can enact this aspect of professionalism by appreciating your advisor. The advising relationship is a reciprocal one. Just as you'd like to have your needs met and to achieve certain outcomes in the advising relationship, so does your advisor. Your advisor wants to feel that she's not just giving and giving and getting nothing in return.

One way to show appreciation is to do your best to follow your advisor's guidelines, expectations, and advice (always remembering, of course, to defend your ideas when appropriate). Be attentive to your advisor's suggestions for your dissertation and make the revisions he suggests. Nothing irritates an advisor more than to keep correcting the same problem over and over again because you simply haven't attended to it. Another way is to explicitly express your appreciation to your advisor. This can be as simple as a verbal "thank you for all the help and support you give me" at the end of a conversation, putting a thank-you note or card in his mailbox, or bringing him a cup of coffee when you stop for one for yourself on the way to a meeting with him. Your advisor will appreciate it, too, if you talk about him positively to others. You might nominate him for awards in your department, at the university, or in your discipline. Disseminating information about his positive qualities is one way to show your appreciation for what he is doing for you.

Professionalism can spread. If you act like a professional, you model the behavior and encourage the same kinds of behaviors by your advisor.

At minimum, do good work. But you can do even more to present a professional image by respecting ground rules, accepting feedback in a professional manner, and appreciating your advisor.

Assessing Your Relationship

There's one more thing to do to create a good advisor for yourself: Regularly assess your relationship with your advisor. Assess how closely your visions for the dissertation match, whether your needs and those of your advisor are getting met, and how well you are working together.

What are the warning signs to watch for that things aren't going well in your relationship? The primary one is if you aren't making progress on your dissertation. If you are stalled out because of your relationship with your advisor, that's a major warning sign. Another is if you try to avoid communicating with or even seeing your advisor. Maybe you've got a route worked out into your department's building where you don't have to go down the hall that leads past her office. Or is it that you do interact, but the interaction seems to generate misunderstanding and conflict? Does your advisor frequently criticize and disparage you? Do you sense your advisor is competing with you? Is your advisor inaccessible and doesn't respond to your messages? These are other common signs of a poor relationship.

Many of us aren't very good at managing conflict, so to expect you to manage conflict with your advisor in an effective way is a lot to expect from you. There are whole books written on how to manage conflict in productive ways,[5] and professional mediators who resolve conflicts for a living train for a long time to be able to do that successfully. Not to mention that you have less power than your advisor does, so you aren't likely to have the kind of input into the interaction that would allow you to orchestrate a process of conflict resolution.

Although you may not be able to shepherd your advisor through a formal process that will end up with your conflict satisfactorily resolved, there are some things you can do in your interaction to create an environment in which your conflict has a better chance of being worked out. These actions are on a continuum, ranging from small strategies you can use in your everyday interactions with your advisor to strategies that involve taking major and dramatic action. They are: understanding your advisor's perspective, framing issues collaboratively, protecting your advisor's face, planning for action, applying productive chicanery, performing completion, adding a coadvisor, and switching advisors. With the exception of the last one, these can help you make your advisor into a good one for you, even when your relationship is a difficult one.

Understanding Your Advisor's Perspective

Often, in an advising relationship in which you're experiencing conflict, you're so concerned about getting your points across that you don't listen to your advisor. As a result, you don't really understand your advisor's perspective and miss opportunities for resolving or managing the conflict you might be experiencing. Listening is an active process that involves thinking about what you heard, trying to clarify misunderstandings, and providing feedback. It also means attending to the whole meaning of the message—what the person is saying verbally and nonverbally and what the feelings are behind the message. It means listening, in other words, for what your advisor thinks, feels, and wants as well as to what she says.

So how do you listen actively in a conflict situation? One is to simply delay your response. Don't formulate a response to your advisor too quickly—whether in your head or spoken aloud. Think about your response before you offer it, and let it be a response to what you actually heard, not to what you thought you heard. Pondering time gives you the chance to be sure you've understood your advisor's perspective.

Another way to listen actively as you try to understand is to ask questions. To understand your advisor's perspective, try to find out as much as you can about it by asking nonjudgmental questions. This means that you want to ask questions that are genuine questions—not questions dripping with sarcasm designed to reveal your attitude toward what your advisor has just said. If your advisor hasn't explained something in enough detail, ask him to elaborate. If what he's told you is confusing, ask him to explain his perspective again or to give examples to clear up the confusion. You might ask questions such as, "Are there things going on that make it difficult for you to read my chapters in a timely manner?" or "I'm not clear on what you mean when you say that I haven't provided enough evidence for my claims. Can you show me a place where I don't do that?"

You can also indicate to your advisor that you heard what she said and are trying to understand her perspective by restating the content of her comment: "Let me be sure I understand you. You want me to make sure my thesis sentences are broader than my specific examples from my data. Did I get that right?" Sometimes, instead of restating the substance of the message, state the feelings you think your advisor is conveying: "You seem very frustrated with my writing style in this chapter. Is that correct?" In both of these ways, you focus on what your advisor is saying and make a genuine effort to understand her perspective accurately. You also acknowledge her and show respect for her by making a sincere effort to understand what she is saying.

Framing Issues Collaboratively

In a conflict situation, problems and issues tend to get framed as opposing positions. The conflict then becomes a conflict of wills because the positions have to be defended. The more you and your advisor clarify your positions and defend yourselves, the more committed you each become to them and the harder it is to resolve a conflict. To avoid this kind of polarization, try to frame the issue or difficulty you are having in a way that makes it a problem the two of you can solve together. Reframe the issue so that it's not one on which you disagree but is a problem that needs solving.

Suppose you and your advisor are disagreeing about your advisor's lack of responsiveness when you submit chapters for him to read. If you argue over positions, your position might be that you need feedback on chapters you submit within a week, and your advisor's position is that he can't possibly get chapters read that quickly. Talk about the issue without fixing blame or responsibility. Instead of saying, "You take forever to read my chapters, so I don't get the feedback I need," you might say, "It's important that I get feedback to produce a good dissertation. Without that kind of feedback, I'm at a loss as to how to proceed. Is there something we can do to ensure that I get the feedback I need?" You have framed the issue as one that enables the two of you to collaborate. Instead of telling your advisor, "You're trying to make this your project and aren't letting my vision for the study come through," you might say, "One of the things you've taught me is how important it is to honor your own vision for a project because that's what produces original scholarship. How can we work together here to make sure that my vision comes through in a quality dissertation?"

You can also frame the issue as a problem that needs solving by focusing on the interests and goals that you share with your advisor. Focusing on interests means searching for the concerns underlying your different positions. Many possible solutions can come from those interests—not just the positions the two of you originally articulated. When your advisor makes a demand or a suggestion, look beneath it to try to discover what she hopes to gain, what she wants or needs, or what is important to her.

For example, you might articulate to your advisor that your interest is in graduating at the end of the fall semester. Your advisor might articulate several interests: completing a manuscript due to a publisher in two weeks, which means he can't read your dissertation immediately; wanting to give your chapters the time they deserve; and wanting you to graduate this semester. As a result of this identification of your interests, the two of you might come up with solutions such as these: You might volunteer to grade a set of papers or do the copyediting on the manuscript for your advisor so he has time to read your chapter. You might offer to bring him lunch one day so he can hole up in his office and read your chapter. Or perhaps he can dictate his comments about your chapter into a tape recorder instead of having to write them out and thus save time. Try to turn the conversation to a focus on new solutions instead of endlessly defending your respective positions.

Protecting Your Advisor's Face

As you work to manage the conflict, look for ways to preserve your advisor's face. Face is the image of yourself that you want others to see and believe. Just as you want to present yourself in certain ways, your advisor also wants to manage the impressions others have of her. Like you, she wants to be seen as competent, professional, and reputable.

In a conflict situation, you might unintentionally threaten the face of your advisor. You might be inclined to say what's on your mind to get it off your chest, without thinking about how your advisor might receive this information. But criticizing, blaming, attacking, and disparaging are all face-threatening acts that generate embarrassment, shame, or guilt. Work to make sure, then, that your advisor doesn't feel any of these as a result of your interaction.

How can you communicate in ways that save face for your advisor? Start by being tactful—speaking in a thoughtful, gentle, and diplomatic way. Minimize negative information, even if an issue is something very important to you. In talking with your advisor, for example, you might couch the issue as a "minor issue" you'd like to talk about. Be appropriately deferential, acknowledging the contributions of your advisor, and remember to keep showing appreciation—in other words, continue to assert professionalism, as we suggested earlier. And give your advisor an out. If he hasn't read your chapter and has had it for two months, you might preface your request for quicker feedback by saying something as simple as, "I know how busy you've been recently with your responsibilities on the department's search committee."

One way to help yourself remember to help your advisor save face is to imagine how you'll feel in the future as a result of engaging in a particular kind of communication. Embarrassed? Stupid? Silly? Unprofessional? Guilty? Also imagine how your advisor might feel as a result. Angry? Inadequate? Stupid? Thoughtless? Uncaring? Frustrated? Think about the long-term implications of what you want to say as well. Sonja had an advisee tell her once that she was doing the wrong kind of work and that she should be pursuing a different line of research. Actually, the student used much stronger language, but you get the idea. The student clearly had not imagined how he would feel in the future when he encountered Sonja at professional conventions or when he wanted a letter of recommendation from her. Needless to say, he didn't get that letter. Taking a moment to imagine yourself after the conflict ends can help you choose to communicate in ways that foster self-respect and enable your advisor to save face.[6]

Planning for Action

Many conflicts end with participants wondering, "What did we accomplish here?" You and your advisor might have hashed out a topic, you might feel better about your relationship, and perhaps you even feel closer to one another. But you've failed to plan for how to make the agreements you've reached actually happen. If you and your advisor don't devise some action steps to take, you're likely to have to revisit the conflict again. So be sure to end a session in which you work through an issue with action planning. Action planning is the mechanism for changing behavior after you reach an agreement. It means making goals specific, making them doable, and developing them together.

For example, let's say a conflict session ends with your advisor agreeing to read your dissertation chapters more quickly. But what exactly does that mean? You can be right back into the same conflict if you aren't explicit. An action plan might be this statement, which you articulate, and with which your advisor agrees: "Reading chapters more quickly means that you will get them back to me no later than two weeks after I give them to you, and when I turn them in, we'll set an appointment to meet two weeks from that date so that I can pick them up."

If a discussion doesn't result in this kind of a major decision, you and your advisor can still commit to take some smaller steps. You can agree to meet again to continue discussing the issue, for example, and you can set the time and place for that meeting. You can agree that each of you will try to define your interests instead of your positions for the next meeting and that you'll e-mail them to each other the day before that meeting. These small commitments are still action steps that can move a relationship forward.

Applying Productive Chicanery

Strategies of deceit are typically not a good way to create an effective relationship with your advisor. Sometimes, though, a little deception can be just what is needed. We call the deception we sometimes recommend *productive chicanery*, and it can be used to solve a number of conflict situations in advising relationships. Productive chicanery is the use of clever action to deceive in ways that are beneficial to you. Using productive chicanery, you verbally reinforce your advisor's perspective of how the dissertation process is supposed to go while doing something different. What you are doing is creating a means of identification between the two of you that works to your benefit.

Productive chicanery is a good strategy to use when your advisor believes a dissertation should take a long time and should be a protracted struggle. Let's say you want to finish much more quickly than your advisor believes is possible, your dissertation is flowing easily, and you are being very productive. Articulating to your advisor how quickly and easily things are going is not likely to generate positive results. It will only increase the cognitive dissonance she is likely to feel. She probably will see whatever you submit to her as inadequate because it didn't require the hard work over a long period of time that she expected. Before you turn in chapters that are completed much more quickly than she believes is possible, engage in talk of struggle and weariness when you're around her. Drop into her office and tell her how hard you're working, that you never imagined a dissertation would take so much hard physical and intellectual work, and that you're working long hours to get it done. When you do give her a chapter to read, this context is likely to frame her perceptions of your work, and she'll be able to fit your fast pace into her experience. She'll be able to equate the extraordinary nature of your effort with the extraordinary speed of your production.

Another version of productive chicanery involves turning in your first version of a proposal or a chapter after multiple drafts done in response to your advisor's suggestions. Often, the suggestions your advisor makes for revision aren't requests for revision but things to think about or ideas to consider. He may believe that he should be as helpful as possible, which means demonstrating that he always has ideas to share with you. Because you're likely to be trying to satisfy your advisor, you, of course, are doing your best to address each of his suggestions. As a result, your vision for your study and your voice can begin to disappear. As Catharine Randazzo described the result, "In my case, the revisions drew me further and further from my vision. I felt like my dissertation was being dragged out to sea, with me in tow, as a new ersatz was being installed, by my own hand and against my will." When Catharine looked for the lost vision and tried to regain her voice, she found it in the first version of her dissertation. She resubmitted a newly printed copy of that first version, which she felt was her best work. Her chair gave her just one comment on it, "This is what I've been looking for."[7] Your advisor may be tossing you ideas to be helpful, but he may not intend for you to follow up on all of them, especially if it means losing your way and your voice in your own dissertation. Sometimes, resubmitting your first or an earlier draft does the trick.

There's no doubt about it: Productive chicanery is an audacious strategy to use in whatever form it takes. But sometimes, the use of this strategy brings positive results that would be difficult to get in other ways—it helps you get done in a timely fashion or helps you retain your voice and vision in the dissertation. Certainly, there's a bit less deference and respect being shown to your advisor if you choose this strategy. You aren't being completely honest with her, and you're taking advantage of the fact that your advisor is busy and not always as attentive as she should be. But you sometimes help your advisor be the best advisor she can be for you by gently helping her out of the way of your progress.

Performing Completion

One of the most successful strategies we've found for dealing with difficult advising relationships is to perform completion. This means submitting your entire dissertation to your advisor in perfect form, with virtually no feedback from him along the way. When you perform completion, you write your entire dissertation, edit and polish it as much as you can, and put it in perfect form according to your university's guidelines. Then have others—fellow students and friends—read it for content, style, and form. You want nothing missing, no citations to be filled in later, no ideas left hanging that you want to develop further. The entire dissertation is as complete and as perfect as you can make it. You then turn it in to your advisor. Sometimes, when an advisor sees your dissertation completed and knows the conflicts that are plaguing the relationship can stop, he will happily approve it.

Performing completion is an excellent strategy to use in a couple of situations. One is when you've been ABD for a long time, your advisor has lost interest in you and your project, and you feel you aren't getting any real help from her. Another is when you and your advisor have an ongoing major conflict that is impeding progress on your dissertation. It also can work when you can't get your advisor to respond to you in a meaningful or timely way.

Obviously, there's a risk here because, with this strategy, you've ratcheted up the stakes. Your advisor may reject your dissertation and want you to redo major parts of it, and you've spent a lot of valuable time performing completion. But there are a couple of things students tend to forget about advisors that you have on your side here. Advisors are busy people, and if they don't have to get you through multiple drafts, doing all that reading and editing and perhaps engaging in contentious interactions along the way, they are likely to be very relieved. Also don't forget that advisors accrue benefits from finishing graduate students. They get to list a graduating dissertation student on their annual merit reports and gain credit for getting that student done. If you can have yourself "count" for your advisor and he doesn't have to do that much work to have you count, that may be very appealing to him.

Let's say you perform completion and your advisor's response is that major revisions have to be made. You still are likely to be farther ahead than you would have been without using this strategy. Your advisor has a specific product to which to respond and make suggestions. Also remember to defend what you have done to your advisor if her response is that major changes are required. If you believe you have a logical research design, insightful findings, and a high-quality dissertation, argue for what you've produced.

Asking for Help from a Mediator

There are some instances when a conflict has gone on so long or involves such major issues that you may need a mediator to help you resolve it. The chair or the director of graduate studies in your department or your university's ombudsman can serve this function. Remember, though, that going outside of the advising relationship is not going to endear you to your advisor. He will lose face with others in the university, including his own chair, and he may very well become defensive and hostile as a result. Sometimes, though, advisees are being treated very unjustly and truly are being abused emotionally and intellectually, and if that's what is happening to you, you may need the outside help that an external mediator can provide.

Adding a Coadvisor

If you're having trouble with your advisor or your advisor isn't responsive to your needs, another solution is to add a coadvisor. Some students start out with a coadvisor just in case some difficulty arises with an advisor or because they want the expertise that two faculty members bring to the project. Conflicts can arise between coadvisors, of course, if the two have very different visions for your project. But the benefits are typically positive, especially if you select as coadvisors faculty members who respect one another and get along well.

But let's say you started with only one advisor and now want to add a coadvisor to resolve a conflict you're having with your original advisor. You have to be careful about this strategy politically because it's not likely to make your advisor very happy. It can also be a politically dangerous strategy for the faculty member you take on as a coadvisor because she can incur the wrath of the original advisor, which may work against her later, especially if she is untenured. But making your advisor into a coadvisor can be a way for your advisor to save face because you are also retaining him as an advisor. You are able to finish because you're getting the assistance you need to finish from your new coadvisor.

Switching Advisors

If you really believe that you won't finish your dissertation if you continue with your advisor and you've tried all other available options, your only remaining option is to change advisors. Clearly, such a decision is not to be made lightly. Both you and your advisor have invested a lot of time and energy in the advising relationship and in your dissertation. The decision may have political ramifications in your department and perhaps later for your career. Plus, don't forget that switching to another advisor may slow you down because a new advisor may want a very different kind of dissertation from the one you had planned.

If you believe, however, that no strategies you can use with your advisor will allow you to finish or to finish in a timely manner, make the request to your advisor that you discontinue your advising relationship. Although students tend to think that the advisor in such an instance will be angry or disturbed, a very real option is that he may feel great relief. If you perceive that your advising relationship is unsatisfactory and ineffective, he is likely to feel the same. He may be happy to turn you over to someone else. If you do decide to end the relationship with your advisor, try to end it on a positive note. Thank him for his mentoring and his assistance. And, of course, before you have this conversation, be sure you've lined up someone else to serve as your new advisor.

Key to an effective working relationship with your advisor and to making progress on your dissertation is that you do what you can to help your advisor be a good advisor for you. Five communication practices are particularly useful in enabling you to have a significant influence on the advising relationship: asking someone to be your advisor at the right time and in the right way, agreeing on a vision, articulating needs, enacting professionalism, and assessing your relationship. When we work with students who are having difficulty with their advisor and suggest some of the strategies in this chapter, they often respond with, "My advisor won't go for that." But they usually do. If you engage in communication behaviors that encourage good advising on the part of your advisor, you are likely to be surprised at how different your advisor's responses are from what you predicted. By engaging in effective communication behaviors, you can help your advisor be as helpful as possible to you.

Notes

1. Mark L. Knapp and Anita L. Vangelisti, *Interpersonal Communication and Human Relationships*, 5th ed. (Boston: Allyn & Bacon, 2005), 31–67.

2. Pamela J. Kalbfleisch, "Communicating in Mentoring Relationships: A Theory for Enactment," *Communication Theory* 12 (2002): 63–69.

3. Dawn O. Braithwaite, Department of Communication Studies, University of Nebraska–Lincoln.

4. Karen A. Foss, Department of Communication & Journalism, University of New Mexico.

5. See, for example: Stephen W. Littlejohn and Kathy Domenici, *Communication, Conflict, and the Management of Difference* (Long Grove, Ill.: Waveland, 2007).

6. For more on saving face, see Kathy Domenici and Stephen W. Littlejohn, *Facework: Bridging Theory and Practice* (Thousand Oaks, Calif.: Sage, 2006).

7. Catharine E. Randazzo, "Don't Throw It Away!" *ABD Survival Guide* [electronic newsletter] (17 April 2006): 3, www.abdsurvivalguide.com.

CHAPTER TWELVE
AVOIDING DELAYS AND ANNOYANCES: ENACTING THE SCHOLAR ROLE

espite careful planning, few trips are flawless. They involve unexpected annoyances and obstacles that the traveler must circumvent to have a successful trip. You might get lost trying to reach a destination. Maybe your plane sits on the runway for a couple of hours, you miss your next plane, and you don't arrive when you thought you would. Maybe you feel overwhelmed with all the new stimuli you're experiencing, and you long momentarily for a familiar routine. Maybe you need something and don't know how to ask for it because you can't speak the local language. We believe that, by following the processes covered in the first eleven chapters of this book, you'll avoid many of the common difficulties with your dissertation. But students like you are creative. You have the capacity to innovate endless ways to impede your progress on your dissertation and spoil your trip. We hope this chapter will redirect this kind of creativity so that your trip is a fun and productive one.

Granted, there's a major difference between the delays and annoyances you experience while traveling and those you experience while writing your dissertation. The stakes are much higher with your dissertation. If you get stuck and can't get unstuck, there are major life consequences. But there's another difference, too. While traveling, the delays you encounter are usually not your fault. In your dissertation, they often are. Although the fact that you generate most of the delays and annoyances you encounter in the dissertation process can be a major problem, it's also a wonderful relief. Because you generate them, those delays and annoyances are under your control. You're the one who can get yourself moving and back to enjoying the trip.

The way out of the delays and annoyances that you may be creating for yourself is to enact the role of the scholar. This means actually doing the things that make you a scholar. Scholars are scholars because of what they do, not who they are. You may be bright and enrolled in a graduate program, but you aren't a scholar until you begin to live your life and approach the work of your dissertation so that you actually enact the scholar role. As writer Marge Piercy said about writing, "The real writer is one who really writes."[1] Likewise, the scholar is one who really does scholarship.

So what's involved in enacting the role of a scholar? What do you have to do to be one? Being a scholar involves two major kinds of work—coming up with ideas and sharing them with others. Many people have excellent ideas that could very well change the way people think about something or that might introduce exciting new constructs to a field, but until they document those ideas so they can be scrutinized and tested by others, those ideas don't become part of the conversation of a discipline. They are ephemeral and fleeting and are never offered in a way that can be assessed, applied, and extended by others. If you want to adopt the scholar role, then, you must come up with ideas and make them permanent by writing them down. We like how Scot McKnight describes a scholar as "a person who constantly gives expression to his or her own thoughts in an academic setting."[2]

Incomplete-Scholar Roles

If you are like many students, the most common way in which you are likely to respond to the exigency of the dissertation is by enacting an incomplete-scholar role. You enact the first part of the scholar—you generate ideas—but you don't complete the role by writing them down in a dissertation so they can be shared. Your enactment of the scholar role is thus incomplete.

The incompleteness is due to the fact that you have assumed a role that makes you into something other than a scholar. You are doing dissertation work that isn't—work that seems relevant to the work of the dissertation but isn't helping you share the ideas you have with others.

Incomplete-scholar roles provide some rewards to you at a time when you feel the need for some kind of reward—after all, you aren't getting the rewards that would come if you were making progress on your dissertation. But we contend that actually adopting the role of the scholar offers fuller, more complete, and longer lasting rewards.

Here are eight of the most common incomplete-scholar roles. In all of them, the potential scholar has good ideas but never gets around to documenting and sharing them. Do you recognize yourself in any of these self-generated, self-sabotaging roles?

Housekeeper

Does this sound familiar? You sit down to work on your dissertation and decide that your kitchen cupboards need cleaning or the laundry needs to be done or the newspapers need to be put in the recycling stack or the plants need to be watered or the fringe on the rug in your office needs to be straightened or your files need to be cleaned out or your books need to be rearranged. One of our favorite examples of this kind of reasoning comes from Mark Matloff, who believes he must walk his dog a few times before he starts writing because, after all, "isn't a walked dog a happy dog, and isn't a happy dog a quiet dog? If my dog doesn't make noise, it will be so much easier to concentrate."[3] And then there's e-mail. If you could just get your in-box cleared out, you would feel psychologically free to write.

What is going on with all of these variations on the housekeeper role is that you are doing things other than the dissertation in the belief that their completion will make writing easier. You believe that the conditions in your environment must be perfect before you can write, so you spend your time making those conditions perfect. Your dissertation always gets pushed to a back burner because there is always something you can do to improve your working conditions to make them more conducive to writing. Instead of making yourself into a scholar, these activities, of course, are making you into a housekeeper.

The motivation for engaging the role of the housekeeper is obvious. You feel helpless trying to write a dissertation. Cleaning up your environment, in contrast, makes you feel helpful and valuable. And you are rewarded with completed projects, cleaned-up messes, and order when you do not see how you can clean up the mess you perceive your dissertation is in, see only disorder in the project, and don't see any completion date in sight. But if you can write only when conditions around you are perfect, you're never going to be able to write. Writing is not dependent on external conditions but on what you do as a scholar. As we've discussed earlier, when conceptualized as small tasks, scholarly activities can be done in the midst of virtually any conditions, including when you have a few minutes in a car while waiting for your kids, between classes if you are teaching, or while waiting to get the oil changed in your car.

Model Employee

You enact the role of the model employee when you have a job to do—paid or otherwise—and let the demands of that job push your dissertation aside. When you adopt the role of the model employee, you spend an inordinate amount of time doing an exemplary job in some area other than the dissertation. You believe this other area of your life is so important that it can't be compromised in any way, so the dissertation must take a back seat to it. Because there is never an end to what you can do on the job when you are busy being a perfect employee, the tasks multiply to fill the time available. If you try to cut back at all from your job, you feel guilty and believe you will be judged inadequate or incompetent.

Graduate students often adopt the role of the model employee in their teaching. In part because you usually haven't been at it very long and in part because you like doing it, you may find yourself spending a great deal of time overteaching—preparing way too much for each class. You know you've adopted this role when you create complex and time-consuming methods for grading, when every lecture is a glitzy media presentation, and when you radically redesign every class each time you teach it. Your students are undoubtedly profiting from your teaching, but guess what? They may not be noticing or appreciating all of that superb teaching as much as you think.

Students' inattention to teaching vividly hit home for Sonja when she met a young woman at a cocktail party who had just graduated from a nearby university with a degree in Sonja's field. Sonja knows many of the professors at that university, so she asked her who some of her professors had been. The newly graduated student couldn't name a single one. Not one. Her professors are very competent teachers, but their excellent teaching did not have the impact on this student that we suspect they think they're having. To help get you out of enacting the role of model employee in your teaching, you might want to read *My Freshman Year* by Rebekah Nathan. An anthropological study of today's students written by an anthropology professor who enrolled in her own university as a freshman, it provides revealing insights about students' responses to higher education.[4]

You can also be a model employee in your personal life. You can choose to be the perfect spouse, partner, parent, or child. "My kids and husband need me!" is likely to be your anthem in the most common version of the role. You believe that if you don't devote your time to what needs to be done at home, your children will suffer irreparable damage or your marriage will fail. Your dissertation takes a back seat to planning play dates, helping your kids with their homework, making a new dress for your daughter for her first day of school, painting the living room, cooking elaborate meals, and hosting Thanksgiving dinner.

What is happening with the model-employee role is that although you know your priority is to finish your dissertation, you keep busy with less important, short-term tasks. These tasks are a means of avoiding the anxieties of the high-priority, long-term task of the dissertation. Once you are immersed in the busyness of some other area of your life, there seems to be no room for any other high-priority task. If you attempted to work on the dissertation in the midst of everything else you are doing that is important, your thinking goes, it would severely impact your performance in another area of your life.

And let's not forget how much support you get for enacting the role of the model employee. Your boss (or spouse or partner) tells you that you are doing an exemplary job in this area of your life. At a time when rewards are hard to come by, such rewards are precious. It takes a long time to begin to feel competent doing your dissertation, but, as a model employee, you are already demonstrating your skills and competence. It feels so good to have someone say she needs you, can't do without you, and requires your full time and attention. But the role of the model employee doesn't produce a dissertation. And, in fact, in the long run, not working on the dissertation may actually increase tensions between you and your work or family. Wider rewards will come with finishing the dissertation. Then you can choose to engage in exemplary behaviors in all aspects of your life *and* enjoy the rewards of being an accomplished scholar.

Undocumented Worker

In the role of the undocumented worker, you can't secure a real job because your dissertation isn't done. Because you don't have the proper papers or credentials—a done dissertation and a doctoral degree—to legitimize you for the job you really want, you aren't allowed to do the work that will pay you appropriately. As a result, you take on many jobs to produce a livable wage. You end up teaching as an adjunct at several colleges and universities, editing papers for students, or working as a server at a local restaurant, with each job earning you far less than you would get for one job if your dissertation were done. And when you work at all of these jobs, you make yourself into an undocumented worker who is too busy and too tired to be a scholar.

In contrast to the model employee, your time as an undocumented worker is being taken up not because you believe you must do such exemplary work in a job other than writing the dissertation but because you are doing so many jobs. Because working at several subsistence jobs takes up all your available time, your dissertation never gets written. When you adopt this role, you believe you must work at all of these jobs to support yourself while writing the dissertation, but these jobs become your work, and the dissertation doesn't get done. The need for a paycheck is used to do anything but write the dissertation.

Another common way in which the role of the undocumented worker is enacted is spending time writing grant proposals to fund the dissertation. The expectation here is that the dissertation will take you so long to write that you need funding to support yourself while you write it. If you actually wrote the dissertation instead of the grant proposals, the dissertation would be done. But because you perceive a lack of finances as something you must address before you write your dissertation, the grant proposal gets done, but the dissertation doesn't.

The role of the undocumented worker has its rewards, of course. Just as in the model-employee role, you gain the rewards that come from work—from demonstrating your competence, from doing a good job, from making money. As you pick up extra shifts or teach more classes and revel in the larger paychecks, you ignore both the larger cost of not finishing your dissertation—tuition, fees, and lower wages—and the larger payoff that awaits you. If you adopt the role of the scholar and finish the dissertation, two things go away—the cost of maintaining your-self in school, and the lack of documentation that keeps you from get-ting a good job.

Patient

The patient is the role you adopt if your dissertation work consists largely of trying to cure yourself of whatever is preventing you from mak-ing progress on your dissertation. You perceive yourself as suffering from an ailment that blocks your progress on the dissertation, and you are un-able to make progress until you are cured. You have constructed a causal relationship between some kind of dis-ease from which you must be healed—physical illness, mental illness, or the dis-ease that comes from lack of progress on your dissertation. This means that an important first step of dissertation work for you is the work that goes into your cure. You feel, as a result, that the work you do to produce a cure is actual disserta-tion work.

You can assume a patient role in various ways. One of the most com-mon is to join support groups related to dissertations—dissertation-support groups or writing groups are typical ones. You spend a significant time each week or month in self-remedy—attending meetings, discussing your problems about the dissertation with others, trying to satisfy the group members' wishes for confession, and bringing in snippets of writing to be critiqued by others who have never written a dissertation before. If you get professional help and go into therapy to try to cure what is keep-ing you from completing your dissertation, you have adopted the role of the patient, too. A focus on physical or psychological ailments as things that can keep you from completing your dissertation is another way in which this role is enacted. Maybe you have ADD, dietary issues, chronic fatigue, or something else. If you use this as the reason why you can't fin-ish your dissertation, you have become the patient.

When you feel like a fraud, suffering from feelings of intellectual fraudulence and chronic self-doubt that prevent you from making progress on your dissertation, you have made yourself into a patient as well. In this role, despite your accomplishments and the fact that you were admitted to and apparently are succeeding in a graduate program, you remain unconvinced that you are capable, intelligent, and competent. One scholar described the phenomenon in this way:

> I am a fraud because I don't work the way everyone else does. I don't read the classics as bedtime reading; hell, I don't read anything except weird novels and stuff that has nothing to do with my "work." I don't sit in the library taking notes; I don't read the journals cover to cover; and what's worse, I don't want to. I am not a scholar. . . . I haven't the commitment to steep myself in the ideas and thoughts of The Masters. I couldn't converse meaningfully about The Literature on any topic including those in which I am allegedly a specialist.[5]

Sound familiar? When you believe you must get over feeling like a fraud to write a dissertation, you have become a patient.

With all of the variations on the patient role, you give power to some condition and allow it to stand in the way between you and a completed dissertation. Your response is to do the work that reinforces, reifies, and highlights the disease so that it becomes the thing to which you respond and on which you focus your attention—not the dissertation. The reward you gain from the patient role is that you feel like you are taking steps toward the completion of your dissertation. You feel like you are making progress. You are rewarded with activity and optimism—you feel hopeful that you can get your dissertation done because you are engaged in healing activities. You have something specific to do and know what it is—whatever it is that will heal you—and you count this as dissertation work.

Everyone has conditions to deal with in their lives. To make them into an excuse that prevents you from accomplishing a significant goal is to give them power and agency that they don't deserve. You are in control—not your disease. People in far worse conditions than you have accomplished amazing things, but they didn't accomplish them by giving power to something outside of themselves. We know students with dyslexia and multiple sclerosis who have successfully completed their dissertations, but they did so not by making their diseases into obstacles that kept them from writing. Their diseases were simply things to be dealt with as quickly and efficiently as possible so that they could turn to the real work of their dissertations. They made themselves into scholars instead of patients.

Good Student

When you adopt the role of the good student, you focus on what you are learning from others instead of developing your own original ideas to share. Yes, we know you are a student, so it probably seems odd that we are suggesting a student role as one of the incomplete-scholar roles. But, at some point in your graduate career, you have to make the switch from student to scholar. You have to stop relying on the ideas that have come from others and begin to develop ideas of your own. In the student role, you continue to learn about others' ideas instead of generating and writing about your own.

The most common enactment of the role of the good student is overreading. When you enact this version of the role, you are always seeking one more source, one more citation, one more way to demonstrate your knowledge. Every new source leads to other sources, of course, and, as the student, you read on and on because, after all, reading is an important part of scholarship. The rewards come easily when you read and read and read because there are always new and exciting materials out there to be discovered. You can always find a book or article you haven't read that sheds light on the subject you are studying. And that new book usually points to three new books. Reading becomes a game—a scavenger hunt for sources.

There's another common way in which the role of the student is acted out and that is by learning complex and sophisticated procedures of some kind prior to doing your dissertation. You might think you have to learn ATLAS.ti software to manage your qualitative data, which means cleaning and entering your data before you can even begin your coding. Perhaps you believe you must learn a new complex way of transcribing interviews. You might have to learn a language to do the translations you want to do or to interview your participants. Maybe you have to learn a whole new research method you never studied in your coursework. In all of these activities, you are learning. You are developing skills you didn't have before and are enjoying the rewards that come with mastering new skills and developing competence. But these are skills that you don't need to develop for your dissertation, and they don't by themselves lead to a completed dissertation. In other words, you stop short of being a scholar by focusing on the accomplishment of skills that don't result in exercise of the scholar role.

If you've come as far as you have, you undoubtedly have been rewarded and reinforced in the past for being a good student. So you continue to engage in the behaviors that gave you those rewards in the past—learning new things, following procedures, getting things right. It's easy, then, to continue to do those things that make you into a good student by constantly learning new things and demonstrating your mastery of them to someone else. But when you don't get past this role to become a scholar, generating and sharing your own ideas, your dissertation doesn't get done.

Proxy Critic

You're writing along on your dissertation. You write a paragraph or a sentence. Then you start to wonder about what you've just written. "This isn't good enough," you say to yourself. "It doesn't flow, my argument isn't strong enough, it isn't eloquent writing, my advisor will never like it." Your indecision stops the writing. You feel like you need approval before you can proceed, but, of course, there's no one who can or will approve every sentence you write at the moment you're writing it. Because you can't get confirmation, you tend to stop writing or your writing proceeds very slowly.

When this happens, you have assumed the role of the proxy critic. What the proxy critic is creating instead of a scholar is an imaginary editor or a fantasy critic who stops the flow, development, and documentation of ideas by assessing them prematurely. As the proxy critic, you are trying to assess and edit your work at the same time that you produce it. Many students believe this is an efficient way to produce high-quality texts. Their reasoning goes something like this: If I don't make any errors while I'm writing my first draft, I won't have to spend any time on revisions. The reality is that you cut yourself off at the pass—you never make progress or you proceed extremely slowly because you are prematurely questioning every organizational structure, every argument, every idea, every paragraph, every sentence, every word.

In the role of the proxy critic, you are standing in for a critic who doesn't exist. Even if such a critic existed, that person probably wouldn't be saying everything you think he is saying. You are forgetting that writing and editing are two separate processes, and the first process is getting the ideas on paper—as rough and unpolished and inelegant as they might be. The second task is to revise, and this is the place where you scrutinize and assess your writing and polish it as much as you can.

Yes, at the point at which you begin to revise, you want to try to imagine what others—such as your advisor—might think about your work. But you can never completely predict how others will react and, more important, even if you could, you don't want your primary criterion for judging your ideas and writing to be whether someone else will like them. Your primary criteria should be the strength of your idea, whether you believe it's useful, and whether you have documented the idea so that others can understand it. Adjusting an idea to suit others makes it no longer original and no longer yours. Dropping the role of the proxy critic and adopting the role of the scholar, primarily by writing multiple drafts and revising after you write, allow you to do the development and documentation of your ideas so crucial to the role of the scholar.

Executor

An executor is someone who is appointed to carry out the provisions and directions in someone's will and to put that person's affairs in order. When you adopt this role as you attempt to write your dissertation, you see yourself as designated by the participants or interviewees of your study to tell their stories or to give voice to their lives and experiences. You believe that the responsibility with which you are entrusted to represent others is so heavy and so significant that you can't possibly fulfill it. Your goal is to uncover stories no one knows and to share them—certainly both noble goals. But when you spend all your time trying to get the stories right from the perspective of those you are studying and believe you can't possibly do justice to their voices, you have adopted the executor role.

One common way in which executors work to get the story right is in the transcribing process. You may believe you must transcribe every word your interviewees say, even though you're only interested in the ideas on a particular topic that the interviewees share with you. You transcribe even vocal nonfluencies like "uh" and "um," every pause, and every cough because you are touched by their stories and want to honor their voices. Obviously, transcribing at this level takes a great deal of time—time not invested in the dissertation itself. Excessive transcribing means you have become an executor and not a scholar. Alternatively, you could simply listen to the tapes until you hear an idea expressed that is relevant to your research question and transcribe that section. (Note: There are times when you want to transcribe every word of an interview—if you are studying the communication behavior of the interviewees, for example, and are interested to know how they talk about the subject and not just what they say about it.)

Another variation of the executor is when you burden yourself with obligations you perceive are incumbent upon you and your dissertation because of a special relationship you have with your advisor. This often takes the form of wanting the dissertation to be extraordinary in some way because you don't want to disappoint your advisor. Another form it may take is wanting to make sure that your dissertation adequately captures your advisor's perspective or philosophy because you consider your dissertation to be part of your advisor's legacy. You feel you are entrusted with special duties, responsibilities, and obligations given your relationship with your advisor.

Where do executors get waylaid? Executors who deal with estates get paid for handling other people's business and, because they get paid, they often drag out that business. They are spending time and energy on the person being represented, but the time and energy don't fulfill the real wishes of the person being represented. In the dissertation, the executor role allows you to extend your relationship with the people whose voices you are representing. You want to maintain what you perceive is a special connection to them, and as soon as you tell the story, that special connection to the participants will vanish. Just as with typical executors, actually handling the estate or telling the story ends the connection. You were special because you were the only one who knew the story, and once you tell it, your uniqueness disappears.

What you don't realize when you adopt the role of the executor is that your uniqueness grows and continues in a more profitable way when you finish your dissertation. Your value and expertise are demonstrated not by telling the stories of those you are representing but by making your own claims about those stories. When you assume the executor role, you are privileging your data over your claims. Your dissertation is made up of your claims and your analysis, and adopting the role of the executor shirks the responsibility of analysis. You do the real work of a dissertation when you use the stories as evidence in support of claims that you develop from your analysis of the data—when you enact not the role of the executor but the role of the scholar.

Maverick

Graduate students sometime adopt the role of the maverick—the lone cowboy who rides into town and stays apart, maintaining independence and refusing to conform to the community. Adoption of this role usually takes the form of believing that you have to figure out everything about a dissertation by yourself—that you don't or can't have access to any resources to help you. You usually don't take advantage of resources your advisor might be prepared to give, the help of other graduate students, or the resources being offered by family members. You go it alone, trying to figure everything out by yourself and doing everything alone.

The rewards gained by the maverick are the rewards that come with figuring out a problem, coming up with a solution, trying and succeeding, and relying on yourself. The costs are high, though, and they take the form of time spent reinventing wheels—constantly re-creating processes and ideas already developed by others. What the maverick creates instead of a scholar is someone who, yes, is independent but who also is engaged in an unnecessary struggle that creates disconnection and isolation from a scholarly community.

Enacting the Scholar Role: Writing Regularly

Perhaps you've recognized yourself in one of the incomplete-scholar roles, and you see how the role is delaying the completion of your dissertation. You want to take up the role of the scholar so that you can finish. How do you do that? The primary antidote to any of the roles of the incomplete scholar is writing regularly. Regular writing will help you confront the incomplete-scholar roles head on and will transform you from student, patient, executor, housekeeper, or whatever your chosen role is into a scholar. Because what most of the incomplete-scholar roles have in common is that they allow you to do things other than write, to counter them, you want to make writing a regular, recurrent activity.

Evidence for how effective regular writing can be comes from Robert Boice, who has done a great deal of research on the subject. One of his studies involved 27 faculty members from various universities who were having trouble completing writing projects. Nine of them agreed not to write during the 10-week period of the experiment, another nine were encouraged to write only when they were in the mood, and those in the third group were forced to write during 50 scheduled sessions. This last group produced the highest and most stable outputs. They wrote about three times as much as those who wrote only when they were inspired. Plus, they enjoyed their writing more.[6] In another study, Boice tracked the writing habits and outputs of newly hired professors over six years. He found that participants who wrote daily wrote twice as many hours as those who wrote occasionally in big blocks of time, and they wrote or revised 10 times as many pages.[7]

In response to Boice's research, you're probably thinking of all sorts of reasons why you can't write regularly. One might be that you can't write unless you are inspired or in the mood—when you're excited about what you're working on and know exactly what you're doing. You also probably believe you shouldn't stop writing when you're in such a state because the inspiration might depart, so you need to take advantage of it while you can. But you often have to do things when you're not in the mood, but you do them anyway. Do you always feel in the mood to teach a class? Of course not. But you don't cancel the class. You go to class and often find that, once you start teaching and interacting with the students, you begin to enjoy the experience and do it well. The same goes for writing. You can perform on demand in this situation as well as in any other.[8] Writing regularly in daily sessions means that you don't have to wait to write until you are motivated or inspired. The regular habit of writing provides the stimulus for you to write because it involves you in the writing process first and generates motivation later.

Perhaps you believe you can't write unless you have large blocks of time available. Your rationale here is that you need time to figure out where you are in your project and to get back into it. You can't do this in half an hour or an hour. If you tried writing in small blocks of time, you believe, you would have to stop when you were just getting started and would have to go over the whole process again when you had a little time to write on another day. But the reason you take so long to get started is because you aren't writing regularly. You would easily remember where you were if you wrote even half an hour or an hour each day.

Plus, the processes in this book are designed to make sure you always know exactly where you are, so this problem should no longer be an issue for you. A regular writing schedule also teaches you that you can make good progress under all conditions. You may feel lethargic one day or have a headache another. None of these is reason not to stay with your schedule and to keep making progress during your writing times.

You may believe that you can work only when you are facing an imminent deadline. Using this approach, you delay the start of a writing project until just before the deadline and then binge—writing frantically in a marathon session over several days and perhaps nights, working until you are exhausted. It's very difficult to get your dissertation done by bingeing, though, because the project is just too big. Bingeing also doesn't allow you to reflect on what you've written. Because you don't have sufficient time for revising and editing, bingeing leads to lower quality in what you produce. In contrast, writing regularly requires that you take regular breaks so you can recharge your batteries. You eat regular meals and get enough sleep, providing the energy and concentration required for writing.

With these excuses out of the way, are you ready to begin the regular writing that makes you a scholar? Two things will help—writing on a schedule and focusing on your successes.

Writing on a Schedule

The first thing to do to get yourself writing regularly is to work on your dissertation according to a schedule. Just like you would go to work at a job and work regular hours, do the same with your dissertation. Even if you just have an hour or two to devote to your dissertation each day, schedule it. Make writing during that period a sacred part of your day.

If you feel you have no time during a day for regular writing, try this: Chart your daily activities for a week or two in half-hour blocks. You undoubtedly will discover that you are spending time on nonessential activities not related to your dissertation. You might be chatting with colleagues during a period of the day when you could be writing. You might be spending two hours preparing for a course when you really only need half an hour. Maybe you watch television for an hour in the morning, and you could cut that out. Maybe you play videogames for half an hour after dinner and could use that time for writing. The first step in developing a schedule, then, is to identify some periods of time—even short ones—that you have free and can use for writing.

Sometimes, reconceptualizing how your dissertation fits into your day helps you develop and keep a regular writing schedule. Many people conceptualize their dissertations as something to fit in around their teaching schedules and their family activities. See if you can reverse that thinking. Your dissertation is now your real job. Conceptualize everything else as something that gets in the way of it and disrupts your writing time. When you are working on your dissertation and it's time for you to go teach a class, our guess is that your previous response was likely to have been something like, "Oh, good, I can stop writing on my dissertation because it's time for me to go teach." When you conceptualize your dissertation as your job, your new attitude becomes, "Is it time for class already? Too bad! I'm really making good progress on my dissertation, and I hate to stop. But I'll come back and use that hour I have free after class to keep writing."

As you create a writing schedule and make writing your regular and primary job, take into account when you are at your best. If possible, schedule your dissertation writing times for when you are fresh and alert. Do everything else when you are tired. Prepare for teaching and grade papers, pay bills, do laundry, and read e-mail when you come home at the end of a day of teaching and are tired. Don't do this kind of work in the morning if that's when you feel energized and ready to go.

If you're fortunate and regularly have large blocks of time free over several days to work on your dissertation, establish a schedule that makes the dissertation the major activity you do on those days. Some students implement the schedule we use at our Scholars' Retreats as their schedule for working on their dissertations on their free days. Here's what it is:

- 6:15: Wake up

- 6:30: Exercise

- 7:30: Shower and dress

- 8:00: Breakfast

- 8:30: Writing

- 12:30: Lunch

- 1:30: Writing

- 5:30: Dinner

- 7:00: Writing

- 9:00: Social hour (a time to talk with your spouse or partner or read e-mail)

- 10:00: To bed

If you can't quite conceive of yourself as working in a sustained fashion for such extended periods of time, you might try the 40-minute cycle. This is a system in which you do 40 minutes of sustained work, take a 20-minute break, and then repeat the cycle. You might set a timer for 40 minutes so you know when that period of time is done and it's time for a break. The 40-minute cycle prevents you from becoming physically tired and burned out and also motivates you to write on the days when you don't feel like it. When you feel like you just can't face doing your dissertation, knowing that you just have to complete two 40-minute cycles doesn't sound so bad. It seems like something you can do.

By the way, most people who come to our Scholars' Retreats don't believe it will be physically possible for them to work as many hours as they are required to work at the retreat. But they find that their writing energizes and motivates them, and they discover that they can easily spend 10 hours a day writing. We suspect you, too, will be amazed at how productive you are on a schedule and probably won't need to use the 40-minute cycle after a while.

Maybe you're someone who has trouble keeping yourself on a schedule. You can easily slide into adopting or perpetuating one of those incomplete-scholar roles and never quite get around to making or sticking to a schedule in which you really do work on your dissertation. Here's something that might help: Keep a record of how many hours you write each day, and share those records with someone at the end of every week—your spouse or partner, a fellow graduate student, a relative, or your advisor. Record keeping makes you aware of how much time you are actually writing on your dissertation. Equally important, being accountable to someone else makes a big difference. Without a commitment to share your records with someone else, you can easily convince yourself that you will begin writing tomorrow.

Boice did another study that showed how important keeping track of your writing time and sharing it with others can be. He worked with three groups of writers, requiring different kinds of record keeping of each group. The first group wrote occasionally in large blocks of time, and in one year, they wrote an average of 17 pages. The second group wrote every day and kept a daily record; their average was 64 pages a year. The members of the third group wrote daily, kept a daily record, and were accountable to someone every week; they averaged 157 pages a year.[9] (Actually, we think 157 pages is pretty small output for a year, and we hope the processes in this book allow you to work more quickly than that, but you get the point: Keeping track of your hours and reporting them to someone can increase your productivity.)

Here's another way to help you stay on your schedule: Ask a friend or family member to call you at the start of your designated writing period—not to chat but to ask if you are sitting down to write. Her only goal during the phone call should be to give you a friendly reminder of your obligation. At the end of the writing time, ask her to call again to check in with you to see how your writing session went and to make a new appointment for the next day. Another option is to set up your writing time so that you and a friend have the same writing periods. You can meet somewhere, such as in the library or at one of your houses, to write for a prearranged period.

Be sure family and friends understand your commitment to your dissertation schedule. Don't let them pull you away from it. A friend might suggest, for example, that because you have seven months for writing your dissertation, you surely can go shopping with her for one afternoon. On a dissertation schedule, you can accept such an invitation only if you buy time from yourself and replace that lost time. If you lose two hours of scheduled writing time on one day to go shopping, you need to make up those hours somehow during that week. If you don't, those seven months you allocated for writing your dissertation will quickly slip away, leaving you with anxiety and not much else. It might be easier, then, to just say no to your friend's invitation and stick with your schedule.

One strategy that can help you resist others' efforts to draw you away from your writing is to name your dissertation with a person's name—*Fred* or *Maura*, for example. Then, if someone invites you to do something and you want to stay firmly committed to working on your dissertation, you have an easy way for refusing the invitation: "I'm sorry, I can't go because I have an appointment at that time with Fred."

Don't forget, too, that there are all sorts of resources available to you to complete your dissertation. Taking advantage of some of them can make a big difference in sticking to your writing schedule. The major one is to buy time. That means paying someone else to do things that would take up your time. This could mean, for example, paying someone to gather sources for you in the library or to do an Internet search for you. It might mean paying someone to copy the excerpts you marked in your books and articles for your literature review. You might want to pay someone to transcribe your data or to format your dissertation or to prepare your tables. Or maybe pay someone to do nondissertation tasks you would normally do, such as cleaning the house. Especially if these tasks are ones you aren't good at or don't like to do, paying someone else can really make you much more efficient and keep you on your schedule.

If self-discipline is a real problem for you and you need more drastic measures to ensure that you keep a writing schedule, try this: Turn yourself over to a friend or family member for a period of time so you can focus on your dissertation. Stay at that person's house so you aren't distracted by what usually distracts you at home. Ask that person to keep you on a strict schedule, make meals for you, and make sure you are at your computer during scheduled writing times. Without any distractions, it's easy to stay on a schedule. Some students have even checked into motels for this purpose (be sure to have the television removed if you do this). Paying the daily motel bill is also a strong motivator to get your writing goals accomplished so you can return home.

When you are done with your scheduled writing period for the day, stop. Put your dissertation aside. It's OK! You've met your goals for the day, so there's no reason to feel guilty. Whatever you turn to next, give it your focused attention and have fun with it. You may be tempted to keep going on your dissertation if you are making good progress. But learning to stop at regular times for breaks is an important part of learning to write regularly. Stopping at the end of your designated time keeps you from becoming hungry or exhausted, either of which makes writing much harder. Stopping on time also reduces your feeling of being overwhelmed because you have time to do other tasks you need to do. If you're doing what we've been suggesting in this book, you will never not know where you are, so don't worry about stopping in the middle of a chapter or a section you are writing. Plus, stopping at a point when you are eager to write more makes it easy for you to begin writing at your next session.

Likewise, when you've meet your schedule during a week, you don't have to exceed it by continuing to work. Now is the time to schedule a reward or a miniholiday for yourself. Go see a movie, meet a friend for coffee, run some errands, get up an hour later, or indulge yourself by doing something you really like to do. One of Sonja's rewards, for example, is that she gets to sew something when she has accomplished a major writing goal. Again, when you take this time off, make it time off. Don't be thinking you should be working on your dissertation or try to do something on it when you are supposed to be rewarding yourself. If you do, you won't be productive on your dissertation, and you won't feel relaxed at the end of your reward time.

Writing regularly is a mechanism that helps you do what scholars do—develop ideas and document them. What writing regularly does is put you in your chair. Staying in your chair usually means that, eventually, you will do something productive. One of Sonja's students told her, at the end of a dissertation process that was much more protracted than it should have been, "I could have done it much sooner if I had just sat down." So sit down on a regular schedule. Something will happen. Another way to think about this is, "Butt to seat. You need to sit and write, regardless of whether you feel like it or not."[10]

Focusing on Successes

Writing on a schedule to ensure that you write regularly is a good start to enacting the role of a scholar. But even if you are writing regularly, you may find yourself discouraged and frustrated by your slow progress and by how much remains to be done on your dissertation. After several weeks and months of this, you can begin to feel crushed by your apparent lack of progress. That's where focusing on your successes comes in.

We are both in disciplines (communication and English) that privilege the power of symbols, and we are strong believers in the power of our words to create our realities. There are many different schools of thought and philosophies that support the need to be attentive to how we frame things, including symbolic construction, rational emotive behavior therapy, and even quantum physics.[11] In one way or another, these philosophies posit that whatever we expect or focus on becomes our reality.

The starting point for all of these perspectives is that external things and events don't make us happy or sad, disturbed or upset. Instead, our feelings come from our perceptions and evaluations of these events. The interpretations or meanings we give to them—our view of them—cause our despair, frustration, anger, or whatever we are feeling. The phrases and sentences that we keep telling ourselves are or become our thoughts and emotions. This means that we have the ability to exert control over how we feel and how we respond to what is going on around us. We can control our emotions by changing the internalized sentences or self-talk with which they were created in the first place.[12]

If self-talk can create and sustain emotion, you are probably not surprised at its role in writing problems. What you say to yourself about your dissertation is powerful, and writers "can literally talk themselves into blocking," as Boice explains.[13] You've undoubtedly had the experience of witnessing the role your thoughts play in your experiences in other situations. Have you ever expected not to have a good time at a party and then experienced it that way? The same thing happens in writing. Boice's research has shown that both blocked and unblocked writers talk to themselves about writing, but blocked writers report telling themselves 10 times as many negative as positive things about writing.[14] What we're suggesting is that, by focusing on your successes in your self-talk, you can be a happier writer, and these happy feelings are more likely to keep you writing regularly and productively.

Although you can't maintain perfect control over your thinking, you can significantly change and regulate it and thus change and regulate your experience of writing. You can literally talk yourself into a positive mood, enthusiasm for writing, and confidence that you are taking practical steps to produce writing that will be of high quality and well received. You do this by ferreting out and challenging internalized messages that are negative and replacing them with patterns of self-talk that are more functional for you—patterns that give you new meanings and interpretations for the writing process and thus new feelings about it.

How do you do this? The first step is self-monitoring. Much of what you say to yourself goes unobserved, so jot down your best guess of what your self-talk is like. Work at observing your ongoing inner discourse. One way to figure out what you tend to tell yourself is to observe your mood or how you are feeling. Inner discourse that focuses on themes like victimization or anticipated failures is rarely accompanied by positive affect. Use how you are feeling as a guide to whether your self-talk is positive or negative, functional or dysfunctional. If you feel frustrated or despairing when you sit down to write, chances are your self-talk about writing isn't positive.

Next, stop the thoughts and the talk that you identify as dysfunctional. Merely recognizing negative self-talk sometimes disarms and disrupts it. Generally, though, more active measures are necessary. As silly as it sounds, stopping negative self-talk can be as simple as a command to yourself: "Stop!" When more effort and planning are necessary, try to analyze the self-talk from a detached, objective vantage. Consider what you're saying as though an impartial jury were listening, and assess your self-talk through their eyes. Would they rate your inner discourse as realistic? As helpful? Would they conclude that you're being too pessimistic or too self-critical?[15]

The third phase of regulating your self-talk requires thought substitution. In general, negative self-talk is easier to supplant than to stop. Trying to think about nothing is difficult, but planning to replace negative self-talk with more constructive self-talk can help fill that void. Generate more positive, helpful scripts to replace your negative ones by identifying the positive in a condition or situation and focusing on it. Instead of seeing something as a problem or an obstacle, pivot and look at the situation from a different perspective. The more power and energy you give something, the more it manifests as reality for you. What do you want to become reality? Surely not delays and annoyances. You want your reality around your dissertation to be efficiency and productivity and success. So focus on the doable and the done and choose self-talk that focuses your attention on how much you are accomplishing and how well the process is going.

Some examples might help. Do you tend to make statements such as, "I'm tired, and I don't feel like working on my dissertation today"? Can you replace that kind of statement with something like, "I am tired, but I know I can make progress even when I'm tired. I've also found that making progress energizes me, so I'm going to put in my hours today anyway. I suspect I'll get energy from the process itself to keep me going." Is your advisor the problem? Instead of "I have a lousy advisor, and I'm not getting good advising," you can reframe your statement into, "I'm making good progress without much help from my advisor, and I'm finding all sorts of resources that are making up for the lack of help from my advisor." If your progress is slow and you're tempted to lament how very slow it is, make statements such as these: "I have made consistent progress up until now, and there's no reason to think that won't continue. I know how to chunk the dissertation out so that it's a series of small processes that I know how to do. I will finish if I just keep going through those processes."

Sometimes, looking backward can help you reframe. If you feel overwhelmed by the dissertation process, you can say to yourself, "Well, I haven't written a dissertation before, but I did write some papers for classes that received grades of A, and I did receive a top-paper award at the national convention in my field." Go back and read something you wrote that you like. It will remind you of how well you can think and write. "I did that?" you might find yourself saying. "That's not so bad. I can write something like that again."

Or look to the future. Call trusted friends and tell them about what you are working on, and they are likely to reinforce you and make appropriately comforting noises in response to your ideas. You might tell yourself, as Pamela Richards does, when she begins to doubt her writing:

> Yes, I produce an appalling amount of crap, but most of the time I can tell it's crap before anyone else gets a chance to look at it. And occasionally I produce something that fits, something Lillian Hellman might have written, something that captures exactly what I want to say. Usually it's just a sentence or two, but the number of those sentences grows if I just keep plugging away.[16]

Something else that might help you transform your self-talk is to see yourself simply as joining a conversation. That's all. You don't have to be brilliant. You don't have to have everything figured out. You are simply tuning into the ongoing conversation on this one topic in your field. You know how to enter a conversation: You hold off on speaking when you first join the group, you listen for a while, get informed about what is being talked about, and then make a contribution that takes the conversation into account and adds something to keep it going. That's not so hard, is it? That's what you are doing with your dissertation.

Be sure to follow the strategy of focusing on your successes when you are talking with others about your dissertation. Tales of struggle or of bad advisors can be entertaining to friends and family, and you might be tempted to tell such stories to amuse or gain the sympathy of others. But when you tell such tales, you are making struggle a part of your reality and your experience. Struggling isn't a very fun way to do a dissertation. That's why, when you talk about your dissertation to others, you want to focus on what is going well and on how much progress you're making. If someone asks about your dissertation, it's always "Great!"[17] Tell your questioner about the progress you've made in the last week and how good you feel about your progress. Celebrate your progress with your words.[18]

Use self-talk, too, to get a feeling of success at the end of each workday. Instead of ending a day feeling discouraged, feeling like the endless dissertation stretches before you forever, try to end each day feeling successful and pleased with your progress. That way, you'll get a taste of those rewards that are so hard to come by when you're working on such a large project. At the end of the day, recap what you've done that day. Don't focus on everything that's left to do. Here's how to think about this using our travel metaphor: You are driving from New York to California, and you're currently in Indiana. You can choose to focus on how far from California you still are, get discouraged, and stay in Indiana. Or you can focus on how far you've come and keep going. That's the kind of sense of accomplishment we want you to foster about your own work, and self-talk focused on your successes will help.

There's a concrete way that we like that helps keep your focus on your successes, and that's a reverse calendar. This is a calendar you create by working backwards from your desired graduation date. You can actually post it on your wall, or it can be something you work out on paper and keep close by so that you can review it regularly. Here's how it works. If you want to graduate next May, then you probably have to submit your final version to the graduate school three weeks before that, which means your defense must be two weeks before that to give you time to do any required revisions. Dissertations are usually given to committee members two weeks before the defense, and your chair probably wants a final version a couple weeks before that. Mark these dates on a calendar, going backwards from May.

But there's more. You also want to chart out how much time you can take to complete each chapter of your dissertation before you even get close to those deadlines. Be very specific here. Work expands to fill the time available, and that is certainly true of dissertations. If you give yourself unlimited time to complete a particular process, it will take unlimited time. You will feel that you are never done with a process or a section, and you don't ever finish it. So set limits in your calendar on the amount of time you can spend on each particular chapter—much like you've done in the past with papers for classes. You probably wrote many papers that you thought weren't ready to turn in, but because they were due, they were done.

Conceptualize and work out the time for each chapter in terms of hours, not days. Days are ambiguous. Are you working 5-hour days or 9-hour days? Number of hours clearly tells you how much time you have to put in. Conceptualizing your calendar in terms of hours also visibly reminds you that you can make progress on your dissertation by working for one hour when you have a chance. You get the dissertation done by putting in the hours, and one hour worked means one hour closer to your goal.

You're not done with your calendar yet. Take each of the chapters of your dissertation and divide it up into the major processes that you must complete to finish that chapter. Be very clear as you chart out these processes exactly what each involves and how you'll know when you're done. Instead of putting on your reverse calendar "Do literature review," divide doing the literature review into concrete, discrete processes such as coding a certain number of sources, copying or typing those coded excerpts, creating your conceptual schema for your literature review, and writing up the literature review. If you are planning 140 hours for your literature review, your calendar for that time might look something like this: 40 hours for collecting your literature, 60 hours for coding the literature, two hours for creating a conceptual schema for the literature review, 30 hours for writing up the literature review, and eight hours for editing it.

Here's another example: Let's say one major step on your reverse calendar is to schedule your interviews to collect your data. Divide that task into concrete tasks: Call five interviewees to set up appointments, send reinforcing e-mails to the five interviewees, buy tapes for tape recorder, do test of tape recorder, make 20 copies of consent form, and so on. Identify the component steps of any overwhelming task and complete each step, one at a time.

You can get even more specific with your calendar. Take the amount of hours you have to spend on an activity and divide those up into the various processes you have to complete. For example, if you have 60 hours for coding your books and articles for your literature review and you have 120 sources to code, that means you must code two sources an hour to maintain your schedule. This is the level of specificity you want on your calendar.

As you sit down to write each day, think in terms of small steps. Use your calendar to figure out how much you can accomplish in your hours for that day. You might decide, for example, in a four-hour block of time, to accomplish six tasks. Make each item on your list something very specific, something very clear, and something that you will know when you are done with it. You might say, for example, at the start of your work period, "Today, I will code 15 of my books for my literature review" or "In this hour, I will cut apart all of my notes for my literature review" or "In my writing time today, I will write up the first two sections of my analysis chapter." When you have completed the task, cross it off the list. With each item, you are making steady progress toward completing your dissertation. You feel a sense of accomplishment. You feel positive about what you have done because you know it actually was progress toward your dissertation. You will, if you keep going, as Beth Triplett suggests, finish your dissertation "by completing literally hundreds of mundane tasks and writing approximately 4,000 sentences."[19]

What do you do if you don't know how long the various processes of your chapters should take? After all, you've never done many of them before, so you don't have any idea how long it will take you to do them. We suggest that you take the reverse position. Instead of allowing yourself to take as long as you want to do one of the processes, use the timeline for a nine-month dissertation in chapter 2 to give you an idea of how long you should take. Allot that amount for doing each chore. Act as though that is all the time you have for that activity.

There's another way you can figure out how much time a chapter should take you to write. We discussed this in chapter 7, but it's important enough to explain again. Start with how long each section in the chapter should be. Let's say you are working on one of your analysis chapters. The introduction to the chapter is one page, you have five themes from your data to explain, and your conclusion section should be about two pages. You know that your chapter is expected to be about 35 pages long. That means you only have six to seven pages for explaining each of your five themes. When you are trying to figure out how much time you need to write up one of the themes, think about how many pages it is supposed to be. Six pages. How long should it take you to write that? By the way, this little trick also helps you figure out how in-depth to go on a particular topic or section of your dissertation. If you know it can only be three pages, you can only go in-depth three pages' worth. Thinking this way helps you give proper weight to the various sections of a chapter.

The reverse calendar, then, is a good way to help you stay focused on your successes. You might try another strategy in conjunction with it, and that's to visually keep track of the number of hours you spend working. Let's say, for example, that you want to work on your dissertation 40 hours per week. At the start of a week, put on the wall of your office 40 of those boldly colored sticky bookmarks. When you work an hour (and we mean real work—work that actually moves you along on your dissertation), pull one bookmark off the wall. When you work a second hour, pull a second bookmark off the wall. You always know visually where you are in terms of the number of hours you have left to work that week. And, then, of course, you can play around with your schedule in terms of how you want to accomplish your writing goal for the week. You might decide to work 10 hours in one day to free up another day of the week for doing something else—you can "buy time" from yourself.

What's important is that you get your hours in. Kate was so committed to getting her hours in per week (because she knew that she needed to get the hours in so she could finish by her deadline) that, if she got to Saturday night and didn't have her requisite number of hours completed, she hired a babysitter for her daughter. Instead of going out to dinner or a movie, she stayed in and worked on Saturday night.

So far, we've been acting as though you'll meet every deadline you set. You've made your reverse calendar and have divided it into small processes, allotting particular amounts of time to those processes. We've assumed that you are meeting your weekly writing goals and are rewarding yourself as you do. But, of course, you sometimes won't meet your deadlines and goals. This happens a lot to novice writers who haven't done many of the processes before that a dissertation requires. If you don't meet a deadline, adjust your reverse calendar to reflect the missed deadline, giving yourself lesser amounts of time for future processes. You might feel a bit anxious or panicked when this happens, but don't beat yourself up about it. This happens to even experienced scholars from time to time. Do what you can to compensate for the missed deadline so that you can stay pretty much with the schedule you planned. Do you need to work a few more hours that week? Do you need to reduce the number of interviews you will conduct? Is there a chapter you can drop? Can you pay someone to do some work for you? What kinds of adjustments can you make so that you can stay on schedule?

Certainly, delays and annoyances will happen along the way as you complete the trip that is your dissertation. If your tendency is to respond to those delays and annoyances by adopting one of the incomplete-scholar roles—perhaps a housekeeper, patient, or good student—you avoid doing what you need to do to become a scholar, which is generating ideas and sharing them. To get back to the scholar role, begin writing regularly and track your successes with your self-talk, a reverse calendar, and keeping track of the hours you work. We guarantee that, if you do these things, you'll soon be back to enjoying your trip.

Notes

1. Marge Piercy, "For the Young Who Want To," in *The Moon Is Always Female* (New York: Knopf, 1980), 85.

2. Scot McKnight, "The Professor as Scholar: Exiled to Eden" (address to faculty colloquium, North Park University, Chicago, Ill., 2005).

3. Mark Matloff, "Excuses Are Us," *ABD Survival Guide* [electronic newsletter] (6 Sept. 2002): 2, www.abdsurvivalguide.com.

4. Rebekah Nathan, *My Freshman Year: What a Professor Learned by Becoming a Student* (Ithaca, N.Y.: Cornell University Press, 2005).

5. Pamela Richards, "Risk," in *Writing for Social Sciences: How to Start and Finish Your Thesis, Book, or Article,* by Howard S. Becker (Chicago: University of Chicago Press, 1986), 112–13.

6. Robert Boice, *Professors as Writers: A Self-Help Guide to Productive Writing* (Stillwater, Okla: New Forums, 1990), 82–83.

7. Robert Boice, *Advice for New Faculty Members: Nihil Nimus* (Needham Heights, Mass: Allyn & Bacon, 2000), 143–44. You might find another of Boice's works on this subject useful: Robert Boice, *How Writers Journey to Comfort and Fluency: A Psychological Adventure* (Westport, Conn.: Praeger, 1994).

8. Boice, *Professors as Writers*, 75.

9. Robert Boice, "Procrastination, Busyness and Bingeing," *Behavioral Research Therapy* 27 (1989): 609.

10. Beth Triplett, "Paying It Forward: A Practitioner's Guide to Climbing the Dissertation Mountain," 6. Available from Triplett at btriplett@maryville.edu.

11. Among the sources that articulate this idea in various ways are: Peter L. Berger and Thomas Luckmann, *The Social Construction of Reality: A Treatise in the Sociology of Knowledge* (Garden City, N.Y.: Anchor/Doubleday, 1966); Benjamin Lee Whorf, *Language, Thought & Reality: Selected Writings of Benjamin Lee Whorf*, ed. John B. Carroll (Cambridge: MIT Press, 1956); Albert Ellis and Robert A. Harper, *A Guide to Rational Living* (North Hollywood, Calif.: Wilshire, 1961); Albert Ellis, *Overcoming Destructive Beliefs, Feelings, and Behaviors* (Amherst, N.Y.: Prometheus, 2001); Jonathan Potter, *Representing Reality: Discourse, Rhetoric and Social Construction* (Thousand Oaks, Calif.: Sage, 1996); Fred Alan Wolf, *Taking the Quantum Leap: The New Physics for Nonscientists* (New York: Harper & Row, 1981); Ian Marshall and Danah Zohar, *Who's Afraid of Schrödinger's Cat? An A-to-Z Guide to All the New Science Ideas You Need to Keep Up with the New Thinking* (New York: Quill/William Morrow, 1997); Amit Goswami, Richard E. Reed, and Maggie Goswami, *The Self-Aware Universe: How Consciousness Creates the Material World* (New York: Jeremy P. Tarcher/Penguin Putnam, 1993); Robert Sapolsky, "Sick of Poverty," *Scientific American* (Dec. 2005): 92–99; and Martin E. P. Seligman, *Authentic Happiness* (New York: Free, 2002), esp. chapter 4.

12. Ellis and Harper, 26–27.

13. Boice, *Professors as Writers*, 98.

14. Boice, *Professors as Writers*, 95.

15. Boice, *Professors as Writers*, 101.

16. Richards, 119.

17. Rachna D. Jain, "Self Care in the Dissertation Process," *ABD Survival Guide* [electronic newsletter] (27 April 2001): 3, www.abdsurvivalguide.com.

18. Lynne Berrett, "Motivating Yourself over the Long Haul," *ABD Survival Guide* [electronic newsletter] (19 March 2006): 4, www.abdsurvivalguide.com.

19. Triplett, 1.

INDEX

ABOUT THE AUTHORS

Sonja K. Foss is a professor in the Department of Communication at the University of Colorado at Denver. Her research and teaching interests are in contemporary rhetorical theory and criticism, feminist perspectives on communication, the incorporation of marginalized voices into rhetorical theory and practice, and visual rhetoric. She is the author or coauthor of the books *Feminist Rhetorical Theories, Women Speak: The Eloquence of Women's Lives, Rhetorical Criticism, Contemporary Perspectives on Rhetoric,* and *Inviting Transformation: Presentational Speaking for a Changing World.* Her essays in communication journals have dealt with topics such as invitational rhetoric, feminine spectatorship in Garrison Keillor's monologues, sewing as emancipatory ritual, visual argumentation, and body art. Dr. Foss earned her PhD in communication studies from Northwestern University and previously taught at Ohio State University, the University of Oregon, the University of Denver, Virginia Tech, and Norfolk State University. Dr. Foss is a codirector of Scholars' Retreat, which she started in 1997.

William Waters is coordinator of composition, director of the writing center, and an assistant professor in the English Department at Northwest Missouri State University. His research and teaching interests are in writing theory and practice, the history of the English language, linguistics, and modern grammar. He was the managing editor of *La Puerta: A Doorway into the Academy* and has published several poems in national journals. Dr. Waters earned his PhD in language and linguistics from the University of New Mexico and previously taught at the University of Maine; University College in Galway, Ireland; and Cheongbuk National University in Korea. Dr. Waters is a codirector of Scholars' Retreat. He and Dr. Foss conduct a variety of workshops for graduate students and faculty on writing and publishing.